D0850594

"*This book is different! Hummel's* Emancipating Slaves, Enslaving Free Men *challenges both time-worn and current interpretations of the Civil War era. Not every reader will agree with his fresh interpretations, but they are thoroughly grounded in the facts and the literature of the period.*"

—ERIC WALTHER
Professor of History,
University of Houston
Author of *The Fire-Eaters*

"*Jeffrey Rogers Hummel has mastered an astonishing range of material in constructing his provocative interpretation of the Civil War as a watershed in shaping the meanings of freedom in the United States. Even veteran students of the conflict will find much to challenge their thinking in this forcefully argued and clearly written study. Apart from Hummel's engaging text, the perceptive bibliographical essays alone make the book well worth reading.*"

—GARY W. GALLAGHER
Professor of American History,
Penn State University
Author of *Stephen Dodson Ramseur: Lee's Gallant General*

"*Hummel presents a very lucid history of the Civil War era, enlivened by his own subtle interpretation.* Emancipating Slaves, Enslaving Free Men *is immeasurably enhanced by the comprehensive bibliographical essays that follow each chapter, providing the scholar with invaluable historiographical information. The book should appeal to the general reader with its colorful quotes and anecdotes that capture the feel of the times it surveys so well. At the same time the author's vast knowledge of the literature makes his work a priceless resource for students and professional historians.*"

—JANET SHARP HERMANN
Author of *The Pursuit of a Dream* and *Joseph E. Davis, Pioneer Patriarch*

"This is a lucid, edifying account of the Civil War era. Mr. Hummel has an impressive command of the relevant contemporary literature. His interpretations are thoughtful, often provocative, always well worth considering. Civil War buffs will want this book on their shelves."

—KENNETH M. STAMPP
Morrison Professor of History Emeritus,
University of California, Berkeley
Author of *The Peculiar Institution*

"In this fresh, provocative survey, Jeff Hummel combines synthesis and interpretation in admirable fashion. Not everyone will agree with his arguments, but they will stimulate discussion as they challenge orthodoxy."

—BROOKS D. SIMPSON
Professor of History,
Arizona State University
Author of *Let Us Have Peace: Ulysses S. Grant and the Politics of War and Reconstruction, 1861–1868*

"Jeffrey Hummel's book Emancipating Slaves, Enslaving Free Men *is a very stimulating and original analysis of slavery and the American Civil War. Stimulating because it incorporates an exceptional blend of economic and political analysis; original because the bibliographic essays at the end of each chapter alone are worth the price of the book."*

—DOUGLASS NORTH
1993 Nobel Prize in Economics for work in economic history of the United States
Author of *The Economic Growth of the United States, 1790–1860*

EMANCIPATING SLAVES, ENSLAVING FREE MEN

EMANCIPATING SLAVES, ENSLAVING FREE MEN

A History of the American Civil War

JEFFREY ROGERS HUMMEL

OPEN COURT
Chicago and La Salle, Illinois

Open Court Publishing Company is a division of Carus
Publishing Company

© 1996 by Jeffrey Rogers Hummel

First printing 1996
Second printing 1996

Printed and bound in the United States of America

Library of Congress Cataloging-in-Publication Data
Hummel, Jeffrey Rogers.
    Emancipating slaves, enslaving free men: a history of the
American Civil War/Jeffrey Rogers Hummel.
        p.   cm.
    Includes bibliographical references and index.
    ISBN 0-8126-9311-6 (cloth: alk. paper).—ISBN 0-8126-9312-4
(paper: alk. paper)
    1. United States—History—Civil War, 1861–1865.   2. United
States—Politics and government—1815–1861.   3. United
States—History—Civil War, 1861–1865—Causes.   4. United
States—History—Civil War, 1861–1865—Influence.   5. State
rights—History—19th century.   6. Reconstruction. I. Title.
E468.H94 1996
973.7—dc20   96-19332
                                                                         CIP

CONTENTS

Preface

Ken Burns's eleven-hour PBS documentary, *The Civil War,* was first televised in 1990. It dramatically transposed to an exciting medium all the limitations of popular Civil War literature. Technically and artistically the documentary was brilliant, and there is no denying its vivid power to bring the conflict to life. Unfortunately, its presentation of the war's origins was superficial; it unreflectively subscribed to the cult of Lincoln idolatry; it slighted the war's broader political and social context; and even from a narrow military perspective, its focus was almost exclusively on major conventional campaigns, giving short shrift to such critical problems as logistics and guerrillas.

This book is a narrative history of the Civil War that transcends the confines of popular literature. It is short, yet comprehensive, covering both the war's causes and consequences as well as its course, its political and social as well as its military aspects. The book is basic, so that someone unfamiliar with the subject can easily follow it. But it takes issue with prevailing interpretations in several respects.

Some of the most innovative of my challenges to established views arise from weaving the latest economic theory into the historical narrative. I have tried my best to make these arguments accessible even for readers untutored in economics. But those who find economic reasoning an irritating distraction from the story should feel free to skim lightly over the second through fifth sections of chapter 2.

The book's organization is basically chronological but shifts to topical for important subjects at appropriate points. The reader will thus find that the second chapter steps out of the historical sequence to explore black slavery in detail. Or that chapters 6, 7, and 11 contain most of the book's treatment of military events, but not all of it.

The notes are at the book's end to make them as unobtrusive as possible. This also befits their relative significance. Those conscientious readers who hate flipping between text and endnotes can rest assured that the notes only cite sources for quotations and numbers. Except when discussing the derivation of certain economic statistics, they contain no textual matter.

Bibliographical essays, on the other hand, follow each chapter. Although general readers may prefer to skip these, the essays provide guides to further study and let scholars know on what works I relied. They also emphasize my own interpretations by contrasting my views to the many alternative interpretations of historians, past and present. Above all, they permit me to acknowledge my enormous intellectual debt to others. Even when I vehemently disagree with an author's conclusions, I hope my profound admiration for previous scholarship comes across clearly. Without these arduous but loving labors to draw upon, a book such as mine would be impossible.

The personal debts I incurred while completing this project exceed even my intellectual debts. It is hard to imagine that any author has received more support and assistance from family, friends, and associates. Thanking them eventually became the part of the book I was most eager to write.

Gary W. Gallagher, Wendy McElroy, and Michele Schwartz commented extensively on earlier incarnations of this work. More complete versions of the manuscript were given scrupulous and thorough attention by Lois Allen, Shearer Davis Bowman, Cindy Cox, Williamson Evers, George B. Forgie, Buzz Grafe, Mike

Grossberg, Janet Sharp Hermann, David Hoefer, Ross Levatter, Robert Middlekauf, Chuck Myers, Dyanne Petersen, Tom Reid, Theodore P. Savas, Kenneth M. Stampp, and Joe Stromberg. David Friedman, David Henderson, William D. Hermann, John Robbart, and Richard K. Vedder all offered their economic expertise in looking over chapters 2, 13, or both for me. Everyone mentioned tried his or her best to get me to make this an accurate and readable product; any remaining errors or infelicities are due entirely to my own stubbornness.

I also wish to express my gratitude to Charles W. Baird, Director of the Smith Center for Private Enterprise Studies at California State University, Hayward, and his assistants, Jenny Reid and Donna Mittelstedt, for providing me convenient access to that university's library. Delores Neese of the main library at Golden Gate University processed an inordinate number of inter-library loan requests. I did most of the actual writing of this book in Golden Gate University's computer labs, and four successive directors—Lee Thompson, Mark Phillips, Harlan Bernhardt, and Siriporn Usanakornkul—along with their entire staffs, were courteous, cooperative, and accommodating beyond the call of duty.

Although he may not recall it, Milton Friedman first suggested this book idea to me. I wish to thank him for that and for indirectly putting me in touch with my agent, Tom Cole, who was instrumental in many ways, but particularly in molding the book's concept. My editor at Open Court, David Ramsay Steele, was an intellectual delight to work with, as well as unusually sympathetic to an author's perspective. I owe Michele Hubinger an extra debt for her proof-reading, while Fabbian George Dufoe III permitted me to test a program he was developing for creating indexes.

So many others were vital in maintaining my morale during rough periods while I worked on this manuscript that space and the reader's patience would not permit mentioning them all by name. They know who they are. But I would be remiss not to give special recognition to Joe and Martha Fuhrig, an indispensable couple. Behind me almost from the beginning, with encouragement and confidence through it all, Joe and Martha more than anyone ensured that this book was completed.

Prologue

America's Crisis

Towering genius . . . thirsts and burns for distinction; and, if possible, it will have it, whether at the expense of emancipating slaves or enslaving freemen.

ABRAHAM LINCOLN, 1838[1]

After little more than a month in office, Abraham Lincoln faced the most serious crisis that ever beset a President of the United States. Seven southern states had withdrawn from the Union even before he took the oath in front of the unfinished Capitol Dome on a brisk, sunny day early in March of 1861. Setting up a rival central government, they had proceeded to seize United States property within their borders. A rumored assassination plot required the humiliating precaution of having the President-elect sneak into Washington in the dead of night wearing a disguise. During the inauguration, the streets were lined with soldiers; riflemen watched from prominent rooftops and from windows in the Capitol wings; and four batteries of howitzers stood guard at City Hall. A Philadelphia newspaper reported that, for the first time, a President delivered his inaugural address "safely esconced [*sic*] out of the people's reach, within a military cordon bristling with bayonets."[2]

Although long active in the rough-and-tumble frontier politics of Illinois, the fifty-two-year-old Lincoln was practically a novice in public office. His only prior elected posts involved eight years as a state legislator and a single term in the House of Representatives. This prairie lawyer of humble origins had absolutely no previous administrative experience. Leading members of Lincoln's own

1

Cabinet looked upon him as an indecisive upstart and crude buffoon, ripe for their adroit manipulation.

Then at 4:30 A.M. on the 12th of April, rebel guns opened fire. Their target: a small federal garrison besieged within Fort Sumter, on an island situated right at the mouth of Charleston harbor in South Carolina. Lincoln did not hesitate. The shelling of Fort Sumter brought forth an immediate presidential proclamation. "Whereas the laws of the United States have been for some time past and now are opposed and the execution thereof obstructed in the States of South Carolina, Georgia, Alabama, Florida, Mississippi, Louisiana, and Texas by combinations too powerful to be suppressed by the ordinary course of judicial proceedings or by the powers vested in the marshals by law," it began, "now, therefore, I, Abraham Lincoln, President of the United States, in virtue of the power in me vested by the Constitution and laws, have thought fit to call forth, and hereby do call forth, the militia of the several States of the Union to the aggregate number of 75,000, in order to suppress said combinations and to cause the laws to be duly executed."[3]

The proclamation was an unprecedented exertion of presidential authority. Seventy-five thousand militia constituted the largest military force ever yet assembled on the North American continent. Moreover, the United States Congress was out of session. Lincoln acted entirely on his own; he neither consulted with nor asked leave of the national government's legislative branch.

The President's militia call signaled open warfare between the northern and southern states. Contrary to the expectations of most leaders on either side, the ensuing Civil War would rage for four soul-wrenching years. Before it was over, the number of troops engaged would dwarf the first call. The total killed on both sides— 620,000, with an additional 400,000 wounded—would rank the conflict as the bloodiest in all of United States history. That figure is half again the number of American deaths that resulted from World War II and represents six times as many on a per capita basis. One of the Civil War's major battles, Gettysburg, alone yielded more American casualties than the fighting in all previous U.S. wars combined.

What sectional disagreement could have provoked this unmatched internal bloodletting? Northerners and Southerners were indistinguishable in so many ways. With respect to politics, both paid homage to the same Constitution. With respect to economics, both were tied together through the same international market. With respect to language, both spoke the same mother tongue. With respect to religion, both worshipped the same Protestant creeds— except for the newly arriving Catholic immigrants in the North, who were among the South's strongest sympathizers. And with respect to race, both practiced the same white supremacy, the black minority being either enslaved or legally discriminated against. None of the most common leavens for civil strife were evident.

Historians and buffs debate the fundamental causes of the American Civil War almost as hotly today as the combatants did then. More has been written on the subject than almost any other event in human history: by one estimate, 50,000 separate books. "There are more Civil War controversies than there were battles between 1861 and 1865," observes one participant in these de-bates.[4] Americans cannot even agree about what to call the conflict. "War of the Rebellion" is the U.S. government's official name, but Southerners have always preferred "The War Between the States," or the more partisan "War for Southern Independence." No single, short explanation therefore can capture all the facets of this complex, difficult, and encompassing cataclysm.

We can simplify our understanding of the Civil War's causes, however, if we follow the advice of one eminent historian, Eric Foner, and ask two separate questions. Why did the southern states want to leave the Union? And why did the northern states refuse to let them go?[5] The answer to at least the first of these questions necessarily revolves around what Southerners called their "pecu-liar institution": black slavery.

Prologue
Bibliographical Essay

The literature about the Civil War is unsurpassed in vastness and richness. There are specialized monographs on nearly every campaign and battle, every major figure and institution, and every phase and facet of the entire war. In these bibliographical essays, I will identify some important works relating to each chapter and survey the changing fashions of historical interpretation. All essays of this sort are necessarily selective, and this applies many times over when confronting the Civil War. Since I wish to highlight my own interpretations, the invariable caveat comes with added emphasis.

The Civil War has inspired many multi-volume studies, and three cover almost all its aspects, from beginning to end. The seven volumes of businessman-turned historian James Ford Rhodes, *History of the United States From the Compromise of 1850 to the Restoration of Home Rule in the South in 1877* (New York: Harper & Brothers, Macmillan, 1896–1906), was a definitive work of thorough scholarship when published at the turn of the century. Now out of date, it manages to combine a nationalist bias against secession with a racial bias against blacks. More current are the eight volumes of Allan Nevins, under three different titles: *Ordeal of the Union*, 2 v. (New York: Charles Scribner's Sons, 1947); *The Emergence of Lincoln*, 2 v. (New York: Charles Scribner's Sons, 1951); and *The War for the Union*, 4 v. (New York: Charles Scribner's Sons, 1959–1971). Nevins's account is magnificently researched and detailed, but unfortunately, once he gets to the Civil War itself, he focuses on the Union and almost forgets the Confederacy. A less imposing treatment that historians sometimes unjustifiably slight because its author was a spellbinding journalist is the three volumes of Bruce Catton, *The Centennial History of the Civil War* (New York: Simon & Schuster, 1961–65), v. 1, *The Coming Fury;* v. 2, *Terrible Swift Sword;* and v. 3, *Never Call Retreat.* Catton—and Nevins with much ambiguity—blame the war on incompetent and opportunistic politicians who lacked the sense or ability to compromise between the irresponsible demands of fanatics on both sides.

Single volumes that attempt a comprehensive account of the Civil War are still often dauntingly long. James McPherson, *Battle Cry of Freedom: The Civil War Era* (New York: Oxford University Press, 1988), is a bestseller in this category that incorporates all the latest research into a compelling, chronological narrative, but I personally prefer his comparable textbook, *Ordeal by Fire: The Civil War and Reconstruction*, 2nd edn. (New York: Alfred A. Knopf, 1992). Peter J. Parish, *The American Civil War* (New York: Holmes & Meier, 1975), is a graceful book by an English historian. James G. Randall's classic and invaluable text, as updated by David Donald, *The Civil War and Reconstruction*, 2nd edn. (Lexington, MA: D. C. Heath, 1969), is 866 closely printed, topically organized pages of infelicitous prose. McPherson,

Parish, and Randall-Donald all contain excellent bibliographical essays; Randall-Donald's is the most extensive but dated, whereas McPherson's are the most up-to-date. Robert Leckie's recent *None Died in Vain: The Saga of the American Civil War* (New York: HarperCollins, 1990), is a shallow narrative that matches these other works only in length. Finally, we have the volume based upon Ken Burns's PBS documentary: Geoffrey C. Ward, *The Civil War: An Illustrated History* (New York: Alfred A. Knopf, 1990), perhaps the finest of the myriad coffee-table books on the subject.

Now for my competitors—Civil War histories that are both comprehensive but short. Among the newest, Charles P. Roland, *An American Iliad: The Story of the Civil War* (Lexington: University Press of Kentucky, 1991), overly concentrates for my taste on the war's military dimension, while short-changing economics and finance. Six previous volumes that offer innovative perspectives are Richard H. Sewell, *A House Divided: Sectionalism and Civil War, 1848–1865* (Baltimore: Johns Hopkins University Press, 1988); David Herbert Donald, *Liberty and Union* (Boston: Little, Brown, 1978); William L. Barney, *Flawed Victory: A New Perspective on the Civil War* (New York: Praeger, 1975); William R. Brock, *Conflict and Transformation: The United States, 1844–1977* (Baltimore: Penguin Books, 1973); Emory M. Thomas, *The American War and Peace, 1860–1877* (Englewood Cliffs, NJ: Prentice-Hall, 1973); and Robert Cruden, *The War That Never Ended* (Englewood Cliffs, NJ: Prentice-Hall, 1973). If I had been entirely satisfied with any of them, I might not have written a book of my own.

There are so many other manageable, single-volume histories of the period—some part of distinguished multi-author series, usually with competent coverage of the war—that there is little point in listing them all. But two do merit special attention. The economist, Roger L. Ransom, has given us *Conflict and Compromise: The Political-Economy of Slavery, Emancipation and the American Civil War* (Cambridge, U.K.: Cambridge University Press, 1989). It is quite useful as an overview of the contributions that economic historians have made to our knowledge of the Civil War, but when Ransom ventures into other fields, his account becomes pedestrian, not to mention riddled with minor factual errors. Ludwell H. Johnson, *Division and Reunion: America, 1848–1877* (New York: John Wiley, 1978), boldly bills itself as a "neo-Confederate" interpretation. In other words, Johnson believes that a defense of secession necessitates blasé indulgence of black slavery, censuring animosity toward abolitionists, and fawning apologetics for Jefferson Davis's despotism. In these pages, I hope to prove him wrong. In a class by itself is James Street, *The Civil War: An Unvarnished Account of the Late but Still Lively Hostilities* (New York: Dial Press, 1953), a wonderfully irreverent, journalistic survey that professional historians have totally ignored.

Jim Cullen, *The Civil War in Popular Culture: A Reusable Past* (Washington: Smithsonian Institution Press, 1995), is a sagacious romp through the popular media, including movies, that have molded American perceptions about the rupture between North and South. A full catalog of the conflicting explanations of historians and contemporaries, up to the time of its publication, is Thomas J. Pressly, *Americans Interpret Their Civil War* (Princeton, NJ: Princeton University Press, 1954). Some of the best, more recent historiographical surveys are chapters within Eric Foner, *Politics and Ideology in the Age of the Civil War* (New York: Oxford University Press, 1980), and Kenneth M. Stampp, *The Imperiled Union: Essays on the Background of the Civil War* (New York: Oxford University Press, 1980). In addition to these compilations from two of our most eminent Civil War historians, also worthy of mention is William W. Freehling's collection, *The Reintegration of American History: Slavery and the Civil War* (New York: Oxford University Press, 1994), despite its annoyingly frequent genuflections to the ephemeral shibboleths of political correctness.

Classifying schools of historical interpretation is inherently imprecise and arbitrary, but I would identify six alternative perspectives on the Civil War: nationalist, revisionist, economic, cultural, neo-Confederate, and neo-abolitionist. All six, unfortunately, tend to approach the war's causes as a single issue; none differentiates sufficiently between the two distinct questions posed in the text: why did the South wish to leave the Union, and why did the North decline to let it go? These questions are muddled together usually because American historians approach the Civil War with an implicit and unchallenged prejudice in favor of national unity, as David M. Potter has pointed out in his insightful discussion of "The Historian's Use of Nationalism and Vice Versa," from *The South and Sectional Conflict* (Baton Rouge: Louisiana State University Press, 1968).

Thus, the traditional nationalist interpretation of, most notably, James Ford Rhodes attributes the war to one factor: slavery. Slavery caused the southern states to secede, and Rhodes almost unreflectively assumes that the national government had no option but to suppress them. The revisionists, in contrast, deny that slavery necessitated war, usually because they believe that slavery was dying of its own accord. This school, which blames the war on a "blundering generation," includes not only Bruce Catton, as mentioned above, but also James G. Randall, who originated that phrase in an article of the same title that was incorporated into his collection, *Lincoln: The Liberal Statesman* (New York: Dodd, Mead, 1947), as well as Avery O. Craven, author of *The Repressible Conflict, 1830–1861* (University: Louisiana State University Press, 1929) and other works cited below and in future chapters. David Donald has given us an institutional variation on revisionism, in "An Excess of Democracy: The American Civil War and Social Process," from his collection, *Lincoln Reconsidered: Essays on the Civil War Era*, 2nd edn., (New York: Random House, 1956), which faults the extreme decentralization in antebellum America for its failure to provide enough institutional bonds. Yet the revisionists usually share the nationalist presupposition that letting the South go in peace was unthinkable.

The economic interpretation of the Civil War, in which a capitalist North subdued an agrarian South, owes its fame to Charles A. and Mary R. Beard. In the relevant chapters of their *Rise of American Civilization*, 2 v. (New York: Macmillan, 1927), they refer to the conflict as a "Second

American Revolution." Beard is supposed to have remarked that slavery hardly merited a footnote in Civil War history (according to Nathaniel W. Stephenson, "California and the Compromise of 1850," *Pacific Historical Review*, 4 [June 1935], 115). Similarly, Barrington Moore, Jr., in chapter 3 of his influential *Social Origins of Dictatorship and Democracy: Lord and Peasant in the Making of the Modern World* (Boston: Beacon Press, 1966), identifies America's sectional conflict as "The Last Capitalist Revolution." Allan Nevins (who himself vacillates between revisionist, cultural, and neo-abolitionist views) has summarized the prevailing verdict on Beard's economic determinism in *The Emergence of Lincoln*, v. 2, p. 465, where he calls it "the flimsiest" of "all the monistic explanations for the drift to war." But Beard's focus on economic causes still echoes today in writings that stress the war's interaction with American modernization, including James McPherson's histories. And a full refurbishment, cognizant of the latest scholarship, can be found in Charles C. Bright, "The State in the United States During the Nineteenth Century," in Bright and Susan Harding, eds., *Statemaking and Social Movements: Essays in History and Theory* (Ann Arbor: University of Michigan Press, 1984).

The cultural interpretation, best articulated in Arthur Charles Coles's social history, *The Irrepressible Conflict, 1850–1865* (New York: Macmillan, 1934), brings slavery back in as one of a constellation of factors making the North and South increasingly divergent societies. A stimulating restatement of the cultural approach is Bertram Wyatt-Brown's series of essays, *Yankee Saints and Southern Sinners* (Baton Rouge: Louisiana State University Press, 1985), while the most sustained critique is Edward Pessen, "How Different From Each Other Were the Antebellum North and South," *American Historical Review*, 85 (December 1980), pp. 1119–149, which finds the sections identical except for slavery.

But the only school even willing to entertain the possibility of secession's legitimacy is the neo-Confederate. Beyond that difference in value judgment, this currently unfashionable approach has not originated any causal explanations of its own. Such unreconstructed Southerners as Frank L. Owsley, in "The Irrepressible Conflict," from Twelve Southerners, *I'll Take My Stand* (New York: Harper & Brothers, 1930), or more recently Ludwell H. Johnson, instead justify secession by downplaying slavery and calling upon revisionist, economic, or sometimes cultural themes from the other schools. This makes them vulnerable to the recent research of neo-abolitionist historians, among whom I would include Allan Nevins, James McPherson, Eric Foner, and Kenneth Stampp. The neo-abolitionists have exhaustively reaffirmed the nationalist school's contention that slavery was the root cause of secession. In fact, the two schools differ hardly at all on the war's causes except that the neo-abolitionists have jettisoned the frequent racism of the nationalists and therefore show more concern about the status of blacks (leading to markedly different opinions about postwar Reconstruction, of which more toward the end of this book). But this merely reinforces their automatic rejection of secession. Whereas the nationalist school justifies force in order to preserve the Union, the neo-abolitionist school prefers the moralistic justification of freeing the slaves. This is most explicit in one of the original neo-abolitionist salvos: Arthur M. Schlesinger, Jr., "The Causes of the American Civil War: A Note on Historical Sentimentalism," *Partisan Review*, 16 (October 1949), pp. 968–981, which compares the Union crusade against slavery to the Allied crusade against the Nazis.

Yet slavery and secession are separate issues, as John S. Rosenberg has pointed out in his remarkably clear-headed "Toward a New Civil War Revisionism," *The American Scholar*, 38 (Spring 1969), pp. 250–272. Even if slavery explains why the southern states left the Union, it does not necessarily either explain or justify the national government's refusal to recognize their independence. The New-Left historian, William Appleman Williams, in *America Confronts a Revolutionary World, 1776–1976* (New York: William Morrow, 1976), recognizes as much, and this is the interpretive niche I seek to occupy. Not only does slavery fail to explain why the northern states resorted to coercion, but letting the lower South go in peace was a viable, untried antislavery option. As the most militant abolitionists themselves demonstrated, there was no contradiction between condemning slavery and advocating secession. In this connection, I must acknowledge above all my deep indebtedness to Joseph R. Stromberg, "The War for Southern Independence: A Radical Libertarian Perspective," *Journal of Libertarian Studies*, 3 ([Spring] 1979), pp. 31–53. Although not in total agreement, much of my own thinking parallels Stromberg's on nearly every issue that the Civil War touches. Many of my arguments he perhaps could have made more effectively, although of course he cannot be blamed for the directions in which I have taken his insights.

1

Slavery and States' Rights in the Early Republic

The American Revolution's Assault on Human Bondage

Slavery had not always divided the South from the North. Prior to the American Revolution, all British colonies in the New World legally sanctioned the practice. Nearly every colony counted enslaved blacks among its population. And most colonists accepted this as normal and inevitable. A full 42 percent of New York City households possessed slaves at the end of the seventeenth century. As late as 1770, nearly twice as many blacks were in bondage throughout the colony of New York as within Georgia, even though blacks were a much larger proportion of less populous Georgia.

John Jay, a prominent New Yorker who coauthored the famous *Federalist* papers and was first Chief Justice of the Supreme Court, remembered the widespread acceptance of slavery among both Northerners and Southerners: "Prior to the great revolution . . . the great body of our people had been so long accustomed to the practice and convenience of having slaves, that very few among them even doubted the propriety and rectitude of it. Some liberal and conscientious men had . . . drawn the lawfulness of slavery into question, and they made converts to that opinion;" Jay conceded, "but the number of those converts compared with the people at large was then very inconsiderable."[1]

The Revolution, however, dislocated slavery both directly and indirectly. Virginia's royal governor ushered in the direct dislocation on November 7, 1775, when he proclaimed free any slave who would bear arms against the rebellious colonists. At least eighteen thousand freed blacks accompanied British forces as they evacuated Savannah, Charleston, New York City, and other places at the end of the war. South Carolina, the only colony with a slave majority when independence was declared, lost as much as one-third of its black population to flight or migration.

The indirect impact was still more profound, as the Revolution's liberating spirit induced many white Americans to challenge slavery. Quakers organized the world's first antislavery society in Philadelphia in 1775, and soon similar organizations dotted the colonies. Some states offered freedom to blacks who enlisted in the military. Vermont in its constitution of 1777 became the first to abolish the institution. The Pennsylvania legislature enacted gradual emancipation in 1780, while the Massachusetts courts pronounced slavery inconsistent with the state's declaration of rights in 1783. State after state followed with either outright abolition or gradual emancipation. The Continental Congress meanwhile passed the Ordinance of 1787, prohibiting slavery in the western territories north of the Ohio river. New Jersey in 1804 became the last remaining state above the Mason-Dixon line to put chattel slavery on the road to extinction.

Slavery was more economically entrenched in the former southern colonies, where 90 percent of British America's 460,000 blacks had resided. But even there, the Revolution's ideological assault upon any form of human bondage made significant inroads. Many southern states banned the importation of slaves; southern societies encouraging masters to free their human chattel flourished; and several states relaxed legal obstacles to such voluntary manumissions. These actions spawned the first substantial communities of free blacks, concentrated in the upper South. Delaware saw the process furthest; three-quarters of the state's blacks were out of bondage by 1810.

Enlightened southern statesmen, such as Thomas Jefferson, a slaveholder himself, condemned slavery as evil and endorsed steps towards its ultimate extinction. "Nothing is more certainly written in the book of fate than that these people are to be free," pronounced Jefferson, yet like so many of his neighbors, he also had strong reservations about the two races living side by side after emancipation. "Nor is it less certain that the two races, equally free, cannot live in the same government. Nature, habit, opinion have drawn indelible lines of distinction between them." Sending former slaves out of the country seemed the only solution. "It is still in our power to direct the process of emancipation and deportation, peaceably, and in such slow degree that the evil will wear off insensibly, and their place be, *pari passu*, filled up by free white laborers."[2]

The first cooling of antislavery fervor became evident in the drafting of the Constitution in 1787. On the one hand, the Constitution never acknowledged slavery's existence by using the term, and it contained a clause permitting Congress to outlaw the Atlantic slave trade after twenty years. On the other hand, this gave the states of the lower South plenty of time to replenish their diminished slave populations, and during this time imports would exceed those in any other two decades in American history.

The Constitution also made two other key concessions to slaveholders. First, Article IV, Section 2, compelled the return of fugitive slaves even if they escaped to states that had abolished the institution: "No person held to Service or Labour in one State, under the Laws thereof, escaping into another, shall, in Consequence of any Law or Regulation therein, be discharged from such Service or Labour, but shall be delivered up on Claim of the Party to whom such Service or Labour may be due." This in effect required the national government to subsidize the enforcement of the slave system with resources from slaveholders and non-slaveholders alike. Second, the Constitution counted three-fifths of a state's enslaved population to determine its representation in the House of Representatives. This "federal ratio," although applied to direct taxes as well, principally increased the political power of slaveholders in proportion to the number of enslaved blacks.

Congress's final abolition of the slave trade with other countries took effect in 1808, during Jefferson's presidency and just after the British Parliament enacted a similar prohibition. This was the last triumph within the United States for the Revolutionary surge against slavery. Southerners had begun to draw back from any commitment to the institution's eventual demise. This reversal ironically owed much to the international spread of Revolutionary ideals. Embraced in the French Revolution of 1789, these radical ideals soon helped spark a bloody slave insurrection in the French West Indies. By New Year's Day, 1804, the successful black rebels had established the Republic of Haiti, the second independent nation in the New World. Southerners looked on in horror as surviving white refugees fled to American shores. They suddenly felt more uneasy about the racial consequences of too strict an adherence to the principles of the American Revolution.

At the same time that the apparition of slave revolts was haunting Southerners, American slavery enjoyed an economic resurgence. Prior to the Revolution, it had been mainly viable along the seaboard South, in areas suitable for tobacco and rice cultivation. But Eli Whitney's invention of the cotton gin in 1793 helped slavery transcend these geographical limits. A cotton boom enticed settlers into the rich lands of the Gulf, converting the formerly slave-free southern frontier to plantation agriculture. In 1820 the United States slave population was three times what it had been at the outset of the Revolution. Thus, while slavery was disappearing throughout the rest of the world, it was expanding in the American South.

Missouri—"A Fire Bell in the Night"

Not until the decade following the War of 1812 did slavery fully divide the South from the North. The northern states still contained some 3,000 slaves as late as 1830, but these blacks would shortly join the 125,000 of their race in those states who were free. Opponents beat back last efforts to legalize the institution in Indiana and Illinois. Simultaneously, the free states were beginning to overwhelm the slave states in total population. Already in 1819, the North outvoted the South in the lower house of Congress, 105 to 81. Only the Senate maintained a balance between the country's two sections: eleven free states to eleven slave states.

At this point, Missouri petitioned Congress for admission to the Union. One-sixth of its 60,000 inhabitants were slaves. Representative James Tallmadge, Jr., of New York proposed several conditions on Missouri's statehood: additional slaves would be prohibited from entering Missouri, and the children of those slaves already there would be freed when they reached the age of twenty-five. Tallmadge's amendment did not touch any of the blacks already in bondage within Missouri. His plan of gradual emancipation would have taken half a century to complete. Still it provoked a fierce debate that kept Congress hopelessly deadlocked for a year. The House, with its free-state majority, approved Tallmadge's amendment. But the Senate rejected it. The elderly Thomas Jefferson best expressed the ominous dread for the future of the Union that this deadlock evoked. "This momentous question, like a fire bell in the night, awakened and filled me with terror. I considered it at once as the knell of the Union."[3]

Many northern politicians, however, were more worried about the additional political influence southern interests would receive through the federal ratio if new slave states were admitted. "The disproportionate power and influence allowed to the slave-holding states, was a necessary sacrifice to the establishment of the constitution," admitted the aging Senator Rufus King of New York, a veteran of the Constitutional Convention. "But the extension of this disproportionate power to the new states would be unjust and odious. The states whose power would be abridged, and whose burdens would be increased by the measure, cannot be expected to consent to it."[4]

Eventually Henry Clay, a Kentucky slaveowner serving as Speaker of the House, used the immense powers of his office to push through a compromise in February 1820. Missouri was admitted as a slave state. Maine, which had been a district of Massachusetts, was admitted as a free state. This maintained the sectional balance. The remainder of the national government's Louisiana Territory was divided along a line that ran parallel to Missouri's southern border. South of the line was open to slavery. The territory north of the line, except for the new state of Missouri, was closed to slavery.

Clay was hailed as the "Great Pacificator." This convivial, hard-drinking late-night gambler had saved the Union. But the Missouri crisis revealed fundamental shifts in the terms of Union. Southerners were now wholeheartedly committed to the expansion of their peculiar institution. Only expansion into new territories could mitigate the South's minority status. But because of that status, Southerners still needed the votes of some northern representatives. Called "doughfaces" by John Randolph of Roanoke, a Virginia Congressman, these northern men with southern principles made passage of the Missouri Compromise possible. Whereas Southerners had united behind slavery's spread, Northerners were not yet united behind restrictions upon it.

Southerners furthermore became advocates of inviolate states' rights. What particularly disturbed them was that Tallmadge's amendment would have imposed antislavery upon a full-fledged state, and not just a territory. Previously states' rights had been an ideological issue with support and opposition in all parts of the country. But once the Missouri controversy exposed the South's vulnerability as a minority, states' rights increasingly turned into a sectional issue. Southerners came to realize that only strict limits upon national authority could protect their existing slave system from hostile interference.

No one understood the reinforcing relationship between states' rights and slavery better than John Randolph of Roanoke. Although nearly all the influential speeches that he made during the House debates on Missouri were never recorded, he reiterated the same theme very soon thereafter when opposing nationally financed roads, canals, and other internal improvements. "If Congress possesses the power to do what is proposed in this bill," Randolph lashed out in his shrill, piercing soprano, "they may emancipate every slave in the United States—and with stronger color of reason than they can exercise the power now contended for." His warning to fellow Southerners about emancipation under the cover of the Constitution's war powers was prophetic. "I ask gentlemen, who stand in the same predicament as I do, to look well to what they are doing—to the colossal power with which they are now arming this Government. The power to do what I allude to is, I aver, more honestly inferrible [sic] from the war-making power, than the power we are now about to exercise. Let them look forward to the time when such a question shall arise, and tremble with me at the thought that the question is to be decided by a majority of the votes of this House."[5]

South Carolina Nullifies the Tariff

Clay's compromise quieted the controversy over slavery in the territories for nearly a quarter of a century but not the controversy over states' rights. No southern state was more locked into slavery than South Carolina. It had the densest concentration of slaves, with blacks well outnumbering whites. A small planter aristocracy monopolized political power. Even during the American Revolution, South Carolina had stoutly resisted any efforts to weaken the peculiar institution. Within less than a decade after the Missouri crisis, the state was militantly defying national power.

The issue that brought forth this defiance was not slavery but the tariff. Even though the Constitution authorized a tariff for revenue purposes, that did not mean, according to those who wished to interpret the document strictly, that it also authorized a tariff to protect domestic producers from foreign competitors. Southerners generally had come to oppose the steady rise in protectionist duties after the War of 1812; they correctly recognized that any restraints on free trade economically exploited an exporting region such as the South. When Congress passed in 1828 what came to be known as the Tariff of Abominations, raising duties to their highest level prior to the Civil War, the South's minority status received further confirmation. The legislature of South Carolina denounced the tariff as "unconstitutional, oppressive, and unjust," and printed up a lengthy essay on the subject of states' rights entitled *The South Carolina Exposition and Protest*.[6]

Vice-President John C. Calhoun had secretly authored the *Exposition and Protest*. Nothing better illustrates the way states' rights was being transformed into a sectional issue than the political swings of this South Carolina statesman. The Scots-Irish, Yale-educated, upcountry Southerner had started his political career as an extreme nationalist, supporting the War of 1812 and an expansive central government. Initially he favored a large standing army, a strong navy, a national bank, federally funded internal improvements, and a protective tariff. But by the time he wrote the

Exposition and Protest, Calhoun had abandoned all these earlier positions.

Calhoun's *Exposition and Protest* defended what has become known as the compact theory of the Constitution. This theory contends that the Constitution was a compact, or contract, among sovereign states. The states had established the central government as their agent to perform specific delegated powers, such as national defense. "The general Government," explained Calhoun in a later public address, "emanated from the people of the several States, forming distinct political communities, and acting in their separate and sovereign capacity, and not from all of the people forming one aggregate political community."

Not only was the central government strictly limited, but if any dispute arose over the extent of these powers, it was the creators of the compact, the states—not their agent, the central government— that should be the final arbiter. "The Constitution of the United States is in fact a compact, to which each State is a party," and "the several States or parties, have a right to judge of its infractions."[7]

The compact theory had a long history running back to the Philadelphia Convention of 1787. To ease the Constitution's ratification among an American populace decidedly unfriendly to a consolidated government, the framers had been deliberately vague about the document's exact nature. The Virginia and Kentucky Resolutions of 1798, written by James Madison and Thomas Jefferson, had enunciated the compact theory, as had representatives of the New England states at the Hartford Convention during the War of 1812. But the *Exposition and Protest* added an additional twist: the doctrine of nullification. Calhoun argued that state conventions, the bodies that had first ratified the Constitution, could also nullify within individual states any federal law they thought unconstitutional.

The only way the central government could override such state nullifications was through a new constitutional amendment approved by three-fourths of the states. Although this cumbersome doctrine may appear to take states' rights to a logical extreme, the South Carolina political theorist actually intended nullification as a moderate compromise. Rather than promoting disunion, he saw it as the best way to preserve the Union. According to the compact theory, each state still retained the sovereign right to secede. Nullification gave the southern states an alternate way of protecting themselves from majority tyranny while remaining within the Union. Calhoun believed that only recognition of this "fundamental principle of our system, resting on facts historically as certain, as our Revolution itself, and deductions as simple and demonstrative, as that of any political or moral truth whatever" could ensure "the stability and safety of our political institutions."[8]

South Carolina did not immediately test the doctrine of nullification. But the doctrine received a full hearing in one of the most famous debates on the Senate floor. South Carolina's Robert Hayne faced off against Bostonian Daniel Webster in 1830. Vice-President Calhoun silently presided over the debate. The Senate galleries were filled with spectators, and so many Congressmen attended the debate that the House lacked a quorum to conduct business.

Webster's ideological career had been almost a mirror image of Calhoun's, demonstrating again the steady ascent of sectionalism. A staunch opponent of national power during the War of 1812, the New England orator now contemptuously disparaged states' rights. He argued that the Constitution was *not* a compact establishing a voluntary federation among sovereign states. The American people, not the states, had ratified the Constitution and thereby created a consolidated government. Hence the states had no right to nullify a national law or secede from the Union.

Webster, massive, craggy, with jutting brows, pounded home the chaos that would follow from frequent nullification at every state's whim. "The doctrine for which the honorable gentleman contends leads him to the necessity of maintaining . . . that this General Government . . . is the servant of four and twenty masters, of different wills and different purposes, and yet bound to obey all. This absurdity (for it seems no less) arises from a misconception as to the origin of this Government in its true character. It is, sir, the people's constitution, the people's Government, made for the people; made by the people; and answerable to the people."[9]

Webster closed his arguments with a spread-eagled appeal to American nationalism. "When my eyes shall be turned to behold, for the last time, the sun in heaven, may I not see him shining on the broken and dishonored fragments of a once glorious Union; on States dissevered, discordant, belligerent; on a land rent with civil feuds, or drenched, it may be, in fraternal blood! Let their last feeble and lingering glance, rather, behold the gorgeous ensign of the republic, . . . not a stripe erased or polluted, nor a single star obscured; bearing for its motto no such miserable interrogatory as, What is all this worth? Nor those other words of delusion and folly, Liberty first, and Union afterwards: but every where, spread all over in characters of living light, blazing on all its ample folds, as they float over the sea and over the land, and in every wind under the whole heavens, that other sentiment, dear to every true American heart,—Liberty *and* Union, now and forever, one and inseparable!"[10]

The cry of "Liberty *and* Union" has since reverberated down through the history books, and to be sure, Webster's assertion of national supremacy possessed some historical validity. A permanent consolidated government had been what many of the Constitution's framers had hoped for. But the remarkable fact remains that Webster's theory did not have a venerable tradition to match that of the compact theory. Prior to the challenge of nullification, American nationalists had never systematically defended perpetual Union.

The nullification controversy reached a climax two years after the Webster-Hayne debate. Congress passed a new tariff lowering duties slightly. But the tariff was still protectionist and not low enough to suit South Carolina. The state's legislature called a convention, which promptly nullified both the Tariff of Abominations and the new Tariff of 1832. State and federal officials were prohibited from collecting duties within South Carolina after February 1, 1833. The state vowed to secede if the national government tried to coerce it.

The hot-tempered Andrew Jackson was President. A Tennessee slaveholder himself, he favored strict construction of the Constitution and sympathized with South Carolina on the tariff. But he drew the line at nullification and dismemberment of the Union. He issued a proclamation accusing South Carolina of treason, while he privately threatened to lead an invasion and hang Calhoun, who had finally revealed his authorship of *The South Carolina Exposition and Protest*. A force bill, permitting the President to use the army and navy to enforce the laws, began making its way through Congress. In response, South Carolina's government started raising a military force of its own.

An armed clash was averted when the Great Pacificator wielded his persuasive charm again. Clay put together a tariff that would reduce duties by 20 percent over nine years. It passed Congress at the same time as the Force Act. South Carolina accepted the Compromise Tariff of 1833 yet, conceding nothing in principle, nullified the Force Act. Helping to prevent the state's plunge toward disunion was its temporary isolation from the other southern states. South Carolina stood alone against the national government in 1833.

The Ideological Rift Over Slavery

Although South Carolina challenged the national government over the tariff, protection of slavery was the hidden agenda. "I consider the Tariff act as the occasion, rather than the real cause of the present unhappy state of things," Calhoun himself admitted in a letter. "The truth can no longer be disguised, that the peculiar domestick *institution* of the Southern States, and the consequent direction, which that and her soil and climate have given to her industry, has placed them in regard to taxation and appropriations in opposite relation to the majority of the Union." Without the protection of states' rights, Calhoun warned, Southerners "must *in the end* be forced to rebel, or submit it to have their paramount interests sacraficed [*sic*], their domestick institutions subordinated by Colonization and other schemes, and themselves & children reduced *to* wretchedness."[11]

The "Colonization scheme" that disturbed Calhoun was the last expression of Revolutionary antislavery. Entailing the removal of freed blacks to Africa, it remained the panacea of those opponents of slavery such as Jefferson who believed that a biracial American society was untenable. Prominent national leaders, many from the upper South, Henry Clay and John Randolph of Roanoke among them, had founded the American Colonization Society after the War of 1812. With endorsements from five slave-state legislatures and some financial aid from the national government, the society established the nation of Liberia on the west African coast in 1822. By 1860 it had transported over six thousand blacks.

Extreme Southerners such as Calhoun were not the only ones who opposed colonization. Free blacks themselves were generally unenthusiastic about voluntary deportation. But no one attacked colonization with greater vehemence than a group of young, radical abolitionists who burst upon the national scene in the 1830s. Exasperated at the betrayal of the Revolutionary promise that American slavery would wither away, and marshaling all the evangelical fervor of the religious revivals then sweeping the country, they demanded immediate emancipation.

The most vitriolic of these abolitionists was William Lloyd Garrison. The son of a drunken sailor who had abandoned his family, Garrison grew up in a poor but piously Baptist household in Newburyport, Massachusetts. He served as a printer's apprentice and then made his first notable mark on antislavery activism when he went to jail rather than pay a fine for libeling as a "highway robber and murderer" a New England merchant who shipped slaves between Baltimore and New Orleans. From Boston on January 1, 1831, the near-sighted, prematurely balding, twenty-five-year-old editor brought out the first issue of a new weekly paper, *The Liberator*. Garrison left no doubt about his refusal to compromise with the sin of slavery:

"I *will be* as harsh as truth, and as uncompromising as justice. On this subject, I do not wish to think, or speak, or write with moderation. No! No! Tell a man whose house is on fire, to give a moderate alarm: tell him to moderately rescue his wife from the hands of the ravisher; tell the mother to gradually extricate her babe from the fire into which it has fallen;—but urge me not to use moderation in a cause like the present. I am in earnest—I will not equivocate—I will not excuse—I will not retreat a single inch— AND I WILL BE HEARD."[12] Garrison conceded that the elimination of slavery would take time in practice. But that should not inhibit forthright condemnation of moral evil. "Urge immediate abolition as earnestly as we may, it will alas! be gradual abolition in the end. We have never said that slavery would be overthrown by a single blow; that it ought to be we shall always contend."[13]

The crusading editor called not only for immediate emancipation of all slaves, without any compensation to slaveholders, but also for immediate and full political rights for all blacks. Colonization was to him a blatantly racist sop that would only strengthen slavery. Garrison, however, did not look to direct political action to eradicate slavery. Moral suasion and non-violent resistance were his strategies. By agitation, he hoped to shame slaveholders into repentance. Indeed, he went so far as to denounce the Constitution for its proslavery clauses as "a covenant with death and an agreement with hell." During one 4th of July celebration, he publicly burned a copy, proclaiming: "So perish all compromises with tyranny!" He believed that if anything the North should secede. That way it could become a haven for runaway slaves. The slogan "No Union with Slave-Holders" appeared on the masthead of Garrison's *Liberator* for years.

Garrison helped organize the American Anti-Slavery Society in 1833. Two thousand local societies with 200,000 members had sprung into existence by 1840. Supporting this network was the northern community of free blacks. Frederick Douglass, a former slave who had escaped from Maryland in 1838, became their preeminent spokesman. Over six feet tall, broad-shouldered, with long hair and a majestic face, he was a striking and popular draw at abolitionist meetings throughout the North. His melodious and rich voice boldly informed white audiences that slavery "brands your republicanism as a sham, your humanity as a base pretense, and your Christianity as a lie."[14]

Although abolitionists were only a tiny minority in the North, they definitely were heard—especially in the South. Southern slaveholders viewed American abolitionists as part of an international movement steadily encircling them. Most of the new nations of Central and South America abolished slavery when they gained their independence from Spain. British abolitionists, who were intimately linked with their American counterparts, pressed Parliament into implementing compensated emancipation in its West

Indian colonies in 1833; France and Denmark followed in 1844. By 1850, slavery persisted only in the United States, Puerto Rico, Cuba, and Brazil, although the total slave population in the Western Hemisphere was larger than it had been half a century earlier.

Slaveholders were even a minority within the southern states. Only one-fourth of white households owned slaves, and about half of those owned fewer than five. The typical Southerner was a yeoman farmer or herdsman. Yet political power was concentrated in the hands of large planters, who held the allegiance of other southern whites by relying on the issue of race. "We have but little interest in the value of slaves," a North Carolina mountaineer subsequently wrote to his Civil War governor, "but there is one matter in this connection about which we feel a very deep interest. We are opposed to negro equality. To prevent this we are willing to spare the last man."[15]

Confronted with mounting moral condemnation, Southerners ceased apologizing for their peculiar institution as a "necessary evil." They instead began boldly to defend it as a "positive good," to use Calhoun's very words. The hierarchical premises of the proslavery defense ironically had originated after the Revolution among New England conservatives of the Federalist Party and been carried south by clergymen of the so-called Benevolent Empire, a loose association of philanthropists and reformers determined to impose Yankee culture on the rest of the country—the same Benevolent Empire within which many young abolitionists had gotten their start. Not until the 1830s did Southerners take this proslavery argument to heart.

The Virginia legislature during the winter of 1831–32 became the last official body within the slave states to debate gradual, compensated emancipation—coupling it with expulsion of all freed blacks. Calhoun could therefore announce in 1838 that most Southerners, goaded by abolitionist propaganda, had now adopted the new attitude toward slavery. "This agitation has produced one happy effect at least; it has compelled us to the South to look into the nature and character of this great institution, and to correct many false impressions that even we had entertained in relation to it. Many in the South once believed that it was a moral and political evil; that folly and delusion are gone; we see it now in its true light, and regard it as the most safe and stable basis for free institutions in the world."[16]

The proslavery defense was built upon a belief in Negro inferiority. "In all social systems, there must be a class to do the menial duties, to perform the drudgery of life," stated Senator James Henry Hammond, another South Carolinian. "It constitutes the very mud-sills of society and of political government." This class requires "but a low order of intellect and but little skill," yet "fortunately for the South, has found a race adapted to that purpose to her hand."[17]

Southerners did not stop with an open defense of slavery. They went on to attack northern society for its "wage slavery" and "exploitation of workers," using arguments repeated by socialist critics of capitalism. The southern writer who developed these arguments most extensively was George Fitzhugh, a Virginia planter and lawyer. His two books were provocatively entitled *Sociology for the South: Or the Failure of Free Society* and *Cannibals All! Or Slaves Without Masters.* In them, Fitzhugh defended slavery as a practical form of socialism that provided contented slaves with paternalistic masters, thereby eliminating harsh conflicts between employers and allegedly free workers. Liberty, he believed, places classes in a position of antagonism and war, whereas slavery identifies the interest of rich and poor, master and slave, begetting domestic affection on the one side, and loyalty and respect on the other. "A Southern farm is the beau ideal of Communism; it is a joint concern, in which the slave consumes more than the master, of the coarse products, and is far happier, because although the concern may fail, he is always sure of support."[18]

The Virginia author's enthusiasm for slavery led him explicitly to reject the radical principles behind the American Revolution. "The best governed countries, and those which have prospered the most, have always been distinguished for the number and stringency of their laws," he wrote; "liberty is an evil which government is intended to correct." Denying that men are "born entitled to equal rights," Fitzhugh turned around a metaphor employed in Jefferson's last letter before his death: "It would be far nearer the truth to say, 'that some were born with saddles on their backs, and others booted and spurred to ride them'—and the riding does them good. They need the reins, the bit and the spur.''[19]

If slavery were justified, it followed that there could be nothing wrong with the African slave trade. Since the Missouri controversy, American law had made slavers subject to hanging as pirates, although the U.S. navy was never as assiduous in hunting them down as the much larger British navy. Slave traders smuggled their cargoes mainly into Cuba and Brazil, but most of them hid behind the American flag, because the United States was one country that would not permit British patrols to search its vessels. By the 1850s the most provocative proslavery agitators were clamoring to reopen this traffic into the ports of the South. "If it is right," asked William Lowndes Yancey, an Alabama fire-eater, "to buy slaves in Virginia and carry them to New Orleans, why is it not right to buy them in Cuba, Brazil, or Africa, and carry them there?"[20] The primary forum for this agitation was a series of commercial conventions held annually at varied locations throughout the southern states, and finally the 1859 convention in Vicksburg demanded the repeal of all prohibitions on the Atlantic slave trade. Already southern juries were refusing to convict participants in this illicit commerce whom federal officials had apprehended.

Many Southerners held back from this proslavery extreme, especially in the northern tier of slave states, where the peculiar institution was less entrenched and the "positive good" argument never won universal acceptance. Nevertheless, as more and more embraced the morality of slavery at the very time that abolitionists became more and more confrontational, religion in America could not bear the strain. Until the second decade of the nineteenth century, most Protestant churches had cautiously conceded the contradiction between slavery and Christianity. But the Methodists, after futile attempts to paper over increasingly acrimonious controversy within the ranks, split into northern and southern branches in 1844. The next year the Baptists divided, leaving the country's two largest denominations broken in halves. The Presbyterians already had a theological schism only tangentially related to slavery between Old School and New School, and each school was able therefore to maintain a semblance of sectional unity well into the next decade. The trend however was unmistakable. Slavery was dissolving ideological and institutional bonds between North and South.

Abolitionists—From Unpopularity to Politics

Moral condemnation was not what alarmed Southerners most about the small number of radical abolitionists in the North. Far more unsettling was the growing southern conviction that any antislavery activity inevitably fanned the ubiquitous fires of servile insurrection. Back in 1800 a black bondsman named Gabriel, having imbibed Jeffersonian rhetoric, had carefully planned an attack on Richmond involving thousands of his compatriots, only to be betrayed by an informer. In 1822 South Carolinians had uncovered Denmark Vesey's plot among some of Charleston's most trusted house servants and hanged thirty-five blacks. Nine years later Nat Turner led about seventy slaves on a bloody rampage through Southhampton County, Virginia.

To squelch any further resistance, Southerners extended many of slavery's totalitarian controls to the free blacks and eventually to whites. Virginia required any slave, upon receiving freedom, to leave the state within twelve months, while South Carolina put all black sailors who landed at Charleston into jail until their ships departed. If no one paid the costs of detention, the authorities would sell such foreign sailors into slavery for reimbursement. Nearly every slave state reintroduced or tightened restrictions upon whites privately emancipating their chattels. Seven simply outlawed manumission unless the legislature granted specific permission, and courts increasingly overturned wills that freed slaves upon the owner's death. Throughout the South, free blacks had their movements watched and regulated, their right to testify against whites denied, and the types of jobs they could do limited. Sometimes they were literally forced to work, being re-enslaved in all but name.

The South's siege mentality turned it into a closed society. Advocating abolition became a felony in Virginia in 1836. The Georgia legislature offered a reward of $5,000 for anyone who would kidnap Garrison and bring him south for trial and punishment. Louisiana established a penalty ranging from twenty-one years hard labor to death for speeches and writings "having a TENDENCY to promote discontent among free colored people, or insubordination among slaves."[21] All slave-state legislatures except Kentucky's passed similar laws censoring free speech. The surveillance and violence of private vigilance committees made the region unsafe for even the most restrained critic of the peculiar institution. A theology student from the Lane Seminary in Cincinnati who carried abolitionist literature into Tennessee in 1835 was lucky to escape with a public whipping of twenty lashes, while one Virginia newspaper editor was gunned down in a duel in 1846 because of his alleged antislavery sympathies.

When northern abolitionists employed new and cheaper printing technologies to flood the South with antislavery tracts, mobs seized and burned much of this mail. Southerners even appealed to northern officials to cooperate in the suppression of abolitionist agitation. In this case, President Jackson shared the concern of his fellow slaveholders. He asked Congress in 1835 for a law barring abolitionist propaganda from the mail. Although the House of Representatives failed to heed Jackson's request by a narrow margin, his postmaster general acquiesced in the illegal refusal of local postmasters to deliver antislavery literature. Moreover, Congress did bow to southern outrage over the antislavery petitions now pouring in, most commonly demanding an end to slavery in the District of Columbia. It instituted a "Gag Rule" that automatically tabled such petitions.

Both measures were possible because abolitionists were unpopular in the North too. Although slavery had passed out of existence there, racism, already prevalent, was on the rise among northern workers. Alexis de Tocqueville, the perceptive French commentator on 1830s America, observed that "race prejudice seems stronger in those states that have abolished slavery than in those where it still exists, and nowhere is it more intolerant than in those states where slavery was never known."[22] Only five New England states allowed blacks to vote on an equal footing with whites, and New York allowed them to vote only if they could meet a special property qualification. Several western states emulated the common southern prohibition upon free blacks entering the state. Most northern locales had legally mandated discrimination of some sort. One infamous incident involved a Quaker schoolmistress named Prudence Crandall, who decided in 1833 to racially integrate her private academy for girls in Canterbury, Connecticut. The state legislature passed a special act that threw her behind bars. Nowhere could blacks serve on juries before 1860. The abolitionist championing of racial equality therefore received a cool reception.

The abolitionist disrespect for the Union did not sit well in the North either. Even when abolitionists did not share Garrison's explicit repudiation of the Constitution, their stridency still seemed to be provoking southern sectionalism. The abolitionists thus incurred the animosity of those Northerners who put their American nationalism above any opposition to slavery. One northern Congressman gave vent to both anti-abolitionist sentiments. "When gentlemen pretending to love their country would place the consideration of the nominal liberation of a handful of degraded Africans in the one scale, and this Union in the other, and make the latter kick the beam, [I] would not give a fig for their patriotism."[23]

Within the hostile atmosphere of the 1830s, abolitionist lecturers, presses, and property were frequent targets of northern violence, often instigated and directed by gentlemen of prominence and high rank. A Boston mob dragged Garrison through the streets and almost lynched him. One anti-abolitionist riot in New York City went on for half a week, during which crowds of day laborers damaged several churches, invaded black neighborhoods, and sacked the home of Lewis Tappan, a wealthy silk importer who generously financed antislavery organizations. These assaults finally reached a fateful culmination in 1837. Elijah Lovejoy, an abolitionist editor, was killed while defending his press from an Illinois mob. The Lovejoy murder marked a turning point, however, "a shock as of an earthquake throughout the continent," remarked former President John Quincy Adams.[24] An increasing number of Northerners began to sympathize with the abolitionists as courageous defenders of civil liberties, and they began to fear that slaveholders harbored contempt for the freedom of white as well as black Americans.

Hope for greater public sympathy helped splinter the abolitionist crusade into doctrinal factions. One source of discord was the role of women. Many remarkable female abolitionists, such as the Grimké sisters, Angelina and Sarah, Quaker converts from a wealthy South Carolina family who had fled north, made major contributions as speakers and organizers, but only Garrison and his followers were willing to flout prevailing mores by permitting women to participate on equal terms with men. Similarly, many abolitionists in their quest for respectability turned away from Garrison's pacifism and anarchism to take up political activity. Delegates from six states organized the Liberty Party in 1839 and, for their presidential candidate, choose James G. Birney, a former slaveholder from Alabama who had moved north after converting to abolitionism.

Rather than viewing the Constitution as a proslavery document, the Liberty Party viewed it as antislavery in spirit. The party's leaders accused the South of betraying an implicit constitutional understanding that slavery should disappear within the United States. Their 1844 platform, written by Salmon Portland Chase, a Cincinnati lawyer, expounded this new interpretation. One of the platform's most important planks resolved that "it was understood in the time of the Declaration and the Constitution, that the existence of slavery in some of the States, was in derogation of the principles of American Liberty, and a deep stain upon the character of the country, and the implied faith of the States and the Nation was pledged, that slavery should never be extended beyond its then existing limits; but should be gradually, and yet at no distant day, wholly abolished by State authority."[25]

As Libertymen hammered out this interpretation's concrete implications, very few would go along with Boston freethinker Lysander Spooner, who insisted that the national government directly abolish slavery in the southern states. Spooner contended that, whatever the intention of the framers, the inherent language of the Constitution—when properly interpreted within a natural-law framework—made slavery automatically unconstitutional throughout the Union. Most members of the new party instead settled for policies designed by Chase to bring about "the absolute and unqualified divorce of the General Government from slavery."[26] This involved abolition of slavery in the territories, in the District of Columbia, and in interstate and coastal commerce. No new slave states would be admitted, no slaveholder would be appointed to federal office, and no slaves would be employed in federal construction projects. The Liberty Party believed that if the national government cordoned off slavery in this rigid fashion, abolition by the South would have to follow.

Birney received a negligible number of votes in the 1840 presidential election and not many more in 1844. Most political abolitionists preferred to support antislavery candidates from the two major parties. During the 1830s, John Quincy Adams, or "Old Man Eloquent" to his admirers, had led a lonely fight against the Gag Rule on the House floor, where the ex-Chief Executive modestly sat as a Massachusetts Whig for the last seventeen years of his life. But with the arrival of the 1840s, several newly-elected members of both the Whig and Democratic Parties centered their political careers around antislavery stands right out of the Liberty Party's program. By the end of 1844, the House had lifted the Gag Rule. The Liberty Party was thus a harbinger of the future direction of antislavery. The resort to the ballot box would bring both a broadened appeal and a dilution of purity.

Chapter 1
Bibliographical Essay

After the civil rights movement of the 1950s and 1960s, slavery became one of the most well mined topics relating to the Civil War. We now have a splendid synthesis of all this scholarly labor: Peter Kolchin, *American Slavery: 1619–1877* (New York: Hill and Wang, 1993). With an outstanding bibliography, it is where to start investigating any aspect of the peculiar institution. More specialized studies on slavery's economic and social features will be deferred until next chapter. Here we are concerned with political and ideological developments.

On the origins of the crusade against slavery, consult the magisterial treatises of David Brion Davis: *The Problem of Slavery in Western Culture* (Ithaca, NY: Cornell University Press, 1966) and *The Problem of Slavery in the Age of Revolution, 1770–1823* (Ithaca, NY: Cornell University Press, 1975). The third volume in the trilogy, *The Problem of Slavery in the Age of Emancipation, 1815–1890*, is still eagerly awaited; until then we must be content with Davis's preliminary *Slavery and Human Progress* (New York: Oxford University Press, 1984).

Bernard Bailyn, *The Ideological Origins of the American Revolution*, rev. edn. (Cambridge, MA: Harvard University Press, 1992), an enormously influential investigation of the American Revolution's radical ideals, offers the most succinct introduction to how those ideals undermined slavery. More detail on this ideological impact is in Duncan J. MacLeod, *Slavery, Race and the American Revolution* (Cambridge, U.K.: Cambridge University Press, 1974). Arthur Zilversmit, *The First Emancipation: The Abolition of Slavery in the North* (Chicago: University of Chicago Press, 1967), covers the Revolution's legal and institutional impact, while Edgar J. McManus, *Black Bondage in the North* (Syracuse: Syracuse University Press, 1973), offers background on slavery's extent and operation within the northern colonies. Sylvia R. Frey, *Water From the Rock: Black Resistance in a Revolutionary Age* (Princeton, NJ: Princeton University Press, 1991), discusses the actions of blacks themselves during the Revolution.

Recent writings sometimes minimize the American Revolution's anti-slavery import. No doubt, slavery was only eliminated in those areas where it was less entrenched, and many northern states freed slaves within their borders very gradually. New Jersey still contained thirteen blacks in bondage in 1860, the year of Lincoln's election. But often the same authors who discount this early emancipation warn that slavery would have been viable in the Old Northwest or other territories if legally permitted. Abolition, before it could triumph everywhere, had to start somewhere, and the fact that it did so where opposition was weakest is unsurprising. What was left undone in no way diminishes the revolutionary nature of this assault upon a labor system that, as David Brion Davis reminds us, had remained unchallenged for millennia.

For the politics of slavery from the Revolution through the Constitutional Convention on up to the Missouri Compromise, see Donald L. Robinson's exhaustive *Slavery in the Structure of American Politics, 1765–1820* (New York: Harcourt Brace Jovanovich, 1971). Glover Moore, *The Missouri Controversy, 1819–1821* (Lexington: University of Kentucky Press, 1966), has become standard on that crisis. A short but valuable analytical overview that starts with the Missouri controversy is Don E. Fehrenbacher, *The South and Three Sectional Crises* (Baton Rouge: Louisiana State University Press, 1980).

A competent but neglected popular history of the compact theory of the Constitution, as employed by both Northerners and Southerners, is James Jackson Kilpatrick, *The Sovereign States: Notes of a Citizen of Virginia* (Chicago: Henry Regnery, 1957). William W. Freehling, *Prelude to Civil War: The Nullification Controversy in South Carolina, 1816–1836* (New York: Harper & Row, 1966), is a pioneering demonstration that slavery was the animating motive behind South Carolina's nullification of the tariff. But Freehling must be supplemented with Merrill D. Peterson, *Olive Branch and Sword—The Compromise of 1833* (Baton Rouge: Louisiana State University Press, 1982), and Richard E. Ellis, *The Union at Risk: Jacksonian Democracy, States' Rights, and the Nullification Crisis* (New York: Oxford University Press, 1987). In particular, Ellis reveals how President Jackson's belligerence carried him beyond the mainstream of his party and that the compromise was more a victory for the nullifiers than previous writers had realized.

Ellis's work is also important because it alone has detected that Northerners generally had not yet become comfortable with a Union held together by force, a finding consistent with Kenneth M. Stampp's outstanding article on the belated development of a constitutional argument against secession: "The Concept of a Perpetual Union," reprinted as chapter 1 of *The Imperiled Union* (cited in the prologue). Although historians have extensively researched southern motives for the transformation of states' rights into a sectional issue, they have not done as good a job with northern motives. Nationalist bias elevates perpetual union to an automatic and almost unquestioned standard. Exactly *how* Northerners came to embrace this standard is recounted in several intellectual histories that I will mention in the fifth chapter, but none are satisfactory in answering *why* this ideological development took place. My hunch is that a thorough investigation would resurrect certain features of Beard's economic interpretation, with a new public-choice emphasis on northern rent-seeking. It is probably no coincidence that Henry Clay, the Great Pacificator who did so much to hold the Union together, was also (as our third chapter will explore) the author of the American System, a lavish banquet of federal subsidies and privileges designed for various special interests.

The eloquent chronicler of Andrew Jackson's life, Robert V. Remini, has now given us a splendid biography of the Great Pacificator: *Henry Clay: Statesman for the Union* (New York: W. W. Norton, 1991). Among several biographies of John C. Calhoun, you cannot beat for completeness the older, sympathetic three volumes from Charles M. Wiltse, *John C. Calhoun*, (Indianapolis: Bobbs-Merrill, 1944–1951); whereas the shorter, newer Richard N. Current, *John C. Calhoun* (New York: Washington Square Press, 1966), is more critical. Alexander Tabarrok and Tyler Cowen, in "The Public Choice Theory of John C. Calhoun," *Journal of Institutional and Theoretical Economics*, 148 (December 1992), pp. 655–674, credit Calhoun's political ideas with anticipating some of modern public-choice economics. Recent scholarly biographies of Daniel Webster are Maurice G. Baxter, *One and Indivisible: Daniel Webster and the Union* (Cambridge, MA: Harvard University Press, 1984), and Irving H. Bartlett, *Daniel Webster* (New York: W. W. Norton, 1978).

My favorite introduction to nineteenth-century abolitionism is James Brewer Stewart, *Holy Warriors: The Abolitionists and American Slavery* (New York: Hill and Wang, 1976), primarily an intellectual history. Other introductory volumes include Ronald G. Walters, *The Antislavery Appeal: American Abolitionism After 1830* (Baltimore: Johns Hopkins University Press, 1976); Merton L. Dillon, *The Abolitionists: The Growth of a Dissenting Minority* (DeKalb: Northern Illinois University Press, 1974); and Gerald Sorin, *Abolitionism: A New Perspective* (New York: Praeger, 1972). To flesh out narrative events, the most oft-cited larger volume is Louis Filler, *The Crusade Against Slavery, 1830–1860* (New York: Harper & Row, 1960). Unfortunately, although historically reliable, Filler's study, part of the New American Nation Series, is much more clumsily written than it should be. Another history, violently partisan, that covers the antislavery movement all the way back to the colonial period is Dwight Lowell Dumond, *Antislavery: The Crusade for Freedom in America* (Ann Arbor: University of Michigan Press, 1966). Dumond's earlier and briefer *Antislavery Origins of the Civil War in the United States* (Ann Arbor: University of Michigan Press, 1939) prefigured many of the findings of his longer work.

For a history of the American Colonization Society, see P. J. Staudenraus, *The African Colonization Movement, 1816–1865* (New York: Columbia University Press, 1961). Alison Goodyear Freehling examines the South's last serious consideration of emancipation before the Civil War in *Drift Toward Dissolution: The Virginia Slavery Debate of 1831–1832* (Baton Rouge: Louisiana State University Press, 1982). An emphasis on abolition's evangelical underpinnings is provided by Lawrence J. Friedman, *Gregarious Saints: Self and Community in American Abolitionism, 1830–1870* (Cambridge, U.K.: Cambridge University Press, 1982); while Betty L. Fladeland, *Men and Brothers: Anglo-American Antislavery Cooperation* (Urbana: University of Illinois Press, 1972) explores the connections between British and American abolitionism. Carleton Mabee, *Black Freedom: The Nonviolent Abolitionists From 1830 Through the Civil War* (New York: Macmillan, 1970), is a sensitive treatment of abolitionist tactics.

One contribution to understanding abolitionism that cannot be praised too highly is Aileen S. Kraditor, *Means and Ends in American Abolitionism: Garrison and His Critics on Strategy and Tactics, 1834–1850* (New York:

Random House, 1969). Prior to her work, the all-too-common inclination was to disparage William Lloyd Garrison and his followers. This goes back to Gilbert H. Barnes, *The Antislavery Impulse, 1830–1844* (New York: American Historical Association, 1933), and tainted the works of both Filler and Dumond. They portrayed Garrison as a vituperative and intolerant zealot whose actual antislavery activities were far less constructive than the those of other, more respectable but less visible figures, such as Lewis Tappan and Theodore Dwight Weld. Kraditor has reestablished the centrality of the Garrisonians and, in the process, shows that they were often more tolerant and less sectarian than conservative opponents in their willingness to welcome all factions within the abolitionist fold.

Another seminal work that looks into Garrison's anarchism and non-resistance is Lewis Perry, *Radical Abolitionism: Anarchy and the Government of God in Antislavery Thought* (Ithaca, NY: Cornell University Press, 1973). More recently, Daniel J. McInerney, *The Fortunate Heirs of Freedom: Abolition & Republican Thought* (Lincoln: University of Nebraska Press, 1994), has grounded abolitionism's ideological heritage not in evangelical religion but in the radical republicanism of the American Revolution. Both works are good antidotes to the tendency—most recently manifest in the study by Lawrence Friedman—to associate radical abolitionism with the Benevolent Empire's paternalistic and often statist reforms (e.g., mandatory Sunday closing, alcohol prohibition, and compulsory government schools). This is not to deny that there were many institutional and personal connections between the two movements. But their more fundamental, ideological antagonisms ultimately predominated. It is best to think of abolitionism as a crusade that drew its recruits primarily from those who were culturally prone toward elitist conservatism but then radicalized them ideologically. Herbert Aptheker, however, carries this approach too far in *Abolitionism: A Revolutionary Movement* (Boston: Twayne, 1989), where he tries to paint abolitionists as class-conscious, anti-property precursors of Marx.

The Kraditor volume is essential for another reason; Garrison has not been adequately served by his biographers. Walter Merrill, *Against Wind and Tide: A Biography of Wm. Lloyd Garrison* (Cambridge, MA: Harvard University Press, 1963), at least is not hostile toward its subject, as is John L. Thomas, *The Liberator, William Lloyd Garrison: A Biography* (Boston: Little, Brown, 1963). An impressive biography of one of the more conservative abolitionists is Bertram Wyatt-Brown, *Lewis Tappan and the Evangelical War Against Slavery* (Cleveland: Press of Case Western Reserve University, 1969).

The participation of free blacks in the abolitionist crusade is the subject of Benjamin Quarles, *Black Abolitionists* (New York: Oxford University Press, 1969), and Jane H. Pease and William H. Pease, *They Who Would Be Free: Blacks Search for Freedom, 1830–1861* (New York: Atheneum, 1974). Frederick Douglass has attracted many biographers, most recently, William S. McFeely, *Frederick Douglass* (New York: W. W. Norton, 1991). Blanche Glassman Hersh, *The Slavery of Sex: Feminist Abolitionists in America*

(Urbana: University of Illinois Press, 1978), chronicles the contributions of women to the antislavery movement, while the life of the Grimké sisters is told in Gerda Lerner, *The Grimké Sisters from South Carolina: Rebels Against Slavery* (Boston: Houghton Mifflin, 1967).

General descriptions of the antebellum South begin with Clement Eaton's addition to the New American Nation series, *The Growth of Southern Civilization, 1790–1860* (New York: Harper & Row, 1961). For detail, move on to the two volumes from the *History of the South* series: Charles S. Sydnor, *The Development of Southern Sectionalism, 1819–1848* (Baton Rouge: Louisiana State University Press, 1948), and Avery O. Craven, *The Growth of Southern Nationalism, 1848–1861* (Baton Rouge: Louisiana State University Press, 1953). Bruce Collins, *White Society in the Antebellum South* (London: Longman, 1985), ably incorporates recent scholarship to argue that the section displayed more consensus than conflict. But William W. Freehling's opening volume to his own new series, *The Road to Disunion*, v. 1, *Secessionists at Bay, 1776–1854* (New York: Oxford University Press, 1990), finds less uniformity and greater diversity, particularly between the upper and lower South. It also contains one of the most extensive treatments of the Gag Rule controversy.

The classic work on the ideological defense of slavery is William S. Jenkins, *Pro-Slavery Thought in the Old South* (Chapel Hill: University of North Carolina Press, 1935). But Jenkins's conclusions require significant modification in the light of Larry E. Tise, *Proslavery: A History of the Defense of Slavery in America, 1701–1840* (Athens: University of Georgia Press, 1987). Tise's discovery of the New England origin of the proslavery ideology during the neglected period prior to 1830 is of monumental importance, although he has come in for justifiable criticism because of his penchant for defining practically all hierarchical thought as proslavery. Nonetheless, Tise's book identifies the true intellectual sources of antebellum America's counter-revolutionary conservatism and helps further dissociate abolitionism from the Benevolent Empire.

Some of Tise's conclusions were foreshadowed in Bertram Wyatt-Brown's artful essay on the evolution of proslavery thought, "From Piety to Fantasy: Proslavery's Troubled Evolution," in his collection, *Yankee Saints and Southern Sinners* (already cited in the prologue). The one major foundation for the proslavery ideology that was, in fact, indigenous to the South was obviously the assumption of black inferiority, whereas racism was often explicitly rejected by the New Englanders composing the Benevolent Empire. For an intriguing argument that the proslavery ideology was the defensive response of the planter class to the contemporaneous extension of suffrage and other democratic processes, see the commanding comparative study by George M. Fredrickson, *White Supremacy: A Comparative Study of American and South African History* (New York: Oxford University Press, 1981).

Historians have long debated just how representative of southern thought George Fitzhugh was. See, for the view that the Virginia theorist was atypical, C. Vann Woodward, "A Southern War Against Capitalism," in his *American Counterpoint: Slavery and Racism in the North-South Dialogue* (Boston: Little, Brown, 1971). A rejoinder is the second essay in Eugene D. Genovese, *The World the Slaveholders Made: Two Essays in Interpretation* (New York: Random House, 1969), whereas Drew Gilpin Faust calls attention to several other Southerners she finds more typical in *A Sacred Circle: The Dilemma of the Intellectuals in the Old South, 1840–1860* (Baltimore: Johns Hopkins University Press, 1977). Harvey Wish, *George Fitzhugh: Propagandist of the Old South* (Baton Rouge: Louisiana State University Press, 1943), tells us the little we know about Fitzhugh's life. For more depth on another proslavery theorists, take a look at Faust's *James Henry Hammond and the Old South: A Design for Mastery* (Baton Rouge: Louisiana State University Press, 1982).

Ronald Takaki, *A Pro-Slavery Crusade: The Agitation to Reopen the African Slave Trade* (New York: Free Press, 1971), surveys this extreme clamor. On United States suppression of the African slave trade, see Warren S. Howard, *American Slavers and Federal Law, 1837–1862* (Berkeley: University of California Press, 1963). Also, David R. Murray, *Odious Commerce: Britain, Spain and the Abolition of the Cuban Slave Trade* (Cambridge, U.K.: Cambridge University Press, 1980), and David Eltis, *Economic Growth and the Ending of the Transatlantic Slave Trade* (New York: Oxford University Press, 1987), contain useful information.

The growth of proslavery thought in southern churches is covered in H. Shelton Smith, *In His Image, But . . . : Racism in Southern Religion, 1780–1910* (Durham, NC: Duke University Press, 1972). For the abolitionist counterattack, see John R. McKivigan, *The War Against Proslavery Religion: Abolitionism and Northern Churches, 1830–1864* (Ithaca, NY: Cornell University Press, 1984). Donald G. Matthews, *Slavery and Methodism: A Chapter in American Morality, 1780–1845* (Princeton, NJ: Princeton University Press, 1965), recounts the struggle within one major denomination. C. C. Goen, *Broken Churches, Broken Nation: Denominational Schisms and the Coming of the Civil War* (Macon, GA: Mercer University Press, 1985), argues that the ruptures within the Protestant churches significantly contributed to the subsequent rupture of the Union.

The dampening impact of Haiti's revolution on southern attitudes is well covered in Alfred H. Hunt, *Haiti's Influence on Antebellum America: Slumbering Volcano in the Caribbean* (Baton Rouge: Louisiana State University Press, 1988). Herbert Aptheker, *American Negro Slave Revolts* (New York: Columbia University Press, 1943), is notoriously exaggerated on slave uprisings in the United States. Joseph C. Carroll, *Slave Insurrections in the United States, 1800–1865* (Boston: Chapman & Grimes, 1938), is more reliable. Douglas R. Egerton, *Gabriel's Rebellion: The Virginia Slave Conspiracies of 1800 and 1802* (Chapel Hill: University of North Carolina Press, 1993), unearths this early outburst from obscurity and misconception. On Denmark Vesey's rebellion, see John Lofton, *Insurrection in South Carolina: The Turbulent World of Denmark Vesey* (Yellow Springs, OH: Antioch Press,

1964). Stephen B. Oates, *The Fires of Jubilee: Nat Turner's Fierce Rebellion* (New York: Harper & Row, 1975), is probably the best of several books on that episode.

For the treatment of southern free blacks, see Ira Berlin, *Slaves Without Masters: The Free Negro in the Antebellum South* (New York: Random House, 1974). Leon F. Litwack, *North of Slavery: The Negro in the Free States 1790–1860* (Chicago: University of Chicago Press, 1961), does the same for northern free blacks. George M. Fredrickson, *The Black Image in the White Mind: The Debate on Afro-American Character and Destiny, 1817–1914* (New York: Harper & Row, 1971), is relevant on racism North and South.

Clement Eaton, *The Freedom of Thought Struggle in the Old South,* covers general violations of civil liberties in the South; Russel B. Nye, *Fettered Freedom: Civil Liberties and the Slavery Controversy, 1830–1860,* 2nd edn., (Ann Arbor: Michigan State University Press, 1963), deals with the country overall. W. Sherman Savage, *The Controversy Over the Distribution of Abolition Literature, 1830–1860* ([Washington]: Association for the Study of Negro Life and History, 1938), treats suppression via the post office. On northern violence directed at abolitionists, Leonard L. Richards, *"Gentlemen of Property and Standing": Anti-Abolition Mobs in Jacksonian America* (New York: Oxford University Press, 1970), is a short analysis relying on statistical techniques.

A new detailed narrative about the Gag Rule debates is William Lee Miller, *Arguing About Slavery: The Great Battle in the United States Congress* (New York: Alfred A. Knopf, 1996). Richard H. Sewell, *Ballots for Freedom: Antislavery Politics in the United States, 1837–1860* (New York: W. W. Norton, 1976), is an excellent discussion of political antislavery and the Liberty Party, but also see Aileen S. Kraditor, "The Liberty and Free Soil Parties," in Arthur M. Schlesinger, Jr., ed., *History of U.S. Political Parties,* v. 1; *1789–1860: From Factions to Parties* (New York: Chelsea House, 1973), pp. 741–763. William M. Wiecek, *The Sources of Antislavery Constitutionalism in America, 1760–1848* (Ithaca, NY: Cornell University Press, 1977), thoroughly compares the conflicting abolitionist interpretations of the constitutionality of slavery and also covers the more mainstream interpretations of the period. A biography of the Liberty Party's presidential candidate is Betty Fladeland, *James Gillespie Birney: Slaveholder to Abolitionist* (Ithaca, NY: Cornell University Press, 1955).

2

The Political Economy of Slavery and Secession

"No Union With Slave-Holders"

William Lloyd Garrison is easily dismissed as hopelessly naive. His opposition to government was so intense that he and his followers refused even to vote. But this appearance of strategic naiveté is misleading. Once it became clear that Southerners were not inclined to repent and free their chattels voluntarily, the Garrisonians fully understood that abolition would require some political act. They further realized, however, that the politics would take care of itself—indeed only could take care of itself—after moral suasion had first created a powerful antislavery constituency.

Yet one of Garrison's proposals remains difficult to fathom. How could northern secession from the Union help the slaves? To appreciate the true sophistication of this tactic, a sophistication that Garrison himself may not have grasped entirely, we must navigate the lively controversy about the economics of American slavery. Much of the ink in this controversy has been spilt over whether slavery was profitable. Although some abolitionists and later historians pictured cotton plantations as decreasingly lucrative enterprises to which Southerners clung for cultural reasons, the current consensus is that slaves did yield a return comparable to other

37

investments at the time. But this does not close the question, because the word "profitable" has several meanings.

The Profitability of Slavery*

Human bondage has been a source of forced labor since the dawn of civilization. People have sought slaves on every continent and for every conceivable task. Islamic slavery, which arose during the Middle Ages and forcibly transported across the Sahara many more millions of souls than were seized for the transatlantic trade, satisfied a large demand for luxury goods. These black Africans were compelled to serve as retainers, servants, or concubines. Even when not directly satisfying their masters' desires, many slaves in the medieval and ancient worlds engaged in household production only. New World slavery, in contrast, produced tobacco, sugar, rice, cotton, and other commodities for world markets.

The ultimate consumers of the cotton that black slaves grew in the American South were workers in England and elsewhere who wore clothes manufactured from it. The price of these slaves therefore was like the price of any other capital good, including corporate stock, farm land, or cattle. The planter held title to the slave's future labor. This labor produced an income stream equal to the value of output minus the slave's subsistence, maintenance, and management. Market competition would drive prices to the present sum of this expected future income, discounted at the prevailing rate of interest. Because the future was uncertain and information costly, this income stream would occasionally diverge from expectations. But since there was no reason to expect these entrepreneurial errors to be systematic in either direction, slaves were as profitable on average as any other asset traded in the market.

Southerners also bought slaves for conspicuous personal consumption. Indeed, a particular bondsman might work both as a field hand and domestic servant. Thus, two sources of demand were impinging on the same market. But the record of pre-Civil War slave prices confirms that very few purchases were for mere consump-

---

*The next four sections employ some economic analysis. Those readers uninterested should feel free to skip ahead to page 52, the section on "The Runaway Slave."

tion. Prime field hands by the mid-1850s cost upwards of $1,200, or $21,000 in today's prices, and the figure was sensitive to anything that could affect the field hand's future labor: health, skills, gender, reliability—with age being the most important. Prices generally peaked when a slave reached his or her mid-to-late twenties, and then fell off along with the expected number of remaining productive years. A skilled blacksmith commanded a 55 percent premium over this average, whereas a disabled or unreliable slave would sell at a discount of up to 65 percent. Twenty-seven-year-old females averaged 80 percent of the cost of male slaves the same age.

These prices were flexible enough to keep the return on slaves in the South hovering between 8 and 12 percent, comparable to the antebellum return on the capital of New England textile firms or railroad companies. At any one time, a particularly astute planter might exceed these rates, while one who was particularly inept might face insolvency. Over the passage of time, above-normal returns during a cotton boom might signal slaveholders generally to expand cultivation in order to satisfy mounting industrial demand, as happened during the 1850s; below-normal returns might encourage slaveholders to shift resources away from cotton, as for instance during the deflation of the early 1840s.

But overall, rather than facing economic demise, slavery was thriving right up to the Civil War. Cotton was the American economy's leading sector, constituting half of all exports. For ambitious white Southerners, the primary avenue to greater wealth and status remained slave ownership. "Never before has the planting been more profitable than in the last few years," wrote Professor C. F. McCay of South Carolina in 1860. "The planters have been everywhere rich, prosperous and happy."[1] Yet just because the peculiar institution was profitable to planters, it does not follow that it was beneficial to everyone living in the region.

To appreciate how individual profit might fail to generate economy-wide advantages, consider another contentious issue that tended to alienate Southerners from Northerners: the tariff. A protective trade barrier such as the 1828 Tariff of Abominations, which pushed up prices of competing imports, clearly benefited some domestic producers. Yet it hurt domestic buyers because they now had to pay the higher prices. Economic theory proves, with only a few technical exceptions that almost never obtain in the real world, that the losses from trade restrictions exceed the gains. The Tariff of Abominations not only redistributed income from Southerners and other consumers to northeastern manufacturers but in the process made the average American poorer. While profitable to protected interests, the tariff was harmful for the country. Slavery worked out similarly.

The Social Cost of Slavery

The most salient economic feature of the South's peculiar institution is that it was like theft. It involved a compulsory transfer from black slaves to white masters. Whereas free workers exchanged labor for market wages, a slaveowner could rent out slaves at the same wage, force them to do the same work, but grant them only a portion of the earnings in money or in kind and keep the difference. The amount the owner kept constituted the transfer and gave slaves a positive price.

Economists cannot quantify a transfer's effect on well-being precisely. After the Atlantic trade was shut down and replacement of slaves became expensive, the planter had more incentive to promote his chattels' health and productivity. The food, clothing, shelter, and other payments in kind that slaves received came to an average of about $30 per year at 1860 prices.[2] This was adequate to give the American slave a life expectancy of thirty-six years, slightly less than rural whites, but comparable to urban populations, and higher than in Europe. Yet surely these expenditures did not provide the same subjective satisfaction to the slave as an equal monetary wage. Free laborers have far more opportunity to exchange money on the market for goods and services tailored to their unique preferences. Making this comparison would be no more valid than pricing all the food, clothing, housing, and medical care received by present-day prisoners and claiming it equivalent to the same number of dollars earned on the outside.

A joke once told about an escaped slave from Kentucky who was brought before an Indiana justice of the peace illustrates the difficulty:

Judge: "Were you unhappy there?"

Slave: "Oh no. I had a good life there."

Judge: "Were you mistreated?"

Slave: "No. Old Masa and me was the greatest friends. Fished and hunted together."

Judge: "Did you have good food and housing?"

Slave: "Sure enough. Ham and 'taters. Molasses. My little cabin had roses over the door."

Judge: "I don't understand. Why did you run away?"

Slave: "Well your Honor, the situation is still open down there if you'd like to apply for it."[3]

Besides this unquantifiable burden, the peculiar institution diminished southern welfare in other ways. Forced transfers have secondary effects. The pirates who plagued colonial waters until the middle of the eighteenth century enriched themselves with captured cargoes. If they sunk merchant ships in the process, then the losses of merchants exceeded the gains of pirates. Economists call this excess burden "deadweight loss," and it is the reason they consider theft inefficient. Pure transfers are assumed to cancel out between gainers and losers, but people nonetheless are worse off on average.

Most deadweight loss results not from damage done during theft but from the way people alter their behavior in response. They reallocate resources either to seek transfers or avoid them. The major net losses from piracy were not ships sunk but all the expenditures on protecting cargoes that merchants could have made on other things, and all the unrealized gains from the ocean trade that piracy scared away, as well as all the ships and sailors that pirates devoted to stealing that otherwise could have furthered mutually beneficial pursuits. Notice that despite these losses, stealing was still profitable to the pirates. Theft, after all, is the quintessential case where individual incentives do not lead to socially optimal outcomes.

Part of the peculiar institution's deadweight loss resulted from how it changed the behavior of blacks. Because human bondage replaced the enticement of a wage with the threat of violence, the quantity and quality of work differed from what free laborers would have provided. The South's aggregate output was consequently worth less, even if we treat all dollar transfers as having made slaveholders better off to the exact same degree that slaves were worse off.

Slaveholders, of course, mixed positive and negative incentives. Not all the bondsman's labor was coercively extracted. Slaves were fed and received other payments, as already noted. Slaveholders could decide whether to try to induce additional work with rewards (pecuniary and non-pecuniary) or with punishments. They would usually only resort to force when it was less expensive. Because coercion itself uses up labor, as well as other scarce resources, not to mention possible loss of output from injuring or killing the slave, it was not always cheaper than paying an implicit wage.

Slaveowners found positive incentives less costly for jobs requiring greater skill, initiative, or self-discipline. In towns and cities, where such jobs predominated, the practice of hiring out slaves and giving them a fixed sum or percentage became well established. Slaves who were skilled carpenters, masons, or other artisans often could "hire their own time," that is, choose their own employers and thereby engage in entrepreneurship. Many lived separately from their masters. Charles Ball, a black undertaker in Savannah, Georgia, was even able to hire other slaves to help with his jobs, paying his master $250 a year in monthly installments. "A city slave," observed black leader Frederick Douglass, "is almost a free citizen" because he "enjoys privileges altogether unknown to the whip-driven slave on the plantation."[4]

These practices were so remunerative for slaveowners that they persisted despite countless municipal and state ordinances outlawing them. This made bound labor adaptable to a diversity of occupations. Lumber camps, sawmills, coal mines, rock quarries, textile mills, riverboats, cattle ranches, and railroads throughout the South employed black slaves, who also comprised half the work force at the Tredegar Iron Works in Richmond, Virginia, while over two thousand were iron workers in the Cumberland River region of Tennessee. One exceptional case involved a Mississippi slave named Simon Gray, who during the 1850s became captain of a Natchez flat boat, managing and paying a crew that included white men. He also conducted other business for his company, requiring that he carry firearms, travel freely, and handle large sums of money. Out of his salary Gray could afford to rent a house for himself and his family. His owners even permitted him a vacation in Arkansas for his health.

To the extent that bondsmen worked for explicit or implicit wages, the system operated like free labor. "Whenever a slave is made a mechanic," complained James Henry Hammond of South Carolina, "he is more than half freed."[5] What distinguished slavery was the master's option to wield brutality and terror. Theoretically he could add sufficient force to induce a slave to do any task that could be induced with a wage. Flogging was the most common method. This power was legally limited only by unenforceable state laws protecting human chattel from murder and mutilation and setting minimum standards for subsistence.

Imagine, however, the security costs of employing a typical slave as a boat captain, and you can understand why the case of Simon Gray was rare. Bondsmen usually were not useful for jobs requiring extensive travel, wide dispersion, use of firearms, or high degrees of trustworthiness, especially when lots of cash was involved. "The point here is not that one incentive system," either rewards or punishments, "was categorically more efficient than the other," notes economist Thomas Sowell. Which of the two was cheaper "differed according to the work and to the cost of knowledge to those who held the decision-making power."[6] Given the existing technology of force, there were many jobs in the South where hiring free laborers was invariably less costly than coercing slaves. But these very often tended to be jobs requiring initiative, discretion, and diligence, where close monitoring was prohibitively expensive—in other words, jobs that commanded higher wages because the output was more valuable.

Many blacks, if free, might have done these well-paid jobs. They therefore could produce either of two possible streams of future output—one less valuable while slaves and one more valuable while free. Wherever such a discrepancy arose, it became a mutually profitable deal for the slave to buy his freedom from his owner. Despite the refusal of state laws to recognize the bondsman's right to hold property, his higher asset value once free should have enabled him to borrow the purchase price, under all sorts of risk and repayment plans, either from his master or a third party.

Varied institutional arrangements have facilitated slave self-purchase historically. Throughout ancient Greece and Rome, manumission and ransom prices were frequently higher than market prices for slaves, and slave self-purchase became so common that it may have been one factor in the institution's decline during the Pax Romana, after supplies of fresh captives dried up. The right of slaves to buy their freedom in many Latin American countries became formalized in a practice known as *coartación*. Manumission by slaveowners practically eliminated slavery in Mexico long before formal abolition in 1829. Even in Brazil and Cuba, where sugar plantations made bound labor far more commercially vital, the number of free blacks was approaching the number of slaves by the nineteenth century.

Manumission through self-purchase was not unknown in the United States, being most common in the upper South. But as the distinguished historian of slavery, David Brion Davis, has noted, "the most important distinction between the legal status of slaves in British and Latin America" was the extensive barriers to manumission in British-settled areas. "Only in the Southern United States did legislators try to bar every route to emancipation and deprive masters of their traditional right to free individual slaves."[7]

Except when temporarily relaxed during the Revolutionary era, these barriers severely inhibited self-purchase. Between 1790 and 1800, the population of free blacks in the Atlantic slave states nearly doubled. If that increase had continued at the same rate until 1860, almost the entire slave population of the country would have become free. In actuality the number of southern free blacks by the 1850s was rising more slowly than the number of slaves.[8] Even when laws against manumission could be evaded, the widespread legal disabilities faced by free blacks, especially requirements that they leave the state, reduced their potential incomes and made self-purchase less viable.

Because of all these legal obstructions, slavery necessarily misallocated labor into less productive uses. Slaves were not only worse off, but the South's aggregate output was lower than otherwise. This does not justify slaves having to buy their own liberty but merely acknowledges that the market provided a route to eliminate this inefficiency and simultaneously erode the peculiar institution. Why planters should erect such barriers when it was in their individual self-interest to permit self-purchase is a question to which we will return.

Unfortunately not all bondsmen had the potential to be more productive as freedmen. But the opportunities for manumission through self-purchase were not confined to those cases. Most individuals have what John Moes has called a "sentimental attachment" to their own body.[9] A slave therefore would value a dollar's worth of wages more highly once free. Blacks may have been willing to do the same physical work for less retained income just to avoid the humiliations and hardships of bondage. This would have still left enough from their wages to buy out their owners. Because of the obstacles put in the way of manumission, however, it is impossible to know for how many this was realistic.

Overworking the Slaves

Nearly three-quarters of America's slaves toiled on plantations or farms in 1860, and the proportion was climbing. Most of these bondsmen were in the South's cotton belt; others grew sugar in lower Louisiana, rice along the coast of South Carolina and Georgia, or tobacco in Virginia. For the greater number of them, self-purchase was almost certainly unfeasible even had it been legal. Large plantations were the one place where free white labor could not compete effectively against black slave labor. The reason? The threat of the lash compelled field hands to work longer, or perhaps harder, than anyone would for market wages.

During peak seasons, black drivers herded gangs of men and women into agricultural assembly-lines that labored from sunup to sundown. Edmund Ruffin, a militant apologist for the peculiar institution, saw this as the source of its superior productivity: "Slave labor, in each individual case, and for each small measure of time, is more slow and inefficient than the labor of a free man. . . . But the slave labor is continuous. . . . Free laborers, if to be hired for the like duties, would require at least double the amount of wages to perform one-third more labor in each day."[10] Planters moreover put women into the fields, even when pregnant or soon after childbirth, and children beginning around ages eight to twelve. Slaves too old for field work took over the care of infants along with other light household duties. As a result of the plantation's "full employment" regime, two-thirds of slaves participated in the labor force, compared with only one-third for free populations, North and South.

These slaves were being worked well beyond the point where the value of their output could cover a wage that would attract free laborers. One implication of Robert William Fogel and Stanley L. Engerman's well-known and much-criticized study of American slavery is that a single field hand's labor on large plantations was worth $52 per year *more* than the cotton he produced.[11] If free and receiving the full value of their output, these blacks would have done less work and consumed more leisure, or perhaps done work that produced less but was more fun or interesting or had other non-pecuniary rewards.

In these instances, where planters compelled laborers to give up leisure or on-the-job rewards, slavery did raise the economy's physical output. This too, however, represented a misallocation of labor, a misallocation that made aggregate production too high rather than too low, because the extra output came at the expense of total well-being. Each additional hour of labor was producing less than its value to the laborer as leisure. In other words, for every dollar that slavery drove up southern output it drove up deadweight loss as well. Fogel and Engerman put this loss for the South overall at $74 million in 1850 alone.[12]

The ultimate gainers from this increased cotton production were primarily consumers. Higher output drove down cotton prices and caused a redistribution from black slaves to American, English, and continental wearers of clothing. But since there were many more of them, these benefits were thoroughly dispersed. One estimate is that every dollar gained by a typical user of cotton cloth imposed a welfare loss of $400 on some individual slave.[13] Although the planter usually earned a competitive return on his chattels, American blacks were being deprived of leisure so that millions of workers elsewhere could live slightly better.

To summarize, so long as we concentrate on the behavior of blacks, the peculiar institution pushed the South's aggregate production of goods and services in two conflicting directions. Insofar as slavery forced laborers to work at less valued jobs, it lowered output. Insofar as slavery forced laborers to work more hours or more intensely, it raised output. Since increased output predominated in southern agriculture, it undoubtedly swamped the reduction in output, which must have been most common in the South's urban areas. The adverse impact on aggregate well-being was unambiguous, however. For calculating slavery's deadweight loss, the two tendencies, rather than counteracting each other, add together. And while bondsmen bore most of this burden, their effective exclusion from more highly valued jobs hurt some white Southerners as well.

The Enforcement of Slavery

Everybody knows that bondage hurt the slave. But recall that deadweight loss is more than harm to one person or a group. It implies that, even after an implausibly generous allowance for offsetting benefits to the masters, the loss to the slaves was so great that it exceeded those gains, making everyone on average poorer in the Old South. Furthermore, we have yet to consider any deadweight loss from the way the peculiar institution changed the behavior of slaveowners.

Masters had two ways to motivate their chattels. When they used (implicit or explicit) wages, the cost to them was a gain for the slaves. Every dollar an employer paid out in wages was a dollar that an employee received. In contrast, when owners used violence, the cost of that was not a receipt to the slaves. It therefore constituted more deadweight loss, converting all the slave system's enforcement into a social burden for the region. Without slavery, these resources would have been used in other endeavors.

The most that can be said about this additional net loss was that it fell exclusively on the slaves—so long as each individual planter had to cover his own enforcement costs. His expected returns from the coerced labor would then be greater than these costs. Even this ceased to be true, however, if slaveholders could impose part of the costs on non-slaveholding whites. Given that wealth, prestige, and power were becoming increasingly concentrated in the hands of large planters, it is no surprise that such was in fact the case.

The chief way that the South's slaveholding elite externalized the costs of the peculiar institution was slave patrols. Established in every slave state, these patrols enforced black codes by apprehending runaways, monitoring the rigid pass requirements for blacks traversing the countryside, breaking up large gatherings and assemblies of blacks, visiting slave quarters randomly, inflicting impromptu punishments, and as occasion arose, suppressing insurrections. The patrollers generally made their rounds at night and were more active and regular in areas with many slaves. Loosely connected with the local militia, patrol duty was compulsory for most able-bodied white males. Exemption usually required paying a fine or hiring a substitute. The slave patrols thereby affixed a tax that shifted enforcement costs to small slaveholders and poor whites who owned no slaves.

Proslavery theorist George Fitzhugh was acutely conscious of the slave patrol's crucial function in an era and region where professional police were unknown. "The poor . . . constitute our militia and our police. They protect men in possession of property, as in other countries; and do much more, they secure men in possession of a kind of property which *they could not hold a day* but for the supervision and protection of the poor [emphasis added]."[14] This aspect did not escape the bondsmen themselves, who had a healthy and well-warranted fear of the patrollers. They "are poor white men" said one fugitive slave who had fled to Canada, "who live by plundering and stealing, getting rewards for runaways."[15]

Consider the consequences of imposing these security costs on whites owning no slaves. Coercion was now less expensive for each slaveholder, so that the trade-off between positive and negative incentives was shifted toward coercion. Not only did this worsen the bondsmen's lot, but expenditures on enforcement were now driven to the point where they well exceeded any gains to planters. Deadweight loss went up still further with free whites bearing some of the burden. Since patrol duty fell more heavily on the poor, the subsidy to slaveholders was matched by a tax on free labor. Manumission through self-purchase became still less attractive to masters because of the subsidy. As slavery's enforcement costs were thus socialized, owners experienced capital gains, although the higher slave prices left the rate of return unaltered.

The desire to reduce slavery's enforcement costs also explains the seeming anomaly of laws hindering slave self-purchase. A large and prosperous free black community would make it easier and more appealing for slaves to escape or resist. As the free black populations grew in Delaware and Maryland after the Revolution, for instance, the threat of runaways sped up the process of voluntary manumission. The gradual emancipation laws of many northern states did not free any slaves alive when enacted, and those born afterwards were held in bondage until their mid-twenties, allowing owners to recoup the costs of raising them. Nonetheless, these laws inexorably drove up the number of free Negroes in the North, and slaves could abscond more easily. Slaveowners found that manumission through self-purchase or a promise of early liberty were better ways to salvage returns than trying to hold slaves for as long as the law allowed. Prohibitions against manumission, restrictions on free blacks, indeed the promotion of racial prejudice itself, all helped planters coerce their chattels more cheaply. The same purpose was behind the laws that forbade teaching slaves to read and write, although by discouraging the formation of human capital, these laws likewise made the South poorer.

Some of slavery's critics have charged that it absorbed southern savings and retarded economic development; the money planters invested in slaves could have been invested in railroads or factories. This charge confuses monetary with real phenomena. The money used to purchase a slave did not disappear but continued to circulate. Trading slaves from one owner to another no more absorbed savings than trading land or any other real asset. Nor does the lack of southern industrialization, relative to the North, necessarily reflect a cost of slavery. True, fewer than one Southerner in ten lived in a town of at least 2,500 inhabitants in 1860, compared with one in three New Englanders. But urbanization in the South was not far behind the Midwest. It was more efficient for a region like the South to specialize in agriculture, in which it had a comparative advantage, and permit the North to specialize in manufacturing.

Nevertheless, the peculiar institution did have a real resource cost that can be thought of as similar to the absorption of savings. Enforcing the slave system required the use of labor and capital.

Every dollar that Southerners spent this way, beyond what they would have spent otherwise to protect life and property, was deadweight loss. This reduction in welfare, moreover, translates unambiguously into a fall in output. In real terms, the entire southern economy, including both whites and blacks, was less prosperous.

How much less? Modern measures of national income are inherently imprecise, despite all that governments nowadays do to collect and refine these statistics. Imagine how much more riddled with imprecision must be estimates for periods like the Civil War, long before governments regularly gathered the data. Nonetheless, if we accept the tentative conjectures of economic historians, per capita income in the South, counting slaves as part of the population, was almost one-third lower than in the North in 1840—$74 as compared with $109 (at 1860 prices). Southern per capita income had risen by 1860 to $103, while that in the North had risen to $141, reducing the percentage difference only slightly.[16] These gaps are consistent at least with the perceptions of contemporary outside observers, who almost uniformly commented on the economic backwardness of the slave states compared to the free states.

Not all of this backwardness was attributable to the peculiar institution. Despite a steady decline in import duties, tariffs fell disproportionately on Southerners, reducing their income from cotton production by at least 10 percent just before the Civil War.[17] But more important, regional disparities understate slavery's harm. Remember that compulsion artificially stimulated the South's production of cotton and other staples. The fact that output per capita was still noticeably lower than in the North, even though the black population was forced to work longer or harder, is a stunning indictment of the peculiar institution.

To be clear, the South was neither stagnant nor impoverished. Since the 1830s, the entire United States had been experiencing the sustained economic growth associated with the Industrial Revolution. Capital accumulation, technological innovation, and material abundance were transfiguring the landscape. These were the natural outcomes from the country's prior advances toward free trade, unrestricted migration, and virtual *laissez faire*. Unencumbered by domestic restraints on the flow of goods and services, the South was an integrated part of this dynamic and vibrant marketplace. Even though southern per capita income was lower than northern, it climbed slightly faster between 1840 and 1860.

Some have pointed to this rapid growth as evidence that slavery was not burdensome to the economy. But with capital mobility between North and South, we would expect the peculiar institution's cost to register only in relative income figures, especially during a decade with a cotton boom. Indeed, most of the South's growth resulted from shifting slaves and other resources into the high yield lands of the southwest. What is more telling is that the North maintained its lead at a time when its population was increasing nearly twice as fast, having doubled over the two decades, due to the most extensive relative influx of immigrants in American history. Even white Southerners—at least 200,000 between 1840 and 1860—were leaving the slave states to settle in the free states.

We can now appreciate the real horror of slave exploitation. Slavery inflicted on blacks tremendous pain, suffering, and sometimes death, along with other more mundane burdens, such as lost income. The American South not only was poorer overall as a result, but non-slaveholding whites were also poorer. Wealthy planters, extracting enormous transfers from black slaves and smaller transfers from poor whites, earned rates of return no greater than northern merchants and manufacturers. In fact, competition probably ensured that few of the perpetrators of this vile system secured exorbitant profits. The flexible price for females made any breeding of slaves for the market receive the going rate, as no doubt did the transatlantic slave trade, when we adjust for risks, such as capture after British suppression. Only during the colonial period, when European governments granted slave-trade monopolies to privileged companies, might returns have risen above normal, but these too would have been capitalized into the price of the companies' shares. We may even reasonably speculate that the profits for the African rulers who first captured the slaves were somewhat competitive, since there were several black states bidding for European buyers. The major beneficiaries were those who could now buy cheaper cotton textiles or other consumption goods made from slave labor.

Although slaveowners merely earned market returns, they had powerful incentives to perpetuate the peculiar institution. The total value of all slaves in the United States as of 1860 is estimated at between $2.7 and $3.7 billion.[18] Immediate abolition would have instantly transferred this entire sum from slaveholders to the freed slaves. Because of slavery's deadweight loss, moreover, emancipation's welfare gains for blacks would far exceed this amount. Not just abolition but any step that increased enforcement costs consequently threatened slaveholders with massive capital losses, as it depressed the value of the income stream expected from their chattels. "Were ever any people civilized or savage, persuaded by any argument, human or divine, to surrender voluntarily two thousand millions of dollars?" the slaveowner James Henry Hammond asked the abolitionists.[19] And so, the slavocracy was willing to invest considerable political resources and eventually fight tooth and nail to preserve a system that in the long run benefited very few Americans.

The Runaway Slave

The runaway slave was the system's Achilles heel. Each fugitive did more than deprive the slaveholder of a valuable capital asset; if running away became easier, enforcement costs rose. This in turn reduced the value of remaining slaves. Manumission through self-purchase would become more appealing to slaveholders, but if they were to succumb to this appeal, the dissolution would accelerate. More manumissions meant more free blacks which further eased escape and raised costs until the viability of the peculiar institution itself came into question.

The predominately rural South was not all that densely populated to begin with, especially along the frontier. One major reason that Indians proved less desirable as slaves than blacks was because it was so much easier for natives to disappear into a wilderness they already knew well. Colonial Massachusetts and South Carolina collected lots of captives during Indian wars, but most were sold to the West Indies, where escape was harder. As late as the 1850s, inaccessible parts of the South, although rapidly receding, harbored some maroon colonies, groups of fugitive blacks who remained at large for years. Individuals most frequently ran off for short periods, either hiding out in the woods, swamps, or other impenetrable terrain, or visiting neighboring holdings where they might have friends or family. Without the system of slave patrols, local runaways would have been more numerous.

But slave patrols alone could not dim the allure of fleeing permanently to a free state. Hence Southerners had insisted upon a fugitive slave clause in the Constitution; escaping slaves would then fear recapture even in the North. And just as the compulsory patrol imposed slavery's enforcement costs on non-slaveholders in the South, the fugitive slave clause imposed these costs on Northerners. It was the prime way the United States government subsidized the peculiar institution. Congress had initially passed legislation enforcing the fugitive slave clause back in 1793, at the end of President Washington's first term. The recovery of runaways was put under joint supervision of national and state courts. Not only did the free states willingly cooperate, but many of them allowed Southerners to bring along slaves on visits, sometimes for up to nine months.

Radical abolitionists put this Fugitive Slave Law under fire during the 1830s and 1840s. They legally challenged it in the courts and illegally evaded it. The illegal evasion led to the famous underground railroad, in which white abolitionists and free blacks spirited runaway slaves to freedom in Canada. Well known are the exploits of Harriet Tubman, who after escaping from bondage herself returned repeatedly to Maryland's Eastern Shore to bring out others. The free blacks (as well as fellow slaves) responsible for the bulk of such assistance, however, remain mostly unsung. Better remembered are the underground railroad's smaller number of white operatives, a few of whom hazarded serious dangers. Calvin Fairbanks, an Oberlin graduate, went south again and again, despite a first sentence that confined him for five years, until he was apprehended a second time. He languished in a Kentucky prison for another twelve years, finally gaining release at the Civil War's close. Charles Turner Torrey, a New England minister, is credited with rescuing four hundred slaves from Virginia before being caught and then dying in jail in 1846.

The legal challenges to the Fugitive Slave Law earned Liberty

Party leader Salmon P. Chase the nickname of "attorney general for runaway Negroes" in Ohio. One challenge from Pennsylvania finally found its way to the Supreme Court in 1842. The Court's decision in *Prigg v. Pennsylvania* was a pro- and antislavery mixture. It granted slaveholders the right to recapture slaves using private force, without going through any legal process, state or federal. The Constitution "manifestly contemplates the existence of a positive, unqualified right on the part of the owner of the slave, which no state law or regulation can in any way qualify, regulate, control, or restrain," wrote Justice Joseph Story in rendering the Court's opinion. "Upon this ground we have not the slightest hesitation in holding, that . . . the owner of a slave is clothed with the entire authority, in every State in the Union, to seize and recapture his slave, whenever he can do it without any breach of the peace, or any illegal violence."[20] The Pennsylvania law that treated such private seizures as kidnapping was therefore struck down.

In another part of his opinion, however, Story conceded that the state governments were under no positive obligation to assist enforcement of the fugitive slave provision. Seven northern legislatures responded with personal liberty laws. These either prohibited state officials from participating in a recapture or forbade holding fugitive slaves in state or local jails. In the face of these hostile enactments, the legal privilege to head north and personally retrieve slaves did not amount to much.

That is why Southerners demanded a tougher fugitive slave law. Preventing flight was of dire importance to the slave system. If blacks could simply obtain freedom by slipping across an open border, enforcement throughout the upper South was compromised, and the lower South would feel the repercussions. This southern concern about runaways had been one motive for U.S. acquisition of the Floridas immediately before and after the War of 1812. Spain had not outlawed slavery there, but slaveholders found it less convenient to hunt down fugitives in this unsettled borderland so long as it was under foreign jurisdiction. Similar concerns led the national government two decades later to initiate the army's most costly and protracted Indian war, against Florida's Seminoles, who provided safe refuge to runaways.

Although the peculiar institution was expanding in the southwest, it was retreating along the South's borders and from its cities. Delaware, Maryland, Kentucky, Missouri, and the western counties of Virginia had seen the proportion of slaves out of their total populations steadily decline after 1830 until it was approaching that of New York at the time of the Revolution. Kentucky, with the highest slave proportion of these regions, chose delegates for a state constitutional convention in 1849, and a full 10 percent of the voters supported a gradual-emancipation plan similar to the one previously adopted in New York.

One Virginian who served both in his state legislature and Congress, Charles James Faulkner, understood quite well the implications of Pennsylvania's new personal liberty law. It "has rendered our slave property . . . utterly insecure. . . . slaves are absconding from Maryland and this portion of Virginia in gangs of tens and twenties and the moment they reach the Pennsylvania line, all hopes of their recapture are abandoned. The existence of such a law on the Statute Book of any State is not only a flagrant violation of the spirit of the Federal Constitution and indeed of its *express provisions*, but is a deliberate *insult* to the whole Southern people, which . . . would amongst nations wholly independent and disconnected by Federal Relations be a *just cause of War*."[21]

Faulkner and other Southerners probably exaggerated the number escaping to the free states, but we will never know for sure. The accepted estimate is not higher than a thousand per year, nearly all from the border states, although many more tried and failed. The only certainty is that without a fugitive slave law, the number would have soared. Since the Constitution explicitly required their return, we can now understand why Garrison's call for disunion posed such a danger to the peculiar institution. Northern secession represented an effective way to eliminate this subsidy to slaveholders. The abolitionists realized that this would help make the North an asylum for runaways.

Slavery flourished because the country's political and legal structure socialized its enforcement costs. Like the incomes enjoyed by today's tobacco growers, which depend on munificent subsidies from the U.S. government, the economic viability of the peculiar institution rested on political power. Removing the free states out from under the Constitution's fugitive slave provision would at first undermine slavery in the upper South. But the lower South faced a potentially fatal domino effect. Once the supports provided by local, state, and central governments were knocked out, a combination of market forces and a black thirst for liberty could bring the system down.

But the planter oligarchy had far too much at stake to let those props go easily. Again, let us quote Faulkner, our legislator from Virginia: "No proposition can be plainer than that the slaveholding interest in this country is everywhere one and the same. An attack upon it *here* is an attack upon it in South Carolina and Alabama. Whatever weakens and impairs it *here* weakens and impairs it *there.* The fanaticism of Europe and Northern America is embarked on a crusade against it. We must stand or fall together."[22]

Black Resistance

David Walker was born a free black in North Carolina in 1785. After traveling widely, he settled in Boston, where he owned a shop near the wharves. But this active member of the Massachusetts General Colored Association had much more on his mind than bartering and trucking old clothes. In 1829 Walker penned and printed at his own expense *An Appeal to the Coloured Citizens of the World,* described by one northern Quaker as the most inflammatory publication in history. It plainly advocated violence and revolution. "We must and shall be free," Walker warned white Americans. Unless slavery was ended "for your good," blacks would resort to "the crushing arm of power. . . . And wo, wo, will be to you if we have to obtain our freedom by fighting." As soon as bondsmen abandoned their habitual servility, "I do declare it, that one good black man can put to death six white men."[23] Walker managed through his brisk business with sailors to smuggle his pamphlet into the South.

The timing of Walker's message was providential. It appeared little more than fifteen months before the premier issue in January of 1831 of Garrison's *Liberator,* a publication which eventually would reprint Walker's *Appeal* in its entirety. That August, Nat Turner launched in Virginia the bloodiest slave insurrection the United States had yet experienced, an event Southerners widely credited to the writings of Walker and Garrison. The same year, slave rebellion swept through British Jamaica. The nullification crisis between South Carolina and the central government was coming to a head. Then at the beginning of 1832, Virginia voted down the South's most considered effort at dismantling the peculiar institution, while a year later, partially impelled by what happened in Jamaica, Parliament approved compensated emancipation in British possessions. Walker, however, was not alive to see this rapid unfolding of events. He had been found dead in his shop's doorway in June 1830, under mysterious circumstances still unsolved by historians.

This early black revolutionary had touched a raw nerve. Outright resistance was another way, the most emphatic of all, to increase slavery's enforcement costs. Slave rebellions in the United States were never as frequent, large, or successful as in the Caribbean and South America, a fact that has long intrigued historians. Argument still goes on over where slavery was harsher, but we do know that the North American slave population was already growing rapidly through natural reproduction well before the slave trade was closed in 1808, whereas virtually everywhere else in the New World slavery depended upon the continuing importation of blacks. Thus, Brazil and the Caribbean islands received more than 85 percent of the ten million Africans forcibly shipped across the Atlantic from the sixteenth through the nineteenth century, but by 1825 the U.S. slave population of 1,750,000 accounted for more than one-third of all slaves in the Western Hemisphere.

One major difference between the American South and other slave societies in the New World was that only in the states of South Carolina and Mississippi did slaves ever constitute a majority of the population, whereas in the British and French Caribbean, blacks were 90 percent of inhabitants from 1770 on. Those economies, dependent upon slave imports, always contained a large number born in Africa and a preponderance of males. Native-born blacks, in contrast, had dominated the sexually balanced slave population in British North America since the end of the seventeenth century, and by 1860 they were all but 1 percent. U.S. slaves were also in closer proximity with whites. Nearly half worked on holdings of twenty or fewer slaves, whereas in Jamaica, on the eve of emancipation, one-third of the slaves worked on plantations of two hundred or more, and three-quarters on plantations of at least fifty. North American blacks often lived and toiled side-by-side with resident masters. Many Caribbean planters were absentee owners, residing as far away as the mother country. Their large holdings were managed by hired agents and overseers, who had less incentive to maximize the slave's long-term capital value and more to go after short-term revenues. All of these factors supplied fewer opportunities and provocations for servile insurrection in the United States.

Any rebellion faces a severe problem with free riders. Overturning a slave system presumably benefits all held in bondage, whether they participated in the rebellion or not. Since revolutionary activity entails enormous personal risks, each individual slave had an incentive to free ride on the revolutionary activity of others. Rather than wonder why slave revolts were so few, we should marvel that they took place at all. The only fully successful servile insurrection in all of human history was the one in Haiti. Escape, on the other hand, was a form of resistance that concentrated nearly all its gains on the individual runaway, except for some external gains that arose when more frequent running away drove up slavery's security costs.

In addition to insurrection and escape, there were many forms of passive resistance, and slaveholders and former slaves alike attest that American blacks tried them all. Shirking, working carelessly, faking illness, being absent, abusing tools and other property, committing petty "theft," and feigning stupidity or incompetence were all difficult to prevent or detect. Sometimes these would shade into more violent protests involving vandalism, arson, poisoning, or physical confrontation. Each of these stratagems helped to reduce the master's return from coercing his "troublesome property." They thereby subtly shifted his ideal mix of rewards and punishments toward positive incentives, bringing collective benefits for all slaves. If applied relentlessly and courageously enough, black recalcitrance could encroach on the peculiar institution's economic viability. A bondsman who could not be compelled to work very hard was not worth much.

One thing that might have moved slaves from hidden noncooperation to open revolt was encouragement and assistance from outsiders. But even free blacks in the North did not wholeheartedly endorse Walker's call for resistance. Frederick Douglass adhered consistently to the pacifism of Garrison through most of the 1840s, and his influence caused a National Negro Convention meeting in Buffalo to reject by a single vote a resolution calling for slavery's violent overthrow. Nonetheless, as time passed without any withering away of the peculiar institution, the acceptance of forceful opposition slowly percolated throughout antislavery circles.

An unlikely white convert was William Leggett. Editor of the *New York Evening Post,* Leggett had been the intellectual inspiration behind the Locofocos, the local Democratic Party's radical, *laissez-faire* wing. At first he shared the prevailing Jacksonian suspicion of abolitionists, because they diverted attention from the political battle against government privilege. But the New York journalist's uncompromising support for civil liberties eventually won him over to antislavery. In one of Leggett's last editorials, appearing in an 1837 issue of the *Plaindealer,* he admitted that "the oppression which our fathers suffered from Great Britain was nothing in comparison with that which the negroes experience at the hands of the slaveholders." Leggett would not "raise a finger in opposition" if "an extensive and well-arranged insurrection of the blacks should occur in any of the slave states. . . . The obligations of citizenship are strong, but those of justice, humanity and religion stronger." Indeed, he confessed the "keenest mortification and chagrin" that the U.S. government would be required under the Constitution to help suppress such an insurrection and prayed "that the battle might end in giving freedom to the oppressed."[24]

By the last decade before the war, militancy became commonplace among abolitionists, and the theorist who carried these revolutionary ideas furthest was Lysander Spooner. He had always been impatient with the "tame, cowardly, drivelling, truckling course pursued by the abolitionists" who wasted their energies "talking to women and children about the churches and the clergy."[25] In 1858 he circulated plans for fomenting slave rebellions in the South. Northern conspirators would assist with money, arms, training, and volunteers. He hoped that non-slaveowning whites could also be enlisted through the expropriation of slaveholders' property. With implacable legalistic logic, the Massachusetts attorney maintained that, rather than being due any compensation, slaveholders in fact owed compensation to their slaves for past exploitation. Blacks therefore could justly seize plantations as their own private property, to parcel out to any who had assisted them. Spooner also envisaged vigilance committees supplanting southern state and local governments. He optimistically looked forward to rapid success, if this insurrection were properly planned, but was also undaunted by the prospect of protracted guerrilla warfare.

Chapter 2
Bibliographical Essay

The premier work on the economics of U.S. slavery remains Robert William Fogel and Stanley L. Engerman, *Time on the Cross*, v. 1, *The Economics of American Negro Slavery*; v. 2, *Evidence and Methods—A Supplement* (Boston: Little, Brown, 1974). Although well-subsidized with government grants, backed up by an army of research assistants, and relying on what were then the latest computer techniques to analyze mountains of data, *Time on the Cross* eventually bore an "avalanche of criticism," which in the words of Jonathan Hughes, *American Economic History*, 3rd edn. (New York: HarperCollins, 1990), pp. 231–32, "in fineness as well as vigor and volume has rarely been known in the scholarship of economic history."

As practitioners of the "new economic history" or in fancier terms "cliometrics," Fogel and Engerman set out to demolish what they called the "traditional interpretation" of American slavery, which can be thought to have begun with Ulrich Bonnell Phillips, *Negro Slavery: A Survey of the Supply, Employment and Control of Negro Labor as Determined by the Plantation Regime* (New York: D. Appleton, 1918). Overtly racist, Phillips portrayed slavery as a civilizing influence on blacks but nonetheless offered the first solid historical treatment of the subject. On the basis of trends in slave and cotton prices, he also argued that slavery was unprofitable. Phillips inspired several state studies that confirmed his evaluation of slavery's profitability, the most important of which was Charles Sackett Sydnor, *Slavery in Mississippi* (New York: Appleton-Century, 1933). Actually, the only necessary implication of Phillips's claim was that slave prices needed to fall to equilibrate returns with other investments. But Charles W. Ramsdell, "The Natural Limits of Slavery Expansion," *Mississippi Valley Historical Review*, 16 (September 1929), pp. 151–171, came along and concluded that therefore slavery was economically doomed. It "had reached its limits in both profits and land," and this conclusion, in turn, bolstered the revisionist interpretation of the Civil War as an unfortunate and avoidable calamity.

Meanwhile, Lewis Cecil Gray produced his two-volume *History of Agriculture in the Southern United States to 1860* (Washington: Carnegie Institution, 1933), a work of such ponderous and overwhelming scholarship that even today there is hardly an aspect of the antebellum agrarian South on which it is not the first, and sometimes the last, word. Gray suffered no illusions about slavery's economic frailty, fully anticipating the cliometricians. Later, Kenneth M. Stampp gave us *The Peculiar Institution: Slavery in the Ante-Bellum South* (New York: Alfred A. Knopf, 1956), still one of the best general works on American slavery, which replaced Phillips's benign regime with a harsher picture and, like Gray, concluded that slaveholding was quite profitable.

Other notable contributions that pre-dated *Time on the Cross* include Stanley M. Elkins, *Slavery: A Problem in American Institutional and Intellectual Life,* 1st. edn. (Chicago: University of Chicago Press, 1959), whose thesis that American slavery resembled a modern concentration camp stirred up a hornets' nest; Eugene D. Genovese, *The Political Economy of Slavery: Studies in the Economy & Society of the Slave South* (New York: Pantheon Books, 1965), an analysis from a Marxist historian who argued that slavery was economically moribund; and John W. Blassingame, *The Slave Community: Plantation Life in the Antebellum South,* 1st edn. (New York: Oxford University Press, 1972), which relied on slave narratives to reconstruct the slave community.

Not Fogel and Engerman themselves, but two other economists, Alfred H. Conrad and John R. Meyer, actually touched off the cliometric revolution with their 1958 *Journal of Political Economy* article, "The Economics of Slavery in the Ante Bellum South," which is reprinted in Fogel and Engerman, eds., *The Reinterpretation of American Economic History* (New York: Harper & Row, 1971), along with several of Fogel's and Engerman's subsequent articles on slavery. Conrad and Meyer attempted to prove, empirically and rigorously, that slavery was indeed remunerative for the slaveowner, and after much back-and-forth debate in the technical literature, that finding at least was firmly established.

Fogel and Engerman went much further, however, claiming that slave plantations were 40 percent more efficient than northern free farms, that planters relied less heavily on coercion than previously supposed, that historians had exaggerated slave breeding and the separation of slave families, and that generally slavery in the South was a model of economic rationality. The best of the attacks on *Time on the Cross* can be found conveniently in two volumes: Herbert G. Gutman, *Slavery and the Numbers Game: A Critique of "Time on the Cross"* (Urbana: University of Illinois Press, 1975); and Paul A. David, Herbert G. Gutman, Richard Sutch, Peter Temin, and Gavin Wright, with an introduction by Kenneth Stampp, *Reckoning with Slavery: A Critical Study in the Quantitative History of American Negro Slavery* (New York: Oxford University Press, 1976). An economically literate yet readable summary of the criticisms is Thomas L. Haskell, "The True and Tragical History of 'Time on the Cross'," *New York Review of Books,* 22 (2 October 1975), pp. 33–39. Gavin Wright presents an alternative to Fogel and Engerman's view of the plantation economy in *The Political Economy of the Cotton South: Households, Markets, and Wealth in the Nineteenth Century* (New York: W. W. Norton, 1978), but as Robert Higgs warns in his review for the *Journal of American History,* 66 (June 1979), p. 153, Wright is an economist prone to "the construction of heavy deductive structures on factual quicksands" and therefore must be approached with some caution, perhaps with as much as Fogel and Engerman.

And what is the final verdict after all this controversy? My admittedly impressionistic judgment is that it depends upon whether you ask professional historians or economists. Most historians would agree with Eugene Genovese's appraisal that *Time on the Cross* was a "creative failure." Peter

Kolchin, professor of history at the University of Delaware, in "More *Time on the Cross?* An Evaluation of Robert William Fogel's *Without Consent of Contract*," *Journal of Southern History,* 58 (August 1992), pp. 491–501, reports that Fogel and Engerman are left "with few defenders among professional historians"; *Time on the Cross* "was a flash in the pan, a bold but now discredited work that added little to the important stream of slavery revisionism that welled forth in the 1970s."

The verdict of professional economists, in contrast, can be gauged by Fogel's sharing the 1993 Nobel prize in economics. They generally seem to believe that subsequent research sustained *Time on the Cross.* For instance, Donald McCloskey, a professionally trained economist at the University of Iowa, in "Little Things Matter" [a review of Fogel's *Without Consent or Contract*], *Reason,* 22 (June 1990), pp. 51–53, reports that Fogel and Engerman "won the debate, demonstrating beyond scientific doubt what was merely plausible in 1974." This dichotomy is symptomatic of the hyper-specialization of modern academe, with the two disciplines failing to talk to each other enough.

Among the significant general works on American slavery since *Time on the Cross,* we should mention Eugene D. Genovese, *Roll, Jordan, Roll: The World the Slaves Made* (New York: Pantheon Books, 1974); Leslie Howard Owens, *This Species of Property: Slave Life and Culture in the Old South* (New York: Oxford University Press, 1976); James Oakes, *The Ruling Race: A History of American Slaveholders* (New York: Alfred A. Knopf, 1982); John B. Boles, *Black Southerners, 1619–1869* (Lexington: University Press of Kentucky, 1983); and Oakes, *Slavery and Freedom: An Interpretation of the Old South* (New York: Alfred A. Knopf, 1990). This list hardly scratches the surface, because I am here concerned with slavery's political economy, but those who wish to delve deeply into other aspects should either consult the bibliography (recommended in our first chapter) from Peter Kolchin's survey, *American Slavery, 1619–1877,* or peruse Peter J. Parish's very fine historiographical volume, *Slavery: History and the Historians* (New York: Harper & Row, 1989).

Recently Fogel has returned to the fray with a new work: *Without Consent or Contract: The Rise and Fall of American Slavery* (New York: W. W. Norton, 1989). Reinforced this time by no less than three supporting volumes, subtitled *Evidence and Methods; Technical Papers: Markets and Production;* and *Technical Papers: Conditions of Slave Life and the Transition to Freedom* (although two of these supplements mainly reprint previously published articles), the text of *Without Consent or Contract* itself is really two separate books cleaved together. In the first half Fogel silently revises the more egregious *faux pas* in *Time on the Cross* and softens his tone while maintaining the same general economic evaluation of American slavery. The second half of Fogel's new book is an unexceptional but wide-ranging history of the antislavery movements in Britain and America.

Mainly theoretical works on the economics of slavery include John R. Hicks, *A Theory of Economic History* (Oxford: Clarendon Press, 1969), chapter 8; Evsey D. Domar, "The Causes of Slavery or Serfdom: A

Hypothesis," *Journal of Economic History*, 30 (March 1970), pp. 18–32; Robert Evans, Jr., "Some Notes on Coerced Labor," *Journal of Economic History*, 30 (December 1970), pp. 861–66; Theodore Berstrom, "On the Existence and Optimality of Competitive Equilibrium in a Slave Economy," *Review of Economic Studies*, 38 (January 1971), pp. 23–36; Stanley L. Engerman, "Some Considerations Relating to Property Rights in Man," *Journal of Economic History*, 33 (March 1973), pp. 43–65; Giorgio Cannarella and John Tomaske, "The Optimal Utilization of Slaves," *Journal of Political Economy*, 35 (September 1975), pp. 621–29; Ronald Findlay, "Slavery, Incentives, and Manumission: A Theoretical Model," *Journal of Political Economy*, 83 (October 1975), pp. 923–933; Yoram Barzel, "An Economic Analysis of Slavery," *Journal of Law and Economics*, 20 (April 1977), pp. 87–110; and Stefano Fenoaltea, "Slavery and Supervision in Comparative Perspective: A Model," *Journal of Economic History*, 44 (September 1984), pp. 635–668.

With the notable exception, however, of Fenoaltea's brilliantly conceived and executed analysis in the last cited article, I have found the most enlightening theoretical contributions to have been unjustifiably ignored by both sides of the *Time on the Cross* debate: viz., Ludwig von Mises, "The Work of Animals and of Slaves," in *Human Action: A Treatise on Economics*, 3rd edn. (Chicago: Regnery, 1960), pp. 628–634; John E. Moes, "The Economics of Slavery in the Ante Bellum South: Another Comment," *Journal of Political Economy*, 68 (April 1960), 183–87; Moes, "Comment," National Bureau of Economic Research, *Aspects of Labor Economics: A Conference of the Universities-National Bureau Committee for Economic Research* (Princeton, NJ: Princeton University Press, 1962); Gordon Tullock, "The Political Economy of Slavery: Genovese and Davis," *Left and Right*, 3 (Spring-Summer 1967), pp. 5–16; Thomas Sowell, "The Economics of Slavery," chapter 5 in *Markets and Minorities* (New York: Basic Books, 1981). Also important is Mark Thornton's recent "Slavery, Profitability, and the Market Process" *Review of Austrian Economics*, 7 (1994), pp. 21–47.

Most of these neglected contributions follow in the classical tradition of Adam Smith, who included some critical remarks about slavery in *An Inquiry Into the Nature and Causes of the Wealth of Nations* (Indianapolis: LibertyClassics, 1976), v. 1, pp. 386–390. This tradition reached its apogee with the indictment of American slavery by John Elliot Cairnes, a nineteenth-century British economist and abolitionist, in *The Slave Power: Its Character, Career, and Probable Designs: Being an Attempt to Explain the Real Issues Involved in the American Contest*, 2nd edn. (London: Macmillan, 1863). The classical economists tended to conclude that bound labor was *always* less physically productive than free labor because they implicitly assumed that slavery operated like a tax on work. They were not sufficiently attuned to the fact that slavery's coercion not only taxed the slave's work and passed the proceeds on to the slaveholder, but also operated like a tax on the slave's leisure, causing the slave to work more or harder than otherwise. This feature is what made slavery particularly attractive when labor was scarcer in relation to land, such as in the New World. Fogel and

Engerman veer in the opposite direction, almost concluding that slavery is always more physically productive, and then they mistakenly apply the welfare term "efficiency" to this overproduction generated by a labor misallocation.

Stefano Fenoaltea, "The Slavery Debate: A Note From the Sidelines," *Explorations in Economic History*, 18 (July 1981), pp. 304–08, was one of the first to expose the logical tension between Fogel and Engerman's conclusions about the productivity of slavery and how well slaves were treated. If slave labor was more physically productive in agriculture than free labor, this could not possibly be the consequence of planters using positive incentives, because those are the precise incentives slavery has in common with free labor. The ability to coerce the slave is its only possible advantage over free labor. Without admitting as much, Fogel has incorporated this correction into *Without Consent or Contract*.

My own approach in this chapter is not fully consonant with either Fogel and Engerman or their critics. Most economists will immediately recognize that I have simply taken the standard analysis of political rent-seeking and applied it to slavery. Some, however, might object to my suggestion that welfare economics depends upon translating all transfers into money and assuming that the marginal dollar is of equal value to everyone. John R. Hicks and Nicholas Kaldor are supposed to have overcome the problem of comparing utility between individuals with what is known as a "potential Pareto improvement." But I have been convinced by David D. Friedman's arguments in *Price Theory: An Intermediate Text*, 2nd edn. (Cincinnati: South-Western, 1990), chapter 15, "Economic Efficiency," and in "Does Altruism Produce Efficient Outcomes? Marshall Versus Kaldor," *Journal of Legal Studies*, 17 (January 1988), pp. 1–13, that the Hicks-Kaldor criterion hides its implicit comparisons behind a confusing veil of words about how the gainers "could have compensated" the losers but did not. If no compensation is actually accepted or turned down, there is no way to know if it was sufficient unless we make an interpersonal utility comparison. Without the assumption that the subjective value of the marginal dollar is equal for everyone, welfare economics can say almost nothing—positive or negative—about transfers, whether through private theft, government intervention, or outright enslavement. Those critics of Fogel and Engerman, such as Paul David and Peter Temin, who argue that welfare economics is completely irrelevant to slavery, do not seem to realize that their objection would also rule out a welfare analysis of any government policies, including tariffs or tax-financed public goods. See also Murray N. Rothbard, "Toward a Reconstruction of Utility and Welfare Economics," in Mary Sennholz, ed., *On Freedom and Free Enterprise: Essays in Honor of Ludwig von Mises* (Princeton, NJ: D. Van Nostrand, 1956).

Strictly speaking, this chapter has shown only that southern slavery was inefficient compared to a Pareto-optimal labor market—not compared to the actual labor market that might have existed had the South abolished the peculiar institution. Someone could argue that free labor would have been less efficient in the real world because of potential market failures that slavery overcame, and indeed, Engerman skirts toward this argument when he refers in "Some Considerations Relating to Property Rights in Man" to slavery's possible reduction of certain transaction costs. I stand ready to revise my evaluation of slavery's efficiency when a more developed presentation comes along. A similar but more plausible approach could pick on government failures in the Old South's labor market. Occupational restrictions on free blacks were inefficient, and if slaves could be admitted into jobs from which blacks otherwise were excluded, then to that extent slavery reduced inefficiencies.

This chapter has also over-simplified the pay-offs from manumission through self-purchase. Even monetary gains (let alone non-pecuniary psychic gains) are not confined to cases where the slave could earn a higher income once free—because coercion costs the master something too, but unlike the payments for a slave's subsistence, these costs are not passed on to the slave. With the master's savings from eliminating enforcement costs, the freed slave no longer has to be both willing and able to earn an income that exceeds the value of his output as a slave. For there to be monetary gains from self-purchase, the former slave's future income must merely exceed that total *minus* the cost of coercing him. On the other hand, I have also ignored any transaction costs associated with the slave's financing his self-purchase, which push required post-manumission income in the opposite direction. What factor predominates is impossible to know *a priori.*

John Moes has implied in "The Economics of Slavery and the Ante Bellum South" that manumission through self-purchase may have been theoretically viable even for field hands. He points out in a footnote that "the relevant comparison is not that between the productivity of a free man and a slave but between the productivity of a slave with and without the hope of freedom." In other words, the wage required to induce free laborers to do plantation work is not necessarily the lowest wage that slaves would have accepted if offered a chance to buy their freedom. This does raise an important puzzle. Why would field hands not be willing voluntarily to do the same work in return for less than their current implicit wages with their liberty thrown into the bargain?

Engerman and others have suggested one possible answer. The high wage demanded by free laborers indicates that these were the very jobs where negative incentives dominated positive incentives. We could therefore reasonably expect that the implicit wage (including what field hands are allowed to consume in leisure) was already close enough to subsistence to leave the slave very little to offer in exchange for freedom. I find much more probable an explanation hinted at by Fenoaltea. The debt contract of the field hand who purchases his own freedom is more costly to enforce than outright enslavement, in light of the fact that the former slave has almost as much incentive and much more opportunity to evade paying the debt than to escape slavery. The fact that this was an era of imprisonment for unpaid debts lends further credence to this explanation.

I have provisionally accepted many of Fogel and Engerman's numerical estimates, not because I am convinced that they are flawless, but because few alternatives are available, and moreover, even significant changes would not alter much my theoretical conclusion—completely at odds with Fogel and Engerman—that slavery entailed significant deadweight loss. Taking a more convoluted route to the same place, two articles have tried to show that slavery dampened saving in the Old South: John E. Moes, "The Absorption of Capital in Slave Labor in the Ante Bellum South and Economic Growth," *American Journal of Economics and Sociology*, 20 (October 1961), pp. 535–541, and Roger L. Ransom and Richard Sutch, "Capitalists Without Capital: The Burden of Slavery and the Impact of Emancipation," *Agricultural History*, 62 (Summer 1988), pp. 133–160. These authors make the intriguing observation that whereas the costs of raising free children are consumption expenditures for the parents, those same costs for slave children appear to slaveowners as investment expenditures. Therefore, even if people in the slave states did save the same proportion of their aggregate income as those in the free states, less ended up actually invested in physical capital because of this antebellum analog to the "bond illusion" some economists think modern government debt generates. Engerman, on the other hand, speculates in "Some Considerations Relating to Property Rights in Man" that slavery may have raised savings by permitting slaveholders to capture more of the externalities associated with the formation of human capital. I remain agnostic over the secondary issue of how slavery may have affected southern saving; either way its deadweight loss necessarily constituted a significant welfare burden.

Like the classic prisoners' dilemma, slavery created an incentive structure where slaveholders gained from making society worse off. Even Fogel and Engerman acknowledge that the coercive transfers received by masters were less than the damages inflicted on slaves. A trickier question is how this negative-sum redistribution affected non-slaveholding whites in the South. Unfortunately, quantifying the answer would require a more rigorous, empirical study. Although *Time on the Cross* correctly identifies the consumers of cotton clothing as the ultimate beneficiaries of slavery's increased output, there no doubt were others. If worldwide demand for southern cotton was elastic, imported goods were cheaper for all Americans. Whites with scarce talents complementary to slavery, e.g., the overseer who was not nearly as good at anything else, had higher salaries. Owners of land suited to slave agriculture were also wealthier. These gains to non-slaveholders must be offset against the losses they suffered from externalized enforcement costs and misallocated black labor.

If the peculiar institution made non-slaveholding whites in the South poorer, the result would not necessarily appear in the average income of white Southerners, because white slaveowners were made richer. Richard A. Easterlin was the first to construct income estimates for the various regions of the United States in "Regional Income Trends, 1840–1950," reprinted in *The Reinterpretation of American Economic History*. His figures for the South have been challenged by Gerald Gunderson, "Southern Ante-Bellum Income Reconsidered," *Explorations in Economic History*, 10 (Winter 1973), pp. 151–176. Fogel and Engerman already had refined Easterlin's estimates, picking out the South's rapid growth between 1840 and 1860 as evidence of slavery's efficiency. My interpretation, as the text makes clear, is just the opposite. These numbers show the South still one-third poorer than the North despite the fact that slavery artificially raised southern output. The authors of *Time on the Cross* also compare the free populations of the two regions. According to their numbers, leaving out slaves results in a slight northern lead in per capita income in 1840 but a reversal of that in 1860, $150 for the South as compared with $144 for the North. These numbers, however, assume that slaves consumed only $20 per year. Since this does not jibe with the contention in *Time on the Cross,* v. 2, p. 117, that annual per capita income for slaves averaged $34.13, it is hard to understand why Fogel and Engerman settled on a $20 adjustment (even though it did yield a slightly lower rate of economic growth for the South) and continue to do so as recently as Fogel's *Without Consent or Contract.*

If free income per capita is recalculated using higher slave consumption, the North maintains its lead for 1860 as well. In other words, not only were all Southerners, free and slave, on average poorer, but also free Southerners were on average poorer than Northerners, despite the planters' exploitation of the slaves. This seems to confirm that the losses of non-slaveholders far exceeded their gains. What may be more telling is the net internal migration from South to North. Free laborers do not generally move from economies where wages are high to where wages are lower.

Leonard Liggio of the Institute for Humane Studies first suggested to me the importance of the Constitution's fugitive slave clause to slavery's enforcement costs. Fogel in *Without Consent or Contract,* p. 39, is aware that slavery "flourished only where political and legal conditions kept the cost of operating gang-system plantations low." But he never goes on to explore fully how those political and legal preconditions affected slavery's efficiency. Indeed, much of the historical and theoretical work on slavery proceeds as if enforcement costs were zero. Theodore Berstrom, for instance, in "On the Existence and Optimality of Competitive Equilibrium in a Slave Economy," gives a general-equilibrium model that is rigorously mathematical but that implicitly makes this erroneous assumption.

A recognition of slavery's enforcement costs may shed light on the ultimately sterile debate over whether we refer to planters as "seigniorial" or "capitalistic." Genovese, a Marxist historian, has been the most emphatic in labeling southern planters as a pre-capitalist, paternalistic class, whereas Fogel and Engerman go furthest in viewing them as modern, rational businessmen. Bear in mind that every producer of goods and services is a consumer as well. Except among the economically self-sufficient, most production is for markets and thus faces outside discipline. Those who fail to heed the market cannot maintain their wealth for long, whether they are slaveowning planters or modern corporate executives. With respect to their purely productive activities, therefore, planters were necessarily market-oriented. As consumers, on the other hand, slaveholders could indulge whatever preferences their wealth permitted. These were obviously influenced by culture and may very well have been pre-capitalist, however we wish to define that term.

What Genovese and the historians who share his view of the paternalistic South, however, seem to have in mind is the planters' ability to escape market discipline through political power. Nearly all producers, under all social systems, turn to the State for subsidies and other special privileges. Some are more successful than others, but the South's large planters were among the successful. They had to be, because as they were well aware, slavery's economic viability depended upon political power. And in their ability to socialize slavery's enforcement costs, slaveholders do strikingly resemble feudal lords or mercantilist magnates.

One dispute I did not even try to address was the relative productivity of free farms versus slave plantations. Many critics, especially David and Temin, have rightly dismissed Fogel and Engerman's calculations of relative productivity as theoretically untenable. The correct procedure would have required plugging in physical quantities of inputs and outputs to compare factor productivity between the regions. Since northern free farms produced no cotton, Fogel and Engerman had to fall back on the monetary value of differing outputs, which completely invalidates any results.

The debate nevertheless has some interesting implications about whether plantation slavery forced its field hands to work longer or harder. Fogel and Engerman believe that slaves worked more intensely rather than more hours, and this greater intensity resulted from the significant economies of scale they allege that cotton cultivation enjoyed. The large plantations, which used slave gangs exclusively, were much more productive per hour of labor than small slaveholdings in the South or even free farms in the North. Gavin Wright and others have countered that cotton production only enjoyed constant returns to scales. My best guess would be that any real economies of scale inhered in the costs of coercion rather than in cotton growing *per se*. A single overseer could cow twenty slaves nearly as easily and cheaply as one slave. Cannarella and Tomaske imply as much in "The Optimal Utilization of Slaves" when they misleadingly refer to the external economies of using force. I say "misleadingly" because these are not true externalities unless they operated across plantations. After all, one of the main reasons large firms, including plantations, exist in the first place is because they capture gains that would be otherwise out of reach.

A necessary theoretical implication of Fogel and Engerman's conclusion, which they fully recognize, is that free laborers could have earned higher hourly wages working in gangs on plantations than working on small family farms. Fogel and Engerman point to the psychic benefits of being self-employed on one's own land to explain why these higher wages could not attract any free laborers. But this will not do. If plantations in fact could offer higher wages, they did not have to bid away all free farmers but just some workers at the margin. To argue that almost none could be enticed in an era in which over three million immigrants took risky voyages across the Atlantic just for slight expected increases in real wages is wildly implausible. In effect, Fogel and Engerman have replaced the old argument that planters were maintaining the slave system by unprofitable conspicuous consumption with a new argument in which free farmers (and free blacks after emancipation) become the irrational conspicuous consumers. One does not have to wholeheartedly embrace the efficient markets and rational expectations of the New Classical economists to realize, as John Moes has so aptly put it (in another context in his comment for *Aspects of Labor Economics*, p. 248) that "the assumption that people will attempt to maximize" is far less heroic than "some of the assumptions that have to be made in the calculation process" to arrive at Fogel and Engerman's results.

In short, Kenneth Stampp got it backwards in *Reckoning With Slavery*, p.30, when he accused Fogel and Engerman of "a desire to make everything fit comfortably in a neo-classical behavioral model." Quite the opposite! Their problem is not being neo-classical enough. Fogel, in particular, views coercion and wages as *merely* two alternative ways to motivate workers. Free labor during this period often "is to the modern mind still brutal and exploitative" (*Without Consent or Contract*, p. 388). Thus his analysis fails to comprehend the fundamental economic distinction between a voluntary transaction, which with its mutual gains moves the transactors toward greater efficiency and welfare (given initial endowments), and a coercive transfer, which with its nearly inevitable deadweight loss must reduce efficiency and welfare. (Admittedly, if voluntary transactions impose costs on third parties, this may reduce efficiency. The slave trade itself, for instance, benefited the trading parties only by inflicting harm on the slave. But as this extreme instance illustrates, serious negative externalities usually arise from a link between a voluntary transaction and a coercive transfer.)

This conceptual failure leaves Fogel pathetically ill-equipped to make a moral case against slavery. The best he can marshal, in the Afterword of *Without Consent or Contract*, is a four-part indictment resting on slavery's "unrestrained personal domination" (whatever that means, domination being more vague a concept than coercion) and its denial to blacks of economic opportunity, citizenship, and cultural autonomy. If these are really the worst things that Fogel can say against slavery, no wonder he has trouble finding a qualitative difference between it and free labor. William Lloyd Garrison and the other radical abolitionists, in contrast, did clearly recognize such a qualitative difference, and to that extent, they exhibited a far more profound appreciation of the economic way of thinking.

To return to historical works, a brief but measured comparison of slavery in the United States with slavery elsewhere is David Brion Davis, "Slavery," in C. Vann Woodward, ed., *The Comparative Approach to American History* (New York: Basic Books, 1968). There are also more details in the first of Davis's intellectual histories, *The Problem of Slavery in Western Culture* (cited ch. 1). The slim volume that kicked off the debate on where in the New World slavery was the most horrible is Frank Tannenbaum, *Slave and Citizen: The Negro in the Americas* (New York: Alfred A. Knopf,

1946). Two further contributions to this debate are Herbert S. Klein, *Slavery in the Americas: A Comparative Study of Virginia and Cuba* (Chicago: University of Chicago Press, 1967), and Carl N. Degler, *Neither Black nor White: Slavery and Race Relations in Brazil and the United States* (New York: Macmillan, 1971). See also Richard S. Dunn, *Sugar and Slaves: The Rise of the Planter Class in the English West Indies, 1624–1713* (Chapel Hill: University of North Carolina Press, 1972), and Herbert S. Klein, *African Slavery in Latin America and the Caribbean* (New York: Oxford University Press, 1986).

Eugene D. Genovese, *From Rebellion to Revolution: Afro-American Slave Revolts in the Making of the New World* (Baton Rouge: Louisiana State University Press, 1979), tries to answer the question of why there were fewer slave revolts in the United States. Very insightful on the general subject of slave resistance is George M. Fredrickson and Christopher Lasch, "Resistance to Slavery," a *Civil War History* article that has been reprinted in one of the most useful collections on American slavery: Allen Weinstein and Frank Otto Gatell, eds., *American Negro Slavery: A Modern Reader*, 2nd edn., (New York: Oxford University Press, 1973). Almon Wheeler Lauber, *Indian Slavery in Colonial Times Within the Present Limits of the United States* (New York: Columbia University, 1913), is the standard work on that subject. For the role of fugitive blacks in the U.S. government's most expensive Indian war, see Kenneth Porter, "Negroes and the Seminole War, 1835–1842," *Journal of Southern History*, 30 (November 1964), pp. 427–450.

For my knowledge of slavery in the ancient and medieval worlds, I have relied on William L. Westermann, *The Slave Systems of Greek and Roman Antiquity* (Philadelphia: American Philosophical Society, 1955); Moses I. Finley, ed., *Slavery in Classical Antiquity: Views and Controversies* (Cambridge, U.K.: W. Heffer & Sons, 1960); chapter 3 of Finley, *The Ancient Economy*, 2nd edn. (Berkeley: University of California Press, 1973); Garlan Yvon, *Slavery in Ancient Greece*, rev. edn., (Ithaca, NY: Cornell University Press, 1982); and William D. Phillips, Jr., *Slavery From Roman Times to the Early Transatlantic Trade* (Minneapolis: University of Minnesota Press, 1985). A. M. Duff, *Freedmen in the Early Roman Empire* (Oxford: Clarendon Press, 1928), contains valuable information on Roman manumission, while Moses I. Finley, *Ancient Slavery and Modern Ideology* (London: Chatto & Windus, 1980), makes direct comparisons between ancient and New World slavery.

Some recent works on slavery in black Africa are Paul E. Lovejoy, *Transformations in Slavery: A History of Slavery in Africa* (Cambridge, U.K.: Cambridge University Press, 1983), and Robin Law, *The Slave Coast of West Africa, 1550–1750: The Impact of Atlantic Slave Trade on an African Society* (Oxford: Clarendon Press, 1991). David W. Galenson, *Traders, Planters, and Slaves: Market Behavior in Early English America* (Cambridge, U.K.: Cambridge University Press, 1986), does a cliometric analysis of the Atlantic slave trade at the time of Royal African Company's monopoly and finds the trade still quite competitive. Orlando Patterson, *Slavery and Social Death: A*

Comparative Study (Cambridge, MA: Harvard University Press, 1982), is a masterly comparative study that draws from the history of slavery in nearly all periods and places.

The little that is known about manumission through self-purchase in the United States can be found in Sumner Eliot Matison, "Manumission by Purchase," *Journal of Negro History*, 33 (April 1948), pp. 146–167, and in sections of Luther P. Jackson, "Manumission in Certain Virginia Cities," *Journal of Negro History*, 15 (July 1930), pp. 278–314. Most of the recent works on southern slave codes and their barriers to manumission—such as Andrew Fede, *People Without Rights: An Interpretation of the Law of Slavery in the U.S. South* (New York: Garland, 1992); Alan Watson, *Slave Law in the Americas* (Athens: University of Georgia Press, 1989); and Mark V. Tushnet, *The American Law of Slavery, 1810–1860: Considerations of Humanity and Interest* (Princeton, NJ: Princeton University Press, 1981)—have fascinating interpretations but are narrowly focused on special issues. Only Thomas D. Morris's new *Southern Slavery and the Law, 1619–1860* (Chapel Hill: University of North Carolina Press, 1996), is truly comprehensive and definitive.

The South's compulsory slave patrols are one of the gaping holes in the slavery literature, and what has been written, quite understandably, tends to be concerned more with the patrol's impact on the slaves than on free whites. Besides brief sections in such general works on slavery as Kenneth Stampp's and Leslie Howard Owens's, there are good discussions in John Anthony Scott, "Segregation: A Fundamental Aspect of Southern Race Relations, 1800–1860," *Journal of the Early Republic*, 4 (Winter 1984), pp. 421–442; Peter H. Wood, *Black Majority: Negroes in Colonial South Carolina From 1670 Through the Stono Rebellion* (New York: Alfred A. Knopf, 1974); John Hope Franklin, *The Militant South, 1800–1861* (Cambridge, MA: Harvard University Press, 1956), pp. 72–76; and Howell M. Henry, *The Police Control of the Slave in South Carolina* (Emory, VA: H. M. Henry, 1914), pp. 28–42.

Studies of the general management of plantation slaves include William Kauffmann Scarborough, *The Overseer: Plantation Management in the Old South* (Baton Rouge: Louisiana State University Press, 1966), and William L. Van Deburg, *The Slave Drivers: Black Agricultural Labor Supervisors in the Antebellum South* (Westport, CT: Greenwood Press, 1979). Michael Tadman, *Speculators and Slaves: Masters, Traders, and Slaves in the Old South* (Madison: University of Wisconsin Press, 1989), covers the workings of the domestic slave trade. An essential state study that verifies the retreat of slavery from the South's borders is Barbara Jeanne Fields, *Slavery and Freedom on the Middle Ground: Maryland During the Nineteenth Century* (New Haven: Yale University Press, 1985). John H. Moore, "Simon Gray, Riverman: A Slave Who Was Almost Free," *Mississippi Valley Historical Review*, 49 (December 1962), pp. 472–484, provided my information on that unusual case.

Varied perspectives on slaves in southern cities and factories can be found in Richard C. Wade, *Slavery in the Cities: The South 1820–1860*

(London: Oxford, 1964); Robert S. Starobin, *Industrial Slavery in the Old South* (New York: Oxford University Press, 1970); Claudia Dale Goldin, *Urban Slavery in the American South, 1820–1860: A Quantitative History* (Chicago: University of Chicago Press, 1976); Ronald L. Lewis, *Coal, Iron and Slaves: Industrial Slavery in Maryland and Virginia, 1715–1865* (Westport, CT: Greenwood Press, 1979); and Fred Batemen and Thomas Weiss, *A Deplorable Scarcity: The Failure of Industrialization in the Slave Economy* (Chapel Hill: University of North Carolina Press, 1981). Whether justifiable of not, many Southerners did exhibit a sense of inferiority about their relative lack of industry, often blaming the North. Robert Royal Russel, *Economic Aspects of Southern Sectionalism, 1840–1861* (New York: Russell and Russell, 1960), details concrete manifestations of this reaction.

At least with respect to the tariff's adverse impact, Southerners not only were absolutely correct but displayed a sophisticated understanding of economics. Cliometricians have been tireless in their efforts to discover if the antebellum tariff did indeed fit one of those rare exceptions where it might have raised American income overall. See Paul David, "Learning by Doing and Tariff Protection: A Reconsideration of the Case of the Ante-Bellum United States Textile Industry," *Journal of Economic History*, 30 (September 1970), pp. 521–601; Clayne L. Pope, "The Impact of the Ante-Bellum Tariff on Income Distribution," *Explorations in Economic History*, 9 (Summer 1972), pp. 375–421; Bennett D. Baack and Edward J. Ray, "Tariff Policy and Income Distribution: The Case of the United States, 1830–1860," *Explorations in Economic History*, 11 (Winter 1973/74), pp. 103–121; John A. James, "The Welfare Effects of the Antebellum Tariff: A General Equilibrium Analysis," *Explorations in Economic History*, 15 (July 1978), pp. 231–256; James, "The Optimal Tariff in the Antebellum United States," *American Economic Review*, 71 (September 1981), pp. 726–734; and Mark Bils, "Tariff Protection and Production in the Early U.S. Cotton Textile Industry," *Journal of Economic History*, 44 (December 1984), 1033–045.

After all this effort, we can be confident of the conclusion rendered in two articles by C. Knick Harley: "International Competitiveness of the Antebellum American Cotton Textile Industry," *Journal of Economic History*, 52 (September 1992), pp. 559–584, and "The Antebellum Tariff: Food Exports and Manufacturing," *Explorations in Economic History*, 29 (October 1992), pp. 375–400. The tariff was inefficient; it not only redistributed wealth from farmers and planters to manufacturers and laborers but overall made the country poorer. Jonathan J. Pincus, *Pressure Groups and Politics in Antebellum Tariffs* (New York: Columbia University Press, 1977), is a public-choice analysis of the special interests that clamored for protection. All these studies supersede John G. Van Deusen's earlier but still valuable effort to calculate the *Economic Bases of Disunion in South Carolina* (New York: Columbia University Press, 1928).

Among general works on the antebellum American economy, still unreplaced are the two volumes from *The Economic History of the United States* series: George Rogers Taylor, *The Transportation Revolution, 1815–1860* (New York: Holt, Rinehart, and Winston, 1951), and Paul W. Gates,

The Farmer's Age: Agriculture, 1815–1860 (New York: Holt, Rinehart, and Winston, 1960). Douglass C. North, *The Economic Growth of the United States, 1790–1860* (New York: Prentice Hall, 1961), a more recent work from one of the first of the new economic historians, emphasizes the role of cotton in driving northern industrialization. For organizational details on that industrialization, examine Thomas C. Cochran, *Frontiers of Change: Early Industrialism in America* (New York: Oxford University Press, 1981). A brief, somewhat dated historiographical essay is Peter Temin, *Causal Factors in American Economic Growth in the Nineteenth Century* (London: Macmillan Press, 1975). Far more thorough and up to date is Jeremy Atack and Peter Passell, *A New Economic View of American History: From Colonial Times to 1940*, 2nd edn. (New York: W. W. Norton, 1994), a textbook on the new economic history that devotes a good number of chapters to the antebellum United States, although I do not always share its judgments.

Perhaps some of the cliometricians could turn their attention to the question of how many slaves escaped north, which urgently needs to be reassessed. The most often cited work on the underground railroad, Larry Gara, *The Liberty Line: The Legend of the Underground Railroad* (Lexington: University of Kentucky Press, 1961), contends that its accomplishments were highly overrated. But Gara seems to have an anti-abolitionist ax to grind, and it is surprising that his findings have been accepted so uncritically, especially after the dean of historians of abolitionism, Louis Filler, in his review of Gara's book, *Mississippi Valley Historical Review*, 48 (December 1961), pp. 523–24, expressed grave reservations, finding it "unlikely to content the numerous investigators whose articles and new evidence continue to underwrite the view that the underground railroad was as real and important as the sponsors of the Fugitive Slave Act believed." Gara dismisses the earlier, more glowing volumes, Wilbur H. Siebert, *The Underground Railroad from Slavery to Freedom* (New York: Macmillan, 1898), and William Still, *The Underground Rail Road: A Record of Facts, Authentic Narratives, Letters, etc., Narrating the Hardships, Hair-Breadth Escapes and Death Struggles of the Slaves in Their Efforts for Freedom* (Philadelphia: Porter & Coates, 1872), but Siebert and Still did have the one advantage of interviewing actual participants. One of the few books on the subject to appear since Gara's is Charles L. Blockson, *The Underground Railroad* (New York: Prentice Hall, 1987), a solid compilation of case histories. Also Stanley Harrold, *The Abolitionists and the South, 1831–1861* (Lexington: University Press of Kentucky, 1995), has an excellent chapter on those abolitionists who risked capture below the Mason-Dixon line to rescue slaves.

Thomas D. Morris, *Free Men All: The Personal Liberty Laws of the North, 1780–1861* (Baltimore: Johns Hopkins University Press, 1974), recounts the history of free states' personal liberty laws. A thorough discussion of additional legal and constitutional issues related to fugitive slaves is Paul Finkelman, *An Imperfect Union: Slavery, Federalism, and Comity* (Chapel Hill: University of North Carolina Press, 1981); while his *Civil War History* article, "*Prigg* v. *Pennsylvania* and Northern State Courts: Anti-Slavery Uses of a Pro-Slavery Decision," reprinted in Kermit L. Hall, *The Law of American Slavery: Major Historical Interpretations* (New York: Garland, 1987), examines in depth that major Supreme Court case. For the legal dilemma confronting antislavery judges, see Robert M. Cover, *Justice Accused: Antislavery and the Judicial Process* (New Haven: Yale University Press, 1975).

Vincent Harding, *There Is a River: The Black Struggle for Freedom in America* (New York: Harcourt Brace Jovanovich, 1981), covers the entire range of black resistance, South and North; while Merton L. Dillon, *Slavery Attacked: Southern Slaves and Their Allies, 1619–1865* (Baton Rouge: Louisiana State University Press, 1990), looks at outside encouragement and support for slave revolts. For more on David Walker and the evolving attitude of abolitionists toward violence, the general works on abolitionism mentioned in the previous chapter are still relevant, along with the works on John Brown mentioned below in chapter 4. Unfortunately, there is no book-length biography of Lysander Spooner. Background information can be found in the chapter about him from James J. Martin, *Men Against the State: The Expositors of Individualist Anarchism in America, 1827–1908* (DeKalb, IL: Adrian Allen Associates, 1953), and the short biography from the first volume of Charles Shively, ed., *The Collected Works of Lysander Spooner* (Weston, MA: M & S Press, 1971). Details about Spooner's circular on slave insurrection, along with discussions of the abolitionists' growing militancy, are contained in Lewis Perry, *Radical Abolitionism*, an important work from last chapter's bibliographical essay; Betram Wyatt-Brown, "William Lloyd Garrison and Antislavery Unity: A Reappraisal," in Robert P. Swierenga, ed., *Beyond the Civil War Synthesis: Political Essays on the Civil War Era* (Westport, CT: Greenwood Press, 1975), a collection of assorted articles on politics that originally appeared in *Civil War History;* and Herbert Aptheker, *To Be Free: Studies in American Negro History*, 2nd edn. (New York: International, 1968), which in addition to its essay on "Militant Abolitionism" also contains useful essays on maroon bands in the South and slaves purchasing their own liberty.

3

The Slave Power Seeks Foreign Conquest

American Politics in the Age of Andrew Jackson

The two major political parties that battled each other during the early 1840s, as the abolitionist Liberty Party appeared on the landscape, were not that old themselves. The War of 1812 had left America with a single party, the Republicans, and only in 1828, well after the Missouri crisis, had personal competition for the presidency between Andrew Jackson and John Quincy Adams given rise to distinct political organizations. Final elimination of property qualifications for voting, both North and South, and the direct election of ever more state and local offices was making this an era in which popular participation in politics reached an all-time high. Now that presidential electors were chosen by the people, an astonishing 80 percent of the eligible voters turned out to vote. Two mass-based parties, Whigs and Democrats, were soon firmly demarcated, each with a different ideology.

Adams and Henry Clay were early leaders of the Whig Party. Striving to carry forward the triumphant nationalism of the war years, their program called for the central government to promote economic growth with protective tariffs, a national bank, and aid for internal improvements. All these were part of what Clay called the

American System. "Is there no remedy within the reach of Government? Are we doomed to behold our industry languish and decay yet more and more?" the Kentucky politician had demanded to know after the Panic of 1819, a severe economic depression that introduced the American economy to the modern trade cycle. "But there is a remedy, and that remedy consists in . . . adopting a genuine American system." Domestic manufacturing must have "adequate protection against the otherwise overwhelming influence of foreigners. This is only to be accomplished by the establishment of a tariff."[1]

The Democratic Party was the combined product of Jackson's popular charisma and Martin Van Buren's backroom politicking. In opposition to the Whigs, the Democrats reaffirmed the prewar creed of the Old Republicans and its Jeffersonian ideal of simple and frugal government. To them, Clay's American System wielded political power to benefit special interests. "The rich and powerful too often bend the acts of government to their selfish purposes," lamented President Jackson in his resounding veto of the Second Bank of the United States. Because the bank was a government-chartered monopoly, it aroused within the party that contemporaries called "the Democracy" a deep-seated hostility to political privilege.

"Distinctions in society will always exist under every just government," Jackson's veto conceded. "Equality of talents, of education, or of wealth can not be produced by human institutions. In the full enjoyment of the gifts of Heaven and the fruits of superior industry, economy, and virtue, every man is equally entitled to protection by law; but when the laws undertake to add to these natural and just advantages artificial distinctions, to grant titles, gratuities, and exclusive privileges, to make the rich richer and the potent more powerful, the humble members of society—the farmers, mechanics, and laborers—who have neither the time nor the means of securing like favors to themselves, have a right to complain of the injustice of their Government."[2]

One issue, however, both major parties avoided at all cost. That was slavery. Its potential to divide the Union along geographical lines had been demonstrated during the Missouri controversy. The tariff crisis of 1832 provided a second reminder that sectional interests could take precedence over party. John C. Calhoun had been allied with Jackson as his first Vice-President, but Jackson's belligerent response to South Carolina's nullification had so alienated Calhoun that he, along with several other states' rights Southerners, defected into the Whig Party.

When an independent Texas applied to join the Union in 1836, sixteen years after Missouri, it threatened to inflame the same kind of sectional passions. Anglo-Americans had first settled in Texas at the invitation of the Mexican government during the 1820s. By the mid-1830s, there were 30,000, as compared with 3,500 native Mexicans. The overwhelming number of these immigrants had come from the southwestern United States, bringing with them several thousand enslaved blacks. After a counter-revolution in Mexico proceeded to strip the American settlers of many previous liberties, they took up arms. The Texans soon declared their independence, defeated the Mexican government's armies, and drew up a constitution that sanctioned slavery.

"PEOPLE OF THE NORTH! WILL YOU PERMIT IT?" asked Benjamin Lundy, a northern Quaker who advocated eventual freeing of all slaves. He had been William Lloyd Garrison's mentor and a major precursor during the 1820s of militant abolitionism. Lundy now raised a hue and cry against Texas annexation. "Will you sanction the abominable outrage; involve yourselves in the deep criminality, and perhaps the horrors of war, FOR THE ESTABLISHMENT OF SLAVERY IN THE LAND OF FREEDOM; and thus put your necks and the necks of your posterity under the feet of the domineering tyrants of the South, for centuries to come?"[3]

Although Lundy's abolitionism was not representative of northern opinion, his concern about the political power of the slave states was. President Jackson had tried to purchase Texas from Mexico and was known to have watched the Texas Revolution with satisfaction. Sam Houston, the first president of the Lone Star Republic, was Jackson's political protégé and a former governor of Jackson's home state of Tennessee. But when annexation became a realistic possibility, the American President turned suddenly cool. Despite being a slaveowner, he did not wish to do anything that would endanger the election of his chosen Democratic successor: Van Buren. He refused even to recognize Texas independence until the Little Magician, as that consummate politician was known, had safely won the presidency in 1836.

The new Chief Executive, a widower hailing from the free state of New York, continued Jackson's policy of snubbing Texas overtures. The annexation question consequently languished until an unusual set of circumstances brought John Tyler of Virginia into the White House. Tyler was initially the vice-presidential candidate on the 1840 Whig ticket, headed by William Henry Harrison. The country was emerging out of another financial panic, and Harrison, like Jackson, was an aging military hero from the War of 1812. That fortuitous conjunction helped the Whigs to defeat Van Buren for reelection. But after a month in office, Harrison died.

Tyler thus became the first Vice-President elevated to the highest office. Yet he was not a committed Whig, despite his presence on that ticket. He was one of the southern Democrats who had defected along with Calhoun, and the Whigs had only nominated him to attract the estranged members of the opposite party. Upon Harrison's victory, the representatives of his party in Congress, under Clay's leadership, had eagerly anticipated enactment of the entire American System. But with Tyler in office, an almost comic political opera was repeated over and over. Congress would pass a bill implementing some part of the Whig program, and the President would dutifully veto it. Clay in frustrated fury railed against the reign of "His Accidency."

Tyler on the other hand became a President without a party. Ideologically a Democrat, politically a Whig, he could interest neither in running him for election in his own right. Tyler therefore sought some issue that would appeal over the heads of the party leaderships. By the middle of Tyler's term, his Cabinet was the first to be completely dominated by proslavery Southerners, so the acquisition of Texas seemed perfect for putting the President onto the crest of the country's surge for more territory. Six months before the 1844 election, Tyler's newly appointed Secretary of State, none other than Calhoun, submitted an annexation treaty to the Senate.

Texas and Slavery

More than political opportunism impelled John Tyler. After consistent rebuffs from the U.S., Texas had decided to pursue a foreign policy that would give it a truly independent stature among the world's powers. Britain and the other European nations had granted the new government diplomatic recognition. During eight years of independence, the rich cotton lands of Texas had helped swell its population fourfold, to around 120,000. The Texans began to think seriously about extending their borders through Mexican territory all the way to the California coast. The United States faced the prospect of a rival republic with competing territorial interests.

What made this prospect unnerving was the increasingly intimate ties between Texas and Britain. The Texans were wooing British assistance in dealing with Mexico, which had never conceded the legitimacy of the new government. The potential advantage for Great Britain of aiding the Lone Star Republic was not confined to erecting a barrier against United States expansion in North America. The British government was in the forefront of the worldwide crusade against slavery, having emancipated the slaves in its own colonies while aggressively suppressing the slave trade on the high seas. British influence might induce Texas to abolish the institution, whereupon runaway slaves would have a new haven, and British mills would have a new source of cotton other than the slaveholding South. Former President Jackson was now a staunch supporter of annexation because of just these fears. "Would not . . . our slaves in the great valley of the Mississippi [be] worth nothing, because they would all run over to Texas, and under British influence, [be] liberated and lost to their owners[?]"[4]

The South was feeling increasingly isolated as one of the last citadels of chattel slavery in the entire world. The Texas question linked the country's traditional hatred of Britain with the southern fear of an abolitionist plot to destroy the peculiar institution. "While England . . . desires the independence of Texas, with the view to commercial connections, it is not less so, that one of the leading motives . . . is the hope, that, through her diplomacy and influence, negroe slavery may be abolished there, and ultimately, by consequence, in the United States and throughout the whole of this

continent," warned Secretary of State Calhoun. The South Carolinian had become the dark-eyed, unruly-haired, "cast-iron man"
described by the English commentator, Harriet Martineau, and he
forcefully articulated this conspiracy theory. "In fact, there is good
reason to believe, that the scheme of abolishing [slavery] in Texas
. . . originated with the prominent members of the [abolition] party
in the United States, and was first broached by them in the . . .
Convention, held in London in the year 1840, and through its
agency brought to the notice of the British Government."[5]

Calhoun believed that Britain's motives involved more than just
humanitarian concern for black freedom. Emancipation in the
British West Indies had been an economic disaster, and the British
government needed some way to recoup. "The question is, by what
means can Great Britain regain and keep a superiority in tropical
cultivation, commerce, and influence? . . . Her main reliance is . . .
to cripple or destroy the productions of her successful rivals. There
is but one way by which it can be done, and that is, by abolishing
African slavery throughout this continent." Like Jackson, Calhoun
believed that an abolitionized Texas would be a beacon to fugitive
slaves. "It is unquestionable, that [Britain] regards . . . the defeat of
the annexation of Texas to our Union, as indispensable to the
abolition of slavery there. She is too sagacious not to see, what a
fatal blow it would give to slavery in the United States, . . . and
thereby give her a monopoly in the productions of the great tropical
staples, and the command of the commerce, navigation, and
manufactures of the world, with an established naval ascendancy
and political preponderance."[6]

The foes of Texas annexation, meanwhile, had developed a
conspiracy theory of their own. The most inexhaustible of them was
John Quincy Adams. The Congressman from Massachusetts could
claim forty-two years of distinguished public service, not only as
Chief Executive for one term, but also as an American diplomat
throughout Europe, as a Senator, and as Secretary of State, where
he had been instrumental in acquiring Florida for the United States.
Only during his later career in the House of Representatives was
Adams fully converted to antislavery by Benjamin Lundy, but as a
result, the seventy-six-year-old former expansionist came to see the
entire Texas saga as an elaborate plot of what abolitionists referred

to as "the Slave Power." The plot dated back to before the Texas Revolution and involved Jackson along with Jackson's close friend and personal agent, Sam Houston, who was again serving as president of the Lone Star Republic. If the extensive territory that Texans claimed was added to the Union, it might become as many as four or five new states and carry slavery north of the Missouri Compromise line.

"We . . . feel bound to call your attention . . . to the project . . . intended soon to be consummated—THE ANNEXATION OF TEXAS TO THIS UNION," stated an address to the people that outlined this conspiracy theory and was signed by twenty other Congressmen as well as Old Man Eloquent. Those "interested in the continuance of domestic slavery and the slave trade in these United States have solemnly and unalterably determined . . . that, by this admission of a new slave territory and slave states, *the undue ascendancy of the slaveholding power in the government shall be secured and rivetted beyond all redemption.*" That this was the reason "settlements were effected in the province by citizens of the United States, difficulties fomented with the Mexican government, a revolt brought about, and an independent government declared, *cannot now admit of a doubt.*"[7]

Both conspiracy theories contained elements of truth. The British would have liked to see the end of slavery in Texas, or elsewhere, and southern slaveholders did feel that their future political security hinged upon annexation. Both conspiracy theories were also highly exaggerated. The British government harbored no enmity toward the South, upon which it depended for cotton, and slavery had played only a minor role in the Texas Revolution. But the two conspiracy theories were mutually self-fulfilling. Belief in an abolitionist plot caused Southerners to behave just as the opponents of Texas annexation predicted, and belief in a Slave Power plot caused Northerners to behave just as the advocates of annexation predicted.

Adams, despite having played a large and enthusiastic role in the country's territorial growth, now felt so strongly about slavery that he and his colleagues were willing to threaten northern secession should Texas join the Union: "We hesitate not to say that *annexation*

. . . WOULD BE IDENTICAL WITH DISSOLUTION." Indeed, " it would be a violation of our national compact . . . so deep and fundamental . . . as, in our opinion, not only inevitably to result in a dissolution of the Union, but fully to justify it."[8] Within such a divisive atmosphere, the annexation treaty of Tyler and Calhoun could not gain the necessary approval of two-thirds of the Senate. The Texas question, nevertheless, had been decisively thrown into the midst of the ongoing presidential race.

The U.S. Acquires More Territory

As the Senate considered the Texas treaty, Clay was the front-runner for the Whig presidential nomination, and Van Buren was the front-runner for the Democratic nomination. The two candidates, hoping to eliminate Texas as a campaign issue, met privately for discussions. Shortly after the meeting, they each issued separate public statements expressing qualified opposition to annexation.

Clay's campaign statement represented a sharp departure from his earlier support for territorial aggrandizement, but that did not hurt him within his party. Although both political organizations contained opponents of annexation, the Whigs, home to most of the Benevolent Empire's militant reformers, included the larger such contingent. The Whig convention unanimously nominated Clay. Within the Democracy, however, Southerners turned away from Van Buren. Even Jackson—retired, dying, but still influential— abandoned the New Yorker. Although the Little Magician still held support from a majority of the delegates as the party's convention opened in Baltimore, the convention rules required a two-thirds vote to nominate. After eight deadlocked ballots, the delegates settled on the first dark-horse candidate in American presidential history: James Knox Polk, a Southerner from Tennessee and an ardent expansionist. In order to overcome northern resistance, the Democratic platform cleverly united the acquisition of Texas with occupation of Oregon.

Now that the Democratic Party had embraced territorial expansion, President Tyler's half-hearted bid to retain the presidency was left without an issue. He withdrew and, taking with him most of the states' rights southern Whigs, reentered the Democracy's ranks, following in the footsteps of Calhoun who had already done so. This reunion, along with the convention's prior rejection of the more radical Van Buren wing of the party, marked the beginning of a major political shift. Over the long term the Democrats would be transformed into a sectional party representing the slaveholding South.

The Liberty Party, now four years old, was participating in its second presidential race. Although so minuscule it had no chance of winning, the party did pick up thousands of northern votes as Clay began to equivocate about Texas in a last-minute effort to appeal to Southerners. The Democratic Party ultimately won, but the election was close. Polk got less than a majority of the popular vote. If Clay had received the Liberty Party's antislavery votes in New York and Michigan, he would have carried two more states and claimed victory.

The Democrats, nevertheless, interpreted the results as a mandate for expansion. They closed ranks on Texas annexation, which was completed even before Polk could assume office. Securing the approval of two-thirds of the Senate remained an obstacle, but President Tyler got around it by proposing a joint resolution on annexation instead, which unlike a treaty, required only majority approval of both houses of Congress. The rejected treaty would have brought Texas into the Union as a territory, leaving Congress with unrestricted control over boundaries and new states. Tyler's joint resolution, on the other hand, would bring Texas in directly as a state, with its formerly independent government continuing to function. Texas would now have to grant permission if any additional states were formed out of its territory. The resolution further stipulated that north of the Missouri Compromise line any such states would be free, while to the south the inhabitants could choose to allow or forbid slavery. This was to become a moot point since the state was never partitioned.

The annexation resolution passed the lame-duck Congress on the basis of strict party lines, with all Democrats supporting it, and all but two Whigs in the House and three in the Senate opposing it. Tyler signed on March 1, 1845, three days before leaving office. Polk thus began his term with half the expansionist program implemented. War, however, loomed on the horizon, as the Mexican government immediately broke relations with the United States. Annexation alone was sufficient cause for hostilities.

The Mexicans made one final diplomatic gesture in a bow to British pressure by offering to recognize Texas independence if the Texans turned down U.S. annexation. The Texas government however accepted the terms of the joint congressional resolution and formally entered the Union as a state almost a year after Polk's inauguration. To add insult to injury, the United States supported the new state's claim to the Rio Grande as its border. The boundary when Texas was a Mexican province had been the Nueces River, 130 miles farther north on the Gulf. There had never been any Anglo-American settlements in the disputed zone between the two rivers.

While Mexico and the United States were heading toward war, Polk was simultaneously looking "John Bull straight in the eye," in his own words, over jointly-occupied Oregon. Since Britain in the past had persistently refused to accept a U.S. offer to divide the territory at the 49th parallel, the President now demanded it all. Whig opponents attempted to ridicule this stand by coining the phrase "Fifty-Four Forty or Fight," referring to the latitude line separating Oregon on the north from Alaska, but western Democrats proudly adopted the slogan as their own.

The United States, however, did not ultimately take on both Britain and Mexico. With both powers there were disputed boundaries. In both cases the Polk Administration pushed extensive territorial claims into doubtful regions. Yet the U.S. government reached a peaceful settlement with Britain in mid-June of 1846, at the very moment that war with Mexico had been raging for a month. Some credit for the divergent outcomes belongs to the concessions on the part of the British government. But a full explanation of why the United States fought Mexico and not Britain in 1846 must include the attitude of the Polk Administration.

The President, in negotiations with the Mexican government, assumed a diplomatic intransigence that never marred relations with the British. Southern Democrats had not been keen upon acquiring all of the Oregon territory anyway; the demand for the "re-occupation of Oregon" had merely been a rhetorical ploy to buy western support for the acquisition of Texas. The most important consideration of all was that California belonged to Mexico and not to Britain. For in addition to the Democrat platform's explicit demands for Oregon and Texas, Polk had another foreign policy objective that he never mentioned in public. This hardworking, uncompromising Presbyterian was determined to acquire the port of San Francisco for the United States, peacefully if possible, but through war if necessary.

War it was, and as the United States commenced a military campaign for foreign conquest, the New England lecturer and essayist, Ralph Waldo Emerson, foresaw the dire long-term consequences. "The United States will conquer Mexico, but it will be as the man swallows the arsenic, which brings him down in turn. Mexico will poison us."[9]

Deadlock Over Slavery's Extension

The single issue that commanded for abolitionists the greatest northern sympathy was slavery's extension into new territories. Here was an antislavery position that carried no taint of disunion. It allowed Northerners to take steps against slavery in a distant sphere while honoring their constitutional obligation to leave the local institutions of the southern states alone. Here also was an antislavery position that could be made consistent with Negrophobia. Keeping slaves out of the territories was an excellent way to keep blacks out altogether.

Preventing the admission of new slave states moreover served the political self-interest of Northerners. Southern representatives often voted down the favorite policies of northern special interests on questions unrelated to slavery, such as the tariff and internal improvements. Blocking slavery's spread would contain the South's political influence. So long as abolitionists had talked about the welfare of blacks, their message had limited appeal among northern whites. But when abolitionists directed their attacks at the ominous sounding Slave Power, Northerners paid more attention.

The explosive question of slavery in the territories had remained dormant for twenty-five years after the Missouri Compromise. Although the annexation of Texas threatened to ignite this powderkeg, the Polk Administration had managed to defuse the sectional bomb by linking southern expansion into Texas with northern expansion into Oregon. But when war with Mexico made the addition of vast new territories in the southwest certain, the issue finally detonated.

The spark that set off the explosion was struck on August 8, 1846, barely three months after the Mexican War's outbreak. Congressman David Wilmot, an antislavery Democrat from northeastern Pennsylvania, proposed a rider to a war appropriation bill. The rider provided "as an express and fundamental condition to the acquisition of any territory from the Republic of Mexico by the United States . . . neither slavery nor involuntary servitude shall ever exist in any part of said territory, except for crime, whereof the party shall first be duly convicted," words patterned after the slavery prohibition in the Northwest Ordinance of 1787.[10]

The crisis provoked by the Wilmot Proviso, as this rider was called, bore many similarities to the previous Missouri crisis. The free-state majority in the House of Representatives was greater than ever. It passed the proviso several times in various forms. But like Tallmadge's Missouri amendment, the Wilmot Proviso always failed in the Senate. The organization of new territories remained at an impasse for four years. Despite these similarities, the two antislavery proposals exhibited a critical difference. Tallmadge's amendment would have eliminated slavery in a new state where it already existed. The Wilmot Proviso would have kept slavery out of territory where, under Mexican law, it was already illegal. Wilmot declared himself opposed "now and forever, to the extension of this 'peculiar institution' that belongs to the South." He had voted for Texas annexation; "slavery had already been established there. But if free territory comes in, God forbid that [I] should be the means of planting this institution upon it."[11] This gave the proviso such moral force that every free-state legislature except one endorsed it.

While Northerners were incensed that a United States military victory might introduce slavery into an area previously free, Southerners were incensed at being denied equal access to an area that their money and lives were helping to conquer. A disproportionate share of the American volunteers fighting in Mexico had come from the South. Southern honor was at stake.

On the Senate floor, Calhoun set forth the southern response to the Wilmot Proviso in four proposed resolutions. Calhoun's resolutions did not simply argue that Congress should not exclude slavery from the territories. They asserted that Congress had no constitutional authority to do so, despite such past legislation as the Northwest Ordinance and the Missouri Compromise. "Sir, these territories are the property of the States united; held jointly for their common use." Under the Constitution, citizens of any state must be free to migrate there with their possessions, including slaves. "Is it consistent with justice, is it consistent with equality, that any portion of the partners, outnumbering another portion, shall oust them of this common property of theirs. . . . Would that be consistent, can it be consistent with the idea of common property, held jointly for the common benefit of all? Would it be so considered in private life? Would it not be considered the most flagrant outrage in the world, one which any court of equity would restrain by injunction—which any court of law in the world would overrule?"[12] Only when a territory was ready for statehood could it constitutionally prohibit slavery. Calhoun's proposals therefore required that all the territories be open to the peculiar institution.

The Wilmot Proviso and the Calhoun resolutions defined the extreme northern and southern positions on slavery in the territories. In one, slavery was stigmatized at the national level and legally permitted only at the state level. In the other, slavery was a national institution sanctioned and protected by the central government. These two irreconcilable visions of the Union would continue to clash until the Civil War.

Not every Northerner and Southerner, however, had gravitated to the polar extremes. President Polk was one Southerner who thought the entire debate a dangerous abstraction, because the southwestern territories seized from Mexico were not suitable for plantation agriculture anyway. An anonymous southern Congressman reportedly complained later in exasperation that the "whole controversy over the Territories . . . related to an imaginary negro in an impossible place."[13] The Polk administration therefore suggested extending the Missouri Compromise line to the Pacific. New territory north of the line would be closed to slavery; south of the line open to it. Enough northern Congressmen, however, opposed this measure to prevent its passage.

A Michigan Senator, Lewis Cass, tried to come up with another basis for compromise. Cass was the leading presidential aspirant of the Democratic Party in 1848, and he needed some fourth formula to hold the two sectional wings of his party together. Cass's answer, called "popular sovereignty," was drawn from the unused provision of the Texas annexation resolution that dealt with forming additional states. Popular sovereignty would allow the settlers of a territory to decide about slavery for themselves. It thus invoked the democratic ideal of local self-government and was also sufficiently ambiguous to attract both Northerners and Southerners. In order for it to work, a territory had to be open to slavery at least initially, and Cass never specified at what point prior to statehood the territorial government could prohibit the institution.

But popular sovereignty failed to uphold Democratic unity in the North. Party feuding was most pronounced in New York state. The Democratic supporters of the Wilmot Proviso were called "Barnburners," because of alleged willingness to burn down the party barn to get rid of the rat of slavery. The opposing pro-southern Democrats were called "Hunkers," because of their unprincipled hunkering after political power. Under the leadership of former President Van Buren, the Barnburners bolted the party when Cass secured the nomination.

The northern Whigs experienced a parallel split. In this case it emanated from Massachusetts, where antislavery "Conscience" Whigs vied against pro-southern "Cotton" Whigs. The eminent place of John Quincy Adams among the party's antislavery members had passed at his death in early 1848 to his son, Charles Francis Adams. After the Whig national convention picked Zachary Taylor, a victorious American general during the recent war and a Louisiana slaveholder, to run for President, the younger Adams denounced the entire proceeding as an unholy alliance between "the Lords of Lash," southern slaveholders, and "the Lords of Loom," northern textile manufacturers.

Just three months before the election, organizers from the Liberty Party skillfully united the Barnburners and Conscience Whigs into a more broad-based third party. One abolitionist recalled the crusading mood at the convention for the new Free Soil Party: "I have been almost carried away by the enthusiasm of the thousands, from all parts of our country north of Masons & Dixon's line, by whom I have been surrounded in the last three days . . . A great deal of high Anti-Slavery thought, and deep Anti-Slavery feeling was expressed by many of the speakers . . . [T]he platform of the new political party . . . was received with uproarious, deafening applause. Three times three, three times three, and three times three again; hats and handkerchiefs whirling all over that vast concourse of upturned and happy faces, in concert with huzzas that were coming, like the rush of many waters, from their united voices."[14]

The Free Soil Party ran Van Buren for President and Adams for Vice-President. While the former Democrats and Whigs each got one slot on the ticket, the former Libertymen got to write the platform. Unlike the prior Liberty Party platform, the Free Soil Party platform took stands on issues other than slavery to broaden its appeal, calling for nationally financed internal improvements and free homesteads on public lands. It also included an explicit protection for slavery within the states and ignored the question of equal rights for free blacks. Many Free-Soil Democrats were primarily concerned about keeping the west open for free white laborers. "The negro race already occupy enough of this fair continent," declared Wilmot at a Free Soil rally. "Let us keep what remains for ourselves, and our children—for the emigrant that seeks our shores—for the poor man, that wealth shall oppress—for the free white laborer, who shall desire to hew him out a home of happiness and peace, on the distant shores of the mighty Pacific."[15]

Nonetheless, under the slogan "Free Soil, Free Speech, Free Labor, and Free Men," the new party retained the radical program of divorcing the national government from slavery. The platform not only stood firmly behind the Wilmot Proviso, but Van Buren also assented to such additional antislavery goals as abolition in the District of Columbia. Although Taylor won the 1848 election, and Van Buren did not carry a single state, the Free Soil Party received 10 percent of the popular vote and elected thirteen members to Congress. As the territorial impasse remained unresolved, the House of Representatives upped the antislavery ante by passing a resolution condemning the slave pens and public auctions in the nation's capital.

Temporary Truce Between North and South

The need to do something about the unorganized territories was becoming acute. The lands ceded by Mexico were still subject to direct military rule. This was especially resented in California, where the discovery of gold had brought a deluge of "Forty-Niners" seeking their fortunes. California's population soon numbered 100,000, greater than states such as Florida and Delaware. At the same time, the extravagant claim of Texas to settlements in New Mexico that had always been autonomous seemed likely to produce armed conflict along the upper Rio Grande. And Mormon settlers in Utah had organized an autonomous and theocratic "Republic of Deseret," which to the consternation of many Easterners legalized polygamy.

President Taylor's solution was to encourage settlers to organize state governments directly, bypassing the territorial stage altogether. Californians heeded this suggestion and ratified a state constitution prohibiting slavery in November 1849. New Mexico was following in California's footsteps. These unilateral executive acts left Southerners feeling betrayed by a fellow slaveholder. California's admission would unhinge forever the delicate sectional balance, which now stood at fifteen states each, slave and free.

For the first time, secession received a serious hearing throughout all of the South. The Mississippi legislature called for a convention of the southern states to meet at Nashville in June 1850. The words of Congressman Robert Toombs of Georgia reflected the South's sense of urgency: "I do not, then, hesitate to avow before this House and the country, and in the presence of the living God, that if, by your legislation, you seek to drive us from the territories of California and New Mexico, purchased by the common blood and treasure of the whole people, and to abolish slavery in this District, thereby attempting to fix a national degradation upon half the States of this Confederacy, *I am for disunion.*"[16]

But the southern states did not secede in 1850. Another compromise, perhaps the most difficult of all, saved the Union for ten more years, in a legislative achievement that is one of the dramatic events in American history. The legendary figures of John C. Calhoun, Henry Clay, and Daniel Webster played their final great roles on the congressional stage, ably supported by a new generation of younger actors entering upon the national political scene.

Clay, in his seventy-third year, came out of retirement to again assume the part of the Great Pacificator. On January 29, 1850, he eloquently pleaded before the Senate for a comprehensive settlement of all outstanding controversies. Congress then debated his proposals for over seven months. Calhoun, just twenty-seven days from death, could only sit, wrapped in a blanket, and listen to his final oration read for him by a colleague. The overbearing North, he warned, was snapping the ties of Union, one after another. "It cannot, then, be saved by eulogies on the Union, however splendid or numerous. The cry of 'Union, Union, the glorious Union!' can no more prevent disunion than the cry of 'Health, health, glorious health!' on the part of the physician can save a patient lying dangerously ill." Only the North, politically stronger, could save the Union by agreeing to "a full and final settlement on the principle of justice of all the questions at issue between the two sections." Failing that, "let the States we both represent agree to separate and part in peace. If you are unwilling we should part in peace, tell us so, and we shall know what to do when you reduce the question to submission or resistance."[17]

Webster delivered his last major speech three days later. "I wish to speak to-day," he began, "not as a Massachusetts man, nor as a northern man, but as an American," and then put all his rhetorical power behind Clay's compromise.[18] Webster's appeal disappointed many antislavery Whigs. One of them was Senator William H. Seward from New York, a wily politician, small and slouching, who because of his big-beaked nose was once uncharitably described as "a jay-bird with a sparrow hawk's bill."[19] Seward hoarsely rejected the compromise on the basis of a "higher law than the Constitution," which pronounced all men free.

With all the lofty oratory, the compromise failed when presented as a single omnibus bill. An exhausted and disheartened Clay left sultry Washington to recuperate. Final passage fell to the politically competent hands of Senator Stephen A. Douglas, an

Illinois Democrat. By presenting each part of the compromise separately, he picked up enough extra northern or southern votes to push every part through. Still, President Taylor, who had fallen under the antislavery influence of Senator Seward, would have vetoed the package if he had not conveniently died in office on July 9. His successor, Millard Fillmore of New York, put his weight behind the compromise and signed all the measures by September.

The Compromise of 1850 admitted California as a free state. The remainder of the Mexican Cession was organized into the territories of Utah and New Mexico, both open to slavery under the principle of popular sovereignty. The Texas boundary included no portion of New Mexico, but Texas received $10 million to help pay off its state debt. Slavery was not outlawed in the District of Columbia, but the slave trade was. Finally, a stronger law to enforce the fugitive slave provision of the Constitution was enacted.

The free-state majority in the House had backed down on the Wilmot Proviso in order to secure California's admission as a free state without provoking southern secession. The country rejoiced, as President Fillmore declared the compromise "final and irrevocable."[20] Most of the Free Soil Democrats reentered their original party, which picked Franklin Pierce, a New Hampshire Yankee dependably friendly to the South, as its presidential candidate for 1852. Yet beneath the surface lurked many indications that the Compromise of 1850 was only a temporary sectional truce. Even after the northern capitulation, fire-eating secessionists came close to winning control of four state governments in the lower South. The slave states may have rejected the expediency of secession for the moment. But they were firmly committed to the right of secession in principle.

In the North, abolitionists and loyal Free Soilers bitterly denounced the compromise. Although the 1852 presidential candidate of the Free Soil Party, Senator John P. Hale of New Hampshire, polled half the votes of Van Buren, four years before, the antislavery wing of the Whig Party was stronger than ever. It managed to block the nomination of incumbent President Fillmore. The Whig platform still backed the Compromise of 1850, and the substitute candidate, General Winfield S. Scott, was from Virginia. Be he received very little southern support in the general election. Pierce swept to victory, and the Democrats won a two-thirds majority in the House of Representatives.

The Book That Made the War

The part of the Compromise of 1850 that eventually galled Northerners more than any other was not the territorial settlement. It was the new Fugitive Slave Law. One of the harshest congressional measures ever, the act created a class of federal court officials, called commissioners, to help slaveholders seize runaways. All the slaveholder needed to do was present an affidavit. The alleged fugitive enjoyed no right to a jury trial or even to testify. Furthermore, commissioners had a financial incentive to rule against the fugitive. They received a $10 fee from the government for deciding that a black was an escaped slave, but only $5 for not. To enhance enforcement, Congress empowered commissioners to conscript the physical aid of any private citizen, thereby extending the principle behind compulsory slave patrols into the North. Obstructing the law was subject to a $1,000 fine, six months in prison, and $1,000 civil damages for each escaped slave.

With this law, Southerners put the North on notice that nothing—not due legal process, not civil liberties, not even the cherished principle of state sovereignty—could stand in the way of masters recovering their human chattel. Free blacks were the northern group in greatest jeopardy. They had no legal recourse if a Southerner claimed they were escaped slaves. The law consequently fostered an unsavory class of professional slave catchers, who could make huge profits by legally kidnapping free blacks in the North and selling them into slavery in the South. Panic reigned in the northern black communities, as many fled to Canada.

The pitiful spectacle of helpless blacks being seized in the streets and dragged off to slavery could unsettle the most prejudiced northern white. Then a fictional work that started to appear serially on June 5, 1851, inflamed indignation further. Written by Harriet Beecher Stowe, the daughter, sister, and wife of abolitionist ministers, *Uncle Tom's Cabin* quickly became an all-time best seller when released as a novel. Stowe was overwhelmed at the book's reception. "Ten thousand copies were sold in a few days, and over three hundred thousand within a year, and eight power-presses, running day and night, were barely able to keep pace with the demand for it. It was read everywhere, apparently, and by everybody." For the suddenly famous author, the most "cheering result was in the testimony of many colored persons and fugitive slaves" who told her " 'Since that book has come out, everybody is good to us; we find friends everywhere.' "[21]

When Mrs. Stowe was introduced to Abraham Lincoln a decade later, the President reportedly greeted her saying "So you're the little woman who wrote the book that made this great war."[22] For every four votes that Pierce received from the free states in 1852, one copy of *Uncle Tom's Cabin* was sold. Its adaptation to the stage brought an even wider audience. Such harrowing scenes as the slave Eliza clutching her young son, braving the ice floes of the Ohio River, in order to reach freedom, personally conveyed to northern readers the slave's plight. Stowe, moreover, did not demonize Southerners, but portrayed them as equally helpless victims of the slave system.

Northern mobs, which once had directed their fury at abolitionists, now attacked slave catchers, broke into jails, and rescued fugitive slaves. Frederick Douglass urged that "the only way to make the Fugitive Slave Law a dead letter is to make half a dozen or more dead kidnappers," and an 1851 gun battle in Christiana, Pennsylvania, left at least one dead southern kidnapper.[23] The national government tried vigorously to prosecute the law-breakers responsible for such defiance, but northern juries refused to convict. In some cases, the authorities had to rely upon military force. The seizure in May 1854 of Anthony Burns, an escaped Virginia slave, brought protesters into Boston from the surrounding countryside. Their unsuccessful assault upon the court-house where Burns was being held resulted in the killing of one guard. Soon the government had called out two companies of artillery and one thousand police, militia, and marines to march Burns to the harbor, while a menacing crowd of twenty thousand Yankees looked on. Southerners never successfully recovered a runaway slave from Boston again.

The Fugitive Slave Law of 1850 also inspired stronger personal liberty laws. Beginning with Vermont, nine free states either provided for the legal defense of alleged runaways or openly defied the national government by requiring jury trial, *habeas corpus,* and other procedural safeguards. Not until 1859 did the Supreme Court strike down these state laws, at a time when accelerating sectional strife was eclipsing all the legal niceties.

Attempted Expansion in the Caribbean

President Polk's territorial ambitions had encompassed more than just one half of Mexico. Indeed, he had been furious when Nicholas Trist, the American negotiator, had settled in the Treaty of Guadalupe Hidalgo for just this one million square miles—encompassing all or most of the future states of Texas, California, New Mexico, Arizona, Nevada, Utah, and Colorado. Only growing antiwar and Free-Soil sentiment had induced Polk reluctantly to submit the treaty for ratification. An 1848 rebellion in the Yucatán Peninsula, then independent from Mexico, provided the President with a pretext for additional seizures, except that Congress failed to act in time. Cuba, however, was the territorial trophy that Polk and Southerners coveted most. With vast sugar plantations, worked by almost half a million black slaves, "the Pearl of the Antilles" as a new state could add thirteen to fifteen slaveholding representatives in Congress.

Senator Jefferson Davis, a Democrat from Mississippi, declared that "Cuba must be ours" in order to convert the Gulf of Mexico into "a basin of water belonging to the United States."[24] His Mississippi colleague, Albert Gallatin Brown, was more explicit: "I want Cuba, and I know that sooner or later we must have it. If the worm-eaten throne of Spain is willing to give it up for a fair equivalent, well—if not, we must take it." Brown however would not stop there. "I want Tamaulipas, Potosi, and one or two other Mexican States. . . . And a footing in Central America will powerfully aid us in acquiring those other States. . . . Yes, I want these Countries for the spread of slavery. I would spread the blessings of slavery, like the religion of our Divine Master, to the uttermost ends of the earth." The Mississippi Senator added that "rebellious and wicked as the Yankees have been, I would even extend [slavery] to them," although "I would not force it upon them, as I would not force religion upon them."[25]

But when Polk secretly tried to purchase Cuba for $100 million, the Spanish government contemptuously refused despite facing a possible war against Britain. The Democratic defeat in the 1848 election compelled Southerners to turn to unofficial channels, because Taylor, the Whig President, opposed further expansion. Perhaps Cuba could be eased into American hands in the same way as Florida, Texas, and California, by fostering and aiding revolution. The United States had always been blessed with private adventurers, or filibusters, eager to risk military expeditions for the capture of foreign lands. Whenever these expeditions conveniently fit in with the government's shifting foreign-policy objectives, they received clandestine encouragement and support. Of course, otherwise they might be hastily quashed, as in the case of the notorious conspiracy of the unfortunate Aaron Burr during President Jefferson's second term.

The current leader of émigrés from Cuba was Narcisco Lopez, a Venezuelan soldier of fortune. With assistance from prominent Southerners, Lopez recruited volunteers and raised money for no less than three successive but short-lived filibustering excursions against Cuba, until Spanish authorities finally captured and executed him in 1851, along with fifty of his American followers. Armed bands from Texas and California launched dozens of similar raids into Mexico during the 1850s. Occasionally federal officials would interfere, but the filibusters were heroes to cheering crowds in the South, where juries refused to convict them of violating the neutrality laws. One Virginian organized the Knights of the Golden Circle, a shadowy fraternity looking forward to a "golden circle" of about twenty-five slave states running all the way from the American South down through Mexico and Central America along the northern coast of South America and up again through the West Indies. Perhaps the greatest of all filibusters was William Walker, a shy, Tennessee-born, five-foot-five, 120-pound, "grey-eyed man of destiny." After an unsuccessful occupation of Baja California, Walker with his small "American Phalanx" gained control of Nicaragua in 1855, re-legalized slavery there, and held it for nearly two years before an alliance of Central American republics drove him out. Still unable to abandon his dreams of annexing more territory for the United States, he ended his career in front of a Honduran firing squad in 1860.

Long before this, Pierce had recaptured the White House for the Democracy. The new "Young America" element within the party, inspired by the nationalist movements in Europe and including not only Southerners but such northern expansionists as Stephen Douglas, had ensured that further territorial acquisitions would be the campaign's major issue. Pierce promised that his administration "will not be controlled by any timid forebodings of evil from expansion," and as soon as in office, he began building up the navy.[26] The Senate, however, was unreceptive to Pierce's treaty annexing Hawaii, while the Spanish rebuffed the Administration's renewed efforts to purchase Cuba. The American ministers to Spain, France, and England met in Ostend, Belgium, and drafted a confidential memorandum warning that Cuba might become "Africanized" because of recent labor reforms on the island, and this posed a danger of slave unrest extending "to consume the fair fabric of our Union." If the Spanish continued refusing to sell the island, "by every law, human and divine, we shall be justified in wresting it from Spain if we possess the power."[27] But when the "Ostend Manifesto" was leaked to the public at the end of 1854, Horace Greeley's *New York Tribune* denounced it as the "Manifesto of the Brigands." Northerners saw confirmed their worst fears about the Slave Power's designs for conquest. The Pierce Administration had to disavow the manifesto and pressure former Governor John A. Quitman of Mississippi into disbanding his well financed and heavily manned filibustering expedition against the island. The Democrats, as it so happened, already had enough trouble at home with a storm they had helped raise over Kansas.

Chapter 3
Bibliographical Essay

The normal practice among historians of the United States is to bisect the period covered in this chapter; up through the end of the Mexican War is tacked on to the Jacksonian Era, whereas the war's territorial controversies are lumped together with the coming of the Civil War. Thus, David M. Potter, *The Impending Crisis, 1848–1861* (New York: Harper & Row, 1976), a contribution to the New American Nation series that is widely and deservedly acclaimed as the best single-volume narrative of this era, covers only the events beginning in the second half. The older, revisionist works of Avery O. Craven, on the other hand, cover the entire period, from 1800 in the case of *The Coming of the Civil War*, 2nd edn. (Chicago: University of Chicago Press, 1957), or starting a bit later in the case of his briefer collection of four lectures, *Civil War in the Making, 1815–1860* (Baton Rouge: Louisiana State University Press, 1959). Bruce Levine, *Half Slave and Half Free: The Roots of Civil War* (New York: Hill and Wang, 1992), is a recent effort, not entirely satisfactory, to integrate the era's social history with the political. A short but lucid exposition of the competing conspiracy theories of Northerners and Southerners is David Brion Davis, *The Slave Power Conspiracy and the Paranoid Style* (Baton Rouge: Louisiana State University Press, 1969). Chilton Williamson, *American Suffrage From Property to Democracy, 1760–1860* (Princeton, NJ: Princeton University Press, 1960), offers details on the increasing popular participation in politics during this era.

Unfortunately, most studies of what is called the second-American party system are marred by a presentism that has never fully assimilated the intellectual transition from classical liberalism to social democracy. Consequently when not trying to wrench the Democrats and Whigs into modern ideological categories, historians are often denying the ideological dimension to these parties altogether. They appear unaware that classical liberals, who emerged during the eighteenth century, were both radical opponents of State power and advocates of liberty with the goal of lifting the mass of mankind out of poverty, stagnation, and oppression. Traditional conservatives, on the other hand, were reactionary defenders of statism and hierarchy, of Throne and Altar, in short, of the Old Order. Murray Rothbard has trenchantly pointed out in "Left and Right: The Prospects for Liberty," from his *Egalitarianism as a Revolt Against Nature and Other Essays* (Washington: Libertarian Review Press, 1974), that the socialists (and their variants, particularly social democrats or, in the U.S., modern liberals), when they came on the scene during the nineteenth century, were not *more* radical than the classical liberals but *less*. They represented a middle-of-the-road compromise that attempted to achieve the goals of classical liberalism, greater freedom and prosperity for the masses, but by using the means of conservatism, State intervention. Socialism thus is not only reactionary in practice, as the abysmal failure of the planned economies recently yet so eloquently attests, but also reactionary in its theoretical origins. An excellent bibliographical essay on antebellum American radicalism that is at least consistent with Rothbard's analysis without embracing it is Eric Foner, "Radical Individualism in America: Revolution to Civil War," *Literature of Liberty*, 1 (July/September 1978), pp. 5–31.

Nevertheless, still one of the most insightful studies of American politics during this period is Arthur M. Schlesinger, Jr.'s, Pulitzer-prize winning *The Age of Jackson* (Boston: Little, Brown, 1945). No one has better appreciated the genuine radicalism of the Democratic Party's support for *laissez faire* and hard money, in opposition to the Whig's conservative defense of government intervention, even if Schlesinger did try to attach the Jacksonian ideology to an anti-capitalist, proto-New Deal, working class. Joseph Dorfman, one of the few historians of his generation not to get mired in current ideological categories, emphasized in "The Jackson Wage-Earner Thesis," *American Historical Review*, 54 (January 1949), pp. 296–306, that the Jacksonians were not anti-capitalist but anti-government. It is indicative of the strength and pervasiveness of Marxist class analysis that Richard Hofstadter, in the *American Political Tradition* (New York: Vintage Books, 1948), managed to convert Dorfman's refutation of Schlesinger into a new, inverted class interpretation—one with the Jacksonians as aspiring and rising entrepreneurs. And some historians do not even notice the difference between Dorfman and Hofstadter, such as Charles Grier Sellers, Jr., who in "Andrew Jackson Versus the Historians," *Mississippi Valley Historical Review*, 44 (March 1958), pp. 615–634, misinterprets them as saying the same thing.

Much of the confusion about Jacksonian rhetoric would be resolved with the realization that the Jacksonians subscribed not to Marxist notions of class but to older, libertarian notions. By "Marxist," I mean classes defined on an economic basis, that is, on the basis of people's relationship to the means of production: workers, capitalists, farmers, and so forth. Libertarian class analysis, most explicitly formulated by two French classical liberals, Charles Comte (not to be confused with Auguste) and Charles Dunoyer, defines classes on the basis of people's relationship to the means of coercion: the State. See Leonard P. Liggio, "Charles Dunoyer and French Classical Liberalism," *Journal of Libertarian Studies*, 1 (Summer 1977), pp. 153–178. Ideologically the Jacksonians were neither pro-labor nor anti-labor, but to the extent that labor was a victim of government intervention, they seem pro-labor.

Bray Hammond's highly overrated *Banks and Politics in America: From the Revolution to the Civil War* (Princeton, NJ: Princeton University Press, 1957) shares the Hofstadter thesis of the Jacksonians as capitalists, whereas Marvin Myers, *The Jacksonian Persuasion: Politics and Belief* (Stanford, CA: Stanford University Press, 1957), transforms them into conservatives. The a-ideological, electoral machine interpretation of Jacksonian politics was formulated by Richard P. McCormick, in his state-by-state account, *The Second American Party System: Party Formation in the*

Jacksonian Era (Chapel Hill: University of North Carolina Press, 1966), and infuses the writings of Edward Pessen, particularly *Jacksonian America: Society, Personality, and Politics* (Homewood, IL: Dorsey Press, 1969). Martin Van Buren is usually presented as one of the least ideological of the Democracy's politicos; Robert V. Remini, *Martin Van Buren and the Making of the Democratic Party* (New York: W. W. Norton, 1959), was one of the earliest to grasp that Van Buren was, in fact, one of the most ideological, certainly more so than Jackson. Donald B. Cole's political biography, *Martin Van Buren and the American Political System* (Princeton, NJ: Princeton University Press, 1984), is informed by this understanding, as is Major L. Wilson's magnificent *The Presidency of Martin Van Buren* (Lawrence: University Press of Kansas, 1984) to an even greater extent. Glyndon G. Van Deusen, *The Jacksonian Era, 1828–1848* (New York: Harper & Row, 1959), remains a wonderfully compact but complete survey of the period. Charles Sellers's more recent *The Market Revolution: Jacksonian America, 1815–1846* (New York: Oxford University Press, 1991), is richly detailed and pays homage to Arthur Schlesinger, but manages to resurrect most of his flaws without all of his virtues.

The latest fashion to be applied to the second-party system is the "new political history," which by studying the local and state levels comes to an appreciation of the cultural bases for political loyalties. The new political history has the great virtue of transcending the oppressive classifications of modern politics in order to understand the Democrats and Whigs on their own terms, although I was unable in a chapter of this scope to incorporate many of this approach's fascinating insights into the vital political role of religion and ethnic identity. The new approach was launched by Lee Benson in *The Concept of Jacksonian Democracy: New York as Test Case* (Princeton, NJ: Princeton University Press, 1961), which despite obliviousness to party ideology, was a pioneering use of statistical tools to escape Marxist classes and get at the ethnic core of New York politics. Ronald P. Formisano, *The Birth of Mass Political Parties: Michigan, 1827–1861* (Princeton, NJ: Princeton University Press, 1971), was another seminal local study that develops the ethnoreligious dimension. A general history of American politics from the cultural perspective is Robert Lloyd Kelley, *The Cultural Pattern in American Politics: The First Century* (New York: Alfred A. Knopf, 1979).

Specialized works on the second-party system include John Ashworth, *"Agrarians & Aristocrats": Party Political Ideology in the United States, 1837–1846* (London: Royal Historical Society, 1983); Jean Baker, *Affairs of Party: The Political Culture of Northern Democrats in Mid-Nineteenth Century* (Ithaca, NY: Cornell University Press, 1983); and Daniel Walker Howe, *The Political Culture of American Whigs* (Chicago: University of Chicago Press, 1979). William J. Cooper, Jr., *The South and the Politics of Slavery, 1828–1856* (Baton Rouge: Louisiana State University Press, 1978), is the best study of that section's parties during the Age of Jackson. For a synthesis treating all regions and parties, consult Harry L. Watson, *Liberty and Power: The Politics of Jacksonian America* (New York: Hill and Wang, 1990).

An excellent biography of one of the era's pivotal politicians is Glyndon G. Van Deusen, *William Henry Seward* (New York: Oxford University Press, 1967). Seward is the northern Whig who managed most fully to harness democratic techniques in the service of the party's conservative ideology, after which he went on to become one of the major architects of the Republican Party. Although John M. Taylor, *William Henry Seward: Lincoln's Right Hand* (New York: HarperCollins, 1991), is newer, it concentrates on Seward's Republican activities, so that the Van Deusen biography remains better on Seward's earlier life. For Old Man Eloquent's congressional career, the reliable work is the second volume of the biography by Samuel Flagg Bemis: *John Quincy Adams and the Union* (New York: Alfred A. Knopf, 1970). The abolitionist who influenced Adams and sparked opposition to Texas annexation is examined in Merton L. Dillon, *Benjamin Lundy and the Struggle for Negro Freedom* (Urbana: University of Illinois Press, 1966).

Justin H. Smith's old standby on *The Annexation of Texas*, corrected edn. (New York: Barnes & Noble, 1941), has been supplemented by much additional scholarship. Frederick W. Merk zeros in on slavery's impact on the politics of annexation in *Slavery and the Annexation of Texas* (New York: Alfred A. Knopf, 1972); whereas Randolph B. Campbell, *An Empire for Slavery: The Peculiar Institution in Texas, 1821–1865* (Baton Rouge: Louisiana State University Press, 1989), details slavery's internal role within Texas itself during colonization, the revolution, and statehood. Unlike Merk, however, I find southern concern about Britain inducing abolition in Texas to be quite genuine rather than mere administration propaganda. An outstanding diplomatic history that successfully integrates the policies of all major participants over the questions of Texas and Oregon is David M. Pletcher, *The Diplomacy of Annexation: Texas, Oregon, and the Mexican War* (Columbia: University of Missouri Press, 1973). Thomas R. Hietala, *Manifest Design: Anxious Aggrandizement in Late Jacksonian America* (Ithaca, NY: Cornell University Press, 1985), is a general look at Jacksonian territorial acquisitiveness.

Michael F. Holt, *The Political Crisis of the 1850s* (New York: John Wiley & Sons, 1978), offers an ethnocultural explanation for the collapse of the second-American party system, covering from 1843 to the Civil War. Joel H. Silbey, *The Shrine of Party: Congressional Voting Behavior, 1841–1852* (Pittsburgh: University of Pittsburgh Press, 1967), and Thomas Alexander, *Sectional Stress and Party Strength: A Study of Roll-Call Voting Patterns in the United States House of Representatives* (Nashville: Vanderbilt University Press, 1967), apply statistical techniques to analyze voting in Congress. More tightly focused on the effect of the Wilmot Proviso are William R. Brock, *Parties and Political Conscience: American Dilemmas, 1840–1850* (Millwood, NY: KTO Press, 1979); Chaplain W. Morrison, *Democratic Politics and Sectionalism: The Wilmot Proviso Controversy* (Chapel Hill: University of North Carolina Press, 1967); and Kinley J. Brauer, *Cotton Versus Conscience: Massachusetts Whig Politics and Southwestern Expansion, 1842–1848* (Lexington: University of Kentucky Press, 1967). On the West's coupling of antislavery and anti-black sentiments, see Eugene H. Berwanger, *The Frontier Against Slavery: Western Anti-Negro Prejudice and the Slavery Extension Controversy* (Urbana: University of Illinois Press, 1967).

The formation of the Free Soil Party is well treated in Frederick J. Blue, *The Free Soilers: Third Party Politics, 1848–1854* (Urbana: University of Illinois Press, 1973), and John Mayfield, *Rehearsal for Republicanism: Free Soil and the Politics of Antislavery* (Part Washington, NY: Kennikat Press, 1980), as well as in the relevant sections of Richard Sewell, *Ballots for Freedom* (cited in ch. 1). Joseph Rayback, *Free Soil: The Election of 1848* (Lexington: University Press of Kentucky, 1970), deals with the election itself.

Holman Hamilton, *Prologue to Conflict: The Crisis and Compromise of 1850* (Lexington: University of Kentucky Press, 1964), remains the fullest account of the sectional truce. For Webster's contribution, see Robert F. Dalzell, Jr., *Daniel Webster and the Trial of American Nationalism, 1843–1852* (Boston: Houghton Mifflin, 1973). The South's serious flirtation with secession at this time is recounted in Thelma Jennings, *The Nashville Convention: Southern Movement for Unity, 1848–1850* (Memphis: Memphis State University Press, 1980), and John Barnwell, *Love of Order: South Carolina's First Secession Crisis* (Chapel Hill: University of North Carolina Press, 1982). The administration that was dominated by this sectional crisis is the subject of Elbert B. Smith, *The Presidencies of Zachary Taylor & Millard Fillmore* (Lawrence: University Press of Kansas, 1988), while Roy Franklin Nichols, *The Democratic Machine, 1850–1854* (New York: Columbia University, 1932), elucidates the Democracy's subsequent triumph in the 1852 election.

The Fugitive Slave Law of 1850 is the purview of Stanley W. Campbell, *The Slave Catchers: Enforcement of the Fugitive Slave Law, 1850–1860* (Chapel Hill: University of North Carolina Press, 1970). The very real threat of enslavement to northern free blacks under this enactment, as well as under the previous fugitive slave law, is revealed in Carol Wilson, *Freedom at Risk: The Kidnapping of Free Blacks in America, 1780–1865* (Lexington: University Press of Kentucky, 1994). Jane H. and William H. Pease, *The Fugitive Slave Law and Anthony Burns: A Problem in Law Enforcement* (Philadelphia: J. B. Lippincott, 1975), is a short volume that gives us details on the Anthony Burns episode, and Thomas P. Slaughter, *Bloody Dawn: The Christiana Riot and Racial Violence in the Antebellum North* (New York: Oxford University Press, 1991), goes into much more depth on the Christiana shoot-out. We are lucky to have newly available a biography of the author of *Uncle Tom's Cabin*, which does a superb job of placing her within the history of American literature and publishing: Joan D. Hedrick, *Harriet Beecher Stowe: A Life* (New York: Oxford University Press, 1994). For more about the work that made Stowe famous, consult Thomas F. Gossett, *Uncle Tom's Cabin and American Culture* (Dallas: Southern Methodist University Press, 1985).

The Slave Power's ongoing expansionist designs are discussed in Robert E. May, *The Southern Dream of a Caribbean Empire, 1854–1861* (Baton

Rouge: Louisiana State University Press, 1973). Basil Rauch, *American Interest in Cuba, 1848–1855* (New York: Columbia University Press, 1948), looks into the special desire for Cuba, which dates back as far as Thomas Jefferson. On the filibusters and their expeditions, both Charles H. Brown, *Agents of Manifest Destiny: The Lives and Times of the Filibusters* (Chapel Hill: University of North Carolina Press, 1980), and Joseph Allen Stout, Jr., *The Liberators: Filibustering Expeditions Into Mexico, 1848–1862, and the Last Thrust of Manifest Destiny* (Los Angeles: Westernlore Press, 1973), are valuable. The United States' one expansionist success subsequent to the Mexican War, to which we will briefly allude in the next chapter, is the subject of Paul Neff Garber, *The Gadsden Treaty* (Philadelphia: Press of the University of Pennsylvania, 1923).

4

Emergence of the Republican Party

The Old Political Party System Unravels

Despite resistance to the Fugitive Slave Law, Northerners might have remained broadly satisfied with the Compromise of 1850. But in 1854 they became convinced that Southerners had breached the sectional truce. The person responsible for this breach, paradoxically, was a northern architect of the compromise, Stephen Douglas. And his immediate motivation, a transcontinental railroad, seemed unrelated to slavery.

The 1850s was the most intense decade of rail construction for the United States. Track mileage soared from 9,021 miles to 30,627, as railroads became the country's first billion dollar business. The national government had subsidized some of this construction with land grants, and now that the nation's borders extended all the way to the Pacific, Congress was abuzz with competing schemes for a railway to link the two coasts. President Pierce's Secretary of War, Jefferson Davis, had ordered surveys of two alternate routes, while the U.S. Minister to Mexico, James Gadsden, negotiated a $10 million purchase of additional Mexican territory to facilitate the southern route, the administration's only expansionist endeavor that bore fruit.

Senator Douglas naturally preferred a central route, starting in his home state at Chicago, where he had speculated heavily in real estate. But this route faced what Douglas referred to as a "barbarian wall." Although the land that a southern transcontinental railroad would traverse was, under the terms of the 1850 compromise, organized already the vast territory west of the states of Missouri and Iowa had been reserved for Indian tribes, many of them forcibly removed from the east. The Indian titles had to be extinguished and the area open to white settlement if a Pacific railroad were to be laid down.

"How are we to develope [*sic*], cherish and protect our immense interests and possessions on the Pacific, with a vast wilderness fifteen hundred miles in breadth, filled with hostile savages, and cutting off direct communication[?]" asked the Illinois Senator in correspondence. Revealing the animating continental ardor that led him to be one of the leaders of the Democratic Party's nationalistic "Young America" faction, he insisted that "the Indian barrier must be removed. . . . Continuous lines of settlements with civil, political and religious institutions all under the protection of law, are imperiously demanded by the highest national considerations. These are essential, but they are not sufficient. . . . We must there-fore have Rail Roads and Telegraphs from the Atlantic to the Pacific."[1]

Douglas accordingly submitted a bill to organize the Kansas and Nebraska territories. The Missouri Compromise had long outlawed slavery there. Douglas, however, needed support from southern representatives, one of whom—Senator David Atchison of Missouri—flatly stated he would see Kansas and Nebraska "sink in hell" unless slavery could enter. So Douglas's bill applied the principle of popular sovereignty to these territories and explicitly repealed the Missouri Compromise line.

President Pierce made the Kansas-Nebraska bill a test of party loyalty, and enough northern Democrats fell in line to gain its passage through Congress. But a storm of angry protest blew across the free states. Salmon P. Chase, now a Senator from Ohio, de-nounced the act in a widely printed circular, *The Appeal of the Independent Democrats,* as "a gross violation of a sacred pledge; as a criminal betrayal of precious rights; as part and parcel of an atrocious plot to exclude from a vast unoccupied region immigrants from Old World and free laborers from our own States, and convert it into a dreary region of despotism, inhabited by masters and slaves." Under the Missouri Compromise, this "vast territory" had been "exempt from these terrible evils. . . . Whatever apologies may be offered for the toleration of slavery in the States, none can be offered for its extension into Territories where it does not exist, and where that extension involves the repeal of ancient law and the violation of solemn compact."[2]

Horace Greeley, editor of the *New York Tribune*, later remarked that the Kansas-Nebraska Act created more abolitionists in two months than William Lloyd Garrison had in twenty years. Anti-Nebraska political organizations spontaneously emerged all over the North. Eventually picking the label "Republican Party," the new antislavery coalition dwarfed from the outset its two precursors, the Free Soil and Liberty Parties. Some Republican leaders, like William Seward, were former Whigs. Others, like Chase, had been Democrats or Libertymen. When the 1854 congressional elections returned to office only seven of the fifty-four northern Democrats who had voted for Douglas's act, the overwhelming Democratic control of the House was overthrown. It was one of the most astonishing political turnabouts in American history.

The Whig Party did not even survive the storm. The recent throngs of Catholic immigrants, mainly Irish and German, filling the Democracy's ranks, had aroused a powerful nativist reaction, which coalesced into another new political party in 1854. Bars against immigrants voting and holding office and local or state prohibitions against alcohol were this movement's primary demands. Officially called the American Party, it was widely known as the Know-Nothings, because the secrecy of many anti-Catholic lodges required members to say that they knew nothing about these organizations. The previous presidential election had already crippled the Whigs in the lower South, but political nativism now delivered the *coup de grâce* in the upper South and Northeast. By the time of the 1856 presidential campaign, the tiny Whig remnant had been reduced to endorsing the Know-Nothing candidate, ex-President Fillmore. For a while it remained unclear whether the anti-immigrant Know-Nothings or the antislavery Republicans would become the primary northern successor to the shattered Whig Party. But the American Party eventually ran afoul for the same reason as the Whigs: a futile effort to attract both Northerners and Southerners by straddling the slavery question.

The triumph of the Republicans and preemption of the Know-Nothings in the free states also owed much to the political acumen of Chase, the former Liberty Party leader who had masterminded the Free Soil coalition. In 1855 Chase was elected as a Republican to the critical post of governor of Ohio. Along with Seward, he became one of the new party's major figures, although the two antislavery radicals could not have been personally more different. Not merely did they come from opposing political parties. While Seward was a consummate opportunist, willing to alter his position deftly with the changing political winds, Chase was as rigidly principled as an ambitious politician could be. Where Seward was slender and disorderly, Chase was stout and dignified. Behind Chase's oval brow was a fastidious mind of massive intelligence and energy. Tragedy, however, had hounded his private life; the Ohio lawyer had buried three wives and four of his six children.

The Republicans, however, chose as their first presidential nominee John C. Frémont, whose main political asset was a romantic reputation as western explorer and military leader. The new party's platform condemned slavery, along with polygamy, as "twin relics of barbarism." The congressional duty to prohibit the peculiar institution extended only to the territories, however. By reaffirming the Wilmot Proviso and avoiding any other abolitionist issue, such as the Fugitive Slave Law, the Republican platform reduced political antislavery to the lowest common denominator. The platform simultaneously continued the Free Soil trend of introducing other issues, most notably with a call for a government subsidized transcontinental railroad.

The abrupt alteration in the political contours of the North tightened the southern grip on the Democratic Party. The party's presidential convention rejected President Pierce and Senator Douglas, because of their close association with the Kansas debacle. It instead nominated James Buchanan of Pennsylvania, who had been safely outside the country as minister to England. But Buchanan was also one of the Ostend Manifesto's authors, and his responsiveness to the·party's southern wing made his reputation as a northern doughface equal to that of his predecessor, Pierce. The Democrats united behind popular sovereignty as their territorial policy and derisively warned that their "Black Republican" opponents threatened the Union. "I consider that all incidental questions are comparatively of little importance," Buchanan wrote, "when compared with the grand & appalling issue of union or disunion. Should Fremont be elected, . . . the outlawry proclaimed by the Black Republican convention at Philadelphia against 15 Southern States will be ratified by the people of the North. The consequences will be *immediate* & inevitable."[3]

The 1856 presidential election became almost two separate contests. Because the Republicans were a purely sectional party, Buchanan competed only with Fillmore for votes in the slave states, whereas competition in the free states was primarily between Buchanan and Frémont. The Democrats, as the sole national party, secured a majority of the electoral college. But they won just 45 percent of the popular vote. Frémont carried all but five of the free states, making Buchanan the first presidential winner since 1828 without majorities in both the North and South. The Democratic Party's sectional unity, furthermore, rested upon the fatal ambiguity of popular sovereignty. The fact that northern and southern Democrats applied the principle differently would soon become evident in Kansas itself.

The Race for Kansas

The introduction of popular sovereignty into Kansas touched off a race between antislavery and proslavery settlers. Senator Seward prophetically anticipated this outcome the moment the Kansas-Nebraska Act became law. "Come on, then, gentlemen of the Slave States. Since there is no escaping your challenge, I accept it in behalf of the cause of freedom. We will engage in competition for the virgin soil of Kansas, and God give the victory to the side which is stronger in numbers as it is in right."[4]

The New England Emigrant Aid Company was established to finance colonization from the free states, while "border ruffians" crossed over from the neighboring slave state of Missouri under the leadership of Senator Atchison. He explained why slavery's protection warranted extraordinary efforts. "The State of Missouri is now bounded on two sides by free States; organize this Territory as free territory, then we are bounded on three sides by free States or Territories." Whether Kansas was suitable for plantation agriculture was a secondary consideration. Even with very few slaves, so long as Kansas had a rigid slave code, it would not attract runaways and help undermine the peculiar institution in Missouri. "We are playing for a mightly [sic] stake," Atchison wrote to a fellow southern Senator. "If we win we carry slavery to the Pacific Ocean[;] if we fail we lose Missouri Arkansas and Texas and all the territories, the game must be played boldly."[5]

This scramble only added to the usual frontier turmoil over land titles, town sites, and water rights. When the territorial governor called the first election in 1855, armed Missourians stuffed the ballot boxes with thousands of votes. The territorial legislature they elected instituted a slave code that made opposition to slavery a felony and punished aiding a fugitive slave with death. The more numerous free-state residents drew up a constitution and conducted elections of their own, but the Pierce Administration stood behind the proslavery legislature. Kansas thereby ended up with two rival governments, one fraudulent and the other illegal.

After the free-state settlers began arming in self-defense, bloodshed erupted. An army of seven hundred proslavery men pillaged the free-state town of Lawrence in May 1856. A grim abolitionist named John Brown appointed himself the agent of divine retribution, and his small band hacked to death five proslavery colonists who had nothing to do with the Lawrence raid. The ensuing summer of bushwacking and barn burning resulted in two hundred deaths and $2 million worth of destruction.

Federal troops imposed an uneasy peace in "Bleeding Kansas" before Buchanan's inauguration. But the rival factions continued to jockey for advantage through a succession of complex maneuvers. The ever more numerous free-state residents finally gained control of the legal legislature, but not before the proslavery faction had presided over a constitutional convention. The resulting document, known as the Lecompton Constitution, contained a clause ordaining slavery. The free-state residents had boycotted the referendum that approved this clause, because they were not permitted to vote down the basically proslavery constitution in its entirety.

Events in Kansas had conspired to convince Southerners elsewhere that their future security depended upon admitting another slave state. There had been no such admissions since the annexation of Texas, twelve years earlier. Yet Minnesota and Oregon were preparing to enter the Union as free states. Talk of secession was again rife. Acceding to southern pressure, President Buchanan tried to ram the Lecompton Constitution through Congress as the basis for Kansas statehood. "Kansas is," declared the President, "at this moment as much a slave state as Georgia or South Carolina."[6]

This obvious subversion of popular sovereignty was too much for Douglas and other northern Democrats. The Illinois Senator publicly broke with the administration. "Let me ask you, why force this constitution down the throats of the people of Kansas, in opposition to their wishes and in violation of our pledges[?]" he demanded to know on the Senate floor. "Neither the North nor the South has the right to gain a sectional advantage by trickery or fraud. . . . If Kansas wants a slave-State constitution she has a right to it; if she wants a free-State constitution she has a right to it. It is none of my business which way the slavery clause is decided. I care not whether it is voted down or voted up. . . . But if this constitution is to be forced down our throats, in violation of the fundamental principle of free government, under a mode of submission that is a mockery and insult, I will resist it to the last. . . . I will stand on the great principle of popular sovereignty, which declares the right of all people to be left perfectly free to form and regulate their domestic institutions in their own way."[7]

Douglas's defection contributed to another congressional stalemate. The Senate passed the Lecompton Constitution, but the House rejected it. The Buchanan Administration ultimately saved face with a compromise that sent the constitution back to the Kansas voters. If the voters adopted it, they would gain statehood plus four million acres of federal land. If they rejected it, they could not enter the Union until their population reached 90,000. Despite the brazen bribery, an honest count of Kansas voters found them against the Lecompton Constitution by a margin of ten to one.

The Dred Scott Decision

The territorial status of slavery had been inducing congressional convulsions off and on for nearly forty years, ever since the Missouri crisis. Perhaps the United States Supreme Court could settle the matter. Congress, in both the Compromise of 1850 and the Kansas-Nebraska Act of 1854, had invited a ruling, and the Court finally heard a relevant case in early 1857. It involved a slave named Dred Scott, whose master had taken him to live in the free state of Illinois for two years and the free territory north of the Missouri Compromise line for four more years. Back in the slave state of Missouri, Scott sued for his freedom.

All nine justices rendered separate opinions, and legal scholars still debate the technicalities of the Dred Scott decision. But Chief Justice Roger Taney, speaking for the majority, reached two unmistakable judgments. First, Dred Scott could not sue in a federal court because he was not a United States citizen, and he could not be a United States citizen because he was black. "It becomes necessary . . . to determine who were citizens of the several States when the Constitution was adopted," argued the Chief Justice. "In the opinion of this court, the legislation and histories of the times, and the language used in the Declaration of Independence, show, that neither the class of persons who had been imported as slaves, nor their descendants, whether they had become free or not, were then acknowledged as part of the people, nor intended to be included in the general words used in that memorable instrument. . . . They had for more than a century before been regarded as beings of an inferior order; and altogether unfit to associate with the white race, either in social or political relations; and so far inferior, that they had no rights which the white man was bound to respect."[8] None of the Constitution's protections therefore applied to blacks, whether enslaved or free. An individual state might grant citizenship to free blacks, but that did not entitle them to any rights and privileges in other states, nor to any standing before the national judiciary.

Taney's second major judgment was that residence in federal territory could not free Scott because the Missouri Compromise's prohibition of slavery had been unconstitutional. Congress had no authority to exclude slavery from the territories. The property right of a slaveholder to his slaves merited full protection under the Constitution, particularly the protection of the Fifth Amendment's due process clause. The Chief Justice, a Maryland Democrat, was just reaching his eightieth year. Six-feet tall, with sunken chest, he was once described as having the face of a galvanized corpse. Taney had emancipated all his own slaves thirty years previously. But his decision elevated to supreme law of the land the extreme southern position on slavery in the territories, first enunciated by John C. Calhoun in response to the Wilmot Proviso. The Republicans found their major political tenet declared unconstitutional.

Northerners were stunned. Greeley's *New York Tribune* scorned the Court's decision as "entitled to just so much moral weight as would be the judgment of a majority of those congregated in any Washington bar-room."[9] Many were convinced that the Dred Scott decision was another brazen manifestation of the Slave Power conspiracy, whose ultimate aim was now nothing less than the legalization of slavery throughout the United States. The Kansas-Nebraska Act had opened previously free territories to slavery. The Lecompton Constitution attempted to impose slavery upon a prospective state. The Fugitive Slave Law gave slaveholders authority that penetrated into free states. If the Court could rule that Dred Scott's two-year residence in Illinois did not emancipate him, what was to prevent slaveholders from bringing their slaves into free states permanently? How far away was a Court decision forbidding *any* state interference with slave property?

Abraham Lincoln, a former Illinois Whig who had opposed the Mexican War and recently hitched his wagon to the Republican Party, best captured this growing fear of the Slave Power. Using one of his homespun analogies, he identified the principals in the plot to impose slavery upon the free states. "When we see a lot of framed timbers, different portions of which we know have been gotten out at different times and places and by different workmen—Stephen, Franklin, Roger, and James, for instance," referring to Senator Stephen Douglas, ex-President Franklin Pierce, Chief Justice Roger Taney, and current President James Buchanan, "and when we see these timbers joined together, and see they exactly make the frame of a house or a mill, . . . all the lengths and proportions of the different pieces exactly adapted to their respective places, and not a piece too many or too few—not omitting even scaffolding—or, if a single piece be lacking, we can see the place in the frame exactly fitted and prepared yet to bring such a piece in—in *such* a case, we find it impossible to not *believe* that Stephen and Franklin and Roger and James all understood one another from the beginning, and all worked upon a common *plan* or *draft* drawn up before the first lick was struck."[10]

Lincoln was right in one respect. Democrats had indeed been hoping that the Supreme Court would undercut the Republican Party. But the Dred Scott decision gave Douglas and his party's northern wing more than they had bargained for. Chief Justice Taney ruled that, because Congress could not touch slavery in the territories, neither could it authorize territorial legislatures to do so. This delivered a hard blow to the Illinois Democrat's own territorial solution, popular sovereignty. Lincoln would soon make the most of Douglas's discomfort in their renowned debates during the 1858 Senatorial election.

The Lincoln-Douglas Debates

Douglas, with his short stature—"leonine head and duck legs" commented one reporter—was known as "The Little Giant."[11] He had long dominated politics in Illinois, a northern state favorably inclined toward the South. A major portion of its population had emigrated from the slave states, like Lincoln himself, who had been born in Kentucky. Racism was so rampant that Illinois was one of the free states that never enacted a personal liberty law, and its constitution prohibited the entry of free blacks. Nonetheless, neither the Lecompton Constitution nor the Dred Scott decision had gone over well. Douglas, in his 1858 reelection bid, was fighting for political survival.

The contest between the gaunt, towering "Honest Abe" and the pugnacious, large-headed "Little Giant" was an unprecedented exhibition of American democracy. Senators at the time were still chosen by a state's legislature. Popular conventions had never proposed candidates for this office before a Republican state convention nominated Lincoln. The two opponents then met in seven face-to-face debates, each at a different town, and gave scores of individual speeches. As they crisscrossed the state, braving foul and fair weather, they addressed listeners who could not vote for them directly but only for members of the state legislature. Yet each community turned these appearances into festive pageants, with thousands of farmers traveling long distances to attend.

Lincoln kicked off his campaign with a speech intended to clarify the differences between the two candidates. He pointed out that popular sovereignty had failed abysmally to quiet the unrest over slavery. "We are now far into the *fifth* year, since a policy was initiated, with the *avowed* object, and *confident* promise, of putting an end to slavery agitation. Under the operation of that policy, that agitation has not only, *not ceased,* but has *constantly augmented.* In *my* opinion, it *will* not cease, until a *crisis* shall have been reached, and passed."

Lincoln then took up the Biblical passage, "A house divided against itself cannot stand," as his theme. "I believe that this government cannot endure, permanently half *slave* and half *free.* I do not expect the Union to be *dissolved*—I do not expect the house to *fall*—but I *do* expect it will cease to be divided. It will become *all* one thing, or *all* the other. Either the *opponents* of slavery, will arrest the further spread of it, and place it where the public mind shall rest in the belief that it is in course of ultimate extinction; or its *advocates* will push it forward, til it shall become alike lawful in *all* the states, *old* as well as *new—North* as well as *South.*"[12]

In a later speech, Lincoln again emphasized the issue of slavery. "The real issue in this controversy" springs from a sentiment "on the one part [that] looks upon the institution of slavery as being wrong, and on the part of another class [that] does not look upon it as a wrong. The sentiment that contemplates the institution of slavery as being wrong, is the sentiment of the Republican party. . . . [T]hey nevertheless have due regard for . . . the difficulties of getting rid of it in the States, and for all the constitutional obligations thrown about it." Yet "they insist upon a policy that shall treat it as a wrong[,] and as the mildest policy to that end they look to the prevention of its growing larger."[13]

Douglas countered by painting Lincoln as a dangerous radical. The Illinois Senator employed the race issue quite effectively. "I do not question Mr. Lincoln's conscientious belief that the negro was made his equal, and hence is his brother," Douglas sarcastically jabbed. "But for my own part, I do not regard the negro as my equal, and I positively deny that he is my brother, or any kin to me whatever."[14]

Thrown on the defensive, Lincoln revealed the limits to his support for racial equality. "I will say then, that I am not nor ever have been in favor of bringing about in any way, the social and political equality of the white and black races—that I am not, nor ever have been in favor of making voters of the negroes, or jurors, or qualifying them to hold office, or having them to marry with white people. I will say in addition, that there is a physical difference between the white and black races, which I suppose, will forever forbid the two races living together on terms of social and political equality[;] and inasmuch as they cannot so live, that while they do remain together, there must be the position of superior and inferior, that I as much as any other man am in favor of having the superior position assigned to the white man."[15]

Lincoln went on to add that just "because the white man is to have the superior position" it did not follow that "the negro should be denied everything. I do not understand that because I do not want a negro woman for a slave, I must necessarily want her for a wife. My understanding is that I can just leave her alone."[16] Like Thomas Jefferson, Lincoln favored colonizing emancipated slaves in Africa or Latin America. But he did insist that "in the right to eat the bread, without leave of anybody else, which his own hand earns," the black man "is my own equal and Judge Douglas' equal, and the equal of every living man."[17]

Lincoln's most telling challenge to Douglas was on the Dred Scott decision. He asked Douglas explicitly when, prior to state-hood, a territory could exclude slavery. This compelled the Illinois Democrat to address the contradiction between Taney's opinion and popular sovereignty. Would Douglas come out for defying the Court? Or would he abandon his previous position? Douglas wiggled out of this dilemma with what historians refer to as the Freeport Doctrine. Territories could exclude slavery before becoming states, he contended, not *de jure*, but *de facto*, by refusing to enact protective legislation. It does not matter what "the Supreme

Court may hereafter decide as to the abstract question whether slavery may go in under the Constitution or not," Douglas argued. Showing an understanding of the vital role government authority played in maintaining slavery, he pointed out that "the people of a Territory have the lawful means to admit it or exclude it as they please, for the reason that slavery cannot exist a day or an hour anywhere unless supported by local police regulations."[18]

At the end of the hard-fought campaign, the Democrats retained enough seats in the Illinois legislature to reelect Douglas to the Senate. But Lincoln had been catapulted into national prominence. Moreover, until then candidates for northern office had usually avoided discussing slavery. During the Lincoln-Douglas contest, it was *the* issue. No one talked much about anything else.

Fire-Eaters and Homesteaders

Slavery was erasing the old ideological lines that had divided political parties. In one sense it was ironic that the Democracy should become the northern bastion for the peculiar institution. This party had traditionally been the home of the South's non-slaveholding whites. The slaveowning oligarchy, accustomed to using government to shore up the plantation system, had more naturally gravitated toward the Whig ideology of economic inter-vention. Large planters had tended to support state subsidies for railroads and banks.

Reaction against the Republicans, however, was turning the deep South into a one-party region. Increasingly influential was a group of political mavericks called "fire-eaters"—men such as Edmund Ruffin of Virginia, Robert Barnwell Rhett of South Caroli-na, William Lowndes Yancey of Alabama, and John A. Quitman of Mississippi. Disappointed at the failure of secession in 1850 and suspicious of established political parties, they had campaigned for cultural separatism through such unofficial channels as the south-ern commercial conventions. At a time when slaveholding was becoming more concentrated, the fire-eaters agitated for reopening the Atlantic slave trade, in order to lower prices and make slaves more accessible to the mass of southern whites.

These radical advocates of states' rights mobilized a growing mass movement that attempted to unify the South by identifying slavery's protection with the liberty of all white Southerners. They successfully drew upon the deep-seated, Jacksonian hostility of small farmers to centralized power. In addition to tariff protection, the national government bestowed mail subsidies, bounties to New England fishermen, improvements of rivers and harbors, land grants to railroads, and shipping monopolies. One South Carolina congressman enumerated some of the programs that redistributed income to the North: "The law by which the coastwise trade is confined exclusively to American ships, the practical advantage of which law is confined almost exclusively to the northern States. . . . [T]he law which gives American ship-builders, almost exclusively confined to the northern States, a monopoly of building ships which sail under the American flag . . . . [T]he law which gives codfish bounties to the people of Massachusetts. . . . [T]he law which, under the form of the reciprocity treaty, exempts the people of the North along the Canadian frontier from paying duties."[19] By the end of the 1850s, the South's regular politicians had to heed the fire-eaters' demand that Southern principles take precedence over political expediency.

The same disgust with political corruption to which fire-eaters appealed was also affecting politics in the North. "There was once a time when the Whig and Democratic parties were arrayed against each other upon certain tolerably well defined political issues," recalled George W. Julian, an Indiana Republican and veteran of the Free Soil Party. "That time is past. These issues are obsolete." The Kansas-Nebraska Act illustrated this loss of ideological definition. Northern Whigs had formerly sponsored government-funded internal improvements. But now a Democratic politician, Stephen Douglas, had been driven into a proslavery bargain in order to buy support for a pet project. Nothing was more indicative of how politics was becoming what Julian denounced as "a mere scramble for place and power."[20]

Douglas never did get his transcontinental railroad. A related issue was further weakening his party in the North: homestead legislation, the proposal to allow settlers to acquire unowned land in the West simply by working it. Part of the Democracy's political genius had been to unite a desire for free trade on the part of

Southerners with a desire for free land on the part of Westerners and northern laborers. The natural-rights ideal of first bringing unused resources into ownership by mixing labor with them had also been consistent with the Democratic goal of limiting government power. From the War of 1812 on, sale of public lands was the central government's only source of revenue outside of the tariff. The Whigs on the other hand had always opposed giving away the public domain. Even more than their desire for an ample treasury, the key Whig constituency of northeastern manufacturers wanted high land prices in order to discourage western settlement. Preventing a drain of labor to the west would keep wages low in the east.

Although the homestead principle had yet to be fully implemented, Congress's Democratic majorities had in the past steadily reduced the price of public land and made it easier for squatters to gain title. Southern Democrats, however, had begun shifting their stance as the safety of the peculiar institution increasingly dominated their concerns. Easy access to land was accelerating the settlement primarily of new free states, working to the North's political advantage. "Better for us," exclaimed a Mississippi newspaper, "that these territories should remain a waste, a howling wilderness, trod only by red hunters."[21] Thus Southerners now tried to retard such growth by opposing free homesteads.

This reversal put added stress on the Democracy's alliance between South and West and alienated northern laborers at a time when the financial panic of 1857 was bringing economic adversity. The House of Representatives passed bills for 160-acre homesteads in 1858 and early 1859, but Southerners blocked them in the Senate. If they needed any further incentive, Northerners had just prevented any appropriations toward President Buchanan's revived efforts to purchase Cuba from Spain. Both chambers approved a homestead measure one year later, only to have the President veto it in deference to the South.

Over the same period that Southerners had turned their backs on liberal land policies, William Seward and Horace Greeley had enthusiastically embraced homesteading. These two prominent Whigs, after entering Republican ranks, consequently raised no objections to making this a conspicuous plank in their new party's platform. The land issue also aided the Republicans in outmaneuvering their Know-Nothing opposition by linking the Slave Power to a bread-and-butter threat to native workers. As Republican ranks absorbed the remnant of northern Know-Nothings, New England became almost as much a one-party region as the deep South.

"An Irrepressible Conflict"

The Union had so far successfully withstood four severe sectional crises: the Missouri crisis of 1819 through 1821; the nullification crisis of 1832–33; the crisis initiated by the Wilmot Proviso in 1846 and ended by the Compromise of 1850; and the crisis over Kansas, running from 1854 to 1858. Each crisis had been patched over with a congressional compromise, but each compromise was making it more evident that the North and the South were drifting apart. The final compromise over the Lecompton Constitution abandoned all pretense at resolving the underlying disagreements.

Bleeding Kansas was to be the prelude to civil war. The violence in the territory had already been mirrored in Congress. Senator Charles Sumner of Massachusetts had delivered an impassioned speech on "The Crime Against Kansas," full of invective against an aged South Carolina Senator. A few days later Congressman Preston Brooks, the insulted Senator's nephew, had brutally beaten Sumner unconscious with a cane right on the Senate floor. Sumner was unable to return to his seat for two and a half years. "Bully" Brooks, as he became known throughout the North, received from approving Southerners more than a hundred replacement canes for the one he had broken.

A debate on the same subject two years afterwards ended in a wild sectional fist fight among thirty Congressmen. By the time the House was choosing its Speaker in 1859, Northerners and Southerners were exchanging insults so furiously that members came armed to the sessions. Senator James Henry Hammond of South Carolina reported that as far as he knew "every man in both houses is armed with a revolver—some with two—and a bowie-knife."[22]

A violent mood began to permeate the country. Many abolitionists reluctantly concluded that both moral and political action had failed. They came to share David Walker's and Lysander Spooner's opinions that only revolution could extirpate the peculiar institution. Joshua R. Giddings, an abolitionist Republican elected from Ohio to the House of Representatives, had predicted the day "when the slaves shall rise in the South; . . . when masters shall turn pale and tremble when their dwellings shall smoke."[23]

A wealthy cabal calling itself the Secret Six financed military preparations being made by John Brown, whom New England reformers and literary figures lionized, although the more murderous details of his Kansas exploits were not generally known in the North. On the night of October 16, 1859, Brown's twenty or so heavily armed black and white followers seized the federal arsenal at Harper's Ferry, Virginia. Brown intended to inspire a giant slave mutiny, but his expedition was so ill planned that none of the nearby slaves risked rallying to his banner. After two days of resistance and seventeen deaths, a detachment of United States marines commanded by Colonel Robert E. Lee captured Brown.

The state of Virginia tried Brown for treason, inciting slave rebellion, and murder, and sentenced him to hang. The visionary old Calvinist met his fate unflinchingly. During sentencing, he calmly explained his motives to the court. "This Court acknowledges, too, as I suppose, the validity of the law of God. . . . I believe that to have interfered as I have done, as I have always freely admitted I have done in behalf of His despised poor, is no wrong, but right. Now, if it is deemed necessary that I should forfeit my life for the furtherance of the ends of justice, and mingle my blood further . . . with the blood of millions in this slave country whose rights are disregarded by wicked, cruel, and unjust enactments, I say let it be done."[24]

The leading Republicans all repudiated Brown. Seward declared Brown's execution "necessary and just." But there was enough northern applause for the martyr to appall Southerners. Henry David Thoreau, the New England essayist, delivered a public "Plea for John Brown" that virtually deified him. "Some eighteen hundred years ago, Christ was crucified; this morning, perchance, Captain Brown was hung. . . . He is not Old Brown any longer; he is an angel of light."[25] Nothing more emphatically underscored the terrifying connection between northern antislavery and black insurrection. Southerners became gripped with fear, as unconfirmed reports of slave conspiracies circulated widely. Every obscure death became a poisoning; every unexplained fire an arson.

One year prior to Brown's raid, Seward had delivered a speech in upstate New York spelling out the Republican Party's ideology, with its veneration of free labor and denigration of slave labor. "Our country is a theater, which exhibits, in full operation, two radically different political systems; the one resting on the basis of servile or slave labor, the other on the basis of voluntary labor of freemen. . . . Hitherto, the two systems have existed in different states, but side by side within the American Union." The Union was moving, however, from a loose confederation of states to a consolidated nation. "Thus, these antagonistic systems are continually coming into closer contact, and collision results."

This speech had then branded the phrase "irrepressible conflict" onto the public consciousness, as the widening sectional estrangement now imparted a chillingly literal interpretation to the New York Senator's words. "Shall I tell you what this collision means? They who think that it is accidental, unnecessary, the work of interested or fanatical agitators, and therefore ephemeral, mistake the case altogether. It is an irrepressible conflict between opposing and enduring forces, and it means that the United States must and will, sooner or later, become either entirely a slaveholding nation, or entirely a free-labor nation."[26]

Chapter 4
Bibliographical Essay

The major debate concerning the collapse of the second-American party system is about which was the more fundamental cause: the ideological conflict over slavery or the ethnic conflict over immigration. The most important work emphasizing slavery is Eric Foner's brilliant exposition of the Republican Party's ideology, *Free Soil, Free Labor, Free Men: The Ideology of the Republican Party Before the Civil War* (London: Oxford University Press, 1970). Wading in on the ethnoreligious side is William E. Gienapp's awesome study of the Republican Party's organizational creation, *The Origins of the Republican Party, 1852–1856* (New York: Oxford University Press, 1987).

Readers of this chapter should have little difficulty detecting toward which interpretation I lean. Gienapp *has* demonstrated (1) that the immigration question had eviscerated the northern Whig Party prior to the Kansas-Nebraska Act and (2) that Republican success did require capturing nativist voters. But those who stress ideology would respond (1) that the destabilizing Whig effort to attract northern immigrants was an ill-fated attempt to recover from the major sectional damage already suffered over slavery and (2) that, after the same issue split the Know-Nothings, northern nativists really had no other viable alternative to the Republican Party. Gienapp may have proven that nativists swelled Republican ranks, but Foner is still right about the free-labor ideology of the Republicans never being significantly corrupted by nativist ideas. Chase, Seward, and Lincoln all remained steadfastly aloof from any anti-immigrant expressions.

Paul Kleppner, *The Third Electoral System, 1853–1892: Parties, Voters, and Political Cultures* (Chapel Hill: University of North Carolina Press, 1979), broadly paints the ethnoreligious picture of the new parties, although I find its non-narrative treatment overly abstract. The political dilemma of northern Whigs is covered in Thomas H. O'Connor, *Lords of the Loom: The Cotton Whigs and the Coming of the Civil War* (New York: Charles Scribner's Sons, 1968). There is no general history of the American Party, but Ray Allen Billington, *The Protestant Crusade, 1800–1861* (New York: Macmillan, 1938), remains the basic survey of antebellum nativism, while each sectional wing of the party now has its own study: Tyler Anbinder, *Nativism and Slavery: The Northern Know Nothings and the Politics of the 1850s* (New York: Oxford University Press, 1992), and Darrell W. Overdyke, *The Know-Nothing Party in the South* (Baton Rouge: Louisiana State University Press, 1950). Worthy of note is Anbinder's deemphasis of ethnic motives for the growth of even the American Party; he instead finds slavery to have been crucial.

Important state or local studies include Jean H. Baker, *Ambivalent Americans: The Know-Nothing Party in Maryland* (Baltimore: Johns Hopkins University Press, 1977); John R. Mulkern, *The Know-Nothing Party in*

Massachusetts: The Rise and Fall of a People's Movement (Boston: Northeastern University Press, 1990); Michael F. Holt, *Forging a Majority: The Formation of the Republican Party in Pittsburgh, 1848–1860* (New Haven: Yale University Press, 1969); Stephen E. Maizlish, *The Triumph of Sectionalism: The Transformation of Ohio Politics, 1844–1856* (Kent, OH: Kent State University Press, 1983); and Dale Baum, *The Civil War Party System: The Case of Massachusetts, 1848–1876* (Chapel Hill: University of North Carolina Press, 1984).

It was refreshing finally to have, after decades of neglect and abuse, a decent biography of one of the Republican Party's key organizers: Frederick J. Blue, *Salmon P. Chase: A Life in Politics* (Kent, OH: Kent State University Press, 1987). Now John Niven has given us a second, *Salmon P. Chase: A Biography* (New York: Oxford University Press, 1995). Blue speculates that Chase had been undeservedly slighted because of his career's sheer diversity: abolitionist lawyer; leader of the Liberty, Free Soil, and Republican Parties; Ohio senator and governor; Secretary of the Treasury during the Civil War; and Chief Justice of the Supreme Court. I suspect more to blame is his rivalry with Lincoln, a rivalry that Chase, unlike so many other Republican politicians, never gave up. Two other important Republicans are covered in Rhul Jacob Bartlett, *John C. Frémont and the Republican Party* (Columbus: Ohio State University, 1930), and David Herbert Donald, *Charles Sumner and the Coming of the Civil War* (New York: Alfred A. Knopf, 1974).

On congressional passage of the act that triggered the political turnabout in the North, consult Gerald W. Wolff, *The Kansas-Nebraska Bill: Party, Section, and the Coming of the Civil War* (New York: Revisionist Press, 1977), and James C. Malin, *The Nebraska Question, 1852–1854* (Lawrence: University of Kansas, 1953). George Fort Milton, *The Eve of Conflict: Stephen A. Douglas and the Needless War* (Boston: Houghton, Mifflin, 1934), is a revisionist assessment of the Illinois politician responsible for the Kansas-Nebraska Act, whereas Robert W. Johannsen, *Stephen A. Douglas,* (New York: Oxford University Press, 1973), is more in tune with the current rejection of the revisionist account of the war's outbreak.

Several studies illuminate the crucial background relating to American railways: Carter Goodrich, *Government Promotion of American Canals and Railroads, 1800–1890* (New York: Columbia University Press, 1960); Robert W. Fogel, *Railroads and American Economic Growth: Essays in Econometric History* (Baltimore: Johns Hopkins Press, 1964); Albert Fishlow, *American Railroads and the Transformation of the Ante-Bellum Economy* (Cambridge, MA: Harvard University Press, 1965); and John F. Stover, *Iron Road to the West: American Railroads in the 1850s* (New York: Columbia University Press, 1978).

James A. Rawley, *Race and Politics: "Bleeding Kansas" and the Coming of the Civil War* (Philadelphia: J. B. Lippincott, 1969), describes clearly what happened in Kansas itself, despite a fixation on Republican racism, but also check out Alice Nichols, *Bleeding Kansas* (New York: Oxford University

Press, 1954). James C. Malin, *John Brown and the Legend of Fifty-Six* (Philadelphia: American Philosophical Society, 1942), exposes John Brown's Kansas activities. The outside support from Yankees is examined in Samuel A. Johnson, *The Battle Cry of Freedom: The New England Emigrant Aid Company in the Kansas Crusade* (Lawrence: University of Kansas Press, 1954). Richard H. Abbott, *Cotton & Capital: Boston Businessmen and Antislavery Reform, 1854–1868* (Amherst: University of Massachusetts Press, 1991), shows how these events induced Boston businessmen to begin funding antislavery.

Kenneth Stampp, *America in 1857: A Nation on the Brink* (New York: Oxford University Press, 1990), has given us a microhistory of the year that saw both the final Lecompton settlement and the Dred Scott case. Don E. Fehrenbacher's exhaustive *The Dred Scott Case: Its Significance in American Law and Politics* (New York: Oxford University Press, 1978) supersedes everything that has been previously written about that Supreme Court decision. The standard biography of the Chief Justice who rendered the decision is Carl Brent Swisher, *Roger B. Taney* (New York: Macmillan, 1935). Fehrenbacher has also evaluated Lincoln's campaign strategy against Douglas in *Prelude to Greatness: Lincoln in the 1850s* (Stanford, CA: Stanford University Press, 1962). A widely cited, neo-abolitionist analysis is Harry V. Jaffa, *Crisis of the House Divided: An Interpretation of the Issues in the Lincoln-Douglas Debates* (Garden City, NY: Doubleday, 1959). David Zarefsky, *Lincoln, Douglas, and Slavery: In the Crucible of Public Debate* (Chicago: University of Chicago Press, 1990), is an extended rhetorical study of the Lincoln-Douglas debates.

Full biographies of Abraham Lincoln are legion. I will confine myself to a few. Stephen B. Oates, *With Malice Toward None: The Life of Abraham Lincoln* (New York: Harper & Row, 1977), is engrossing and relatively short. If you want scholarly completeness, pick up the four volumes of James G. Randall, *Lincoln the President* (New York: Dodd, Mead, 1945–1955). David Donald, *Lincoln* (New York: Simon & Schuster, 1995), is the most recent. Also enlightening is Richard N. Current, *The Lincoln Nobody Knows* (New York: McGraw-Hill, 1958). Gabor S. Boritt, *Lincoln and the Economics of the American Dream* (Memphis: Memphis State University Press, 1978), tries to elucidate the man's character through his economic ideas. Boritt has also put together, with the assistance of Norman O. Forness, an anthology of varied perspectives entitled *The Historian's Lincoln: Pseudohistory, Psychohistory, and History* (Urbana: University of Illinois Press, 1988).

Unfortunately, too much of the writing about the sixteenth President is caught up in the cult of Lincoln idolatry. As H. L. Mencken observed in 1931 (in a story reprinted in Marion Elizabeth Rodgers, *The Impossible H. L. Mencken: A Selection of His Best Newspaper Stories* [New York: Doubleday, 1991], p. 423), Lincoln "has become one of the national deities, and a realistic examination of him is thus no longer possible." The perfect remedy is Gore Vidal, *Lincoln: A Novel* (New York: Random House, 1984), which despite being fictional and taking occasional literary license, displays a command of the American past that should do any professional historian proud. Vidal ably if acerbically defends himself from pro-Lincoln critics in his 1988 *New York Review of Books* essay, "How I Do What I Do If Not Why," reprinted in *At Home: Essays 1982–1988* (New York: Vintage Books, 1990).

The critical role of southern fire-eaters is unveiled in William L. Barney's insightful but uneven *The Road to Secession: A New Perspective on the Old South* (New York: Praeger, 1972). For reservations about Barney's psychologizing, see Robert E. May, "Psychobiography and Secession: The Southern Radical as Maladjusted 'Outsider'," *Civil War History*, 34 (March 1988), pp. 46–69. An indispensable, combined biography of nine of these figures is Eric H. Walther, *The Fire-Eaters* (Baton Rouge: Louisiana State University Press, 1992), but also still invaluable is Laura A. White, *Robert Barnwell Rhett: Father of Secession* (Washington: American Historical Association, 1931). On the other hand, David S. Heidler's recent *Pulling the Temple Down: The Fire-Eaters and the Destruction of the Union* (Mecanics-burg, PA: Stackpole Books, 1994), is an unfortunate retrogression to the revisionist denunciation of these alleged swaggering hotheads. One of the most important institutional conduits for the fire-eaters' propaganda is the topic of Herbert Wender, *Southern Commercial Conventions, 1837–1859* (Baltimore: Johns Hopkins Press, 1930).

Several works offer differing perspectives on the emergence of Southern nationalism generally. Jesse T. Carpenter, *The South as a Conscious Minority, 1789–1861: A Study in Political Thought* (New York: New York University Press, 1930), focuses on southern thinking about politics, construing that term narrowly. John McCardell, *The Idea of a Southern Nation: Southern Nationalists and Southern Nationalism, 1830–1860* (New York: W. W. Norton, 1979), throws a broader net, looking into cultural and economic concerns, and exploring the manifestation of Southern nationalism in such divergent institutions as schools and churches. For McCardell, the peculiar institution is central to southern identity, as it is in Kenneth S. Greenberg, *Masters and Statesmen: The Political Culture of American Slavery* (Baltimore: Johns Hopkins University Press, 1985), an analysis of the South's political culture stressing the persistence of old Republican ideals. Rollin G. Osterweis, *Romanticism and Nationalism in the Old South* (New Haven: Yale University Press, 1949), concentrates on the Romantic features of this development within South Carolina.

Joel H. Silbey intriguingly links the growth of southern nationalism to the North's ethnoreligions changes in " 'The Surge of Republican Power': Partisan Antipathy, American Social Conflict, and the Coming of the Civil War," from his *The Partisan Imperative: The Dynamics of American Politics Before the Civil War Era* (New York: Oxford University Press, 1985).

Widespread disillusionment with political corruption, both South and North, is the theme of Mark W. Summers, *The Plundering Generation: Corruption and the Crisis of the Union, 1849–1861* (New York: Oxford University Press, 1987). Economic depression heightened this reaction, and James L. Huston scrutinizes the relationship between *The Panic of 1857 and the Coming of the Civil War* (Baton Rouge: Louisiana State University Press, 1987).

For more on the homestead issue as well as background on government land policies, consult Raynor G. Wellington, *The Political and Sectional Influence of the Public Lands, 1828–1842* (Cambridge, MA: Riverside Press, 1914); George M. Stephenson, *The Political History of the Public Lands From 1840 to 1862: From Pre-Emption to Homestead* (Boston: Richard G. Badger, 1917); Malcolm J. Rohrbough, *The Land Office Business: The Settlement and Administration of American Public Lands, 1789–1837* (New York: Oxford University Press, 1968); and Daniel Feller, *The Public Lands in Jacksonian Politics* (Madison: University of Wisconsin Press, 1984). Most of these studies, unfortunately, cut off before the 1850s, so that the finest discussion of how land reform was transformed from a Democratic to a Republican issue remains that found in Roy M. Robbins's overview, *Our Landed Heritage: The Public Domain, 1776–1936* (Princeton, NJ: Princeton University Press, 1942). Paul Wallace Gates, *Fifty Million Acres: Conflicts Over Kansas Land Policy, 1854–1890* (Ithaca, NY: Cornell University Press, 1954), unravels the complex interplay between public land and Bleeding Kansas.

Too many economists look upon homesteading as a government subsidy, similar to land grants to railroads and tariffs for manufacturers. This implicitly assumes that the State initially has a just title to all these resources. But in the natural-rights philosophy of John Locke, such land qualifies as "unowned" (except in those cases where American Indians held a prior, just claim). The first user, therefore, becomes the legitimate title holder. Homesteading was not a subsidy to farmers but merely a recognition of their property rights, whereas the sale of public lands was an expropriation of squatter rights—i.e., a tax. Murray N. Rothbard is one of the few modern economists to defend homesteading as the proper application of free-market principles. See his essay, "Justice and Property Titles," reprinted in *Egalitarianism as a Revolt Against Nature and Other Essays* (cited ch. 3), and chapters 10 and 11 from his book, *The Ethics of Liberty* (Atlantic Highlands, NJ: Humanities Press, 1982).

A superb account of John Brown's life is Stephen B. Oates, *To Purge This Land With Blood: A Biography of John Brown* (New York: Harper & Row, 1970). But Oswald Garrison Villard, *John Brown: A Biography, 1800–1859* (Garden City, NY: Doubleday, Doran, 1910), contains still more facts. On Brown's backers and supporters, see Edward J. Renchan, Jr., *The Secret Six: The True Tale of the Men Who Conspired With John Brown* (New York: Crown, 1995); Jeffery S. Rossbach, *Ambivalent Conspirators: John Brown, the Secret Six, and a Theory of Slave Violence* (Philadelphia: University of Pennsylvania Press, 1982); and Benjamin Quarles, *Allies for Freedom: Blacks and John Brown* (New York: Oxford University Press, 1974). Tildon G. Edelstein, *Strange Enthusiasm: A Life of Thomas Wentworth Higginson* (New Haven: Yale University Press, 1968), is a captivating biography of one of the Secret Six. Eric Foner has remarked that John Brown, in all things, was *sui generis*. Thus, unlike other radical abolitionists, Brown was indeed an egalitarian, who favored seizing southern plantations so they could be held as common property.

One good way to approach this period is through the presidential administrations that it encompasses. Roy Franklin Nichols, *Franklin Pierce: Young Hickory of the Granite Hills*, 2nd edn. (Philadelphia: University of Pennsylvania Press, 1958), and Larry Gara, *The Presidency of Franklin Pierce* (Lawrence: University Press of Kansas, 1991), explore the President whose term was dominated by not only the Kansas-Nebraska Act but also fugitive-slave enforcement and the Ostend Manifesto. For Pierce's successor, see Elbert B. Smith, *The Presidency of James Buchanan* (Lawrence: University Press of Kansas, 1975).

5

The Confederate States of America

The Election of 1860

The Democratic Party, the last remaining institution with significant strength in both sections of the country, could no longer hold together through the crucial election year of 1860. The Freeport Doctrine may have salvaged Stephen Douglas's political fortunes in the free states, but it scuttled them in the slave states. It thereby drove a final wedge into the party. Just four years before, Southerners had looked upon Douglas as a reliable northern ally. But the Illinois Senator's break with the Buchanan Administration over the proslavery Lecompton Constitution, in combination with his equivocation over the Supreme Court's proslavery decision in Dred Scott, had left the South feeling more isolated than ever. Southern Democrats, under the prompting of Senator Jefferson Davis of Mississippi, were no longer content to have Congress leave the territories open to slavery. They now demanded a congressional slave code that would explicitly protect the peculiar institution in all territories.

When northern Democrats refused to go along with this demand at the party's 1860 convention in Charleston, southern delegates walked out. The Alabama fire-eater, William Yancey, played an instrumental part in this rejection of the Illinois politician. The party's two wings eventually nominated separate presidential candidates. The Northern Democrats stuck with Douglas and popular sovereignty; the Southern Democrats opted for John C. Breckinridge of Kentucky and a federal slave code. This split in the Democracy climaxed a reinforcing cycle of southern isolation and escalation. As the concrete political power of the slave states had declined, they had escalated their demands for guarantees to their peculiar institution. But each successive guarantee, running from the Fugitive Slave Law through the Kansas-Nebraska Act and the Dred Scott decision to the Lecompton Constitution, alienated greater numbers of Northerners. The cumulative impact was to foster the Republican Party.

The leading contender for the Republicans' 1860 presidential nomination started out as William Seward. The New York Senator's reputation as an antislavery radical, however, became a political liability. Many party members decided that the more moderate Lincoln would have greater appeal. He had not been nationally prominent long enough to make political enemies. On the third ballot at the Republican convention, held in a specially built "Wigwam" in Chicago, the delegates nominated the Illinois rail-splitter.

Still another political party also joined the contest with the high-minded purpose of eschewing sectional extremism and preserving the Union. Called the Constitutional Union Party, it consisted mainly of old Whigs and Know-Nothings from the upper South. Its candidate was John Bell of Tennessee. As in 1856, the presidential election in 1860 became essentially two separate races, one in the North and one in the South. But unlike 1856, there were four rather than three candidates. And not one of the four commanded substantial support in both regions. The race in the North was between Lincoln, the Republican, and Douglas, the Northern Democrat. The race in the South was between Breckinridge, the Southern Democrat, and Bell, the Constitutional Unionist.

Some Democratic optimists believed that the party's two candidates might pick up more total support than one would, thereby throwing the election into the House of Representatives. Lincoln did not carry a single slave state. Within ten of them, he did not get a single recorded vote. Nationwide, he carried only 40 percent of the popular vote. Yet he won the election. He did so by receiving the electoral votes of every free state except New Jersey, where he got four out of the state's seven electoral votes. This gave him an overwhelming majority in the electoral college. The contest in the South between Breckinridge and Bell had been irrelevant. Even if the votes of all Lincoln's opponents had been combined, he would still have won.

Nothing could make the looming political impotence of the slave states more stark. Since the adoption of the Constitution, a southern slaveholder had held the office of President for forty-nine out of seventy-two years, or better than two-thirds of the time. Twenty-four of the thirty-six Speakers of the House and twenty-five of the thirty-six presidents *pro tem* of the Senate had been Southerners. Twenty of thirty-five Supreme Court Justices had come from the slave states, giving them a majority on the court at all times. Lincoln's election was a bitter pill to swallow for a section of the country that had hitherto dominated the national government.

South Carolina acted swiftly. Before the year was out a state convention unanimously passed an ordinance of secession. Within another six weeks, Mississippi, Florida, Alabama, Georgia, Louisiana, and Texas had followed South Carolina out of the Union. The South Carolina convention cited northern evasion of the Constitution's fugitive slave clause as its foremost grievance. The deliberate violation of this obligation, as far as the South Carolinians were concerned, had made the Constitution a dead letter already. The convention's "Declaration of Causes" concluded that the Republican election victory now threatened slavery within the very states. A sectional party, "observing the *forms* of the Constitution," had elected "a man to the high office of President of the United States whose opinions and purposes are hostile to Slavery. . . . On the 4th of March next this party will take possession of the Government." It intended to exclude "the South . . . from the common territory" and wage "a war . . . against Slavery until it shall cease throughout the United States. . . . The Slaveholding States will no longer have the power of self-government, or self-protection, and the Federal Government will have become their enemy."[1]

Did South Carolina have grounds for its fears? Lincoln, after all, was not an abolitionist. Between his election and his inauguration, he refused to compromise on keeping slavery out of the territories, but throughout his campaign he had steadfastly opposed any other antislavery policies. He promised to enforce the Fugitive Slave Law and respect slavery in the existing states. The Republicans, moreover, had not gained a majority in either house of the new Congress. Many loyal unionists in the South thought that the seven seceding states were over-reacting.

Southern fire-eaters, however, recognized that a major faction within the Republican Party did endorse further steps to divorce the general government from slavery. Lincoln appointed to his cabinet at least two of these radical Republicans: Seward as Secretary of State and Salmon P. Chase as Secretary of the Treasury. Chase, for one, had long been firmly committed to a whole series of antislavery initiatives. "Restrict slavery in the slave States!" he had urged in 1849, "prevent its ingress to territories! repeal the Fugitive Slave law! put the general government on the side of freedom! and emancipation will spring up in the Southern States!"[2] Even if the radicals did not immediately get their way, the Republican Party now controlled federal patronage, the postal service, military posts, and judicial appointments. Lincoln could put Republicans, abolitionists, and even free blacks into public office all over the South. The fact that a national administration—for the first time—morally condemned the peculiar institution might, in and of itself, trigger slave resistance. And the Republican commitment to a territorial policy that the Supreme Court had declared unconstitutional showed that slaveholders could not rely upon paper guarantees.

The editors of the *Richmond Enquirer* described how Lincoln's victory must in the long term destroy slavery. "Upon the accession of Lincoln to power, we would apprehend no direct act of violence against negro property," the editors conceded. But "the use of federal office, contracts, power and patronage" would result in "the building up in every Southern State of a Black Republican party, the ally and stipendiary of Northern fanaticism, to become in a few short years the open advocate of abolition." Already a Missouri Congressman, Frank Blair, Jr., whose family had long been powerful within Democratic circles, had gone over to the Republicans and delivered 10 percent of that border state's presidential vote to Lincoln.

The *Enquirer* also understood that the eventual "ruin of every Southern State by the destruction of negro labor" would be accomplished through the increase in fugitive slaves after tampering with the peculiar institution in the upper South. "By gradual and insidious approach, under the fostering hand of federal power, Abolitionism will grow up in every border Southern State, converting them into free States, then into 'cities of refuge' for runaway negroes from the gulf States. No act of violence may ever be committed, no servile war waged, and yet the ruin and degradation of Virginia will be as fully and fatally accomplished, as though bloodshed and rapine had ravished the land. There are no consequences that can follow, even forcible disunion, more disastrous to the future prosperity of the people of Virginia."[3]

Secession was a risky gamble. By leaving the Union, Southerners were abandoning the Constitution's protections for slavery. But with Republicans in control, many whites in the deep South felt they had nothing to lose. Their peculiar institution was certainly doomed otherwise, and for them that conjured up inevitable images of racial apocalypse. Slaveholders could better depend upon an independent central authority to provide those protections and police the new borders. As one Georgian explained, independence would permit Southerners to erect "an impassable wall between the North & the South so that negroes could not pass over to the North or an abolitionist come to the South to annoy us any more."[4] Anyone urging caution or delay found themselves overwhelmed by the surging tide of secession. "The prudent and conservative men South," admitted Senator Judah P. Benjamin of Louisiana, are not "able to stem the wild torrent of passion which is carrying everything before it. . . . It is a revolution . . . of the most intense character . . . and it can no more be checked by human effort, for the time, than a prairie fire by a gardener's watering hose."[5]

A Rival Government

Incumbent President James Buchanan still had four months left to serve after Lincoln's election. Despite blaming Republicans for provoking the South, he believed that no state had a legal right to leave the Union. But he also doubted that the President had sufficient power to coerce a seceding state. This gave the lame-duck

Congress time to consider various stop-gap compromises. One that gained Lincoln's acceptance was a proposed constitutional amendment that would prohibit interference with slavery in the states and that would be unamendable.

The seceding states were uninterested. Delegates assembled in Montgomery, Alabama, in early February of 1861 and drew up a constitution for the Confederate States of America. The Confederate Constitution was in most respects a carbon copy of the United States Constitution. The few changes either weakened the central government or strengthened slavery. The new document affirmed that the states were "sovereign and independent" and omitted a general welfare clause. The Confederate government could not impose protective tariffs, grant subsidies, or finance internal improvements. The Confederate Congress must pass all appropriations by two-thirds vote, unless they were explicitly requested by the executive branch, which was granted a line-item veto. The clause establishing the Confederate post office required it to become financially self-sufficient. States could now more easily initiate constitutional amendments, but Congress could no longer do so at all. And officials of the central government could be impeached by the state legislatures as well as by the House of Representatives.

Unlike the Philadelphia convention of 1787, the Montgomery convention was not squeamish about the term "slavery." The Confederate Constitution explicitly protected "the right of property in negro slaves." The Confederate Congress had to provide a slave code for any Confederate territory. Another provision permitted the citizens of each state to "transit and sojourn" in other states with their slave property "unimpaired." This new supplement to the fugitive slave clause demonstrated a willingness to sacrifice even states' rights for the peculiar institution.

Forty-nine-year-old Alexander H. Stephens of Georgia was the newly elected Confederate Vice-President. A frail, sickly man, weighing less than one hundred pounds, he had served as a Whig in Congress, where his eloquence had once brought Lincoln to tears. Stephens had no doubts that the Confederate Constitution's most valuable innovations involved slavery. "The new constitution has put at rest, *forever*, all the agitating questions relating to our peculiar institutions—African slavery as it exists among us—the proper *status* of the negro in our form of civilization," he told a Savannah gathering. "This was the immediate cause of the late rupture and present revolution." The new Government's "foundations are laid, its corner-stone rests, upon the great truth, that the negro is not equal to the white man; that slavery—subordination to the superior race—is his natural and moral condition. This, our new government, is the first, in the history of the world, based upon this great physical, philosophical, and moral truth."[6]

What the Montgomery convention failed to do was almost as noteworthy as what it did do. The fire-eaters who had instigated the secessionist revolution were conspicuously absent from positions of leadership within the new government. The man elected Confederate President was aristocratic Jefferson Davis, an affluent cotton planter in his mid-fifties and Democratic Party regular. He looked his new part: a shade under six feet and ramrod straight, slender and graceful, aloof and severe, with thin lips, high cheekbones, and deep-set eyes. Yet Davis had been only a reluctant secessionist, while Vice-President Stephens had actually fought against his state's withdrawal from the Union. Of the six appointees to the new Confederate cabinet, only two could be considered radicals— Robert Toombs of Georgia, as Secretary of State, and Leroy Pope Walker of Alabama, as Secretary of War—and neither of them held these posts for long. Davis's most trusted subordinate would become Judah P. Benjamin, a former Whig Senator from Louisiana. Foreign-born and Jewish, Benjamin started out as Confederate Attorney General, heading a Department of Justice that was the country's first—since the Federal government during George Washington's presidency had established the position but not the department to go with it. Benjamin would later ably serve as Davis's Secretary of War and then Secretary of State, remaining in the cabinet until the very end. But this successful sugar planter had initially upon Lincoln's election denigrated "the absurd and self-contradictory charge that we seek to dissolve the Union."[7]

The crest of the secessionist wave had hurled out many southern appeals to the natural right of revolution as well as to the compact theory of the Constitution. "We are in times of revolution," pronounced one delegate to the convention that had taken Louisiana out of the Union, "and questions of form must sink into insignificance."[8] After the moderates seized the political helm, however, the legalistic justification for southern independence predominated. Jefferson Davis later denied that secession involved revolution at all: "Ours is not a revolution. . . . We are not engaged in a Quixotic fight for the rights of man; our struggle is for inherited rights."[9]

Demands of the fire-eaters were voted down at the constitutional convention as well. Allowing slave imports from Africa would bring down prices and reduce the current wealth of large slaveholders. It would also offend border states yet to secede because they sold their excess slaves into the cotton South and would not be happy to face foreign competition. The Confederate Constitution accordingly obligated Congress to proscribe the international traffic in black chattels and legalized such trade only with those slave states that remained in the Union. It also kept the three-fifths Federal ratio rather than increasing the congressional representation of districts to the full proportion of their slaves.

The most heated controversy at the Montgomery convention was whether or not the Constitution should permit only slave states to join the Confederacy. The fire-eaters wanted to ensure a permanent separation from the North. They feared that the admission of free states would enable the moderates to reconstruct the old Union under the new Constitution. A compromise, however, left the admission of new states to the discretion of two-thirds of the Confederate Congress. The Montgomery convention, which met behind closed doors, even rejected a constitutional sanction of either nullification or secession. On the contrary, the new document muddied any implicit incorporation of these doctrines with the preamble's reference to a "permanent federal government," something that was never part of the United States Constitution. This increasing political conservatism eventually rendered the Confederate government into a mirror image of its Union counterpart.

Union authority meanwhile evaporated from the deep South. Federal officials resigned in droves. State troops took possession of customhouses, post offices, arsenals, revenue cutters, and military posts. Louisiana grabbed the New Orleans mint, along with $500,000 in hard money. The major general commanding all United States forces in Texas simply surrendered them on his own initiative. Only Fort Sumter in Charleston and three other forts along the Florida coast had garrisons of sufficient size and determination to keep them in Union hands. When President Buchanan tried to ship provisions and reinforcements to Fort Sumter in the unarmed *Star of the West*, South Carolina's shore batteries opened fire and drove the vessel away. Buchanan slipped out of office still refusing to turn over these last vestiges of federal presence.

Abraham Lincoln Assumes Office

Protection of the South's peculiar institution had induced the first wave of secession. But as Lincoln took the oath of office, the Union still contained eight slave states, more than had left. Secession had so far failed in the upper South, where the black population was less dense. Even in a few states of the lower South, disunion had triumphed only by narrow margins. But southern unionists made clear their conviction that no state should be forced to remain.

Some Northerners agreed that the new Gulf Coast Confederacy should be allowed to depart in peace. Militant abolitionists such as Garrison had championed separation from the slave states for twenty years, and their biggest worry was that southern secession might just be a bluff. The withdrawal of the deep South's representatives from Congress made free-state control over the national government more pronounced than ever. The Republicans would have a free hand in the territories, whereas the economic viability of a small, independent slave republic was in doubt, especially if it could not expand. Even Greeley's *Tribune* had briefly come out for letting the cotton states go, hoping "never to live in a republic whereof one section is pinned to the residue by bayonets."[10] Within Lincoln's cabinet, Secretary of State Seward was the leading spokesman for conciliation. He predicted "voluntary reconstruction" of the seceding states given patience and time.

Lincoln, nevertheless, was determined to preserve the Union by force if necessary. "I hold that . . . the Union of these States is perpetual," he asserted in his first inaugural address, cautiously revealing this unyielding posture. "The Union is unbroken, and to the extent of my ability I shall take care, as the Constitution itself expressly enjoins upon me, that the laws of the Union be faithfully executed in all the States." Lincoln, however, seemed to be promising not to initiate coercion against the seceding states. "There needs to be no bloodshed or violence, and there shall be none unless it be forced upon the national authority. The power confided to me will be used to hold, occupy, and possess the property and places belonging to the Government and to collect the duties and imposts; but beyond what may be necessary for these objects, there will be no invasion, no using of force against or among the people anywhere."[11]

Lincoln's determination received the hearty applause of powerful northern interests. Westerners feared the closing of the lower Mississippi River, even though the Confederate government promised free navigation. Eastern manufacturers worried that they would lose southern markets to European competitors because of the Confederacy's free-trade policy. Yankee merchants and ship builders faced an end to a monopoly on the South's coastal trade that the government granted to United States vessels. Holders of government securities were edgy about the Union's loss of tariff revenue. But in the final analysis, American nationalism proved to be the most compelling opponent of southern independence. Abolitionists had failed to win over the North because they had put their opposition to slavery ahead of the Union. Republicans had succeeded because they had put the Union ahead of their opposition to slavery. Now that the Union was imperiled, the Republican Party had to take decisive action or face political oblivion.

The deep South's refusal to abide by the outcome of a fair and legal election struck northern voters as a selfish betrayal of the nation's unique mission. "Plainly the central idea of secession is the essence of anarchy," argued Lincoln. Indeed, his inaugural equated secession with despotism. "A majority held in restraint by constitutional checks and limitations, and always changing easily with deliberate changes of popular opinions and sentiments, is the only true sovereign of a free people. Whoever rejects it does, of necessity, fly to anarchy or to despotism," because "unanimity is impossible.

The rule of a minority, as a permanent arrangement, is wholly inadmissible."[12] Worse still, the successful breakaway of the lower South raised the possibility of other regions separating.

Yet Lincoln also wished to preserve the loyalty of the upper South. He therefore settled upon a defensive strategy to uphold national authority. The government would for the moment make no effort to retake federal posts. Like Buchanan, Lincoln would merely hang on to those posts still under the government's control. Simultaneously, United States ships stationed off the Confederate coast would attempt to collect duties. The new President could thus close his inaugural with a moving plea for peace: "In *your* hands, my dissatisfied fellow-countrymen, and not in *mine,* is the momentous issue of civil war. The Government will not assail *you.* You can have no conflict without being yourselves the aggressors. . . . We must not be enemies. Though passion may have strained it must not break our bonds of affection. The mystic chords of memory, stretching from every battlefield and patriot grave to every living hearth and hearthstone all over this broad land, will yet swell the chorus of the Union, when again touched, as surely they will be, by the better angels of our nature."[13]

Fort Sumter and Secession's Second Wave

The day after his inauguration, Lincoln received distressing news. Major Robert Anderson reported that his garrison of about seventy soldiers would have to abandon Fort Sumter within six weeks unless resupplied. After extensive and lengthy consultations with his cabinet, the President ordered an armed relief expedition to sail. He notified the governor of South Carolina, however, that transports would land "provisions only," not reinforcements, so long as the state offered no resistance.

The defiant American flag flying over Fort Sumter had been a smoldering affront to the citizens of Charleston, the center of southern militancy. Secretary of State Seward unofficially was reassuring Confederate representatives that the government would abandon the post. This helped Confederate President Davis persuade the South Carolinians to wait and starve the Union garrison out. But with relief pending, he could stall no longer. Major Anderson refused one final demand to vacate, whereupon the Confederate guns opened fire.

Mary Boykin Chesnut, the wife of South Carolina's former United States Senator, was in Charleston at the time and left a vivid description in her diary. "I do not pretend to go to sleep," she wrote. "How can I? If Anderson does not accept terms—at four—the orders are—he shall be fired upon. I count four—St. Michael chimes. I begin to hope. At half-past four, the heavy booming of a cannon. I sprang out of bed. And on my knees—prostrate—I prayed as I never prayed before." Eventually she joined other citizens of Charleston on the rooftops of their waterfront mansions, observing the bombardment. She heard "the regular roar of cannon—there it was. And who could tell what each volley accomplished of death and destruction. The women were wild, there on the housetop. Prayers from the women and imprecations from the men, and then a shell would light up on the scene."[14] The bombardment lasted thirty-four hours. Having suffered no casualties but with his ammunition exhausted, Anderson surrendered on April 14.

The Confederate attack on Fort Sumter electrified the free states. Lincoln could now count on enthusiastic northern support for his appeal to arms, as he issued his proclamation calling up the militia. Ohio's Republican governor did not even wait to receive a quota of men from the War Department, but fired a telegram directly off asking: "What portion of the 75,000 militia you call for do you give to Ohio? We will furnish the largest number you will receive. Great rejoicing here over your proclamation."[15]

But the President's call for state militia garnered an opposite reaction in the slave states. It of course wiped out any lingering unionism in those that had already seceded. But still more decisive was its impact upon the wavering states of the upper South. "The militia of Virginia will not be furnished to the powers at Washington for any such use or purpose as they have in view," replied Virginia's governor, John Letcher. Originally critical of South Carolina's impetuosity, he now laid squarely upon Lincoln's shoulders full responsibility for starting a civil war. "Your object is to subjugate the Southern States, and a requisition made upon me for such an object—an object, in my judgment, not within the purview of the Constitution or the [militia] act of 1795—will not be complied with. You have chosen to inaugurate civil war, and having done so, we will meet it in a spirit as determined as the Administration has exhibited toward the South."[16]

Virginia, North Carolina, Tennessee, and Arkansas all promptly transferred their allegiance to the Confederate States of America. Previously unwilling to secede over the issue of slavery, these four states were now ready to fight for the ideal of a voluntary Union. Out in the western territory that would someday become Oklahoma, the sedentary Indian tribes—Cherokees, Choctaws, Chickasaws, Creeks, and Seminoles—also joined the rebellion. The Confederate government relocated its capital from Montgomery to Richmond, Virginia, one hundred miles from Washington. More federal installations fell into rebel hands, including the major arms factory at Harper's Ferry and the large naval shipyard near Norfolk. At a single stroke of the pen, Lincoln had more than doubled the Confederacy's white population and material resources.

Holding Maryland and Missouri

Four slave states on the border remained to be heard from: Delaware, Maryland, Kentucky, and Missouri. Only tiny Delaware was unquestionably loyal. In Maryland popular sentiment was bitterly divided. The governor was timidly pro-Union, whereas the majority of the legislature leaned toward secession. Maryland, however, was vital to the Lincoln Administration. It not only contained Baltimore, the country's third largest city; the state also isolated the nation's capital, itself a southern town, from the free states further north. No sizable regular army units were on hand for Washington's defense, and with Confederate flags already visible across the Potomac River to the south, Lincoln feared he might have to flee.

The arrival of the first regiment to answer Lincoln's call, the 6th Massachusetts, did nothing to dispel the panic. A mob had attacked the troops in Baltimore as they shuttled between train stations. In the ensuing melee shots were exchanged. Four soldiers and at least nine civilians died, with many more injured. While the 6th Massa-chusetts limped into Washington, Baltimore officials burned the railroad bridges and cut the telegraph wires.

Not until more regiments began pouring into the beleaguered capital a week later was it truly secure. Lincoln then suspended the writ of *habeas corpus* along "the military line" between Philadel-phia and the District of Columbia and clamped a military occupa-tion down upon Maryland. The governor convened the legislature in the northwest part of the state, where unionism was strong. Although the legislature rejected secession, it came out for "the peaceful and immediate recognition of the independence of the Confederate States"; the state "hereby gives her cordial consent thereunto, as a member of the Union." The legislature also de-nounced "the present military occupation of Maryland" as a "flagrant violation of the Constitution."[17]

The military authorities soon began imprisoning prominent secessionists without trial. The writ of *habeas corpus* was a constitu-tional safeguard to prevent such imprisonments without sufficient legal cause, and one of the incarcerated Marylanders, John Merry-man, attempted an appeal on that basis. Chief Justice Roger B. Taney, sitting as a circuit judge, ordered Merryman released, but federal officials, acting under Lincoln's orders, refused. The aging Chief Justice, just three years from death's door, thereupon issued a blistering opinion holding that only Congress had the constitutional right to suspend *habeas corpus*. The President "certainly does not faithfully execute the laws, if he takes upon himself legislative power, by suspending the writ of habeas corpus, and the judicial power also, by arresting and imprisoning a person without due process of law," declared Taney. If Lincoln's action was allowed to stand, then "the people of the United States are no longer living under a Government of laws, but every citizen holds life, liberty and property at the will and pleasure of the army officer in whose military district he may happen to be found."[18]

Lincoln simply ignored Taney's opinion. He also wrote out standing orders for the Chief Justice's arrest, although these were never served. The President did not ignore, however, the increas-ingly outspoken Maryland legislature when it lodged a sharp protest with Congress. Rather, Secretary of State Seward ordered a lightning statewide raid that jailed thirty-one legislators, the mayor of Baltimore, one of the state's Congressmen, and key anti-Administration publishers and editors. At the state's next election in the fall of 1861, federal provost marshals stood guard at the polls and arrested any disunionists who attempted to vote. The outcome was further rigged by granting special three-day furloughs to Marylanders who had joined the Union army so they could go home and vote. Unsurprisingly, the new legislature was solidly behind the war.

Events in Maryland inspired the words to one of the Confederacy's favorite marching songs, "Maryland, My Maryland." Written by James Ryder Randall, they were adapted to the music of "O Tannenbaum":

> The despot's heel is on thy shore,
>   Maryland!
> His torch is at thy temple door,
>   Maryland!
> Avenge the patriotic gore
> That flecked the streets of Baltimore,
> And be the battle queen of yore,
>   Maryland! My Maryland!
> . . . .
> I hear the distant thunder-hum,
>   Maryland!
> The Old Line's bugle, fife, and drum,
>   Maryland!
> She is not dead, nor deaf, nor dumb—
> Huzza! she spurns the Northern scum!
> She breathes! she burns! she'll come! she'll come!
>   Maryland! My Maryland![19]

The song with only minor changes eventually became the state's official anthem, but Maryland was never able to come to the Confederacy.

Farther west, the border state of Missouri contained a larger population than any other slave state outside of Virginia. A special convention chosen by the people had rejected secession before the attack on Fort Sumter. But the state's newly elected governor, Claiborne Jackson, a former "border ruffian," favored the Confederacy and refused Lincoln's call for troops. The governor controlled

the state militia, which was in spring encampment near St. Louis.
The local Union commander, the impetuous and intolerant Captain
Nathaniel Lyon, precipitated open hostilities by surrounding the
militia encampment with his own force of regulars and hastily
recruited German immigrants. The militia laid down their arms,
but a crowd gathered that was not so peaceful. The raw Union
recruits fired indiscriminately, killing twenty-eight mostly innocent
bystanders.

This provocation converted many Union sympathizers into secessionists. One delegate to the state convention, who had voted
against Missouri's secession, announced his change of heart to a
city crowd. "If Unionism means such atrocious deeds as have been
witnessed in St. Louis, I am no longer a Union man."[20] The Lincoln
Administration's heavy-handed ineptitude had managed to provoke
open hostilities within a state that had not formally seceded. The
legislature rallied behind Governor Jackson and granted him dicta-
torial powers, but Federal troops chased them all out of the state
capital. Missouri ended up with two shadow governments, one in
the Union, the other in the Confederacy. Declaring the governor-
ship vacant and the legislature abolished, the anti-secessionist
members of the state convention operated without elections as a
provisional government loyal to the Union for the next three years.
The remnant of the legislature, meanwhile, joined the deposed
governor in aligning with the Confederacy.

The real power in Missouri was the Federal military, which
gained nominal control over most of the state. A ferocious guerrilla
war devastated the countryside, however. John C. Frémont, who
assumed command of the Union's Western Department, imposed
martial law at the end of August. "Circumstances, in my judgment,
of sufficient urgency render it necessary that the commanding
general of this department should assume the administrative powers of the State." On his own authority, Frémont freed the slaves of
those in rebellion and confiscated all their other real and personal
property. He also proclaimed the death penalty for any captured
guerrillas. "All persons who shall be taken with arms in their hands
within these lines shall be tried by court-martial, and if found guilty
will be shot. . . . All persons who shall be proven to have destroyed,

after the publication of this order, railroad tracks, bridges, or telegraphs shall suffer the extreme penalty of the law."[21]

The President countermanded the precipitate emancipation and replaced Frémont in order to placate what loyal sentiment was left in the various border states. But Missouri remained under martial law. The internecine warfare was further aggravated as Kansas "jayhawkers" crossed the border and took revenge for the earlier efforts of the Missouri "border ruffians" to extend slavery into Kansas. What one historian has called a "maelstrom of retaliation and counter-retaliation" built to a howling crescendo.[22] During the war's second summer, the most notorious band of Confederate partisans, led by William C. Quantrill, descended upon Lawrence, Kansas, burned the business district to the ground, and murdered in cold blood every male inhabitant they could locate—183 in all.

Union commanders responded with such harsh measures as General Order No. 11, which forcibly relocated nearly all the residents of four western counties in Missouri, destroyed their crops, and razed their homes and barns. The relocation made no effort to distinguish between citizens loyal to the Union and those disloyal. Only six hundred persons were left in Cass County, which before the war had a population of ten thousand. After observing a boat that "was crowded full" of deportees, one Federal colonel expressed the bitterness widespread among Union soldiers toward a populace that had spawned "Bushwackers." "God knows where they are all going for I don[']t nor do I care," he wrote his wife. "I think if we get rid of the women" then "it will not be hard to get rid of [the Bushwackers]."[23] This legacy of hatred, dating back six years before Fort Sumter, would continue to plague Kansas and Missouri long after the rest of the country attained peace. Many of the desperate young boys whose families were banished and who rode with Quantrill, such as seventeen-year-old Jesse James, would not abandon their violent grudges until they reached the grave.

Kentucky and West Virginia

The Union handling of Kentucky, birthplace of both Lincoln and Davis, was initially more tactful than its handling of either Missouri or Maryland. Fear that this border state would join the Confederacy was one of the major reasons that Lincoln had revoked Frémont's emancipation proclamation. "The Kentucky Legislature would not budge till that proclamation was modified," he confided in private correspondence. "I think to lose Kentucky is nearly the same as to lose the whole game. Kentucky gone, we can not hold Missouri, nor, as I think, Maryland. These all against us, and the job on our hands is too large for us. We would as well consent to separation at once, including the surrender of this capitol."[24]

Although Kentucky's governor favored secession and refused to supply Lincoln with militia, the state's unionists were numerous enough to get the legislature to declare neutrality. This kept Kentucky free from either side's armies for four months. When Confederate troop movements violated the neutrality, the legislature invited Union forces to expel the invaders. Many individual Kentuckians, however, had already enlisted in the Confederate ranks. They elected a convention that passed an ordinance of secession and set up an alternative state government. Thus Kentucky, like Missouri, was represented in both the Confederacy and the Union.

The Confederate military never could consolidate control over Kentucky, and the Union embrace squeezed tighter as the war heated up. Federal authorities declared martial law; required loyalty oaths before people could trade or engage in many other daily activities; censored books, journals, sermons, and sheet music; and crowded the jails with Rebel sympathizers. By 1862 the military was interfering with elections, preventing candidates from running, and dispersing the Democratic convention at bayonet point. The net result was that the people of Kentucky felt greater solidarity with the rest of the South at the war's end than at its beginning.

The Lincoln Administration carved still another border state out of the mountains of northwestern Virginia. Owning very few slaves, the region's residents had long been disaffected from Virginia's tidewater oligarchy. Moreover, the strategically crucial Baltimore and Ohio Railroad ran through the region. Confederate guerrillas cut the railroad within the first month after Sumter. But General George Brinton McClellan led about 20,000 Ohio volunteers into western Virginia in one of the war's earliest campaigns. By the end of July he had reopened the railroad and driven out enemy formations.

McClellan was a short, dapper man, of only thirty-five, with a natural military bearing. His conciliatory proclamation to the local populace stood in marked contrast to Frémont's policy in Missouri. *"To the Union Men of Western Virginia:* . . . I have ordered troops to cross the river," McClellan announced. But "they come as your friends and your brothers—as enemies only to the armed rebels who are preying upon you. Your homes, your families, and your property are safe under our protection. All your rights shall be religiously respected." This included property in slaves, "notwithstanding all that has been said by the traitors to induce you to believe that our advent among you will be signalized by interference with your slaves." Indeed, "not only will we abstain from all such interference, but we will, on the contrary, with an iron hand, crush any attempt at [slave] insurrection."[25] Future campaigns would convert McClellan's west Virginia success into a minor skirmish by comparison. But at this early date, it gained him a fawning reputation in northern newspapers as the "Young Napoleon."

Virginia's northwestern counties, however, could not yet legally establish a separate state, because the United States Constitution requires permission from the parent state. So instead, the Lincoln Administration organized the loyal residents of the western counties into a pro-Union government for the entire state. The legislature of this bogus Virginia government then authorized the separation of the northwestern counties in May 1862. When West Virginia entered the Union in 1863, the new state encompassed not only unionist counties but also many that would rather have remained part of Confederate Virginia.

The Confederate government made its own attempt in the far west to do the same as the Union did in Virginia. Settlers in the southern and western parts of the New Mexico territory were sympathetic to the South, so in early 1862 they formed the new territory of Arizona and attached themselves to the Confederacy. This separation did not last long, however. Federal troops recovered these settlements later that summer.

The Civil War experience throughout the entire borderland, in short, comprised variations on a single pattern. While military occupations maintained formal Union sovereignty, popular feelings were torn, setting neighbor against neighbor and sometimes brother against brother. Kentucky, home to the now deceased Henry Clay, sent three of the Great Pacificator's grandsons to fight for the North and four to fight for the South. From Maryland, Missouri, Kentucky, and West Virginia together, about 185,000 white men served in the Union armies, while 103,000 served in the Confederate armies. Occasionally opposing units from the same border state would engage each other on a battlefield. Nowhere was the designation "Civil" War more apt.

Chapter 5
Bibliographical Essay

Was the South's secession a revolution or counter-revolution? Charles Beard's economic interpretation of the Civil War suggests the latter, with the slave states futilely trying to hold back the triumph of bourgeois capitalism. The recent author who explicitly labels the Confederate States as counter-revolutionary is James McPherson, in his two general histories of the war: *Ordeal by Fire* and *Battle Cry of Freedom* (both cited in the prologue's bibliographic essay)—a conclusion that naturally follows from his emphasis on modernization. Emory M. Thomas, on the other hand, in works we will mention below in this or future chapters, argues that the Confederacy's wartime centralization of power was so unprecedented that it qualifies as truly revolutionary.

I find both perspectives incomplete. Modern revolutions often generate counter-revolutions. The American Revolution—and here I do follow Beard—was partially reversed by the counter-revolutionary Constitution. The French Revolution had its Napoleon. The Confederate revolution of 1861, despite deep commitment to the peculiar institution, clearly carried on the radical tradition of '76 in its drive toward self-determination, decentralization, and *laissez faire*. But as Joseph R. Stromberg has so perceptively observed in "The War for Southern Independence: A Radical Libertarian Perspective" (also cited in the prologue), this secessionist revolution had the misfortune to suffer a premature counter-revolution. The "early 'Thermidor' at the Montgomery Convention," in Stromberg's words, "dispossessed the secessionist cadre (Rhett, Yancey *et. al.* . . .) and put legalistic conservatives like Davis in charge." Jefferson Davis thus represented the Confederacy's version of Federalist George Washington, or perhaps, its Napoleon Bonaparte.

The general history of the Confederate States that gives this political reversal greatest attention is Emory M. Thomas's contribution to the New American Nation series, *The Confederate Nation: 1861–1865* (New York: Harper & Row, 1979). E. Merton Coulter, *The Confederate States of America, 1861–1865* (Baton Rouge: Louisiana State University Press, 1950), part of the *History of the South* series, is the most detailed single-volume on the Confederacy. Other worthwhile volumes include Clement Eaton, *A History of the Southern Confederacy* (New York: Free Press, 1954); Charles P. Roland, *The Confederacy* (Chicago: University of Chicago Press, 1960); and Frank E. Vandiver, *Their Tattered Flags: The Epic of the Confederacy* (New York: Harper's Magazine Press Book, 1970).

The 1860 election must figure prominently in any survey of the Civil War, and many of them give it more than adequate coverage. Also some of the political works from the last chapter equally treat events in this one. Three older monographs devoted specifically to the election are Emerson D. Fite, *Presidential Campaign of 1860* (New York: Macmillan, 1911), Reinhard H. Luthin, *The First Lincoln Campaign* (Cambridge, MA: Harvard

University Press, 1944), and Ollinger Crenshaw, *The Slave States in the Presidential Election of 1860* (Baltimore: Johns Hopkins Press, 1945). Roy Franklin Nichols, *The Disruption of American Democracy* (New York: Macmillan, 1948), thoroughly recounts the breaking apart of the Democratic Party.

Dwight Lowell Dumond, *The Secession Movement, 1860–1861* (New York: Macmillan, 1931), and Ralph A. Wooster, *The Secession Conventions of the South* (Princeton, NJ: Princeton University Press, 1962), offer details on the South's decision to leave the Union. For the journalistic angle, look at Donald E. Reynolds, *Editors Make War: Southern Newspapers in the Secession Crisis* (Nashville: Vanderbilt University Press, 1970). Nearly every seceding state has a study of its own, with several having more than one, but some of the more interesting are Steven A. Channing, *Crisis of Fear: Secession in South Carolina* (New York: Simon & Schuster, 1970); William L. Barney, *The Secessionist Impulse: Alabama and Mississippi in 1860* (Princeton, NJ: Princeton University Press, 1974); Michael P. Johnson, *Toward a Patriarchal Republic: The Secession of Georgia* (Baton Rouge: Louisiana State University Press, 1977); J. Mills Thornton, III, *Politics and Power in a Slave Society: Alabama, 1800–1860* (Baton Rouge: Louisiana State University Press, 1978); and Walter L. Buenger, *Secession and the Union in Texas* (Austin: University of Texas Press, 1984). Daniel W. Crofts, *Reluctant Confederates: Upper South Unionists in the Secession Crisis* (Chapel Hill: University of North Carolina Press, 1989), is an important work that provides insight into the states that did not secede until Fort Sumter.

Once the neo-abolitionist historians re-established that slavery was the underlying cause of secession, a new question presented itself. How did the planter class secure the political allegiance of the South's majority of non-slaveholders? Non-slaveholders of course predominated in the four divided border states and in the other four upper-South states that rejected secession until Lincoln's call for troops, but even in the deep South, the proportion of families owning slaves in 1860 approached only slightly more than one third—compared to one fourth for the slave states overall. The highest proportions in Mississippi and South Carolina just reached a majority.

Frank Lawrence Owsley, *Plain Folk of the Old South* (Baton Rouge: Louisiana State University Press, 1949), was the first to tackle this question. Since then it has been fruitfully investigated in both the state studies of secession mentioned above and several superb local studies: Steven Hahn, *The Roots of Southern Populism: Yeoman Farmers and the Transformation of the Georgia Upcountry, 1850–1890* (New York: Oxford University Press, 1983); J. William Harris, *Plain Folk and Gentry in a Slave Society: White Labor and Black Slavery in Augusta's Hinterlands* (Middletown, CT: Wesleyan University Press, 1985); and Lacy K. Ford, Jr., *Origins of Southern Radicalism: The South Carolina Upcountry, 1800–1860* (New York: Oxford University Press, 1988). One book that attempts a more global answer is Laurence Shore, *Southern Capitalists: The Ideological Leadership of an Elite, 1832–1885* (Chapel Hill: University of North Carolina Press, 1986).

Despite all this research, a straightforward analysis of what interests supported secession and why is still not in sight. Race obviously was the factor uniting whites, and the South's version of the country ideology inherited from the American Revolution had come to see slavery as the only firm foundation for true republican independence and equal liberty. But no longer tenable is the older thesis of Seymour Martin Lipset, "The Emergence of the One-party South—The Election of 1860," in his *Political Man: The Social Bases of Politics* (Garden City, NY: Doubleday, 1960). He depicted self-interested planters dragging non-slaveholders into secession—an opinion very similar to the one held by the Republican Party's leadership in the North. Wealthy planters, in many cases, were actually reluctant secessionists, whereas fire-eaters often appealed most to small farmers. Yet we cannot simply turn the picture around. Secession does not appear to consistently represent a revolution on the part of the South's aspiring yeoman either.

One motivation for secession that most historians have failed to weight adequately is the fugitive-slave question. Only William W. Freehling has given this motive its due, in his collection, *The Reintegration of American History: Slavery and the Civil War* (cited prologue)—and particularly in such discerning articles as "The Divided South, Democracy's Limitations, and the Causes of the Peculiarly North American Civil War" and "Toward a Newer Political History—A Reintegrated Multicultural History." The references by Southerners to slaves escaping north are so frequent that no historian has ignored them. Not only was this grievance given the greatest play in South Carolina's Declaration of Causes, but Freehling has found it a prime concern at Virginia's secession convention. In "The Editorial Revolution, Virginia, and the Coming of the Civil War," reprinted in *The Reintegration of American History*, he quotes for instance Leonard S. Hall, a delegate from the northwestern part of the state, as declaring "we have but few slaves—we cannot keep them—the emissaries of the underground railroad are always upon the alert, and the terminus of that road is at our very door." But because of the allegedly few number of actual runaways, historians tend to treat these complaints as merely symbolic. The symbolic interpretation can reach the extremes of Bertram Wyatt-Brown, "Honor and Secession," from his collection *Yankee Saints and Southern Sinners* (cited prologue). While not addressing fugitive slaves directly, this article implies that secession resulted in large part from the wounds to southern pride inflicted by the harsh rhetoric of abolitionists, Republicans, and other Northerners.

I do not doubt that Southerners indeed had an exaggerated sense of honor. Wyatt-Brown has expounded this theme skillfully in *Southern Honor: Ethics and Behavior in the Old South* (New York: Oxford University Press, 1982). Moreover, citing northern failure to comply with the Constitution's fugitive-slave clause gave Southerners the rhetorical advantage of blaming the North for abrogating the constitutional contract. Yet the economic link (which I developed in chapter 2) between the runaway and slavery's enforcement costs makes the issue far more than symbolic. The peculiar institution's ongoing retreat from the South's borders shows that encouragement of fugitives represented a genuine threat. As Freehling points out, in the Compromise of 1850, "southern congressmen surrendered California to the North in exchange for a new Fugitive Slave Law" (p. 170); and again in 1854, southern representatives were more united behind the Kansas-Nebraska Act, which could protect the vulnerable borders of Missouri, than behind the acquisition of Cuba.

A new narrative of the Confederate government's founding, covering until the move to Richmond, is William C. Davis, *"A Government of Our Own": The Making of the Confederacy* (New York: Free Press, 1994). Charles Robert Lee, Jr., wrote the older standard on *The Confederate Constitutions* (Chapel Hill: University of North Carolina Press, 1963)—there were two, a provisional constitution and a permanent one. Marshall L. DeRosa, *The Confederate Constitution of 1861: An Inquiry Into American Constitutionalism* (Columbia: University of Missouri Press, 1991), has given us a political theorist's defense of the Confederacy's constitutional innovations. While I find myself in sympathy with DeRosa's praises for those departures from the U.S. Constitution that limited political power, he unfortunately does not give sufficient weight to the new document's proslavery features.

The latest biography of the Confederate President is William C. Davis, *Jefferson Davis: The Man and His Hour* (New York: HarperCollins, 1991). Hudson Strode, *Jefferson Davis*, 3 v. (New York: Harcourt, Brace, 1955–1964), is the longest and is laudatory, but also worthy is Clement Eaton's more critical *Jefferson Davis* (New York: Free Press, 1977). Thomas Edwin Schott, *Alexander H. Stephens of Georgia: A Biography* (Baton Rouge: Louisiana State University Press, 1988), is an excellent study of the Confederate Vice-President. For the Confederate cabinet, see Rembert W. Patrick, *Jefferson Davis and His Cabinet* (Baton Rouge: Louisiana State University Press, 1944). Eli N. Evans, *Judah P. Benjamin: The Jewish Confederate* (New York: Free Press, 1988), is a biography particularly sensitive to the difficulties of a Jewish statesman in nineteenth-century Protestant America.

The northern reaction to the Confederacy's creation is well narrated in Kenneth M. Stampp, *And the War Came: The North and the Secession Crisis, 1860-61* (Baton Rouge: Louisiana State University Press, 1950), probably the best consideration of why the North insisted on crushing secession. While there is no monograph on some of the surprising northern sentiment to let the South go, William C. Wright, *The Secession Movement in the Middle Atlantic States* (Rutherford, WI: Farleigh Dickinson University Press, 1973), discusses the desire for outright secession prior to Sumter in, among other places, New York, New Jersey, and Pennsylvania. David M. Potter, *Lincoln and His Party in the Secession Crisis*, 2nd edn. (New Haven: Yale University Press, 1962), looks at the development of Republican policy, while Robert Gray Gunderson, *Old Gentlemen's Convention: The Washington*

Peace Conference of 1861 (Madison: University of Wisconsin Press, 1961), recounts the failure of one of the last-ditch efforts at compromise.

Far more fundamental to the North's reaction, however, is how it came to identify liberty with Union. The starting point for understanding this phenomenon is Hans Kohn, *American Nationalism: An Interpretative Essay* (New York: Macmillan, 1957). Paul C. Nagel, *One Nation Indivisible: The Union in American Thought, 1776–1861* (New York: Oxford University Press, 1964), traces the intellectual development of the Union as an absolute deity, but does not really explain *why* this occurred. Major L. Wilson, *Time, Space and Freedom: The Quest for Nationality and the Irrepressible Conflict, 1815–1861* (Westport, CT: Greenwood Press, 1974), comes somewhat closer to answering the question. George B. Forgie, *Patricide in the House Divided: A Psychological Interpretation of Lincoln and His Age* (New York: W. W. Norton, 1979), despite its Freudian framework, is a fascinating look into the psychological roots of American nationalism. A short but provocative suggestion that the Republican Party rejected America's revolutionary heritage in reaction to socialism and the European revolutions of 1848 is John Higham, *From Boundlessness to Consolidation: The Transformation of American Culture, 1848–1860* (Ann Arbor: William L. Clements Library, 1969).

For the policies of the Lincoln Administration, Phillip Shaw Paludan, *The Presidency of Abraham Lincoln* (Lawrence: University Press of Kansas, 1994), pertains not only to this chapter but all that follow, as does Burton J. Hendrick's older study of *Lincoln's War Cabinet* (Boston: Little, Brown, 1946). Two books that treat the military aspects of the Fort Sumter engagement are William A. Swanberg, *First Blood: The Story of Fort Sumter* (New York: Charles Scribner's Sons, 1957), and Roy Meredith, *Storm Over Sumter: The Opening Engagement of the Civil War* (New York: Simon & Schuster, 1957).

The revisionist historian, Charles W. Ramsdell, charged in "Lincoln and Fort Sumter," *Journal of Southern History*, 3 (August 1937), pp. 259–288, that Lincoln maneuvered "the Confederates into firing the first shot in order that they, rather than he, should take the blame of beginning the bloodshed." Both David Potter and Lincoln's biographer, James G. Randall, adamantly disagreed. They not only absolved Lincoln of any duplicity but implausibly claimed that he expected the reprovisioning of Sumter to proceed peacefully. The modern synthesis, most fully defended in Richard N. Current, *Lincoln and the First Shot* (Philadelphia: J. P. Lippincott, 1963), but also shared by Kenneth Stampp, is that Lincoln's sending relief to Sumter was a calculated risk, with a Confederate attack being one possible outcome that Lincoln anticipated. Debating Lincoln's expectations is, in the final analysis, debating an imponderable, but this should not obscure the fundamental fact that Lincoln had already determined to employ military force to prevent Southern independence. It certainly strains credulity to suppose that such an astute politician did not realize that war would be a likely result.

Although many of the multi-volume histories of the Civil War provide some detail about the Baltimore riot against the 6th Massachusetts and Lincoln's holding Maryland in the Union, the best single-volume account is Dean Sprague's lively *Freedom Under Lincoln* (Boston: Houghton Mifflin, 1965), a work many Civil War historians do not like because of its searing judgment of Union policies. An older account that is excellent is the third volume of Thomas J. Scharf, *History of Maryland From the Earliest Period to the Present Day* (Baltimore: John B. Piet, 1879). I should also reference two articles: Charles B. Clark, "Suppression and Control in Maryland, 1861–1865: A Study of Federal State Relations During Civil Conflict," *Maryland Historical Magazine*, 54 (September 1959), pp. 241–271, and Richard R. Duncan, "The Era of the Civil War," in Richard Walsh and William Lloyd Fox, eds., *Maryland, A History: 1632–1974* (Baltimore: Maryland Historical Society, 1974). For the political battles leading up to Maryland's rejection of secession, see William J. Evitts, *A Matter of Allegiances: Maryland From 1850 to 1861* (Baltimore: Johns Hopkins University Press, 1974). Jean H. Baker, *The Politics of Continuity: Maryland Political Parties from 1858 to 1870* (Baltimore: Johns Hopkins University Press, 1973), is a pro-Union history of Maryland's wartime parties that denies the political significance of military occupation.

David M. Silver, *Lincoln's Supreme Court* (Urbana: University of Illinois Press, 1957), looks at the President's relationship with the judicial branch throughout the war. *Ex parte Merryman* appears in Civil War histories from many angles, and a good approach is through the works on wartime civil liberties, which we cover in chapter 10. But almost never brought up is Lincoln's warrant for the arrest of Chief Justice Taney. I have seen this mentioned in only two locations: Frederick S. Calhoun's official history, *The Lawmen: United States Marshals and Their Deputies*, rev. edn. (New York: Penguin Books, 1991), pp. 102–04; and Harold M. Hyman, *A More Perfect Union: The Impact of the Civil War and Reconstruction on the Constitution* (New York: Alfred A. Knopf, 1973), p. 84. Their sources are two independent manuscript collections, which lends credence to the claim's reliability, although I have personally examined neither collection.

On the border states generally, except Maryland and Delaware, Edward Conrad Smith, *The Borderland in the Civil War* (New York: Macmillan, 1927), starts with the 1860 election. The best overview of Missouri is William E. Parrish, *Turbulent Partnership: Missouri and the Union, 1861–1865* (Columbia: University of Missouri Press, 1963). Hans Christian Adamson, *Rebellion in Missouri: 1861, Nathaniel Lyon and His Army of the West* (Philadelphia: Chilton, 1961), is a journalistic defense of the Union military leader whose belligerent blundering "blew the lid off Missouri" (to borrow a phrase from James McPherson, *Ordeal by Fire*, p. 155). For a shocking portrait of the man, who more than any other deserves blame for the state's descent into chaos, see Christopher Phillips, *Damned Yankee: The Life of General Nathaniel Lyon* (Columbia: University of Missouri Press, 1990). A military history that recaptures all the horror and atrocities on both sides is Michael Fellman, *Inside War: The Guerrilla Conflict in Missouri During the American Civil War* (New York: Oxford University Press, 1989).

Because the guerrilla war also reached into Missouri's neighboring state on the west, Albert Castel, *Frontier State at War: Kansas, 1861–1865* (Ithaca, NY: Cornell University Press, 1958), is worth exploring, while Thomas Goodrich, *Bloody Dawn: The Story of the Lawrence Massacre*, (Kent, OH: Kent State University Press, 1991), is an account of Quantrill's raid into Kansas. Jay Monaghan, *Civil War on the Western Border, 1854–1865* (Boston: Little, Brown, 1955), covers the entire theater, starting with Bleeding Kansas.

Discussions of operations in the New Mexico and Arizona territories can be found in Alvin M. Josephy, Jr., *The Civil War in the American West* (New York: Random House, 1991), and Donald S. Frazier, *Blood & Treasure: Confederate Empire in the Southwest* (College Station: Texas A & M University Press, 1995). Laurence M. Hauptman, *Between Two Fires: American Indians in the Civil War* (New York: Free Press, 1995), takes selective looks at Indians who fought for both the North and the South. More particulars on the native Americans allied with the Confederacy are in Annie Heloise Abel's three volume, *The Slaveholding Indians* (Cleveland: Arthur H. Clark, 1919), whereas David A. Nichols, *Lincoln and the Indians: Civil War Policy and Politics* (Columbia: University of Missouri Press, 1978), scrutinizes the Union's Indian policy.

The most complete study of the war's impact on Lincoln's and Davis's state of birth is still E. Merton Coulter, *The Civil War and Readjustment in Kentucky* (Chapel Hill: University of North Carolina Press, 1926). Mary Scrugham, *The Peaceable Americans of 1860–1861: A Study in Public Opinion* (New York: Columbia University, 1921), looks at Kentucky's attempt at neutrality. Lowell H. Harrison, *The Civil War and Kentucky* (Lexington: University Press of Kentucky, 1975), is a brief discussion of military events. Two worthwhile works on the new state that seceded from seceding Virginia are George Ellis Moore, *A Banner in the Hills: West Virginia's Statehood* (New York: Appleton-Century-Crofts, 1963), and Richard Orr Curry, *A House Divided: A Study of Statehood Politics and the Copperhead Movement in West Virginia* (Pittsburgh: University of Pittsburgh Press, 1964).

Many historians have not been kind to General George Brinton McClellan, especially with respect to his military operations after his success in west Virginia. Yet he has attracted some favorably disposed biographers. See for instance Warren W. Hassler, Jr., *General George B. McClellan: Shield of the Union* (Baton Rouge: Louisiana State University Press, 1957). Stephen W. Sears's recent *George B. McClellan: The Young Napoleon* (New York: Ticknor & Fields, 1988) is more critical. Required reading is Joseph L. Harsh's balanced review essay, "On the McClellan-Go-Round," reprinted in John T. Hubbell, ed., *Battles Lost and Won: Essays From Civil War History* (Westport, CT: Greenwood Press, 1975). By focusing on McClellan's ideas, particularly his reticence regarding total war, Harsh renders more sensible many military decisions of this controversial Union commander and partially acquits him of the oft-repeated charges that his operations were invariably slow or that his enemy estimates were invariably exaggerated.

6

Mobilizing for Conflict

The Volunteer Militia

Unlike most European and Latin American governments, the United States did not maintain a peacetime standing army large enough to suppress domestic insurrection. Its forces were barely sufficient to garrison the American frontier. Mexico had a 32,000-man army at the outset of its war with the U.S. in 1846—more than four times larger. To wage that war, the United States government had of course expanded its military but, at the conclusion, had reduced its conquering force of nearly 50,000. The 16,000 regulars that remained were scattered across outposts mainly in the far west and some along the coast, when South Carolina seceded. More than a third of the regular army's officers were Southerners who soon resigned their commissions to follow their states. Consequently, both the Union and the Confederacy, as they vied for the allegiance of the border states, had to create military establishments of gargantuan proportions almost from scratch.

In both cases, the foundation for this unprecedented mobilization was the volunteer militia. Although state militias had always been the American alternative to large standing armies, these systems originally entailed the universal obligation of all males to defend their communities. After the War of 1812, however, the common militia came under sustained criticism. Radical Jacksonians condemned militia fines as falling unfairly upon laborers and the poor, while mandatory training increasingly bore the brunt of an effective campaign of ridicule and civil disobedience.

Abraham Lincoln, during a speech in Springfield, Illinois, back in 1852 before he became President, had recalled how the required "militia trainings" had been "laughed to death." At the head of the local militia parade, "on horse-back, figured our old friend Gordon Abrams, with a pine wood sword, about nine feet long, and a pasteboard cocked hat, from front to rear about the length of an ox yoke, and very much the shape of one turned bottom upwards; and with spurs having rowels as large as the bottom of a teacup, and shanks a foot and half long." Among the "rules and regulations" that Lincoln's militia unit adopted were: "no man is to wear more than five pounds of cod-fish for epaulets, or more than thirty yards of bologna sausages for a sash; and no two men are to dress alike, and if any two should dress alike the one that dresses most alike is to be fined." The unit even had militia flags, with mottoes such as "We'll fight till we run, and we'll run till we die." "That was the last militia muster here," wryly noted the Illinois rail-splitter.[1]

As a result of all these assaults, the compulsory features of the common militia had disappeared. Delaware was the first state to repeal some of its militia fines in 1816. Massachusetts abolished all compulsory militia service in 1840, followed by six other northern states within the next decade. In several states, the fines were no longer enforced or became nominal. The mandatory training days dropped in frequency and degenerated into more social than military events. Only in the South was compulsory militia duty kept on the books, probably because of its vital association with the slave patrols.

Concomitant with this decline in the state governments' common militia was a remarkable growth in the privately organized volunteer militia. The number of volunteer units had been expanding steadily since the American Revolution, but after the War of 1812, it exploded. Three hundred sprang up in California alone between 1849 and 1856. In the District of Columbia, one out of every twenty-nine people was a member of one or another volunteer company. With this burgeoning mass appeal, the volunteer

militia was no longer the preserve of a wealthy elite. As Russell
Weigley has noted in his masterly history of the U.S. Army, units
such as "the New England Guards of Boston, the 7th Regiment of
New York 'National Guards,' the First Troop of the Philadelphia City
Cavalry, the Light Infantry Blues of Richmond, [and] the Washington Artillery of New Orleans" became popular and colorful "fix-
tures of the American scene."[2] Even throughout the South, the
volunteer militia almost completely supplanted the common militia.

In short, the decades before the Civil War had witnessed a
dramatic transformation in the militia system, from compulsion to
voluntarism. Because of this transformation, the Mexican War
become the first in U.S. history to be fought exclusively with
volunteer enlistees. The national government had made no recourse to the militia drafts that had been so frequent during the
War of 1812 and the American Revolution.

This volunteer system left responsibility for organizing, recruit-
ing, and often equipping soldiers to state or local governments, or
even private citizens. The states had many troops already organized
before the firing on Fort Sumter, and once war was certain, local
officials or prominent citizens took the initiative to recruit many
more. Forged into units that were geographically based, the recruits
usually elected their own officers. The states, communities, private
donors, or recruits themselves provided uniforms, mounts, and
sometimes rifles or muskets as well. Especially favored by wealthier
companies was the gaudy Zouave uniform, copied from French
colonial troops in North Africa. Its impractical baggy trousers,
colorful sash, and outlandish red fez made it easily recognizable.
Yet the fact that the 6th Massachusetts, a fully armed regiment of
850 men, was en route to Washington within an astonishing forty-
eight hours of Lincoln's first call, with three more Massachusetts
regiments right behind, attests to the volunteer militia's readiness.

Lincoln's proclamation of April 15 called for 75,000 militia to
serve for three months. That was the longest term he could legally
institute without Congress. The President nonetheless delayed con-
vening an emergency session of the legislature until July 4, and on
his own authority ordered both the regular army and the navy
nearly tripled in strength and asked the states for 42,034 more

volunteers to serve for three years. When Congress finally met, it retroactively approved these measures and increased the authorized number of volunteers to 500,000. The Confederate Congress, meanwhile, had established a tiny regular army supplemented by a 100,000-man provisional army five weeks before it attacked Fort Sumter. After Lincoln's calls, it added 400,000 three-year volunteers.

The rush to fill these quotas in the North and South was overwhelming. Each central government got more volunteers than it requested. "The heather is on fire," wrote George Ticknor, who was teaching history at Harvard. "I never before knew what a popular excitement can be. Holiday enthusiasm I have seen often enough, and anxious crowds I remember during the war of 1812–15, but never anything like this."[3] An Arkansas youth exhibited similar emotions when he admitted that "so impatient did I become for starting, that I felt like ten thousand pins were pricking me in every part of the body, and started off a week in advance of my brothers."[4]

The Union had 235,000 men already under arms as Congress assembled. Its army had multiplied by a factor of fifteen despite defections. That sharply contrasts with the army's mere threefold growth, under a rigid system of conscription, during the four months at the beginning of U.S. entry into World War I. English novelist Anthony Trollope was quite correct in 1862 when he expressed "doubt whether any other nation ever made such an effort in so short a time."[5] The Confederacy did even better. With a white population only one-third that of the Union, it had mobilized forces numbering two-thirds as large. Indeed, the Confederate Secretary of War had to turn away as many as 200,000 volunteers because he could not arm, equip, or feed them. Military historians have endlessly denounced what they perceive as the volunteer militia's unpreparedness and disorganization, yet any objective, quantitative comparison shows Civil War mobilization, North and South, to have been one of the most rapid and effective ever.

The First Battle of Bull Run

Much of the initial enthusiasm stemmed from widespread confidence on both sides that the conflict would be short. Southerners often believed that Yankee "shopkeepers" would not fight at all. Ex-Senator Chesnut of South Carolina had boastfully offered to drink all the blood shed as a result of secession. Most Northerners had never taken the threats of secession seriously, and they were now convinced that the Confederacy would collapse after one good trouncing. The *New York Times* predicted after Sumter that the "treason" in the seceding states could be crushed within *"sixty days, if we will."*[6] This optimism produced a mounting clamor for an immediate advance on Richmond. *"Forward to Richmond! Forward to Richmond!"* screamed the pages of Greeley's *Tribune. "The Rebel Congress must not be allowed to meet there on the 20th of July!* BY THAT DATE THE PLACE MUST BE HELD BY THE NATIONAL ARMY!"[7]

Mobilizing an army was one thing, however; training it another. Although a large number of new military commanders had to come from civilian life on both sides, the Union ended up with a greater proportion of inexperienced political generals, because Lincoln employed military patronage to unify Democrats and other northern factions behind the war effort. Even among professional officers, West Point graduates, and Mexican War veterans, very few had ever commanded units as large as a brigade, which was composed of two or more regiments. The most notable exception, General-in-Chief Winfield Scott, was loyal but unable to take the field. In his seventy-fourth year, he suffered from dropsy and vertigo. Yet Civil War armies became so massive that they would combine brigades into divisions, divisions into corps, and occasionally corps into larger sub-units.

The President finally bowed to the popular pressure in mid-July and ordered the main Union army at Washington to advance. When this undisciplined force of 35,000, under General Irvin McDowell, encountered the Rebels at the meandering stream known as Bull Run, thirty-odd miles from the capital, utter confusion prevailed. The green units in both armies quickly became disorganized and intermingled, and the battle turned into a conglomeration of uncoordinated individual engagements. Soldiers fought randomly with different outfits for up to twelve hours. A bewildering array of colorful uniforms bedecked the field, with some blue and gray in both armies. This led to tragic mix-ups, as soldiers fired on friends or failed to fire on enemies until too late. The civilian spectators, both men and women, who had packed picnic lunches and driven carriages from Washington to observe the Confederate defeat only added to the confusion.

"It was three o'clock, and the soldiers had been engaged upon the march, or in action, during the long period of thirteen hours," reported one Massachusetts captain. "A large number, from various causes, had left their commands and escaped to the rear, or fought without regard to the rules of discipline." He witnessed troops acting "like all novices in the dreadful art of war," executing many "movements with great confusion." Moreover, "the hearts of [the] men" had not yet "by long experience become callous to the sight of human agony," including "the ghastly faces of the dead, and the sufferings of the wounded, who were begging for water, or imploring aid to be carried to the hospital."[8]

Equal confusion reigned on the Confederate side. The Richmond correspondent for the *Charleston Mercury* sent back one report from a spot where the line had been sagging under the Union assault. General Barnard Bee was attempting to rally his South Carolina brigade, "encouraging his troops by everything that was dear to them to stand up and repel the tide which threatened them with destruction." He then pointed out General Thomas J. Jackson's brigade of Virginians, shouting "there is Jackson standing like a stone wall." As Bee's own brigade heeded his commands to turn and advance, "he fell, mortally wounded." But Bee had unknowingly bequeathed an immortal nickname to "Stonewall" Jackson, and it quickly captured the public imagination throughout the South.[9]

Behind the battle's tactical chaos lurked some strategic clarity. The Confederates took advantage of what military theorists call "interior lines," which allowed them to concentrate dispersed forces at the critical place and time. Their army at Bull Run counted only 20,000 troops. When McDowell first attacked, he seemed to carry the day. But the Confederates had deployed another army 12,000 strong fifty miles to the northwest, in Virginia's Shenandoah Valley, commanded by General Joseph E.

Johnston, former Quartermaster General of the U.S. Army and the South's highest ranking officer. A superior Union force that had reoccupied Harper's Ferry on the upper Potomac had been observing this second Confederate army. But Johnston's troops managed to slip away from the Shenandoah Valley and travel rapidly by rail to Manassas Junction, just south of Bull Run.

It was a textbook maneuver upon which the Confederates would rely time and again throughout the war. Thrown into the battle, these Rebel reinforcements turned the tide. What had been a Union advance first became an orderly retreat and then degenerated into a complete rout. Fleeing soldiers mingled with civilians and wagons to clog the roads back to the District of Columbia. The nearly 500 Union dead and over 2,600 wounded and missing finally brought the war's reality home to the North. Lincoln beckoned General George B. McClellan, fresh from his campaign in West Virginia, to the capital to take command of the demoralized troops. The Confederate armies had also suffered heavily—nearly 400 dead and over 1,000 wounded—and were in no condition to follow up their victory. As both governments steeled themselves for a protracted struggle, major military activity on land ceased for the six months remaining in 1861.

The Naval War

The national government did possess a sizable peacetime navy at the beginning of 1861. Forty-two American warships were regularly patrolling stations near and distant. The navy could claim responsibility for such celebrated national exploits as Lieutenant Charles Wilkes's discovery of the Antarctic continent in 1840 and Commodore Matthew Perry's opening up of trade with Japan in 1854. Another forty-eight warships were laid up and could be rapidly put into commission, while federal mail subsidies to private steamship companies since the Mexican War provided vessels that could be converted to wartime use.

Most of these warships still relied upon wind for power. Although steampowered ships predated the War of 1812, not until the United States had launched the world's first propeller-driven man-of-war in 1843 did steam prove truly suitable for naval vessels. Even so, the logistical complications of heavy fuel consumption and the fact that there was no American coaling station beyond the country's shores dictated that the navy's growing number of steamships also carry sails. Southern politicians ironically had been behind appropriations for the eighteen most modern warships in the half-dozen years before the Civil War. They had envisaged these ships as supporting further national expansion into the potential slave territories of the Caribbean. Yet when secession came, the officers of the navy, in stark contrast to those of the regular army, remained predominately loyal.

The Confederacy therefore started out with a marked maritime inferiority. "At the inception of hostilities," Jefferson Davis himself noted, "we had no commercial marine, while their merchant vessels covered the ocean. We were without a navy, while they had powerful fleets."[10] Within a week of Fort Sumter's surrender, Lincoln proclaimed a blockade of Confederate ports. The southern states, however, had 3,500 miles of coastline with 189 harbors and coves where cargo could be landed. Despite unrestrained new construction and the purchase of many private vessels, the Union fleet was never sufficient to cover so much. The blockade only became effective as command of the seas allowed Union troops to take physical possession of the southern coast. Combined army-navy operations picked their targets with seeming impunity during the war's first year. A Union flotilla seized Port Royal and the South Carolina Sea Islands in November 1861. This gave the Atlantic blockading squadrons a much needed base. In February and March of 1862 another amphibious assault drove the Confederates from Roanoke Island and New Bern along the North Carolina coast. Fort Pulaski, commanding the port of Savannah, Georgia, fell to the Federals the following month. But the most spectacular naval expedition fell upon the Confederacy's largest city, New Orleans.

The commander of the New Orleans expedition was Flag Officer David Glasgow Farragut. This sixty-year-old Tennessean of Spanish-American lineage had first joined the navy at age nine and was a veteran of both the War of 1812 and the Mexican War. Now under his command were seventeen wooden warships carrying 210 guns, along with twenty mortar boats and 15,000 soldiers. Farragut faced formidable defenses. Seventy miles down the Mississippi from New

Orleans were two powerful forts on either side of the river. Connecting the two forts was a river barricade consisting of chains and ship hulks. Behind the barricade was a small Confederate collection of converted steamers.

Despite the stiff current against him, Farragut decided to run his fleet single file through a narrow gap in the barricade and past the forts. After he started out at 2:00 A.M. on the morning of April 24, the Rebels released burning rafts down the river, hoping to set the Union ships afire. "We were not discovered until we were well under the forts; then they opened a tremendous fire on us," recounted the letter of a young New Hampshire lieutenant, piloting Farragut's lead ship. "The air was filled with shells and explosions which almost blinded me as I stood on the forecastle trying to see my way, for I had never been up the river before." After making it past the forts, "our ship had received forty-two shots in masts and hull, and six of our men had been wounded; one of the boys had to have one of his legs cut off. All this time, night and day, firerafts and ships loaded with burning cotton had been coming down the river and surrounding us everywhere." When added to the firing from the forts, "the river and shore were one blaze, and the sounds and explosions were terrific. Nothing I could say would give you any idea of these last twenty-four hours!"[11]

An officer with the soldiers who accompanied the expedition gave an even more succinct description of running the forts. "Imagine all the earthquakes in the world," he told an inquiring lady, "and all the thunder and lightning storms together, in a space of two miles, all going off at once; that would be like it."[12] Yet by daybreak most of Farragut's warships were safely past the forts, while the Confederate gunboats were either sunk or captured. New Orleans capitulated within a few days, and Farragut received a promotion that made him the U.S. Navy's first rear admiral.

Unable to match the Union navy, the Confederates turned to technological innovations for harbor protection. They extensively utilized naval mines, which were then called "torpedoes." Sometimes small, quick boats carried these torpedoes at the end of long poles to the target. This could be suicidal for the personnel on the torpedo boat, but even riskier were Confederate experiments with underwater warfare. When the *C.S.S. Hunley* became the first submarine to sink an enemy ship in early 1864, it also took its own eight-man crew to the bottom. The Confederate Secretary of the Navy, Stephen R. Mallory, placed his greatest reliance upon armored vessels. Having served prior to the war as chairman of the Senate Naval Affairs Committee, he was well suited for his difficult post. Ironclad warships were not unknown, but Mallory pushed them with such vigor that by the end of the war the South had thirty-seven completed or under construction.

The first was the rebuilt *Merrimack,* a United States steam frigate that had fallen into Confederate hands along with the Norfolk navy yard. Rechristened the *Virginia,* she was fitted with four inches of iron plate to protect her ten-gun superstructure and carried a cast-iron ram on her prow. Less than a month after the loss of New Orleans, the transformed *Merrimack* surprised the blockading squadron off the Virginia coast near Norfolk. The Confederate ironclad, while suffering no harm herself, sunk two of the largest Union ships and ran three others aground by the end of her first day of action.

The Lincoln Administration had only belatedly recognized the danger posed by Confederate ironclads. It had finally contracted with a Swedish-born private inventor, John Ericsson, for armored steamships of a special design. Ericsson's first delivery, the *Monitor,* reached Norfolk the evening after the devastating unveiling of the *Virginia.* Possessing a revolving turret that mounted two guns, the *Monitor* was frequently described as resembling a "tin can on a shingle." The next day, when the *Virginia* returned to finish off the Federal squadron, she encountered this new nemesis.

Although the *Virginia* and *Monitor* were not the first armored ships, they staged the world's first battle between armored ships. The two battered each other at close range for three hours. "The *Monitor* was firing every seven or eight minutes, and nearly every shot struck," reported one officer aboard the *Virginia.* After more than two hours "we had made no impression on the enemy so far as we could discover, while our wounds were slight." Another officer aboard the Confederate ironclad ordered his section of guns to cease firing at the *Monitor,* observing "I can do her about as much damage by snapping my thumb at her every two minutes and a half."[13] The opposing ironclads soon broke off the indecisive duel. But the Union acquired an entire fleet of Monitors, effectively neutralizing Confederate armor.

Secretary Mallory also tried to weaken the blockade with attacks upon Union merchant ships on the high seas. He hoped this would divert the U.S. Navy to the protection of commerce. At first the Confederates engaged private ships to conduct these attacks. But the blockade made it increasingly difficult to bring maritime prizes profitably back to southern ports, whereas the European nations had recently signed a treaty that no longer sanctioned privateering. Thus as the war went into its second year, the task of commerce raiding shifted from privateers, which sold their captures, to government cruisers, which burned them.

The most successful of these cruisers, the *C.S.S. Alabama,* was launched from a British shipyard. Its commander was the legendary Raphael Semmes, one of the few former United States naval officers to fight for the Confederacy, and its crew was mostly English. Roving over the Atlantic, Indian, and Pacific oceans, the *Alabama* destroyed sixty-two Yankee merchantmen, valued at close to $7 million, and one warship. Not until mid-1864 could the Union navy corner and destroy the raider. By this time, Confederate cruisers had incapacitated the United States merchant marine by sending insurance rates through the roof. What remained of the North's international trade was carried on foreign vessels.

The Union navy, however, never eased up on the blockade and in December 1864 had amassed 671 vessels of all types manned by 68,000 sailors. Still, Federal forces failed to capture and close down the major Confederate ports of Wilmington, North Carolina; Charleston, South Carolina; and Mobile, Alabama, until the war's very end. Better than 90 percent of the vessels that ran the blockade had gotten through during 1861, while two-thirds were getting through three years later. These high figures admittedly do not take into account the many ships that gave up trying, nor the reduced tonnage of the swifter ships that did try. Doubtless the Union navy drastically impeded the Confederacy's overseas trade; nonetheless the blockade remained a leaky sieve that failed to contain resourceful blockade runners.

Early Confederate and Union Diplomacy

Major civil wars have tended to become international wars throughout history. Looking back wistfully to the French alliance during the American Revolution, the Confederate States counted upon eventual assistance from European governments. Southerners believed that France's and Britain's need for cotton imports would bring intervention. The South produced 60 percent of the world's crop by 1840, and half of that went to Britain. "What would happen if no cotton was furnished for three years?" James Henry Hammond of South Carolina had asked on the Senate floor, two years before Lincoln's election. "Old England would topple headlong and carry the whole civilized world with her," he boldly predicted. "No, sir, you dare not make war on cotton. No power on earth dares make war upon it. Cotton is king."[14]

King Cotton became the cornerstone of Confederate diplomacy. Southerners decided to embargo the crop until European nations granted recognition. The Confederate government did not directly enforce this policy, but only because President Davis did not wish to antagonize Britain and France needlessly. Voluntary compliance, local committees of public safety, and state governments policed the cotton embargo instead. This self-inflicted denial did more than the entire Union navy to halt Confederate exports. Southern cotton reaching Europe in the first year of the war dropped to about 1 percent of its peacetime level. Later, production was also cut, as the southern states strictly limited the amount of cotton that planters could grow. Output fell from 4.5 million bales in 1861 to 1.0 million bales in 1862.

The Davis Administration had acceded to the cotton embargo under pressure from radicals, who were emulating the American colonists' successful embargoes against the mother country prior to the Revolution and the Jeffersonian's much less successful peaceable coercion against Britain prior to the War of 1812. The embargo stick, however, was supposed to be coupled with the carrot of free-trade treaties. Most of the fire-eaters wished to see the southern economy reoriented toward Europe. Davis and the conservatives, in contrast, still looked upon the northern states as the Confederacy's natural trading partners. They therefore stalled any measures that might appear to give other nations preferential trading relations.

Britain was the neutral country that mattered most, and slavery was a key issue affecting its reaction. Lincoln, however, had made clear that the war was for the preservation of the Union only. He promised not to interfere with slavery in the states, and many Union commanders during the early campaigns returned runaways to their southern masters, in compliance with the Fugitive Slave Law. As a result, the foreign antislavery movement was reluctant to throw its weight behind the Union, and many Britons openly sympathized with the Confederacy. "The contest is really for empire on the side of the North," concluded the London *Times,* the most important paper reflecting this sympathy, "and for independence on that of the South, and in this respect we recognize an exact analogy between the North and the Government of George III., and the South and the Thirteen Revolted Provinces." The paper further claimed that "these opinions . . . are the general opinions of the English nation."[15]

The Lincoln Administration's official position was that the Confederacy did not legally exist. The United States was suppressing a purely internal rebellion, not waging a war against a legitimate government. But the realities of the fighting made this an increasingly difficult position to sustain consistently. The North, for instance, refrained from executing all prisoners-of-war as traitors. Although Lincoln had announced his intention to hang all Confederate privateers as pirates, he backed down in early 1862 after Jefferson Davis ordered Union prisoners to draw lots for retaliatory hangings. The ambiguity was epitomized in Lincoln's imposition of a blockade, a weapon of war against a sovereign power.

This ambiguity even reached the Supreme Court in 1863. Lincoln had imposed the blockade in April of 1861, but under the Constitution only Congress could declare war. Merchants whose vessels had been seized prior to Congress's recognizing the insurrection three months later sued in what were referred to as the *Prize* cases. Chief Justice Taney, ill yet clinging to life, had secretly written in advance half a dozen or so opinions striking down the President's usurpations. Generally the administration deftly prevented such cases from reaching the Court at all. The wisdom of this strategy was confirmed when the Court sustained the President in the *Prize* cases by only one vote. Three of the five justices in the majority were new Lincoln appointments, moreover, as the Chief Justice now found himself in the minority.

Because the blockade impinged upon commerce with Europe, Britain's Queen Victoria had immediately responded with a proclamation of neutrality, which granted the Confederacy the automatic status of a belligerent. Although falling short of full diplomatic recognition, this allowed Southerners to purchase supplies and contract loans abroad and to engage in naval warfare without being treated as pirates. The other European governments had followed with similar declarations. Secretary of State Seward was livid at this apparent Confederate coup. Months earlier, in a last ditch effort to avert the Fort Sumter crisis, he had entertained wild notions of reuniting the country by provoking a war with assorted European powers. Lincoln had ignored this suggestion, but it had leaked out to the foreign ministries. Seward's diplomacy would continue to be marked by truculence. European leaders remained acutely aware that a formal recognition of Southern independence would involve them in the conflict.

The Union blockade, meanwhile, raised age-old issues of neutral rights. International law required that a blockade must be effective in order to be binding. The mere "paper blockade" at the war's outset put the United states in blatant violation of the enlightened maritime principles that it had espoused during the War of 1812 and that the rest of the world had come to accept. Britain now became the aggrieved neutral, while Washington assumed the ancient and aggressive British stance. London, however, decided not to protest. The dominant naval power still, it might find this American precedent useful in the future. Her Majesty's government even acquiesced when the United States resurrected the old doctrine of "continuous voyage" to confiscate neutral vessels sailing between the West Indies and Europe with cargoes bound ultimately for the Confederacy. The Lincoln Administration went so far as to add a new twist to the "continuous voyage." It seized English ships that traded at the Mexican port of Matamoros under the pretext that they carried contraband that was destined for overland transfer to the southern states.

But one Union seizure that took place three and a half months after the battle of Bull Run caused Britain to draw the line. The British mail packet *Trent* had picked up in Havana, Cuba, two Confederate envoys, James Mason and John Slidell, who were bound for Europe. A Union warship in the area was under the command of Captain Wilkes, the same naval officer who had led the United States scientific expedition to Antarctica. Wilkes on his own authority stopped the *Trent* and seized Mason and Slidell. He then carried them to prison in Boston.

Northerners were ecstatic over Wilkes's display of initiative, but Britain prepared for war. Prime Minister Viscount Palmerston told a tense cabinet: "You may stand for this but damned if I will!"[16] Troops were ordered to Canada and naval reinforcements to American waters. "At present the excitement in England is truly terrific," was the first-hand impression that a secretary of the United States legation in London wrote in his personal diary. "By . . . asserting that Capt. Wilkes' act was an authorized and deliberate insult of our Gov't," he continued, "the journals have lashed the nation into a most indecent rage, and the consequence is that . . . the natural English hatred of the American people, which is ordinarily concealed, has been allowed to gush up in its full bitterness from all hearts, high and low. This polite and calm nation is in the throes of a vulgar and coarse excitement such as one might naturally look for among a crowd of the London Fancy. . . . That pink of modesty and refinement, *The Times*, is filled with such slatternly abuse of us and ours that it is fair to conclude that all the Fishwifes of Billingsgate have been transferred to Printing House Square to fill the ears of the writers there with their choicest phraseology. There is something positively infernal in the way these assassins are goading the nation on to war."[17]

After the delays of trans-Atlantic communication allowed passions to cool, Lincoln concluded that one war was enough for the moment. He ordered the Confederate envoys released on Christmas day, 1861. The British government accepted this in lieu of a formal apology. Although relations remained tense, the crisis was averted, and the Confederacy did not gain the diplomatic recognition it had so hopefully expected.

The South's cotton diplomacy had proved an expensive irrelevancy so far. The bumper crops of the prewar years had given

European textile mills ample stocks. Once the British began to feel the pinch, they developed alternate sources in Egypt and India. They furthermore were making handsome profits supplying both the Union and Confederacy with arms, ammunition, and sundry military equipment. Most important, European governments were not going to let the South's attempt at economic coercion override their own national interests. Events on American battlefields would be much more compelling.

Chapter 6
Bibliographical Essay

The only study of the Jacksonian era's militia reform movement, despite the reform's profound impact on the country's military, is one obscure journal article: Lena Londen, "The Militia Fine, 1830–1860," *Military Affairs*, 15 (Fall 1951), pp. 133–144. Paul T. Smith, "Militia in the United States from 1846 to 1860," *Indiana Magazine of History*, 15 (March 1919), pp. 20–47, recounts the legal changes at the state level but offers nothing on the movement's ideology or composition. Only tantalizingly suggestive is the voting analysis on militia reform that Herbert Ershkowitz and William G. Shade include in their 1971 *Journal of American History* article, "Consensus or Conflict? Political Behavior in the State Legislatures During the Jacksonian Era," reprinted in Edward Pessen, ed., *The Many-Faceted Jacksonian Era: New Interpretations* (Westport, CT: Greenwood Press, 1977). Susan G. Davis, "The Career of Colonel Puck: Folk Drama and Popular Protest in Early Nineteenth-Century Philadelphia," *Pennsylvania Magazine of History and Biography*, 109 (April 1985), pp. 179–202, is about instances where public ridicule enervated the compulsory militia. Robert F. McGraw provides one of the few complete descriptions of a single state's voluntary system in "Minutemen of '61: The Pre-Civil War Massachusetts Militia," from John T. Hubbell, ed., *Battles Lost and Won* (cited previous chapter).

There is not even a decent general history of the American militia. John K. Mahon, *History of the Militia and the National Guard* (New York: Macmillan, 1983), is not up to the standards of thoroughness set by its companion volumes in the "Macmillan Wars of the United States." Mahon's *The American Militia: Decade of Decision, 1789–1800* (Gainesville: University of Florida Press, 1960) is far superior and covers the birth of the volunteer units but cuts off early. William H. Riker, *Soldiers of the States: The Role of the National Guard in American Democracy* (Washington: Public Affairs Press, 1957), is brief and slights the volunteer militia. Jim Dan Hill, *The Minute Man in Peace and War: A History of the National Guard* (Harrisburg: Stackpole, 1964), is a narrative that devotes only one out of its twenty-one chapters to the pre-Civil War period.

The militia's dramatic transformation from compulsion to voluntarism best emerges from broader surveys of American military history. The most complete discussion can be found in Marcus Cunliffe's seminal investigation of antebellum military culture, *Soldiers and Civilians: The Martial Spirit in America, 1775–1865* (Boston: Little, Brown, 1968). But Russell F. Weigley's contribution to the "Macmillan Wars of the United States" series, *History of the United States Army*, enl. edn. (Bloomington: Indiana University Press, 1984), is unsurpassed in scope and authority. And a neglected but important journal article is William L. Shaw, "Conscription by the State through the Time of the Civil War," *Judge Advocate Journal*, no. 34 (October 1962), pp. 1–40.

Weigley is also excellent on Union mobilization. For years, this subject groaned under the professional militarism of Major General Emory Upton, a Union veteran, whose *The Military Policy of the United States* (Washington: Government Printing Office, 1917) was heavy-handed propaganda for a large, regular military. Upton's perspective infected both Fred Albert Shannon, *The Organization and Administration of the Union Army*, 2 v. (Cleveland: Arthur H. Clark, 1928), and A. Howard Meneely, *The War Department, 1861: A Study in Mobilization and Administration* (New York: Columbia University Press, 1928). It took a mathematician, Kenneth P. Williams, to finally correct this misleading impression in *Lincoln Finds a General: A Military Study of the Civil War* (New York: Macmillan, 1949–59), a work that the author never finished despite having written five full volumes before his death. Many mainstream military analysts retain their prejudices in favor of discipline, centralization, and large peacetime forces, but the Civil War gives them scant historical confirmation. I should hastily add, however, that Williams's spirited evaluations of the relative military merits of Lincoln, McClellan, and other Union commanders often differ from mine. Another fair treatment of Union mobilization is in the official U.S. Army study, Marvin A. Kreidberg and Merton G. Henry, *History of Military Mobilization in the United States, 1775–1945* (Washington: Department of the Army, 1955). John Niven, *Connecticut for the Union: The Role of the State in the Civil War* (New Haven: Yale University Press, 1965), is one of the few good studies of northern mobilization at the state level. Recruitment of the foreign born is explored in William L. Burton, *Melting Pot Soldiers: The Union's Ethnic Regiments* (Ames: Iowa State University Press, 1988).

There is almost nothing comparable on the creation of the Rebel army outside of the general Confederate histories mentioned in chapter 5; a biography of the first Confederate Secretary of War, William C. Harris, *Leroy Pope Walker: Confederate Secretary of War* (Tuscaloosa, AL: Confederate Publishing Company, 1962); and the discussion of state mobilization by May Spencer Ringold at the beginning of *The Role of the State Legislatures in the Confederacy* (Athens: University of Georgia Press, 1966). One recent work that illuminates an obscure corner of this topic is Richard P. Weinert, Jr., *The Confederate Regular Army* (Shippensburg, PA: White Maine, 1991).

William C. Davis, *Battle at Bull Run: A History of the First Major Campaign of the Civil War* (Baton Rouge: Louisiana State University Press, 1977), covers both sides of this early major engagement. The most detailed account of prior military operations in the area is R. H. Beatie, Jr., *Road to Manassas: The Growth of Union Command in the Eastern Theater From the Fall of Fort Sumter to the First Battle of Bull Run* ([New York]: Cooper Square, 1961). Before leaving the Union defeat at Bull Run, I also must call attention to a deserving work of fiction: William Safire, *Freedom: A Novel of Abraham Lincoln and the Civil War* (New York: Doubleday, 1987). Accompanied by an "Underbook" in which Safire meticulously separates fact from invention and cites his sources with commentary, this novel details Union policy-making from the Merryman Decision to the Emancipation Proclamation. What makes it noteworthy is Safire's unflinching willingness to pin blame for early Union reverses right where it belongs: on Abraham Lincoln.

The highest commander is assumed responsible under most circumstances for operations under his control. American Presidents can sometimes escape the full force of this dictum because they delegate military responsibilities to subordinates and then take a hands-off attitude except for major objectives and policies. Only Lincoln, of all wartime Presidents, interfered in day-to-day military matters. Yet by casting aspersions in every other direction and spinning out a string of excuses, apologists have managed to gain for him this utterly astounding and unwarranted reputation as a solid military leader. No matter what went wrong, it was never the President's fault. Lincoln emerges as a Commander-in-Chief uniquely blessed with inept subordinates and unlucky surprises.

The next chapter will set forth the Union's overwhelming military advantages at the war's outset, once the Confederacy had decided to fight a conventional war. Given Lincoln's temptation to micro-manage, the conclusion should be inescapable to those not blinded by hero worship. Without explicitly making the argument, Safire conveys better than most the extent to which Lincoln's military incompetence brought on not only the premature advance on Manassas but a whole string of military fiascoes in the east. The President failed to utilize properly the incredible military skills of Winfield Scott, arguably the greatest American general of all time; his vacillation and paranoia about the defense of Washington was a major reason for the Federal defeat on the Peninsula; he then put in command the patently unfit General John Pope, who brought about another Union disaster at Second Bull Run; he finally relieved General George McClellan in the midst of ongoing offensive operations just when McClellan had begun to show greater promise; and the general he shoved in as a replacement, Ambrose E. Burnside, severely doubted his own military capabilities, doubts that another defeat soon justified. Replacing a key subordinate five times within a year and a half, in one case just to switch back to someone previously thought undesirable, only to remove him again subsequently, normally does not earn high marks for management skills, and yet this is precisely what Lincoln did with the command of the main army in the east.

One of the reasons Northern generals in the west usually performed so much better is because they were too far away for Lincoln to foul things up. No commander is perfect, but Grant and Sherman, unlike McClellan, were given more leeway to learn from their costly errors. Indeed, as William L. Barney has recognized in *Flawed Victory: A New Perspective on the Civil War* (p. 17, cited prologue), "the Western theater that Lincoln felt had the greatest political importance, eastern Tennessee, with its predominately Unionist population," a region where "Lincoln devoted an inordinate amount of his attention," became "that portion of the Western front where the federal effort most often bogged down."

Harold and Margaret Sprout, *The Rise of American Naval Policy, 1776– 1918* (Princeton: Princeton University Press, 1946), an administrative and political history of the U.S. Navy, is still essential for putting the Civil War's naval operations in context. A more recent collection that covers the same ground, Kenneth J. Hagan, Jr., ed., *In Peace and War: Interpretations of American Naval History, 1775–1984*, 2nd edn. (Wesport, CT: Greenwood Press, 1984), contains not entirely satisfactory articles on the Union and Confederate navies. The fullest account is the three volumes of Virgil Carrington Jones, *The Civil War at Sea* (New York: Holt, Rinehart, Winston, 1960–62). Single volumes that cover the Civil War's naval aspects are Ivan Musicant, *Divided Water: The Naval History of the Civil War* (New York: HarperCollins, 1995); William M. Fowler, Jr., *Under Two Flags: The American Navy in the Civil War* (New York: W. W. Norton, 1990); Howard P. Nash, Jr., *A Naval History of the Civil War* (New York: A. S. Barnes, 1972); and Bern Anderson, *By Sea and by River: The Naval History of the Civil War* (New York: Alfred A. Knopf, 1962).

Rowena Reed, *Combined Operations During the Civil War* (Annapolis: Naval Institute Press, 1978), and James M. Merrill, *The Rebel Shore: The Story of Union Sea Power in the Civil War* (Boston: Little, Brown, 1957), are written from the Union perspective. The biography by Charles L. Lewis, *David Glasgow Farragut*, 2 v. (Annapolis, MD: United States Naval Institute, 1941–43), sheds considerable light not only on Farragut's capture of New Orleans but also on the United States Navy before the war. Chester G. Hearn, *The Capture of New Orleans, 1862* (Baton Rouge: Louisiana State University Press, 1995), is a fascinating, well-researched, new account.

How the Confederacy faced its naval challenge is told in Tom Henderson Wells, *The Confederate Navy: A Study in Organization* (University: University of Alabama Press, 1971). William N. Still, Jr., has investigated *Confederate Shipbuilding* (Athens: University of Georgia Press, 1969), as well as Confederate ironclads in *Iron Afloat: The Story of Confederate Armorclads* (Nashville: Vanderbilt University Press, 1971), while Milton F. Perry has treated other Confederate naval innovations in *Infernal Machines: The Story of Confederate Submarine and Mine Warfare* (Baton Rouge: Louisiana State University Press, 1965). Two economists, Robert B. Ekelund, Jr., and Mark Thornton, argue that misguided Confederate naval policies had very high opportunity costs in "The Confederate Blockade of the South," from Steven E. Woodworth, ed., *Leadership and Command in the American Civil War* (Campbell, CA: Savas-Woodbury, 1995).

William C. Davis, *Duel Between the First Ironclads*, 2nd edn. (Mechanicsburg, PA: Stackpole Books, 1994), is foremost among several books on the *Monitor* versus the *Virginia*. A detailed look at maintaining the Union blockade is Robert M. Browning, Jr., *From Cape Charles to Cape Fear: The North Atlantic Blockading Squadron During the Civil War* (Tuscaloosa: University of Alabama Press, 1993). Successful efforts to break through are recounted in Stephen R. Wise, *Lifeline of the Confederacy: Blockade Running During the War* (Columbia: University of South Carolina Press, 1988), and Hamilton Cochran, *Blockade Runners of the Confederacy* (Indianapolis: Bobbs-Merrill, 1958). William Morrison Robinson, Jr., *The Confederate Privateers* (New Haven: Yale University Press, 1928), is old but the only work on that subject, while Chester G. Hearn has written about the Rebel government's commerce raiders in *Gray Raiders of the Sea: How Eight Confederate Warships Destroyed the Union's High Seas Commerce* (Camden, ME: International Marine, 1992). Edward C. Boykin, *Ghost Ship of the Confederacy: The Story of the Alabama and Her Captain, Raphael Semmes* (New York: Funk & Wagnalls, 1957), treats the most famous of these raiders.

An Australian historian is responsible for one of the better surveys of Union and Confederate foreign policy: David P. Crook in *The North, the South, and the Powers, 1861–1865* (New York: John Wiley, 1974). But it should be supplemented with the recent and refreshing anthology: Robert E. May, ed., *The Union, the Confederacy, and the Atlantic Rim* (West Lafayette, IN: Purdue University Press, 1995). Hyman Harold, ed., *Heard Round the World: The Impact Abroad of the Civil War* (New York: Alfred A. Knopf, 1969), is a good collection on different countries and regions. An older account of Confederate diplomacy is Frank Lawrence Owsley, *King Cotton Diplomacy: Foreign Relations of the Confederate States of America*, 2nd edn. (Chicago: University of Chicago Press, 1959). For an economist's argument that the Confederacy's suicidal cotton embargo could have effectively exploited an OPEC-like monopoly in order to increase the South's monetary income, if only it had been more ruthlessly enforced, see Stanley Lebergott, "Why the South Lost: Commercial Purposes in the Confederacy, 1861–1865," *Journal of American History*, 70 (June 1983), pp. 58–74.

Early Union diplomacy is the subject of Norman B. Ferris, *Desperate Diplomacy, William Seward's Foreign Policy, 1861* (Knoxville: University of Tennessee Press, 1976). Stuart L. Bernath, *Squall Across the Atlantic: The American Civil War Prize Cases and Diplomacy* (Berkeley: University of California Press, 1970), assesses the international import of the Supreme Court decision relating to the blockade and the Union doctrine of continuous voyage. For the incident that brought the United States and Britain close to blows, see Gordon H. Warren, *Fountain of Discontent: The Trent Affair and Freedom of the Seas* (Boston: Northeastern University Press, 1981). The resulting impact on British naval operations can be found in Regis A. Courtemanche, *No Need of Glory: The British Navy in American Waters, 1860–1864* (Annapolis, MD: Naval Institute Press, 1977). Brian Jenkins, *Britain and the War for Union*, 2 v. (Montreal: McGill-Queen's University Press, 1974), treats British-American relations during the war more generally.

7

The Military Struggle

Confederate Strategy and the Eastern Theater

Was Confederate defeat inevitable? The Confederate States of America faced serious disadvantages in all the conventional measures of military power. Not counting the divided 3.2 million inhabitants of the four border states, the Confederate population was 9.1 million, compared to the Union's 19.1 million. Furthermore, more than one-third of this population consisted of slaves, who were presumably unavailable for military service. The South's economic disabilities were even greater. Per capita income was higher among Northerners, who owned three-quarters of the nation's material wealth. The output of northern industry was ten times that of the South. Indeed, the products manufactured in all eleven Confederate states combined amounted to less than one-fourth the total value manufactured in just New York state. The North had twice the railroad mileage and built fourteen out of every fifteen locomotives. These figures, coupled with Federal naval and maritime supremacy, make the Rebel cause seem hopeless.

Nevertheless, the Confederacy faced no more overwhelming odds than did the thirteen colonies at the beginning of the American Revolution. The South was a rugged and rural country, twice as expansive as the United States in 1776. Fighting a defensive war,

Southerners could count upon high morale, knowledge of the terrain, and interior lines. Military theorists generally agree that an attacking force needs a three-to-one numerical superiority to ensure victory on the battlefield, and a still greater superiority to pacify unfriendly territory.

All these factors led General Pierre G. T. Beauregard, Confederate commander at Fort Sumter and Bull Run, to conclude that "no people ever warred for independence with more relative advantages."[1] George Wythe Randolph, a leading Virginia secessionist who would serve as Confederate Secretary of War for eight months during 1862, reassured his niece in the fall of 1861: "There is no instance in history of a people as numerous as we are inhabiting a country so extensive as ours being subjected if true to themselves."[2] Many foreign observers agreed with Southerners about the Confederacy's ultimate triumph. The London *Times* of July 18, 1861, emphasized that "it is one thing to drive the 'rebels' from the south bank of the Potomac, or even to occupy Richmond, but another to reduce and hold in permanent subjection a tract of country nearly as large as Russia in Europe . . . We have never questioned the superiority of the North for purposes of warfare," the *Times* went on, "but no war of independence ever terminated unsuccessfully, except where the disparity of force was far greater than it is in this case."[3]

A lot hinged, however, on the type of defense the Confederacy mustered. The intervening years had done much to obscure or discredit the creative military expedients dating from America's revolution and to channel thinking, North and South, toward more conventional strategies. The highest ranks of the Rebel military were dominated by former United States officers with West Point training. Their most practical combat experience had been gained in offensive operations against Mexico. President Jefferson Davis himself was a graduate of the U.S. Military Academy who had led a Mississippi regiment during the Mexican-American War and served as Secretary of War under President Pierce. In fifty-five of the Civil War's sixty biggest battles, the commanders on both sides would be West Pointers.

Not all Southerners found this apparent asset a blessing. The Academy aspired to European standards of military professionalism, which some doubted were suitable to the character or cause of the southern rank and file. Robert Toombs, who left his Cabinet post of Secretary of State in July, 1861, to become one of the Confederacy's political generals, complained in a letter to Vice-President Alexander Stephens as early as September of the same year about the Old Army dominance he ran up against all around him. "The army is dying," he warned. Not "the poor fellows who go under the soil," but "the army as an army." The reason? "Set this down in your book, and set down opposite to it its epitaph, *'died of West Point'*."[4]

The Confederate high command never entertained any thoughts of conducting the kind of war for national liberation that Americans had fought during their Revolution and that has become common-place in the modern world. Such a strategy would have entailed leaving the bulk of southern manpower scattered about in guerrilla units. Although much of the South would have remained exposed to invasion, Union willpower would have been patiently worn down through insurmountable logistical obstacles, continual hit and run harassment, and the countryside's implacable hostility. The dispersed Rebel forces would have constituted a huge reservoir, available for concentration only when they could inflict decisive blows.

Vice-President Stephens, also skeptical of what he derided as "the West Point policy," hinted at just such an alternative strategy when he argued that the Confederacy's leaders should "husband our resources" by letting the enemy get "into the midst of our territory and then meeting him with *concentrated* forces."[5] "I looked for the invasion of our country," he admitted in a letter of November 1861. "The superior numbers of the enemy made this almost certain. But invasions, while they do great harm, destroy vast amounts of property, and cause a vast deal of suffering, do but little toward conquering a people who are determined never to submit."[6] After the war was over, the Confederate Vice-President explained that such a defensive policy would have kept "the people alive to the real cause, and zealous in its maintenance."[7]

But Stephens was virtually alone in his recommendations. Instead the Confederacy massed armies along all its borders in an effort to protect every inch of ground. Irregular warfare was not merely alien to the social background and professional training of the Southern officer corps. The conservatives who had gained control of the Confederate central government wished to establish a legitimate nation-state, not unleash a remorseless revolution. Perhaps fears about the South's control over its slaves made the choice of a conventional military strategy inevitable. Whatever the reason, the Confederacy condemned itself to waging a war on the Union's terms, in the realm where the Union had overwhelming predominance.

This Napoleonic focus of Southern strategy was most evident in Virginia. The Confederacy's northern border stretched all the way from the Atlantic Ocean to the Great Plains, but the rugged Appalachians divided this long frontier into two distinct, major theaters. Bounded by mountains on one side and the Chesapeake Bay on the other, the eastern theater constituted a corridor running between Richmond and Washington. It was fated to become the site of the war's most celebrated engagements. Only as far back as the War of 1812, the United States had been so decentralized that a humiliating loss of the nation's capital to the invading British had been of little military significance. But during the Civil War, both Southerners and Northerners viewed their two capitals as *the* major objectives.

The Confederates enjoyed astonishing success within this narrow corridor. General George B. McClellan took a full eight months after the Union defeat at Bull Run to organize and train the 120,000 troops in the Army of the Potomac at Washington. When he finally got moving, instead of driving south toward Richmond, as General McDowell had attempted before him, he took advantage of Union naval superiority to ferry his army down the Potomac River and the Chesapeake Bay to Fortress Monroe on the Virginia coast. From there the Federal forces methodically approached Richmond from the southeast. By the end of May 1861, McClellan had reached the very outskirts of the Confederate capital, closer than any Northern general for another two years. But here he was abruptly checked by the gifted military team of Robert E. Lee and Stonewall Jackson.

The fifty-five-year-old Lee was the scion of an aristocratic Virginia family, a former superintendent of the United States Military

Academy, and a protégé of General-in-Chief Winfield Scott. Lincoln had offered this exemplary career officer command of the Union army in the field at the war's outset, but Colonel Lee preferred to fight for his beloved home state, notwithstanding a dislike for secession. Appointed a Confederate general, he had been languishing as President Davis's top military advisor until given command on June 1st of what he soon designated the Army of Northern Virginia, replacing General Joseph E. Johnston, who had been wounded in battle.

The already famous Jackson, a stern, Old-Testament Presbyterian, became Lee's indomitable subordinate. Initially detached off to the northwest in Virginia's Shenandoah Valley, General Jackson there had outmaneuvered and outfought three independent Union commands. The Valley campaign of Stonewall's "foot cavalry," as his fast-marching infantry became known, spread such alarm about the safety of Washington that Lincoln deprived McClellan of promised reinforcements. Jackson, in contrast, quickly joined up with Lee near Richmond. Although the combined Confederate army was still far smaller than the Federal horde, Lee attacked savagely in a series of sharp engagements lasting a week. At the end of what would become known as the Seven Days' battles, McClellan was in full retreat back to a base of operations on the James River, protected by Federal gunboats. One month later, Lincoln ordered McClellan's troops to re-embark for a return voyage to Washington.

It was a dazzling performance, which Lee and Jackson, although constantly outnumbered, would repeat against a succession of Union commanders. General John Pope was defeated at the second battle of Bull Run in August 1862; General Ambrose Burnside at the battle of Fredericksburg in December 1862; and General Joseph Hooker at the battle of Chancellorsville in May 1863. Not only did Lee keep Federal troops away from Richmond, he was able to mount two brief invasions of Northern territory: the first into Maryland during the autumn of 1862 and the second into Pennsylvania in the summer of 1863.

The architect of these local successes was a model southern gentleman who inspired near reverence in his officers and men. His powerfully-built, white-bearded, dignified frame, poised gracefully atop his gray stallion, Traveller, cut an almost perfect soldierly pose. Devout, humble, and reserved, General Lee became renowned for his courtesy and tact, especially with subordinates. But his aggressive military maneuvers involved breathtaking risks. Strategically on the defensive, the commander of the Army of Northern Virginia consistently strove to assume the tactical offense in battle.

Lee was convinced that this "offensive defense," as President Davis styled it, would enable the Confederacy to recover any territory lost temporarily to the enemy. "It is as impossible for him to have a large operating army at every assailable point in our territory as it is for us to keep one to defend it," the Confederate commander once explained. "We must move our troops from point to point as required, & by close observation and accurate information the true point of attack can generally be ascertained. . . . Partial encroachments of the enemy we must expect, but they can always be recovered, and any defeat of their large army will reinstate everything."[8] In other words, Davis and Lee were relying not simply upon a conventional defense of the new nation's vast boundaries but upon a conventional defense so geographically inflexible that it required immediate counterstrokes to prevent any prolonged Yankee incursions.

Default to Unconventional Warfare in the Western Theater

Unfortunately for the Confederacy, its orthodox strategy did not serve so well in the military theater west of the Appalachian Mountains. First off, it induced the political blunder of violating Kentucky's neutrality in order to seize defensible terrain along the Ohio River. Afterwards Southern forces were still spread too thinly across a 600-mile perimeter, which the Union breached at several points in early 1862, well before McClellan started his Richmond campaign.

The western theater not only was far wider than the eastern theater but also was transected by the Mississippi River and its tributaries, which all ran generally north-south (except for the Ohio). These provided the Union with convenient avenues of advance, as naval control over navigable rivers opened up the

Confederate west in the same way that command of the seas had made the entire southern coast vulnerable. Thus, the most irretrievable rupture of the Confederate perimeter was made at Fort Donelson on the Cumberland River by a Northern army and gunboat flotilla collaborating under General Ulysses S. Grant.

Grant was an undistinguished West Pointer who had abandoned the regular army, despite demonstrating cool-headed courage during the Mexican War. Exaggerated but not entirely unfounded rumors about his drinking clouded his early military career. This Ohio native had not been particularly successful at assorted civilian trades either. The outbreak of the war had gained Grant a new commission with the Illinois volunteers just as he turned forty, but he was still outranked by many other Union generals in the west at the time he invested Fort Donelson. A persistent campaigner, this quiet, slight man did not put much store in military formalities. "The art of war is simple enough," he once claimed. "Find out where your enemy is, get at him as soon as you can, and strike him as hard as you can, and keep moving on."[9] When the commander of the surrounded Confederate garrison requested terms of surrender, Grant sent back a curt reply: "No terms except unconditional and immediate surrender can be accepted. I propose to move immediately upon your works."[10] The reply inspired the popular nickname of "Unconditional Surrender" for U.S. Grant's first two initials and set the tone for his future operations.

While Grant proceeded inexorably south along the Tennessee River, the Confederates resorted again to their railroads and interior lines. They gathered a force of 45,000 from throughout the west in April 1862 for a surprise attack. Striking Grant's army at Shiloh Church, the Rebel soldiers nearly drove their foes into the river on the battle's first day. But reinforced, Union troops recovered all their lost ground on the second day. The more than 20,000 casualties from both sides made the battle of Shiloh the war's bloodiest so far. A subsequent Confederate invasion of eastern Kentucky, timed to coincide with Lee's fall invasion of Maryland, culminated in an inconclusive engagement at Perryville and was no more successful at easing the Federals out of Southern territory.

Yet the Union offensive in the west, after overrunning much of the state of Tennessee, soon bogged down seemingly of its own accord. Rebel forces, unable to pull off successful counter-offensives, spontaneously defaulted to unconventional alternatives with astonishing success. The water invasion routes, except for the giant Mississippi, had reached their natural limits. Further Federal advances would depend upon rail transport for supplies. Although a vast improvement over the wagon ruts and frontier trails that had ensnarled British campaigns in North America during the Revolution and War of 1812, railways could be easily interdicted.

One historian, William L. Barney, has aptly characterized the Civil War army as "a cumbersome amalgam of men, horses, and equipment."[11] Like a city, it needed continual provisions from the outside. The Union Quartermaster's Department estimated that a force of 40,000 men with its 18,000 horses required 250 tons of supplies per day. Northern armies in the field were therefore weighted down with long supply columns composed of between 25 and 35 wagons for each thousand soldiers. Even so, the armies could rarely stray far from their bases located either at railheads or water landings.

An ordinary western steamboat, in contrast, could carry 500 tons alone. This made rivers more logistically robust than railroads. "We are much obliged to the Tennessee," noted one of Grant's division commanders, William Tecumseh Sherman, "for I am never easy with a railroad which takes a whole army to guard, each foot of rail being essential to the whole; whereas they can't stop the Tennessee, and each boat can make its own game."[12]

The Rebel ability to exploit Federal dependence upon railroads was illustrated by Grant's first attempt in December of 1862 to capture Vicksburg, a southern stronghold on the east bank of the lower Mississippi River. An impenetrable maze of swamps and bayous made Vicksburg virtually unassailable down river. So Grant, who had 75,000 soldiers at his disposal, decided to make his main thrust overland. He had not gone far when a Confederate force of no more than 3,500 cavalry—less than a twentieth the size of Grant's columns—swept around him and destroyed his main supply depot at Holly Springs in northern Mississippi. The Rebels even captured Mrs. Grant's horses and burned her carriage.

Another 2,000 Rebel cavalry raided even farther to Grant's rear. Their commander, Nathan Bedford Forrest, was a millionaire slave trader who had enlisted at the age of forty as a private. He rapidly rose to become one of the most innovative Southern generals. Forrest distilled complex military principles down to a single sentence that is still often quoted: "Get there first with the most." His raid demolished sixty miles of railroad and killed, wounded, or captured more than 2,000 garrison troops, while losing fewer than 500 men. Utterly helpless, Grant simply had to give up and turn back, without his main force having seen action at all.

Nearly a year later, Grant was still unable to keep all the railroads open in the area. His memoirs recalled the difficulty of moving the Union army to eastern Tennessee for a new campaign: "Sherman had started from Memphis. . . . His instructions required him to repair the road in his rear in order to bring up supplies. The distance was about 330 miles through a hostile country. His entire command could not have maintained the road if it had been completed. The bridges had all been destroyed by the enemy, and much other damage done. A hostile community lived along the road; guerrilla bands infested the country, and more or less of the cavalry of the enemy was still in the West. Often Sherman's work was destroyed as soon as completed, and he only a short distance away."[13]

The Union commanders not only had to guard railroad lines, they also had to administer conquered territory. The western gains of early 1862 had brought the total area requiring Northern occupation up to the size of France. Already, several hundred guerrillas in Missouri were tying down tens of thousands of federal troops, in a state where the Rebels could not even command the people's unanimous loyalty. For a later try at Vicksburg in early 1863, Grant took 36,000 soldiers down the Mississippi, while leaving behind almost twice as many to protect his rear. If these are added to all the other Union garrisons—holding Missouri, guarding the Baltimore and Ohio Railroad through West Virginia, or securing Washington—their number approaches 200,000. Overall, the North dissipated between one-third and one-half its military manpower on unglamorous but essential tasks away from the front lines.

In other words, the failure of the Confederacy's conventional defense west of the Appalachian Mountains inadvertently led to irregular warfare. No one was more acutely conscious of this

strategic transition than Sherman. "The South has united people
and as many men as she can arm," he noted in frustration. "Every
house is a nest of secret, bitter enemies." Union armies could freely
"pass across and through the land," but "the war closes in behind
and leaves the same enemy behind. We attempt to occupy places,
and people rise up and make the detachments prisoners."[14]

The reversion to unconventional war, whether through the
unsanctioned partisan bands led by such men as William Quantrill
or through formal cavalry raids conducted by such officers as
General Bedford Forrest, brought a resurgence in Confederate
prospects. By the middle of 1862, the Federal offensive had ground
to a halt in the west as well as in the east. "I don't see the end or the
beginning of the end," Sherman lamented.[15] Guerrilla warfare
would remain, however, nothing but a last, unpleasant resort for the
South's West Point-dominated command, to be discarded whenever
resources permitted. As a result, any gains from this effective
strategy were fatally eroded by the stunning impact of new military
technology.

The Devastating Impact of the Rifle

The Civil War was a war of technological innovations. On water, it
introduced, in addition to steam and armor, more powerful and
longer range naval guns. On land, the railroad and telegraph saw
their first extensive military use. But the most revolutionary innovation was the Minie ball, a newly invented bullet. It transformed the
rifle into a serviceable replacement for the smoothbore musket.
The earliest rifles had actually predated the American Revolution,
but until the Minie ball's development, only the smoothbore musket
had been able to bear the full brunt of battle.

The difference between the two infantry arms was the spiral
grooves, or rifling, inside the rifle's bore. Imparting a spin to the
discharged bullet, these grooves gave the rifle more accuracy. The
musket's effective range was only 80 yards (on a still day). Grant
recalled from his duty during the Mexican War that "at a distance of
a few hundred yards a man might fire at you" with a musket "all day
without your finding it out."[16] The effective range of the rifle was at
least 400 yards, five times as great. One gratified New Hampshire

private in a letter to his parents attested to the new weapon's accuracy at even greater distances. "We have not got the Enfield rifles but the Springfield. They are just as good and a good deal lighter. We went out the other day to try them. We fired 600 yards, and we put 360 balls into a mark the size of old Jeff [Davis]."[17]

The problem had been that rifle models before the 1850s took far too long to load. They were therefore only suitable for small or elite units with special missions. The Minie ball changed all that. The new bullet was still inserted at the muzzle and rammed down the barrel, one shot at a time. Nonetheless, a competent infantryman could load and fire two or three Minie balls a minute, slightly better than what was possible with the old muskets. Although breach-loading and repeating rifles also made their appearance during the Civil War, being issued to some Union cavalry units, questions about reliability along with logistical concerns about heavy ammunition consumption prevented their widespread introduction. Single-shot muzzle loaders, therefore, persisted as the staple armament of both sides.

The weapons stored in United States arsenals when the southern states seceded were mostly smoothbores; the national government had barely enough rifles for the regular army. The volunteer regiments of both the North and South consequently carried muskets in such early battles as First Bull Run. The Federal War Department, however, acquired rifles as rapidly as possible. Some were manufactured at the government armory in Springfield, Massachusetts, some were bought from private American firms, and some were purchased abroad. The Confederacy lagged only slightly behind. Its far smaller domestic output was offset by the capture of several hundred thousand Union rifles through the course of the conflict, often scavenged right off the battlefield. By the second year of fighting, most infantrymen on both sides had these modern shoulder arms.

The new bullet's impact on battlefield tactics was immense. With the old, smoothbore musket, the troops needed to stand elbow-to-elbow in rigid formations in order to mass their firepower. Because they still had time to get off only a few volleys before the enemy closed, the shock of a bayonet charge might decide the issue.

With the rifle, infantry formations could be loosened up. Men now could take advantage of the terrain by firing from behind trees or other obstacles. Individual skirmishers were sent out in front of the main body to prevent surprise and break up the enemy's formations.

The bayonet became almost useless, as the rifle's enhanced range inflicted terrible casualties long before the opposing lines physically met. Out of about 245,000 wounds treated by surgeons in Federal hospitals, fewer than 1,000 were from bayonets or sabers.[18] One northern surgeon reported that he "never saw a bayonet wound; . . . there were probably as many men severely kicked by mules!"[19] The offensive power of artillery and cavalry also declined. Field artillery, organized into batteries of four to six guns, with caissons carrying ammunition and horses providing mobility, could shoot farther than rifles but was not yet very lethal at these long distances. Only when near enough to fire grapeshot and canister— rounds which spewed forth a shower of small projectiles as if from a giant shotgun—could the guns tear an advancing infantry line to shreds. But because riflemen could now pick off the gunners outside the range of grape and canister, artillery batteries utilized these rounds best on the defensive, usually with their own infantry in support. Mounted cavalry meanwhile was relegated mostly to scouting and raiding.

The Minie ball helped the citizen soldiers of the Union and Confederacy to rank among the most proficient killers the world has known. During the Mexican War, a unit had suffered severely in action if its casualty rate was over 10 percent. The same would prove true during World War II, when battlefield tactics had once again caught up with the enhanced lethality of new technology. But during the Civil War, a unit that had any fewer than 10 percent killed and wounded was not considered to have been seriously engaged at all. Twenty-five to fifty percent was common, and sometimes the casualties soared higher.[20]

The 1st Minnesota at the battle of Gettysburg seems to have set some kind of wartime record for Northern regiments. On the battle's second day, the 1st Minnesota had just arrived on the field as the Union left wing was dissolving. General Winfield S. Hancock rode up and desperately ordered the regiment to stop an advancing

Confederate line. Although the men had been assigned the daunting task of engaging an entire enemy brigade, they did not hesitate. Their charge broke the Rebel attack, but as one of the regiment's lieutenants recounted, "at what sacrifice. Nearly every officer lay dead or wounded upon the ground. . . . Of the two hundred and sixty-two men who made the charge," eighty-four remained in line. After only fifteen minutes under fire, 68 percent of the 1st Minnesota had fallen.[21]

One North Carolina regiment, the 26th, started the same battle with eight hundred men. It was already down to two hundred by the end of the first day's fighting. Nevertheless, the 26th North Carolina was among the forty-seven regiments participating in Pickett's doomed charge on Gettysburg's third day. Only ninety members of the 26th returned. Total losses for the entire battle were 86 killed, 502 wounded, and 120 captured or missing, for a casualty record of 88 percent.[22]

It is difficult to imagine what could have induced Billy Yank or Johnny Reb to brave such risks. No doubt one major factor was the local, voluntary basis for organizing both armies. The fact that men fight more bravely for each other than for some abstraction has now become a commonplace among military theorists. The companies that made up Civil War regiments were bound together by ties of community and sometimes kinship, which were only strengthened as they carried the same personnel from battle to battle. No modern bureaucracy callously transferred men in and out, ticket punching them through some idealized career path, and disrupting the unit's hometown cohesion in the process.

Of course, major battles did not occur every day. Rather than the sustained combat of more recent wars, armies would go through months of either inactivity or marching and countermarching. One undocumented estimate is that Civil War soldiers spent an average of fifty days in camp for every day in battle. Moreover, while the Civil War brought modern methods of killing, it conformed in many ways to a traditional code of personal honor. Officers still led from the front, urging on their men through a courageous willingness to share the same danger. As a result, the battle's carnage extended all the way up the ranks. More than half of the Confederacy's generals were wounded or killed. Many had been wounded once, twice, or even more times in prior battles. One such fatality was Stonewall Jackson, who was accidentally shot by his own men as he returned from nighttime reconnaissance at the battle of Chancellorsville.

Despite enormous losses, Civil War battles were almost never conclusive. The only way to destroy enemy forces was by attacking, but attacking is almost always more costly than defending. The Minie ball thus could make victory as debilitating as defeat. The beaten army, still intact, merely withdrew to fight another day. As the war lengthened, defending soldiers increasingly would dig entrenchments and build breastworks for protection. And these made assaults still more murderous.

One captain, Henry Dwight, serving with an Ohio regiment in Sherman's army, described what making such an attack was like: "One reads in the papers of the assaults on earth-works, of the repulses, and yet one does not know what is contained in those words. . . . You make up your mind to assault the enemy's works. You have formed a line of battle, with a second and third line behind you for support. You march forth filled with the determination to accomplish the object. . . . Two hundred yards brings you to the picket-line, and here the opposition commences. You dash across the space between the two lines, you lose a few men; and the enemy's pickets, after making as much noise as possible, run back to their main works. By this time the enemy are sure you are really coming, and open on you with artillery, besides a pretty heavy fire of musketry. . . . You commence to lose men rapidly. . . . 'Forward, double-quick!' . . . and while the whole line of the enemy open fire from behind their works, your men, mindless of . . . the death intensified, the bullets and the shells, they dash on with wild cheers."

After the adrenaline of starting the assault came its reality. The attackers must navigate the first defensive obstacle, a barricade of felled trees, called an abatis: "The abatis with its tangled intricacy of sharpened branches snares your line. . . . [T]he firing grows more fierce, the men grow more desperate. Your three lines have been almost reduced to one. . . . You stumble, fall, tear your flesh on these stakes, and must stop to pull them up—stop, when every instant is an hour—stop, when you are already gasping for breath; and here open the masked batteries, pouring the canister into that writhing, struggling, bleeding mass—so close that the flame scorches, that the smoke blinds. . . . Is it any wonder that your three lines are torn to pieces, and have to give back before the redoubled fire of an enemy as yet uninjured comparatively? And then the slaughter of a retreat *there!*" Captain Dwight had bitterly concluded by 1864 "that earth-works can be rendered nearly impregnable . . . against direct assault." Consequently, frontal attacks were now almost futile. "An assault means . . . a slaughter-pen, a charnel-house, and an army of weeping mothers and sisters at home. It is inevitable."[23]

The death toll steadily mounted for both sides, but it imposed more heavily upon the South's smaller population. General Lee's relentless but unavailing quest for a conclusive victory that would "reinstate everything," although successful in the short term, bled the South of manpower. He saved Richmond with his audacious defeat of McClellan during the Seven Days' battles. But he had lost 20,000 men in the process, twice McClellan's loss. After Lee's first four months in command, his Army of Northern Virginia had suffered 47,000 casualties, more soldiers than usually served with the Confederacy's Army of Tennessee in the west.

General Daniel H. Hill could not erase the vivid memory of one assault his division made against federal positions on Malvern Hill during the last of the Seven Days' battles. "I never saw anything more grandly heroic than the advance after sunset of the nine brigades." Unlike so many other of Lee's assaults, this one had failed. "As each brigade emerged from the woods, from fifty to one hundred guns opened upon it, tearing great gaps in its ranks; but the heroes reeled on and were shot down by the reserves at the guns, which a few squads reached. . . . It was not war—it was murder."[24]

These irreplaceable lives were the long-term cost of the Confederacy's offensive defense. Nonetheless, this conventional strategy prevailed within Rebel councils in the west, even after the emergence of irregular warfare had handed out a military stalemate. Southern commanders there tried to emulate Lee throughout 1862 and 1863 by throwing the Army of Tennessee and other concentrations against frequently larger Federal forces. The same pattern repeated itself at Corinth in October 1862, at Perryville the same month, at Stone's River in December 1862, at Chickamauga in September 1863, at Knoxville in November 1863, and still later, around Atlanta in July 1864 and at Franklin in November 1864. Although occasionally bringing tactical victories, these battles never offered any strategic rewards comparable to their expensive losses.

Long after the war ended, General Hill had reluctantly come to this realization. "We were lavish of blood in those days, and it was thought to be a great thing to charge a battery of artillery or an earth-work lined with infantry. . . . The attacks on the Beaver Dam intrenchments, on the heights of Malvern Hill, at Gettysburg, etc., were all grand, but of exactly the kind of grandeur which the South could not afford."[25]

The Toll of Disease

Many deaths had no grandeur at all. Just as in previous wars, disease—not enemy fire—was the primary killer. While 140,000 Union soldiers perished as a result of battle, more than 220,000 died from disease. The same grim two-to-one ratio prevailed in Confederate forces as well. Every concentration of green troops first endured outbreaks of childhood maladies, chiefly measles and mumps. Rural recruits, particularly from the west, had never been exposed to these ailments. No sooner did soldiers develop immunities to this first wave of diseases then a second wave swept through the armies. Including dysentery, typhoid, and malaria, these more lethal illnesses would increasingly bedevil encampments because their underlying causes could neither be eliminated nor, often, ascertained, given the medical knowledge and techniques of the day. As Charles Francis Adams, Jr. remarked, a Civil War military camp was "a city without sewerage, and policing only makes piles of offal to be buried or burned."[26] Bad food, impure water, poor sanitation, exposure to inhospitable climates, and swarms of mosquitoes were unavoidable with so many crowded together.

Even if disease did not kill outright, it put large numbers on the sick list. The 64th and 65th Ohio regiments, for instance, entered national service in the fall of 1861 with a full complement of nine hundred men each. Within less than a year, before seeing any action, both regiments had been reduced almost to half strength. About one hundred in each regiment had died from illness; three hundred more were sick or discharged as unfit. And these figures are merely typical. An extraordinary epidemic could debilitate an entire army. In June 1862, six months prior to Grant's first stab at Vicksburg from the north, Admiral Farragut tried to seize the city by bringing his fleet and 3,200 troops up river from New Orleans. But malaria raised the proportion of incapacitated soldiers and sailors to upwards of two-thirds the Federal force, and he had to abandon the attempt.

Sickness added to the burden placed upon medical services already overtaxed by the wounded. The Union alone had 6,454,834 *recorded* cases of either disease or wounds throughout the conflict. The U.S. Army could claim only 113 physicians at the time of Fort Sumter, serving under a surgeon general who was an eighty-year-old veteran of the War of 1812. Even for civilians, all of New England contained only three hospitals; the entire South, four or five. So both sides had to create extensive medical systems. Northern forces eventually attained one overworked surgeon for every 133 men, supported by 350 new general hospitals. Southern forces managed one surgeon for every 324 men, as well as two of the largest military hospitals in America, both located in Richmond, with 7,800 beds each, and both woefully overcrowded.

As badly as the ill might suffer, they generally fared better than men injured in battle. Often those who received any medical attention whatsoever were lucky. After Second Bull Run, six hundred fallen soldiers lay on the field for nearly a week, bleeding, starving, crying out for help. The Minie ball was a slow-moving bullet of large (usually .58) caliber, and left a ghastly, mangled wound. Next to nothing was known about the role of microorganisms in disease, making the Civil War the last to be fought largely without aseptic and antiseptic care. Thus, amputation was the only way doctors knew to stop gangrene or other infections. Gerald Linderman, in studying the experiences of Civil War soldiers, observed that "almost every Civil War memoir contains a passage descriptive of the author's horror on first encountering the pile of arms and legs outside the field hospital tent."[27] Although ether and chloroform had both come into use as anesthetics in the prior two decades, they were not always available, especially in Rebel hospitals.

Union General Carl Schurz encountered a virtual assembly line at one field hospital near Gettysburg after the battle. "As a wounded man was lifted on the table, often shrieking with pain as the attendants handled him, the surgeon quickly examined the wound and resolved upon cutting off the injured limb," he wrote in his reminiscences. "Some ether was administered and the body put in position in a moment. The surgeon snatched his knife from between his teeth, where it had been while his hands were busy, wiped it rapidly once or twice across his blood-stained apron, and the cutting began. The operation accomplished, the surgeon would look around with a deep sigh, and then—'Next!' And so it went on, hour after hour, while the number of expectant patients seemed hardly to diminish."[28]

With all that, 14 percent of treated Yankees died from their wounds and an even higher percentage of treated Rebels. Yet as grisly as these facts appear, we must ultimately agree with the U.S. Surgeon General who proudly reported at the end of the war that the Union army's mortality rate from both disease and wounds was "lower than had been observed in the experience of any army since the world began."[29] Treatment and prevention during the Civil War scored giant improvements over both the Mexican War, where the ratio of deaths from disease to battle deaths had been seven to one among American soldiers, or the Crimean War in Europe, where the ratio had been four to one among British soldiers. In fact, even during the subsequent Spanish-American War, disease took a higher proportion of American soldiers, the ratio to battle deaths being six to one.

The Civil War's impressive medical achievements can largely be credited to civilian organizations, outside the military bureaucracies. Inspired by the example of Florence Nightingale in the Crimean War, northern women who had been active in the antislavery movement or other reform crusades began as soon as the war broke out to organize what became the United States Sanitary

Commission. The Sanitary Commission had to overcome army hostility to meddling civilians; Lincoln initially dismissed the organization as "fifth wheel to the coach." The commission did achieve official recognition in June 1861 but remained a decentralized, privately funded, voluntary organization. Its locals spread across the North and numbered seven thousand by 1863. They raised money for medical supplies; circulated "Rules for Preserving the Health of the Soldier," an unprecedented hygienic guidebook; distributed food, clothing, and medicine; provided volunteer nurses and doctors; supported lodges and homes for traveling and convalescing soldiers; and even chartered ships to evacuate the wounded from the Shiloh battlefield. Just one of the Commission's sanitary fairs in New York raised the unheard of sum of $1 million.

The Sanitary Commission's leaders were mainly wealthy philanthropists, influential within the Republican Party, and they pressured Congress into appointing the thirty-three-year-old William Hammond as the army's surgeon general in 1862. He began actively staffing the military hospitals behind the lines with salaried, female nurses, who supplemented detailed or convalescent soldiers and the unpaid volunteers. By the end of the war, the army had recruited three thousand women nurses under the stern supervision of Dorothea Dix, the famous reformer of insane asylums. Hammond also instituted, with the aid of General McClellan, another Sanitary Commission goal: a trained, independent ambulance corps that became the model for future armies. The War Department, unfortunately, acceded to the Commission's pressure only begrudgingly, and in early 1864 Secretary of War Edwin M. Stanton court-martialed Hammond on trumped up charges and obtained his dismissal. Many of the Surgeon General's reforms endured, however.

The Sanitary Commission was the largest humanitarian association seen in the country so far but was only one of several relief agencies performing similar tasks in the wartime North. Clara Barton, later to found the American Red Cross, became one of the few women to provide medical assistance right on the battlefields and at field hospitals, independently of both the Commission and army nurses. The Confederacy had no direct counterpart to the

Sanitary Commission, but local and state organizations promoted soldiers' aid and hospital relief. Many of the South's general hospitals were first established through private initiative.

Nursing remained the main avenue for southern white women to assist the war effort, just as it was for northern women. Overcoming strong male resistance, the growing presence of these nurses was a landmark for female social mobility. Their work could be very hazardous on either side of the Mason-Dixon line. Noted author Louisa May Alcott was a volunteer nurse in Washington for a month when she came down with typhoid. The only known treatment, calomel, gave her mercury poisoning. She lost her teeth and hair, suffered slow deterioration of the nervous system, and never entirely recovered before her death in 1888. In spite of such risks, the overwhelming number tending to the sick and wounded, both North and South, were unpaid volunteers. The story of Civil War medical care is moving testimony to the unmatched courage and efficacy of private action.

Chapter 7

Bibliographical Essay

The literature on the Civil War's military aspects is overwhelming, more overwhelming than the literature on slavery. "There must be more historians of the Civil War than there were generals fighting in it," comments David Donald, in "Refighting the Civil War," from *Lincoln Reconsidered* (cited prologue), p. 82. Practically every battle and, indeed, many minor skirmishes have at least one book of their own; practically every commanding general, significant or insignificant, has a least one biography; and practically every regiment, North and South, has at least one unit history. Let us start, however, with the multi-volume military histories, of which the most famous, deservedly, is novelist Shelby Foote's massive but readable *Civil War: A Narrative* (New York: Random House, 1958–74), v. 1, *From Sumter to Perryville;* v. 2, *Fredericksburg to Meridian;* and v. 3, *Red River to Appomattox.* The prolific William C. Davis began his own, less imposing trilogy, *The Imperiled Union: 1861–1865* (Garden City, NY: Doubleday, 1982–83), but only finished v. 1, *The Deep Waters of the Proud,* and v. 2, *Stand in the Day of Battle.* Finally, everyone interested in the Civil War's battles and campaigns eventually gets to the four classic volumes, Robert Underwood Johnson and Clarence Clough Buel, eds., *Battles and Leaders of the Civil War* (New York, Century, 1884–89). The serious researcher's most basic tool, next to the government's official records, these were originally articles written by participants for *Century* magazine.

There is a heavy military emphasis in the three volumes of Bruce Catton's *Centennial History of the Civil War* (cited in the prologue), but that master wordsmith also wrote a one-volume military history of the North, *This Hallowed Ground: The Story of the Union Side of the Civil War* (Garden City, NY: Doubleday, 1956). A popular, primarily military history of the South is Clifford Dowdey, *The Land They Fought For: The Story of the South as the Confederacy, 1832–1865* (Garden City, NY: Doubleday, 1955). Since I find most single-volume military histories that treat both the North and South unsatisfactory, I will list only R. Ernest Dupuy and Trevor N. Dupuy, *The Compact History of the Civil War* (New York: Hawthorn Books, 1960), Harry Hansen, *The Civil War: A History* (New York: Mentor, 1961); and Curtis Anders, *Hearts in Conflict: A One-Volume History of the Civil War* (New York: Birch Lane Press, 1994). Usually it is better to rely upon single-volume histories that also include the war's non-military aspects, and those works I mentioned in the prologue.

But military history is incomprehensible without adequate maps, and a compilation that remains unequaled, whether for ease of use or accuracy of detail, and which includes a narrative built around the maps, is the first volume of Vincent J. Esposito, ed., *The West Point Atlas of American Wars,* rev. edn. (New York: Henry Holt, 1995). After this atlas first appeared in 1959, a special edition, *The West Point Atlas of the Civil War* (New York:

Frederick A. Praeger, 1962), was released, with the Spanish-American War cut off from the end. Be warned that the newer versions contain editorial corrections not present in the original. James M. McPherson, ed., *The Atlas of the Civil War* (New York: Macmillan, 1994), although not quite as useful for major campaigns, often provides more details on less prominent operations.

Civil War buffs love to refight campaigns and battles, second guessing every leader's most minute decision, each decision with its passionate critics and defenders. Although these endless wrangles often worm their way into the scholarly literature, they frequently ignore so many non-military fundamentals as to become completely detached from reality. For just as there is a new economic history and a new political history, so there is a "new military history." And the new military history compels us to remember that military decisions cannot be divorced from their economic, political, and social context. In particular, when armchair commanders mentally redeploy troop concentrations like pieces on a chess board, without any thought as to how these troops will be supplied, or to how these movements might affect the ability of either opponent to raise forces in the first place, they confirm again the old military adage: amateurs talk strategy; professionals talk logistics. To get some understanding of these fundamental factors, three otherwise very different collections are helpful: David Donald, ed., *Why the North Won the Civil War* (Baton Rouge: Louisiana State University Press, 1960); John T. Hubbell, ed., *Battles Lost and Won* (cited ch. 5); and Gabor S. Boritt, ed., *Why the Confederacy Lost* (New York: Oxford University Press, 1992).

The best overall discussion of Civil War strategy, fit within a broader survey, is Russell F. Weigley, *The American Way of War: A History of United States Military Strategy and Policy* (New York: Macmillan, 1973). The influence of West Point can be traced either through James L. Morrison, Jr.'s, general history of the antebellum academy, *"The Best School in the World": West Point, the Pre-Civil War Years, 1833–1866* (Kent, OH: Kent State University Press, 1986), or John C. Waugh's specific chronicle of one graduating class, *The Class of 1846, From West Point to Appomattox: Stonewall Jackson, George McClellan and Their Brothers* (New York: Warner Books, 1994).

On the Union side, traditional military history has tended to obscure Lincoln's prime responsibility for early Union failures—as I have already stressed in the previous chapter's bibliographical essay. The most unbridled case for Lincoln as a military genius can be found in T. Harry Williams, *Lincoln and His Generals* (New York: Alfred A. Knopf, 1952); while the most outlandish effort to shift blame elsewhere is Michael C. C. Adams, *Our Masters the Rebels: A Speculation on Union Military Failures in the East, 1861–1865* (Cambridge, MA: Harvard University Press, 1978), which offers a psychological explanation based upon the alleged inferiority complex of Union commanders in the east. There is more to recommend on the later developments in Union strategy when we get to chapter 11 and total war.

On Confederate strategy, I have been most heavily influenced by Robert L. Kerby, "Why the Confederacy Lost," *Review of Politics*, 35 (July 1973), pp. 326–345, a dazzling argument for irregular warfare. By shying away from this alternative, the South sealed its fate, and all its other strategic debates became secondary. Some will notice overlap between the argument I have adopted from Kerby and that of Grady McWhiney and Perry D. Jamieson, who in *Attack and Die: Civil War Military Tactics and the Southern Heritage* (Tuscaloosa: University of Alabama Press, 1982) blame the South's Celtic heritage for costly offensives against the North. The case against a Napoleonic strategy, however, does not depend upon the South being any more aggressive than the North, and quantitative analysis seems to confirm that there was little difference. See Richard E. Beringer, Herman Hattaway, Archer Jones, and William N. Still, Jr., *Why the South Lost the Civil War* (Athens: University of Georgia Press, 1986), a book that is a gold mine of original and provocative contentions that relate to the next three chapters as well. Two of these authors, Hattaway and Jones, collaborated on an earlier book, *How the North Won: A Military History of the Civil War* (Urbana: University of Illinois Press, 1983), that also emphasizes logistics and guerrillas. (By the way, if you think you have begun to detect an overused and tired theme in Civil War book titles, you are right.)

Once the Confederacy rejected unconventional warfare, it still had four orthodox options: (1) A true offense, which was what Robert Toombs and the fire-eaters advocated after the First Battle of Bull Run. They wanted an immediate attack upon Washington and liberation of Maryland. Whether this was ever realistic, it certainly became less so with the passage of time, although Lee's invasions of the North can be thought to have revived this option temporarily. (2) A perimeter or rigid defense, which is what Jefferson Davis tried initially in the western theater. The Rebels stretched their troops right along the border's edge to prevent any incursions but ultimately did not have sufficient military resources to pull off this kind of defense. (3) An offensive defense, which is what Robert E. Lee practiced and advocated. Its goal was the same as the perimeter defense—to keep Union forces off Southern soil—but the means more economical in the short run. This strategy permits limited enemy incursions but requires prompt counter-offensives. (4) A passive or flexible (or Fabian) defense, which was practiced by General Joseph E. Johnston in front of Richmond, before Lee took command, and later in front of Atlanta. This defense both allows Union incursions and avoids wasteful counter-offensives, in the hope that the enemy will attack and destroy himself.

If the Confederacy had to rely upon a conventional approach, then in my view this last was the best, because it had the most in common with an irregular defense. For what it is worth, Grant considered Joseph Johnston, the West Pointer who honed this strategy, the best of all Confederate generals. A recent account of Johnston's life is Craig L. Symonds, *Joseph E. Johnston: A Civil War Biography* (New York: W. W. Norton, 1992). McWhiney and Jamieson in *Attack and Die* do offer insight into why adoption of Johnston's passive defense was probably politically unacceptable to militant Southerners, whatever the weaknesses of the authors' main thesis about relative aggressiveness.

Much of the debate among Confederate military historians and buffs, however, has focused neither on the basic question of a conventional versus unconventional strategy nor upon the secondary question of what conventional variant was best but on the utterly subsidiary and almost inconsequential question of where the Confederacy should have devoted more resources—the eastern or western theater. A sustained criticism of Davis and Lee for wasting limited military resources on the wrong (i.e., eastern) theater is Archer Jones and Thomas L. Connelly, *The Politics of Command: Factions and Ideas in Confederate Strategy* (Baton Rouge: Louisiana State University Press, 1973). But see the defenses of Lee by Albert Castel and Ludwell H. Johnson in the Hubbell anthology, *Battles Lost and Won;* by Gary W. Gallagher in the Boritt anthology, *Why the Confederacy Lost;* and by Charles P. Roland, "The Generalship of Robert E. Lee," in Grady McWhiney, ed., *Grant, Lee, Lincoln and the Radicals: Essays on Civil War Leadership* ([Evanston, IL]: Northwestern University Press, 1964).

On the South's command bureaucracy, Frank E. Vandiver's older, *Rebel Brass: The Confederate Command System* (Baton Rouge: Louisiana State University Press, 1956), must be consulted. Richard M. McMurry, *Two Great Rebel Armies: An Essay in Confederate Military History* (Chapel Hill: University of North Carolina Press, 1989), which systematically compares the quality of Rebel forces in the east and west, ends up approving of Lee's and Davis's strategic decision to mount the major effort in the east. Steven Woodworth, *Jefferson Davis and His Generals: The Failure of Confederate Command in the West* (Lawrence: University Press of Kansas, 1990), focuses on the western theater.

Two books that explore the guerrilla activity that went on anyway in the east are Virgil Carrington Jones, *Gray Ghosts and Rebel Raiders* (New York: Henry Holt, 1952), and Jeffrey D. Wert, *Mosby's Rangers* (New York: Simon & Schuster, 1990). Chapter 5 already mentioned several works on the guerrilla war in Missouri, yet also worthwhile is Richard S. Brownlee, *Gray Ghosts of the Confederacy: Guerrilla Warfare in the West, 1861–1865* (Baton Rouge: Louisiana State University Press, 1958). But the most notable success of Confederate irregular warfare, east of the Mississippi and west of the Appalachians, after the Union had reached the limits of the river invasion routes, is woefully neglected. There is some information in books that treat cavalry operations, such as Edward G. Longacre, *Mounted Raids of the Civil War* (South Brunswick: A. S. Barnes, 1975); the third volume of Stephen Z. Starr, *The Union Cavalry in the Civil War* (Baton Rouge: Louisiana State University Press, 1979); or William R. Brooksher and David K. Snider, *Glory at a Gallop: Tales of the Confederate Cavalry* (Washington: Brassey's [U.S.], 1993), but these often miss the full strategic significance. There is one chapter on the guerrilla war in Union-occupied Tennessee in Stephen V. Ash, *Middle Tennessee Transformed: War and Peace in the Upper South* (Baton Rouge: Louisiana State University Press, 1988), but that was a sideshow. Still the best way to approach this topic is through biographies of the greatest of the Confederacy's unconventional generals, Nathan Bedford Forrest. Two are fairly new: Jack Hurst, *Nathan Bedford Forrest: A Biography* (New York: Alfred A. Knopf, 1993), and Brian Steel Willis, *A Battle From the Start: The Life of Nathan Bedford Forrest* (New York: HarperCollins, 1992).

The eastern theater has inspired splendid multi-volume histories of the two opposing armies. On the Union side, Bruce Catton has chronicled *The Army of the Potomac* (Garden City, NY: Doubleday, 1951–53): v. 1, *Mr. Lincoln's Army;* v. 2, *Glory Road;* and v. 3, *A Stillness at Appomattox.* Douglas Southall Freeman, a Ph.D. in history who edited the *Richmond News Leader,* produced what still remains the classic study of the Confederate Army of Northern Virginia in the three volumes of *Lee's Lieutenants: A Study in Command* (New York: Charles Scribner's Sons, 1946). Of the many encounters between these two armies, the best known undoubtedly is Gettysburg, which requires a bibliography unto itself. There is even a scholarly periodical devoted to this campaign. The most thorough work on the battle's entire three days is Edwin B. Coddington, *The Gettysburg Campaign: A Study in Command* (New York: Charles Scribner's Sons, 1968). Also worth reading are George R. Stewart on the battle's third day, *Pickett's Charge: A Microhistory of the Final Attack at Gettysburg* (Cambridge, MA: Riverside Press, 1959), and Harry W. Pfanz *Gettysburg: The Second Day* (Chapel Hill: University of North Carolina Press, 1987), a 600-page work that is slightly mistitled, because it really deals with only part of the second day's battle, on the Union left.

Douglas Southall Freeman also wrote the most extensive biography of the Army of Northern Virginia's commander, *R. E. Lee: A Biography*, 4 v. (New York: Charles Scribner's, 1934–35). For a long time Lee appeared to be a rarity in history, a hero with virtually no personal flaws. Two recent attempts at debunking the Lee legend, Thomas L. Connelly, *The Marble Man: Robert E. Lee and His Image in American Society* (New York: Alfred A. Knopf, 1977), and Alan T. Nolan, *Lee Considered: General Robert E. Lee and Civil War History* (Chapel Hill: University of North Carolina Press, 1991), only leave one more impressed with the man's character. This should not divert us, however, from the more important task of critically revising Lee's military reputation, to which both books make enormous contributions. The Confederate general's most recent biographer, Emory M. Thomas, in *Robert E. Lee: A Biography* (New York: W. W. Norton, 1995), returns to a more sympathetic portrait.

Stonewall Jackson has had many biographies, but one that was particularly influential is the two-volume study by the British military scholar, Colonel George F. R. Henderson, *Stonewall Jackson and the American Civil War* (London: Longmans, Green, 1898). I know I will get in trouble with the partisans of General James Longstreet for not saying anything about this other of Lee's Corps commanders, after having given Jackson so much air time. Gary W. Gallagher, "Scapegoat in Victory: James Longstreet and the Battle of Second Manassas," *Civil War History*, 34 (December 1988), pp. 293–307, is one of the notable attempts to reverse the traditional evaluations of these two lieutenants, by arguing that Stonewall was in fact erratic and unreliable while Longstreet was really Lee's dependable War Horse. I am not unsympathetic, and it is certainly true that Longstreet's military reputation was unjustifiably sullied by reaction against his subsequent participation in Republican Reconstruction. In this case, however, I am captive to the dominant fashion. Longstreet is not as conspicuous in history, because it was Jackson's valley campaigns, after all, that fired the southern imagination and excited Lincoln's terror.

Thomas L. Connelly has given us a two-volume history of the South's most important conventional force in the west: *Army of the Heartland: The Army of Tennessee, 1861–1862* (Baton Rouge: Louisiana State University Press, 1967) and *Autumn of Glory: The Army of Tennessee, 1862–1865* (Baton Rouge: Louisiana State University Press, 1971). Works on the Union army in the west and its two prime commanders, Grant and Sherman, are mentioned in chapter 11, but attention must be paid here to the waterways that played so major a role in opening up vast sections of the Confederacy to Federal penetration. Many naval studies from the previous chapter include rivers, but in addition peruse John D. Milligan, *Gunboats Down the Mississippi* (Annapolis, MD: United States Naval Institute, 1965); Fletcher Pratt, *Civil War on Western Waters* (New York: Henry Holt, 1956); and H. Allen Gosnell, *Guns on the Western Waters: The Story of River Gunboats in the Civil War* (Baton Rouge: Louisiana State University Press, 1949).

Walter Millis, *Arms and Men: A Study in American Military History* (New York: G. P. Putnam's Sons, 1956), is an excellent introduction to the influence of military technology. More details on Civil War arms themselves are in Carl L. Davis, *Arming the Union: Small Arms in the Civil War* (Port Washington, NY: Kennikat Press, 1973). Robert V. Bruce, *Lincoln and the Tools of War* (Indianapolis: Bobbs-Merrill, 1956), deals with the developmental side of Union innovations. For an ultimately unconvincing argument that the rifle did not make all that much tactical difference, see Paddy Griffith, *Battle Tactics of the Civil War* (New Haven: Yale University Press, 1989), lightly revised from a 1987 British edition under the title of *Rally Once Again*.

Bell Irvin Wiley pioneered the study of the Civil War's common soldiers in *The Life of Johnny Reb: The Common Soldier of the Confederacy* (Indianapolis: Bobbs-Merrill, 1943) and *The Life of Billy Yank: The Common Soldier of the Union* (Indianapolis: Bobbs-Merrill, 1952). Since then many fine studies have carried this inquiry further. Especially good are James I. Robertson, Jr., *Soldiers Blue and Gray* (Columbia: University of South Carolina Press, 1988), and Reid Mitchell, *Civil War Soldiers: Their Expectations and Their Experiences* (New York: Simon & Schuster, 1988). But I find the most illuminating is Gerald Linderman, *Embattled Courage: The Experience of Combat in the American Civil War* (New York: Free Press, 1987), for the way it manages to unify the Civil War combat experience around the single theme of courage, thereby opening a window onto the culture of that time and facilitating comparison with other wars. Moreover, Linderman emphasizes the vital role that women played in promoting this martial virtue among soldiers. Quite unique but fruitful is Fred Arthur Bailey, *Class and*

Tennessee's Confederate Generation (Chapel Hill: University of North Carolina Press, 1987), which mines interviews of one state's veterans to discover significant social divisions within the Rebel military.

A safe and sometimes entertaining way to share vicariously the soldier's experience is through fiction. Almost every American has at some point in his or her education encountered Stephen Crane's novel, *The Red Badge of Courage: An Episode of the American Civil War* (Charlottesville: University Press of Virginia, 1975). Yet Crane himself never saw combat. More realistic fictional portrayals are in the macabre short stories of Ambrose Bierce, a battle-hardened veteran. There are two modern collections: Ernest Jerome Hopkins, ed., *The Civil War Short Stories of Ambrose Bierce* (Lincoln: University of Nebraska Press, 1970), and William McCann, ed., *Ambrose Bierce's Civil War* (Chicago: Regnery Gateway, 1956). They contain roughly the same stories, although each has a few absent from the other. (Also, the version of "Jupiter Doke, Brigadier-General" in the McCann set inadvertently omits one paragraph.) In contrast, Michael Shaara's popular *The Killer Angels: A Novel* (New York: David McKay, 1974)—which was the basis for the movie *Gettysburg*—although historically accurate, has an inflated reputation both as a novel and as a compelling depiction of battle.

Stewart Brooks provides a good introduction to *Civil War Medicine* (Springfield: Charles C. Thomas, 1966). Studies on various specialized aspects of this topic are Paul E. Steiner, *Disease in the Civil War: Natural Biological Warfare in 1861–1865* (Springfield: Charles C. Thomas, 1968); George Worthington Adams, *Doctors in Blue: The Medical History of the Union Army in the Civil War* (New York: Henry Schuman, 1952); Horace H. Cunningham, *Doctors in Gray: The Confederate Medical Service* (Baton Rouge: Louisiana State University Press, 1958); and Glenna R. Schroeder-Lein, *Confederate Hospitals on the Move: Samuel H. Stout and the Army of Tennessee* (Columbia: University of South Carolina Press, 1994). The literature could profitably use a new study of the United States Sanitary Commission. William Quentin Maxwell, *Lincoln's Fifth Wheel: The Political History of the United States Sanitary Commission* (New York: Longmans, Green, 1956), is haphazardly organized and written, and therefore one must still turn to the older, official history, Charles J. Stillé, *History of the United States Sanitary Commission: Being the General Report of Its Work During the War of the Rebellion* (Philadelphia: J. B. Lippincott, 1866).

Mary Elizabeth Massey, *Bonnet Brigades* (New York: Alfred A. Knopf, 1966), covers not only women nurses, North and South, but the whole range of women's participation in the war effort. That indefatigable biographer, Stephen B. Oates, has most recently related the wartime activities of the founder of the American Red Cross, *A Woman of Valor: Clara Barton and the Civil War* (New York: Free Press, 1994). J. Matthew Gallman, "Voluntarism in Wartime: Philadelphia's Great Central Fair," in Maris A. Vinovskis, ed., *Toward a Social History of the American Civil War: Exploratory Essays* (Cambridge, U.K.: Cambridge University Press, 1990), illustrates the centrality of voluntary action during the Civil War.

8

The War to Abolish Slavery?

Radical Republicans

Southerners had no doubt about the purpose of their lavish expenditure of blood: independence. But Northerners were not so clear about their own goal. Lincoln insisted that he wanted only to preserve the Union, and the newly elected Congress confirmed this war aim shortly after it convened. The Crittenden-Johnson resolutions denied that the government was waging war "in any spirit of oppression, nor for any purpose of conquest or subjugation, nor purpose of overthrowing or interfering with the rights or established institutions of those States" but only "to defend and maintain the supremacy of the Constitution and to preserve the Union."[1] In other words, the resolutions promised to leave slavery untouched in the seceding states.

Northern blacks, abolitionists, and Radical Republicans, however, wanted from the very beginning a crusade against the South's peculiar institution. All these groups strenuously protested when Lincoln revoked General Frémont's punitive emancipation in Missouri. Not that the President promulgated any consistent military policy regarding slavery. Some commanders, such as General McClellan, scrupulously respected this form of southern property. Others, such as General Benjamin Butler, while at Virginia's

Fortress Monroe, refused to return slaves who fled to Federal lines, defining them as "contraband of war" and often putting them to work as teamsters, cooks, nurses, and laborers.

Yet the prospect of wartime abolition had seduced even William Lloyd Garrison and most of his militant followers into abandoning disunion. As the abolitionists found themselves elevated from pariahs into folk heroes throughout the North, Garrison's slogan of "No Union with Slave-Holders" was transformed into "Union without Slavery." The thirty-three-year-old American Peace Society virtually closed up shop as most of its members praised *this* war. Only a handful of slavery opponents went along with George W. Bassett, who proclaimed that "the same principle that has always made me an uncompromising abolitionist, now makes me an uncompromising secessionist. It is the great natural and sacred right of self-government."[2] Novelist Lydia Maria Child did not go quite so far, but she concluded that "even should [the slaves] be emancipated, merely as a 'war necessity,' everything *must* go wrong."[3]

Among the handful of dissenters was Lysander Spooner, an abolitionist so enthusiastic about John Brown's raid on Harper's Ferry that he had earnestly proposed kidnapping the governor of Virginia to hold as hostage in exchange for Brown's life. But although never a pacifist, Spooner saw absolutely no moral analogy between slaves violently rising up to secure their liberty and the central government violently crushing aspirations for self-determination on the part of white southerners. After the war, he would write that the North had fought for the principle that "men may rightfully be compelled to submit to, and support, a government they do not want; and that resistance, on their part, makes them criminals and traitors." "Political slavery" had taken the place of "chattel slavery."[4]

The experience of Moncure Conway illustrates the extent to which most of slavery's opponents threw their support behind the war effort. Conway was a Virginia-born pacifist who at first reluctantly went along with suppressing Southern independence. But the increasing bloodshed sickened him, so that by 1863, when in England as an unofficial representative of American abolitionists, Conway proposed to a Confederate envoy that if the South freed the slaves on its own, the antislavery men in the North would "immediately oppose the further prosecution of the war."[5] The cries of protest on this side of the Atlantic that greeted the proposal's publication made clear that most abolitionists now wanted to subdue and punish the South, slavery or no. For many, this represented the end of an intellectual journey that had come full circle. They had often begun their careers within the Benevolent Empire, working for such conservative reforms as temperance, Sabbatarian laws, or compulsory, tax-financed schools. Antislavery had radicalized many into consistent opponents of government coercion at all levels. But the Civil War then brought abolitionists back into the ranks of those Yankees devoted to State power and social hierarchy.

While the Union cause faltered on the battlefield, the tightly organized Radical Republicans were gaining ascendancy in Congress. Leading this faction in the Senate was Charles Sumner, who had recovered from his beating to retake his Massachusetts seat in late 1859. Carl Schurz, one of the Union's political generals who was a Radical himself, characterized the arrogant Sumner as a "moral agitator." Handsome and articulate, this well-traveled Harvard graduate had no sense of humor. "Mr. Sumner frequently—I might say almost always—failed to see the point of the quaint anecdotes or illustrations with which Lincoln was fond of elucidating his argument," Schurz commented. "Mr. Sumner not seldom quoted such Lincolnisms to me, and asked me with an air of innocent bewilderment, whether I could guess what the President could possibly have meant."[6] Yet Sumner's sense of moral rectitude was so vehement that prior to the war he had avowed on the Senate floor that he was duty bound to disobey the Fugitive Slave Act.

In the House of Representatives, the Radical Republican who loomed largest was the seventy-year-old chairman of the Ways and Means Committee, Thaddeus Stevens of Pennsylvania. Well-built but club-footed, clean shaven with a usually misplaced wig, and grimly sardonic, Stevens was willing that the South "be laid waste, and made a desert, in order to save this Union from destruction."[7] Before a Republican state convention, the former Whig and Know-Nothing declared: "Abolition—*yes!* abolish everything on the face of the earth but this Union; free every slave—slay every traitor—

burn every Rebel mansion, if these things be necessary to preserve this temple of freedom to the world and to our posterity. Unless we do this, we cannot conquer them.''[8]

Under Radical leadership, the Senate expelled four of its members as disloyal, while the House expelled three. Although the rump legislature still balked at repealing the Fugitive Slave Act of 1850, the Radicals pushed through an alteration in the articles of war in March 1862 that forbade all army and navy personnel from enforcing the act. One month later Congress fulfilled the long-term abolitionist goal of eliminating slavery in the District of Columbia— albeit with compensation for the slaveholders. The legislators next added a formal prohibition upon slavery in the territories. Most significantly, the Republican majority passed two confiscation acts directed at persons supporting the rebellion. All their property was forfeited and their slaves freed. The confiscation acts, however, were clumsy in practice, requiring the operation of Federal courts.

The army's attitude toward slavery was simultaneously hardening. Soldiers who had volunteered only to save the Union quickly realized that slave labor behind the Confederate lines was releasing white men for military service. As northern troops penetrated Southern territory, blacks were their only allies in an otherwise hostile land. Treating the Union forces as liberators, slaves often provided valuable military intelligence. The Yankee prisoner of war who escaped could turn to the slave for shelter and aid. In one celebrated exploit, a South Carolina slave named Robert Smalls and his brother hijacked the Confederate side-wheeler, *Planter,* and sailed it out to the Union fleet blockading Charleston.

Lincoln was drifting toward the Radical position as well. By early 1862, the President was urging the border states to institute gradual emancipation, promising them federal financial assistance to compensate slaveholders. And he tried to allay fears about the racial consequences by promoting, with funds supplied by Congress, the colonization of free blacks to central America. But he publicly warned that he would take whatever action he thought necessary to win the war. "My paramount object in this struggle," the President declared—replying to Horace Greeley's "Prayer of 20 Million," published in the *New York Tribune*—"*is* to save the Union, and is *not* either to save or to destroy slavery. If I could save the

Union without freeing *any* slave I would do it, and if I could save it by freeing *all* the slaves I would do it; and if I could save it by freeing some and leaving others alone I would also do that. What I do about slavery, and the colored race, I do because I believe it helps to save the Union; and what I forbear, I forbear because I do *not* believe it would help save the Union." Lincoln added, however, that "I have here stated my purpose according to my view of *official* duty; and I intend no modification of my oft-expressed *personal* wish that all men every where could be free."[9]

The border states shunned all Lincoln's urgings. So after the Union reverses in the Seven Days' battle, the President announced to his Cabinet that he had made up his mind. He would use the immense and unprecedented war powers he now claimed to liberate the slaves in the rebellious states. Secretary of State Seward pointed out that if such a decree was issued while the fighting was going badly for the Union, it would be interpreted as an act of desperation. Lincoln therefore filed away his proposed decree to await victory on the battlefield.

Antietam and Emancipation

President Lincoln was not the only one awaiting the verdict of battle. When Robert E. Lee's army invaded Maryland at the beginning of September in 1862, the French and British governments were on the verge of offering to mediate between the Union and the Confederacy. Napoleon III, ruler of France, was particularly desirous of a permanent division to facilitate intervention he planned in Mexico. If the Union refused mediation, these foreign powers would recognize the Confederate government. All that held them back was the pending news about the Southern offensive.

General Lee's motives for moving north went beyond his continuing desire to deliver a knock-out blow to the Union army. He also wanted to relieve war-ravaged Virginia and was hoping finally to bring Maryland into the Confederacy. But his invasion took him to the border state's western counties, where Union sentiment was strong. Not only did the local inhabitants fail to rally to the Rebel banner, but Lee's campaign on Northern territory was plagued by the same logistical burdens that Union commanders had already encountered in the South.

Lee alleviated these burdens partially by dispersing his forces and keeping them on the move, so that they could live off the land. They dutifully paid Confederate currency for all provisions in order not to undermine the campaign's political objectives too severely; the ragged Army of Northern Virginia was used to living sparsely anyway. The often barefoot southern soldiers, for instance, cleaned out all the shoe stores in western Maryland. One veteran described his fellows as "a set of ragamuffins." "It seemed as if every cornfield in Maryland had been robbed of its scarecrows," he recalled. "None had any under-clothing. My costume consisted of a ragged pair of trousers, a stained, dirty jacket; an old slouch hat, the brim pinned up with a thorn; a begrimed blanket over my shoulder, a grease-smeared cotton haversack full of apples and corn, a cartridge box full, and a musket. I was barefooted and had a stonebruise on each foot." None of his comrades were much better dressed. "There was no one there who would not have been 'run in' by the police had he appeared on the streets of any populous city, and would have been fined next day for undue exposure."[10]

Without a decisive victory, however, the Maryland invasion could amount to nothing more than a large-scale raid. At this critical juncture, the Army of Northern Virginia suffered a stroke of bad luck. A Union corporal stumbled upon a lost copy of Lee's orders wrapped around three cigars. Passed along to General McClellan, whose Army of the Potomac was nearly three times larger, the orders revealed the location of every Confederate unit. Lee was barely able to call the units back together at Sharpsburg, near the Virginia border, before the Federal onslaught fell. The Rebel lines behind Antietam Creek came close to giving way but ultimately held through attack after attack. It was the bloodiest single day of the entire war, with over 23,000 dead and wounded, about evenly divided between the two sides.

A British member of Parliament, Lord Hartington, who visited the battlefield ten days later, was appalled. "In about seven or eight acres of wood," he observed, "there is not a tree which is not full of bullets and bits of shells. It is impossible to understand how anyone could live in such a fire as there must have been there."[11] Tactically, the battle was a draw. Strategically, Lee retreated the next night back into Virginia. Yet McClellan did not pursue for five weeks. Republican legislators, working through a Joint Committee on the Conduct of the War, were already dissatisfied with the Union commander not only for his lack of aggressiveness but also for his politics—he was an outspoken Democrat. When the Army of the Potomac finally did follow the Rebel army, Lincoln relieved McClellan, and Lee's winning streak resumed.

Nevertheless, the battle of Antietam looked enough like a victory for Lincoln to unveil the Emancipation Proclamation. The preliminary proclamation, released on September 22, 1862, gave the seceding states until the end of the year to cease their rebellion. On the first of the year, "within any State" or "part of a State" that had not done so, "all persons held as slaves . . . shall be then, thenceforward, and forever free."[12] For those states that voluntarily rejoined the Union, the proclamation reiterated Lincoln's offers of compensated emancipation and colonization of freed blacks.

Southerners of course did not throw down their arms, and the President issued the final Emancipation Proclamation at the beginning of 1863. But it technically freed no slaves. As a war measure similar to that of the British during the American Revolution, the proclamation only applied to the areas still in rebellion. It did not emancipate any of the slaves in the four border states. Nor did it emancipate any slaves in those sections of the Confederacy that Union armies had already reconquered, including all of Tennessee and large portions of Virginia and Louisiana. The only slaves covered were the ones beyond the reach of Union authority. This anomaly inspired a cynical retort from Seward. "We show our sympathy with slavery," he stated the day after the proclamation was issued, "by emancipating slaves where we cannot reach them, and holding them in bondage where we can set them free."[13] The London *Spectator* dismissed the proclamation because it liberated "the enemy's slaves as it would the enemy's cattle, simply to weaken them. . . . The principle is not that a human being cannot justly own another, but that he cannot own him unless he is loyal to the United States."[14]

Black Soldiers Fight for the North

The peculiar institution was in serious trouble anyway. Even before the Emancipation Proclamation, masters were moving their slaves away from approaching Federal troops. Not only did this disrupt agricultural routines, but the new locations often did not offer comparable profits. Slaveholders hired out increasing numbers of their bondsmen, especially to the expanding war industries in the cities, which gave more blacks the improved opportunities and independence associated with urban slavery.

The Emancipation Proclamation, moreover, did offer freedom to those who fled to Union lines. It therefore struck at slavery as effectively as any measure that encouraged fugitives, accelerating a process already well underway. Congress's previous abolition in the District of Columbia had brought slaves flocking in from the surrounding border state of Maryland. Now they crowded into Union camps from all over the South. Jefferson Davis lost a string of domestic servants, three escaping in the first month of 1864 alone. These usually absconded with some of the President's clothes or silver, although a couple of the more bold tried to burn down the Executive Mansion. By early 1865, at a time when Confederate armies were starved for manpower, the Georgia legislature felt compelled to establish a special cavalry battalion for stopping slaves from escaping to the enemy. The numbers reaching the sanctuary of Federal jurisdiction eventually swelled to over half a million.

Those blacks outside the 20 percent that Union armies directly liberated benefited as well. Some whites had expected the proclamation to incite slave insurrection, and reports of plunder, looting, and arson were not unknown. But since running away was a less dangerous route to liberty, there was very little black violence against former owners. Nevertheless, as fugitives increased enforcement costs for slaveowners, the peculiar institution crumbled in those areas unreached by Federal troops exactly as Southerners had feared would happen without vigorous recapture of runaways. The drain of white males into the Confederate military also contributed to a decline in supervision. Labor discipline on plantations and farms relaxed. Slaves worked less than before, as they escalated their traditional resort to passive resistance, with insolence and intransigence becoming widespread.

One woman desperately trying to run her husband's plantation finally wrote him that "you may give your negroes away if you won[']t hire them, and I'll move into a white settlement and work with my hands."[15] The productivity of bound labor had plummeted. "The institution of slavery is already so undermined and demoralized," wrote Linton Stephens to his brother, the Confederate Vice-President, in October of 1863, "as never to be of much use to us, even if we had peace and independence to day." It had "received a terrible shock which is tending to its disintegration and ruin."[16] In the final analysis, it was not military conquest but the fugitive slave who brought down the South's peculiar institution. Liberation, so often presented as something the Union did for blacks, was as much something they did for themselves.

The desire for freedom among blacks was so powerful that it was not even diminished by some harsh Federal practices. Through no one's direct fault the death rate in contraband camps approached 25 percent. Up and down the Union-controlled areas of the Mississippi River, regulations put able-bodies blacks back to work on plantations. Although the former slaves now could choose among employers, some of whom were Yankee lessees and others Southerners who had taken a loyalty oath, contracts lasted for a year with "respectful, honest, faithful labor" enforced by the military.[17] Idleness and vagrancy were crimes, and those found unemployed had to labor on public works. At other locations, Union authorities coercively impressed contrabands to build fortifications or do other military work. Perhaps several hundred thousand labored for the war in auxiliary capacities.

Lincoln's emancipation policy realized another major objective: the recruitment of former slaves into the North's armies. "Any different policy in regard to the colored man, deprives us of his help, and this is more than we can bear," mused the President in a letter he never ultimately sent, adding that "this is not a question of sentiment or taste, but one of physical force which may be measured and estimated as horse-power and Steam-power are measured and estimated."[18] Although the United States Navy had always enlisted blacks, the regular army would not admit them at the war's beginning. State militia laws also had customarily discriminated against Negroes. With the rising death toll, however, the northern prejudice against black soldiers fell by the wayside.

One Irish officer, writing verse under the pseudonym of Private Miles O'Reilly, published his sentiments in the *New York Herald:*

> Some tell us 'tis a burnin' shame
> To make the naygers fight;
> An' that the thrade of bein' kilt
> Belongs but to the white:
> But as for me, upon my sowl!
> So liberal are we here,
> I'll let Sambo be murthered instead of myself
> On every day in the year.
>
> On every day in the year, boys,
> And in every hour of the day;
> The right to be kilt I'll divide wid him,
> An' divil a word I'll say.[19]

The Union decision to employ black troops brought thunderous outrage from all over the South. This spilled over to affect the treatment of prisoners. Throughout the war's first year, Lincoln had refused to negotiate an exchange of captured soldiers lest that be construed as officially recognizing the Confederacy. Field commanders, however, had arranged informal exchanges until the summer of 1862 when the Union government accepted a formal cartel. Prisoners were traded one for one, except that officers were weighted more heavily according to rank. Any excess on either side was paroled upon promising not to take up arms again until actually exchanged. Thus by the fall of 1862, war prisons on both sides were almost empty.

This agreement broke down in 1863, however, when Jefferson Davis threatened to execute captured officers from black regiments for engaging in "servile insurrection" and to turn black soldiers over to the states for re-enslavement. Union Secretary of War Edwin Stanton therefore suspended the cartel, while Lincoln promised an eye-for-an-eye retaliation. Although the Confederacy never put its threat into systematic operation, its soldiers and officers occasionally took matters into their own hands, murdering black captives or subjecting them to forced labor. Controversy still swirls around the killing of several hundred black soldiers after General Bedford Forrest's recapture of Fort Pillow, Tennessee, in April of 1864.

Nonetheless, nearly 200,000 blacks served in the Union military by the end of the war. Over half were recruited right off plantations along the Mississippi River or the southern coast—a few even drafted at gun point. The army formed them into segregated units with white officers, at first usually confined them to garrison duty, and until June 1864 paid them less than white soldiers. But these black regiments eventually proved their worth at some of the war's severest engagements. One of them, the 54th Massachusetts, led an assault in the summer of 1863 against Battery Wagner, which guarded the entrance to Charleston Harbor. Although the assault failed, the regiment demonstrated as much bravery as any white unit by losing nearly half its men. Black participation in the military may have provided the essential margin necessary for the final Union victory.

Europe Declines to Aid the South

Although intended to placate foreign opinion, the Emancipation Proclamation at first actually heightened the possibility of European intervention in America's war. England's rulers were very disturbed about the prospect for a bloody slave uprising that the proclamation seemed to augur. But the battle of Antietam demonstrated enough Union staying power to persuade the British and French governments to put off their proposed mediation. As the war lengthened, diplomatic recognition of the Confederacy became steadily less likely for Britain, the world power most committed to abolishing slavery.

Still some stormy incidents were ahead. The United States minister in London, Charles Francis Adams, had not been happy about construction at Liverpool of the *C. S. S. Alabama* and other deadly commerce raiders for the South. Although Confederate purchasing agents had been able to slip through English neutrality laws, Adams bombarded Her Majesty's government with mounting claims for damages. More menacing were the "Laird rams," iron-clad warships constructed by the same firm that had built the

Alabama. Equipped with seven-foot, wrought-iron, underwater rams and nine-inch rifled guns, these sea-going fortresses might have smashed through the Union blockade. Confederate ownership was disguised, yet Adams threatened Downing Street with war if they embarked. Finally in September of 1863, the British government detained the two rams and later purchased them for the Royal Navy. The Confederacy retaliated by expelling British consuls from southern cities—no more than a futile gesture. The United States and Britain had navigated the last major crisis of the war.

The *Alabama* claims, however, would continue to be a source of rancor. The Senate rejected a postwar treaty to adjudicate the dispute. Charles Sumner, who was Chairman of the Senate Foreign Relations Committee, suggested that Canada might be fair indemnity. Not until 1872 was a settlement arbitrated. Britain was found not to have exercised "due diligence" and paid the United States $15.5 million.

The United States had already scored a similar diplomatic achievement against France. During the war, French troops had installed Archduke Maximilian of Austria as emperor of Mexico. But in 1867, Seward, still serving as Secretary of State, invoked the Monroe Doctrine to force Napoleon III to withdraw military support from his puppet monarchy. Mexican Liberals promptly overturned Maximilian's shaky regime and executed him. By this time the Spanish troops that had taken advantage of the North American conflict to reoccupy the island of Santo Domingo had also pulled out.

These ultimately unsuccessful European adventures were not all that had kept the U.S. government's interest in the Gulf-Caribbean basin alive during the Civil War. Lincoln, Seward, and other cabinet members thought the area ideal for colonizing emancipated slaves. Congress appropriated $600,000 for this purpose, and the United States conducted preliminary negotiations with Mexico, British Honduras, Guatemala, Honduras, and Costa Rica. These fell through, as did a projected Negro colony at Chiriquí, on the isthmus. The settlement in 1863 of some 450 American blacks at the Isle à Vache in Haiti turned into an utter disaster when starvation and smallpox decimated the colony.

At the close of the war the administration had given up on colonization. But Seward's aggressiveness, having abated not a whit, sought additional outlets. He proposed intervention in Korea, annexation of the Hawaiian Islands, and acquisitions in the Caribbean. His only successes, however, were seizure of the tiny Midway Islands in the Pacific and purchase of Alaska from Russia for $7.2 million. The Republican Congress, far less imperialistic than the Secretary of State, provided the money to buy "Seward's icebox" mainly to avoid alienating Czar Alexander II. This most despotic of Europe's rulers had been the most loyal to the Union. Indeed, the Czar had suppressed a revolt for self-determination, which had broken out among his Polish subjects, at the same time that Federal armies were invading the Confederacy. Fearing British and French intervention himself, he had sent Russia's two feeble fleets to New York and San Francisco for safe refuge in 1863. Grateful Northerners had widely misinterpreted these visits as a gesture of military solidarity. As *Punch,* the London humor magazine, had Lincoln say to Alexander II:

> Imperial son of Nicholas the Great,
> We air in the same fix, I calculate,
> You with your Poles, with Southern rebels I,
> Who spurn my rule and my revenge defy.[20]

Chapter 8
Bibliographical Essay

James M. McPherson, *The Struggle for Equality: Abolitionists and the Negro in the Civil War and Reconstruction* (Princeton, NJ: Princeton University Press, 1964), is the basic study of the abolitionist movement after 1860; while Wendy Hamand Venet, *Neither Ballots nor Bullets: Women Abolitionists and the Civil War* (Charlottesville: University Press of Virginia, 1991), concentrates on the wartime activities of female opponents of slavery. George M. Fredrickson, *The Inner Civil War: Northern Intellectuals and the Crisis of the Union* (New York: Harper & Row, 1965), reports on not just abolitionists but intellectuals generally as they solidified behind the war.

The fullest account of those few radical abolitionists who remained true to their principles by refusing to sell out to the crusade for Union is the penultimate chapter of Carleton Mabee, *Black Freedom* (cited ch. 1). See also Sheldon Richman, "The Anti-war Abolitionists: The Peace Movement's Split Over the Civil War," *Journal of Libertarian Studies,* 5 (Summer 1981), 327–40. More on Moncure Conway is in Peter Walker, *Moral Choices: Memory, Desire, Imagination in Nineteenth-Century Abolition* (Baton Rouge: Louisiana State University Press, 1978). Peter Brock's monumental *Pacifism in the United States: From the Colonial Era to the First World War* (Princeton, NJ: Princeton University Press, 1968) details the collapse of the peace movement generally. Another good chapter on the subject is in Merle Curti, *Peace or War: The American Struggle, 1636–1936* (New York: W. W. Norton, 1936).

Difficult to classify is Edmund Wilson's inspired foray, *Patriotic Gore: Studies in the Literature of the American Civil War* (New York: Farrar, Straus and Giroux, 1964). Delivering both more and less than its subtitle promises, the book reads like the series of *New Yorker* articles it started out as. Wilson's coverage of Civil War literature is idiosyncratic; it leaves out much of what conventionally would be considered belles lettres in order to veer in the direction of more practical, worldly writings. While *Patriotic Gore* gives slight attention to the poetry of Walt Whitman or the novels of Mark Twain and Henry James, it has noteworthy essays on Ulysses S. Grant, Alexander Stephens, and Oliver Wendell Holmes, Jr. In his introduction, Wilson compares Abraham Lincoln to Lenin and Bismarck, and although he does not sustain this interpretation throughout, no work is better at depicting the wartime militarization and brutalization of American culture.

A more conventional study of Civil War literature is Daniel Aaron, *The Unwritten War: American Writers and the Civil War* (New York: Alfred A. Knopf, 1973). Randall C. Jimerson, *The Private Civil War: Popular Thought During the Sectional Conflict* (Baton Rouge: Louisiana State University Press, 1988), reconstructs popular feelings for both sides; Earl J. Hess, *Liberty, Virtue and Progress: Northerners and Their War for the Union* (New York: New York University Press, 1988), briefly attempts an integrated picture of the North's wartime ideology. The way the established Protestant churches fell in behind the war is covered in James H. Moorhead, *American Apocalypse: Yankee Protestants and the Civil War, 1860–1869* (New Haven: Yale University Press, 1978).

The wartime Radical Republicans are depicted as opportunistic politicians using the slavery issue to fasten political and economic controls upon the South in T. Harry Williams, *Lincoln and the Radicals* (Madison: University of Wisconsin Press, 1941). David Donald rises to the defense in "The Radicals and Lincoln," from *Lincoln Reconsidered* (cited prologue). The two historians then go at it again in their selections for Grady McWhiney, ed., *Grant, Lee, Lincoln and the Radicals* (cited the previous chapter). Donald's denial of any sharp divergence between Lincoln and the Radicals also comes through in the second volume of his biography of the Radical leader in the Senate, *Charles Sumner and the Rights of Man* (New York: Alfred A. Knopf, 1970), and this conclusion finds confirmation in Hans L. Trefousse, *The Radical Republicans: Lincoln's Vanguard for Racial Justice* (New York: Alfred A. Knopf, 1968). Fawn M. Brodie, *Thaddeus Stevens: Scourge of the South* (New York: W. W. Norton, 1959), tells the life of the most notorious House Radical, superseding the more critical Richard Nelson Current, *Old Thad Stevens: A Story of Ambition* (Madison: University of Wisconsin Press, 1942).

Henry D. Shapiro, *Confiscation of Confederate Property in the North* (Ithaca, NY: Cornell University Press, 1962), is a short, highly specialized monograph on an important facet of Congress's confiscation acts. For the development of the Union's policy toward the slaves, in addition to works on Lincoln himself already mentioned, see John Hope Franklin, *The Emancipation Proclamation* (Garden City, NY: Doubleday, 1963), and LaWanda Cox, *Lincoln and Black Freedom: A Study of Presidential Leadership* (Columbia: University of South Carolina Press, 1981). Negative northern reaction to the Emancipation Proclamation is discussed in Forrest G. Wood, *Black Scare: The Racist Response to Emancipation and Reconstruction* (Berkeley: University of California Press, 1968), and V. Jacque Voegeli, *Free but Not Equal: The Midwest and the Negro During the Civil War* (Chicago: University of Chicago Press, 1967). Benjamin Quarles, *Lincoln and the Negro* (New York: Oxford University Press, 1972), offers one of the fullest discussions of the administration's continuing flirtation with colonization.

Stephen W. Sears, *Landscape Turned Red: The Battle of Antietam* (New York: Ticknor & Fields, 1983), is the best written modern study of the Civil War's bloodiest day, but James V. Murfin, *The Gleam of Bayonets: The Battle of Antietam and the Maryland Campaign of 1862* (New York: T. Yoseloff, 1965), shows deeper research. A useful collection is Gary W. Gallagher, ed., *Antietam: Essays on the 1862 Maryland Campaign* (Kent, OH: Kent State University Press, 1989). Richard R. Duncan is good on the political implications of Lee's invasion in "Marylanders and the Invasion of 1862," reprinted in John T. Hubbell's *Battles Lost and Won* (cited ch. 5).

The earliest study of blacks during the Civil War, Bell Irvin Wiley, *Southern Negroes, 1861–1865* (New Haven: Yale University Press, 1938), is still much admired. A recent synthesis is Ira Berlin, Barbara J. Fields, Steven F. Miller, Joseph P. Reidy, and Leslie S. Rowland, *Slaves No More: Three Essays on Emancipation and the Civil War* (Cambridge, U.K.: Cambridge University Press, 1992). Leon F. Litwack, *Been in the Storm So Long: The Aftermath of Slavery* (New York: Alfred A. Knopf, 1979), is a massive, pioneering work on black reaction to the transition from slavery to freedom. Three indicative local studies on the wartime crumbling of the peculiar institution are Clarence L. Mohr, *On the Threshold of Freedom: Masters and Slaves in Civil War Georgia* (Athens: University of Georgia Press, 1986); John Cimprich, *Slavery's End in Tennessee, 1861–1865* (University: University of Alabama Press, 1985); and James H. Brewer, *The Confederate Negro: Virginia's Craftsmen and Military Laborers, 1861–1865* (Durham, NC: Duke University Press, 1969).

Various features of early Union policy toward and treatment of liberated slaves are covered in C. Peter Ripley, *Slaves and Freedman in Civil War Louisiana* (Baton Rouge: Louisiana State University Press, 1976); James L. Roark, *Masters Without Slaves: Southern Planters in the Civil War and Reconstruction* (New York: W. W. Norton, 1977); and Lawrence N. Powell, *New Masters: Northern Planters During the Civil War Reconstruction* (New Haven: Yale University Press, 1980). Exemplary at uncovering the frequent harshness of the Union military toward blacks is Louis S. Gerteis, *From Contraband to Freedman: Federal Policy Toward Southern Blacks, 1861–1865* (Westport, CT: Greenwood Press, 1973). Willie Lee Rose, *Rehearsal for Reconstruction: The Port Royal Experiment* (Indianapolis: Bobbs-Merrill, 1964), was a ground-breaking assessment of one area where the Union military put freed blacks to work on government-run plantations.

The military motivation for emancipation is explored in Mary Frances Berry, *Military Necessity and Civil Rights Policy: Black Citizenship and the Constitution, 1861–1868* (Port Washington, NY: Kennikat Press, 1977). Dudley Taylor Cornish, *The Sable Arm: Negro Troops in the Union Army, 1861–1865* (New York: Longmans, Green, 1956), surveys the subject of black troops generally, and Joseph T. Glatthaar, *Forged in Battle: The Civil War Alliance of Black Soldiers and White Officers* (New York: Free Press, 1990), looks into an important aspect more deeply. The attack of the 54th Massachusetts on Battery Wagner is fairly faithfully depicted in the movie *Glory*. A history of this black unit and its white commander is Peter Burchard, *One Gallant Rush: Robert Gould Shaw and His Brave Black Regiment* (New York: St. Martin's Press, 1965), and the latest account of overall Union operations against this southern stronghold is Stephen R. Wise, *Gate of Hell: Campaign for Charleston Harbor, 1863* (Columbia: University of South Carolina Press, 1995).

Many of the works on Civil War diplomacy in chapter 6 cover the Laird rams and emancipation's diplomatic ramifications. A new study, Howard Jones, *Union in Peril: The Crisis Over British Intervention in the Civil War* (Chapel Hill: University of North Carolina Press, 1992), finds that the threat of British mediation was far more serious than previous scholars had realized and that this threat actually persisted after Antietam and the

Emancipation Proclamation. Detailing foreign construction of the Rebel navy are Frank J. Merli, *Great Britain and the Confederate Navy* (Bloomington: Indiana University Press, 1970), and Warren F. Spencer, *The Confederate Navy in Europe* (University: University of Alabama Press, 1983). Specifically on the rams themselves, see Wilbur Devereux Jones, *The Confederate Rams at Birkenhead: A Chapter in Anglo-American Relations* (Tuscaloosa: Confederate, 1961). Merli's article, "The Confederate Navy, 1861–1865," from Kenneth J. Hagan, *In Peace and War* (cited ch. 6), disputes the conventional view that these warships were a serious threat to the Union blockade.

A book that will tell you everything you wanted to know about U.S. relations with France during the Civil War is Warren F. Spencer and Lynn M. Case, *The United States and France: Civil War Diplomacy* (Philadelphia: University of Pennsylvania Press, 1970). More on Louis Napoleon's adventure in Mexico can be found in Alfred Jackson Hanna and Kathryn Abbey Hanna, *Napoleon III and Mexico: American Triumph Over Monarchy* (Chapel Hill: University of North Carolina Press, 1971), and Thomas David Schoonover, *Dollars Over Dominion: The Triumph of Liberalism in Mexican-United States Relations, 1861–1867* (Baton Rouge: Louisiana State University Press, 1978).

Two works on Seward's major territorial acquisition are Ronald J. Jensen, *The Alaska Purchase and Russian-American Relations* (Seattle: University of Washington, 1975), and Paul S. Holbo, *Tarnished Expansion: The Alaska Scandal, the Press, and Congress, 1867–1871* (Knoxville: University of Tennessee Press, 1937). Joe Patterson Smith, *The Republican Expansionists of the Early Reconstruction Era* (Chicago: University of Chicago Libraries, 1933); Donald F. Warner, *The Idea of Continental Union: Agitation for the Annexation of Canada to the United States, 1849–1893* (Lexington: University of Kentucky Press, 1960); and Ernest N. Paolina, *The Foundations of the American Empire: William Henry Seward and U.S. Foreign Policy* (Ithaca, NY: Cornell University Press, 1973), cover the postwar expansionist impulses more broadly. Adrian Cook recounts the final resolution of *The Alabama Claims: American Politics and Anglo-American Relations, 1865–1872* (Ithaca, NY: Cornell University Press, 1975).

9

Republican Neo-Mercantilism Versus Confederate War Socialism

Union Finance

Wars are very expensive. Nearly all governments throughout history have spent more on waging and preparing for war than on anything else. In fact, until recently governments usually spent more on war than all other things combined. Yet Lincoln's Secretary of the Treasury, Salmon Portland Chase, in addition to being a Radical on slavery, was a former Democrat. That meant he despised government debt, paper money, and internal taxes. Good government in Chase's eyes was frugal government. Imagine, then, his mortification when he discovered that the Union's wartime deficit for only the first three months after Fort Sumter would exceed $17 million.

The national government at the time had only two sources of revenue: a very low tariff and the sale of public lands. These had been more than adequate to cover minuscule peacetime budgets, except during periods of financial panic. The highest that annual outlays had reached was $74.2 million in 1858. That translates into little more than $1.3 billion in today's (1995) prices. Adjusting for population, the government in Washington was spending approximately $2.50 per person in 1858, or the equivalent of $44 per person today. This was less than 2 percent of the economy's total output.

We have no good records of how much state and local governments spent at the time, but if we assume twice as much as the national government, which was true in 1902, the first year for which we have good information, then total spending for all levels of government was only 5.5 percent of national income. Compare that with today when all government expenditures account for more than one-third of United States income.

Government overall was thus small and unobtrusive. The national debt, for all intents and purposes, had been completely paid off in 1835. By 1860, mainly as a consequence of the Mexican War, it stood at a bearable $65 million—*less* than annual outlays in 1858.[1] Most Americans paid no taxes whatsoever to federal officials directly, and their only regular contact with any representatives of central authority was probably through the United States Post Office—if they had any contact at all. Indeed, in New York City, the government delivered only one million letters in 1856 as compared with the ten million carried by private companies.

The cost of waging the Civil War, however, would ultimately average $1.75 million per day. These unprecedented expenditures struck at the very moment that anticipated revenues were falling. Although the outgoing Congress had raised the tariff even before President Buchanan left office, the Treasury Department was not going to be able to collect any duties from the South in the foreseeable future. Meanwhile the prices charged for public lands had been declining, and in 1862 a Homestead Act finally passed Congress without a presidential veto, implementing the demand that settlers get free title to 160 acres of government land after five years of settlement.

Chase therefore found himself resorting to a mixture of all the financial expedients he hated. Congress started off in 1861 with a direct tax of $20 million on real estate. This was the first internal tax Americans had paid to Washington in nearly forty years, but it was at least administered through the state governments. Such was not the case with the Internal Revenue Act passed by Congress one year later. As James G. Blaine, an up-and-coming Maine Republican, admitted, the act tried to tax nearly everything. "One of the most searching, thorough, comprehensive systems of taxation ever devised by any Government," he called it. "Spirituous and malt liquors and tobacco were relied upon for a very large share of revenue. . . . Manufactures of cotton, wool, flax, hemp, iron, steel, wood, stone, earth, and every other material were taxed three percent. Banks, insurance and railroad companies, telegraph companies, and all other corporations were made to pay tribute. The butcher paid thirty cents for every beef slaughtered, ten cents for every hog, five cents for every sheep. Carriages, billiard-tables, yachts, gold and silver plate, and all other articles of luxury were levied upon heavily. Every profession and every calling, except the ministry of religion, was included within the far-reaching provisions of the law and subjected to tax for license. Bankers and pawnbrokers, lawyers and horse-dealers, physicians and confectioners, commercial brokers and peddlers, proprietors of theaters and jugglers on the street, were indiscriminately summoned to aid the National Treasury."[2]

In addition to these excise, sales, and license taxes, the Internal Revenue Act of 1862 also introduced stamp taxes on most legal documents and an inheritance tax. Collection required the creation of an extensive Internal Revenue bureaucracy with 185 districts reaching into every hamlet and town. Evasion still became a major problem, especially for the whiskey excise, as bootleg liquor displaced taxed liquor on the market. Congress's most portentous revenue measure, however, was a national income tax. Authorized in August 1861, this was the first such tax in United States history. It ultimately covered all incomes over $600 per year (or $10,500 in 1995 prices) at graduated rates from 5 to 10 percent. To ensure compliance, the government adopted a British practice and withheld money from people's income when it could. The sources most vulnerable to withholding were government salaries, and dividends and interest from the stocks and bonds of banks, railroads, and other corporations.

At the war's close the United States could boast higher taxation per capita than any other nation. But all the new and old taxes combined were just sufficient to cover about one-fifth of the Civil War's monetary cost. Chase therefore borrowed some money directly from the general public, with the aid of an extravagant publicity campaign handled by private financier, Jay Cooke. The Union had to go to the banks for most of its loans, however. And this required that Congress undermine the restraints built into the country's prewar financial structure.

That structure was the ideological handiwork of the Jacksonian Democrats. Its major accomplishment was divorcing the central government from the banking system. There was no nationally chartered central bank, and the Treasury, as much as possible, avoided dealing with the many state-chartered banks. The only legally recognized money was specie, that is, gold or silver coins. The economy's currency consisted solely of bank notes redeemable in specie on demand. Private competition thus regulated the circulation of paper money.

Although traditional historians have subjected this era of unregulated banking to trumped-up charges of financial instability, many economists are coming to agree that it was probably the best monetary system the United States has ever had. The alleged excesses of the fraudulent, insolvent, or highly speculative "wildcat" banks were highly exaggerated. Total losses that bank note holders suffered throughout the entire antebellum period in all states that enacted free-banking laws would not equal the losses for one year from today's rate of inflation (2 percent), if superimposed onto the economy of 1860.[3] Moreover, most of these losses resulted from too much regulation, not too little. Lingering at the state level were prohibitions on branch banking, mandates for minimum specie reserves, restrictions on the issue of small-denomination bank notes, and requirements that banks purchase state bonds, which at this time were among the most dubious investments. The banks were also vulnerable to international flows of specie, especially as orchestrated by the British government's Bank of England, and so the country suffered major bank runs in 1837 and 1857. But no monetary system is perfect. By any objective comparison this one was relatively stable and crisis free.

The Treasury's initial war loan of $150 million, however, put a heavy strain on the northern banks who had subscribed to the loan. After the financial community realized that the war would not be quick or easy, Treasury bonds dropped in value. As gold reserves drained from the banks, governments authorized suspension of specie payments in December of 1861, a resort banks had always depended upon during panics. These fifteen thousand institutions were soon issuing over $100 million worth of irredeemable notes, all depreciating at different rates. The Republicans then drafted the National Currency Acts of 1863 and 1864. These acts fashioned a network of nationally chartered banks, which were required to hold specified quantities of war bonds. In exchange, they could issue national bank notes supplied to them by the new federal Comptroller of the Currency. The state-chartered banks were still allowed to compete by providing other financial services. But a prohibitive 10 percent tax on state bank notes imposed in 1865 made sure that nationally chartered banks had a currency monopoly. In other words, the national banks became privileged intermediaries whereby the Treasury's war debt was converted into a government-managed circulating medium.

Congress meanwhile had passed the Legal Tender Act in early 1862. This empowered Secretary Chase to issue a form of paper money that became popularly known as Greenbacks. The Greenbacks were different from national bank notes in several ways. Although the banks did not resume specie payments for the duration of the war, the national bank notes at least made a contractual promise to be exchangeable for reserves (which meant eventually for gold) and were nominally the liability of private institutions. The Greenbacks were unbacked, directly issued by the government, and made legal tender through fiat for all payments, public and private, except tariff duties and interest on the Treasury's debt. These differences gave Chase extreme misgivings about the Greenback's constitutionality. But he was desperate.

"Is it necessary to incur all the unquestionable evils of inconvertible paper, forced into circulation by act of Congress?" asked Senator Charles Sumner; is it necessary, he wanted to know, "to suffer the stain upon our national faith—to bear the stigma of a seeming repudiation—to lose for the present that credit which in itself is a treasury—and to teach debtors everywhere that contracts may be varied by the will of the stronger? Surely there is much in these inquiries which may make us pause. . . . It is hard—very hard—to think that such a country, so powerful, so rich, and so beloved, should be compelled to adopt a policy of even questionable propriety."

Yet Sumner announced to the Senate that he would vote for the

Legal Tender Act because of the Treasury Secretary's endorsement. "Surely we must all be against paper money—we must all insist on maintaining the integrity of the government—and we must all set our faces against any proposition like the present, except as a temporary expedient, rendered imperative by the exigency of the hour. . . . Others may doubt if the exigency is sufficiently imperative, but the Secretary of the Treasury, whose duty it is to understand the occasion, does not doubt."[4] The final total of Greenbacks put into circulation reached $431 million, supplemented by a small quantity of interest-bearing notes and other currency. All this government paper coupled with the flood of private bank notes doubled the Union's money stock by 1863. The consequent inflation put specie at a premium. Greenback dollars had fallen in July of 1864 to a low of 35 cents worth of gold.

The wartime expansion of paper money caused not only a rise in prices but a rise in counterfeiting, justifying the creation of a new federal agency to hunt down the culprits. This was the origin of the Secret Service, set up, just as the conflict ended, under the unscrupulous adventurer, William P. Wood, who as Capitol prison warden had already done intelligence work for the State Department. Another way the government tightened its control over money was by banning private minting for the first time. Although the official United States mint had issued gold and silver coins since George Washington's presidency, until the Civil War these had competed with coins issued by foreign governments and by privately owned domestic mints. Now, however, Americans would no longer enjoy the freedom to choose these alternative moneys.

The Lincoln Administration even tried to interfere with holding specie as protection from the government's inflation. Banks in the northeast offered deposits denominated either in gold dollars or Greenback dollars. On the west coast, gold was also still the circulating money and Greenbacks only accepted at a discount. In the summer of 1864, Congress shut down trading in contracts promising future delivery of gold. But this threatened further to disrupt foreign commerce, which depended on the metal. Congress had to back off hastily, and thereafter the Treasury confined any efforts at manipulating the gold exchange to the issue of gold certificates, authorized the year before and convertible on demand, but not actually put in circulation until 1865.

Confederate Finance

The Confederacy's conventional military strategy ensured that it, like the Union, would bear staggering wartime expenditures. Chase's Confederate counterpart, Christopher G. Memminger, was also a hard-money man, but he likewise ended up turning to a mixture of heavy taxation, government borrowing, and fiat money. The South however could not call upon wealth as abundant as that available to the North. Taxation consequently covered less than 7 percent of the South's total war costs.[5]

That was not for any lack of trying, even though the Confederacy, like the Union, delayed truly confiscatory measures because it expected a short war. The Rebel government imposed duties on imports, as soon as it was established, and also on exports, something the United States Constitution prohibited. Yet the Federal blockade along with the self-inflicted cotton embargo severely circumscribed any revenue from those sources. The Confederate Congress's first stab at internal taxation, like the Union's, was a direct tax upon the state governments. Yet again most southern states converted this tax into a war loan by issuing state bonds to finance their shares. So eventually in April of 1863 the Confederate government imposed a comprehensive revenue measure that included a graduated income tax, an excess profits tax, license taxes, excise taxes, and a 10 percent tax in kind.

Farmers paid the tax in kind by directly surrendering their agricultural products. The southern economy's lack of monetary development necessitated this expedient, but the high-handed behavior of the TIK men who enforced it engendered widespread resistance, particularly in North Carolina. "We pledge ourselves to each other to resist, to the bitter end, any such monarchical tax" was among many similar resolutions passed at public meetings of the common folk.[6]

Secretary of the Treasury Memminger secured one-fourth of his government's income through borrowing. As in the North, most southern banks ceased paying specie immediately after secession.

They therefore had enough gold and silver left in their vaults to subscribe to much of the first Confederate loan, of $15 million. The South later floated an $8.5 million loan abroad through the French financier Emile Erlanger. Greater amounts came from produce loans, which were fiscally analogous to the tax in kind. At first planters and farmers would subscribe a share of their crop, sell it themselves for hard money, and loan the proceeds to the government. But later they exchanged cotton and other commodities directly for Confederate bonds. Churches, ladies' societies, and patriotic citizens also donated more than $2 million during the course of the war. Finally, a sequestration law, passed in response to the Union confiscation acts, expropriated all northern private property within Confederate jurisdiction and provided the government some additional resources.

But overall Memminger was far less successful with taxation and borrowing than Chase, and therefore relied far more extensively upon paper money. Starting in March of 1861 with $1 million of one-year Treasury notes bearing 3.65 percent, the Confederate Congress by August of the same year had authorized more than $100 million of non-interest bearing notes. Although this paper money was acceptable for most tax payments to the central government, what really helped it circulate was the willingness of the state governments and state banks to receive it. Indeed, Memminger compelled the conservative New Orleans banks, which had continued to pay out gold and silver after the Sumter crisis, to stop doing so in order to prevent specie from competing with Confederate currency.

The Confederate Treasury ultimately issued over $1 billion worth of currency, more than twice the amount of Greenbacks. Its printing presses ran continuously toward the end of the war. This monetary expansion spurred ruinous price increases that made the Union's wartime inflation seem trivial. The blockade, an additional $45 million in paper currency issued by individual southern states, and uncounted "shinplasters" issued by local governments and private companies contributed to the monetary depreciation. A Confederate dollar was worth 82.7 cents in specie in 1862, 29.0 cents in 1863, and 1.7 cents in 1865. Between 1860 and 1864 prices less than doubled in the North as compared with multiplying twenty-seven times in the South. Only southern banks exercised any restraint, having no central bank or national banking system to encourage their monetary expansion. As the war dragged on, bank notes circulated at a premium, despite being immediately redeemable only in Confederate paper.

The Rebel Congress attempted a currency "reform" in February 1864, but this amounted to nothing more than a phased devaluation and repudiation. After January of the following year, the government would not accept its old currency at all, although it continued to issue new currency. "In the winter of 1863–64 Congress became aware of the fact that prices were higher than they should be under a sound currency," was the sarcastic observation of George Cary Eggleston, a non-commissioned officer in the Confederate army. "If Congress suspected this at any earlier date, there is nothing in the proceedings of that body to indicate it. Now, however, . . . [t]he lawgivers took the alarm and sat themselves down to devise a remedy for the evil condition of affairs." But Eggleston was not very impressed with the resulting currency reform: "With that infantile simplicity which characterized nearly all the doings and quite all the financial legislation of the Richmond Congress, it was decided that the very best way to enhance the value of the currency was to depreciate it still further by a declaratory statute, and then to issue a good deal more of it."[7]

The skyrocketing inflation worked a great hardship on the southern people. As this hidden tax diverted resources to the Confederate war effort, prices climbed faster than incomes. Real wages fell by almost two thirds. Food riots swept through Richmond and other southern cities in the war's third year, with wives and mothers at the forefront of the rioters. "My salary of $3000 goes about as far as $300 would do in ordinary times in purchasing all the articles of household necessity, the average of prices being about ten fold," noted a bureau head at the Confederate War Department in his diary. "The consequence is that with an income from all sources of at least $6000 and a good deal of help from my father-in-law, my family is reduced to two meals a day, . . . and they are of the most plain and economical scale."[8]

The state governments attempted to step in and aid suffering families. They blocked debt collection with stay laws and tried to prevent speculative hoarding. Previously relief had been handled at the local level, but now the state legislatures appropriated millions for this purpose. Georgia spent more in 1863 than during the entire decade of the 1850s. Inflation accounted for some of this increase, and nearly half these expenditures were military, but the other half was welfare. By 1864, more than 37,000 families were receiving some form of relief from the state of Alabama—37 percent of all families in the state.[9] Unfortunately, government welfare was powerless to create more real resources and so was doomed to futility as long as the military's appetite remained unabated.

The Rebel government at least never made its paper money legal tender. It did, however, force much of this money into circulation through the impressment of supplies. Commanders in the field initiated the practice, and the Confederate Congress formally systematized impressments in 1863. The Commissary and Quartermaster Bureaus would seize food and other items as needed in exchange for Confederate currency at officially fixed prices, a step beyond anything the Union did. Because the fixed prices were invariably lower than the inflationary market prices, shortages became rampant.

Impressments made Southerners suffer almost as much from the proximity of their own armies as from the invasions of Union armies. One Confederate soldier from Mississippi confided that "I beleave [sic] our troops are doing as much harm in this country as the yankees would do with the exception of burning houses."[10] Moreover, the authorities extensively impressed slave labor. Although these slaves, as well as conscripted free blacks, dug entrenchments and earthworks, served as cooks and teamsters, and otherwise rendered vital service to the war effort, their impressment further destabilized the peculiar institution. Nearly every southern state governor protested. The chief executive of Alabama, for instance, denounced "the impressment of private property" as "always odious" and "disastrous" in its "practical operation." Better "for the Government to pay double price. . . . If we fail to achieve our independence in this contest, the failure will arise from breaking down the spirits of the people by acts of tyranny by our own officers." Impressment only "creates opposition to the Government and our cause."[11]

Economic Mobilization in the North

The Republican Party was an antislavery coalition of both former Whigs and former Democrats. Prior to Fort Sumter, at least eight former Democrats had served as Republican governors, seven as Republican Senators, and many more as Republican Congressmen. Once the fighting got underway, however, Congress implemented the traditional Whig program of government subsidies and economic regulation. Ex-Whigs dominated Republican councils partially because they had nowhere else to go, whereas the Democratic Party was still viable throughout much of the North. Lincoln himself had been a Whig, as had Secretary of State Seward. But mostly, it was the natural dynamics of wartime intervention that subverted the prevailing Democratic regime of free trade and *laissez faire*.

The Whigs, for instance, had been the guardians of the defunct Bank of the United States. Although the Jacksonian legacy was virile enough to block reestablishment of a single central bank, the new National Banking System nevertheless reconstituted the alliance between the banks and the central government. Furthermore, the war brought the United States Treasury into regular contact with the country's capital and financial markets. Similarly the Whigs had long believed in protective tariffs. The new party's 1860 platform had contained an ambiguous plank, which could be interpreted as favoring protection or not, depending upon where the Republicans campaigned. After raising duties in 1861 for revenue purposes, Republican legislators took advantage of the southern departure from Congress to jack up the rates higher and higher. The war's internal taxes helped justify steep tariffs, since domestic industry would otherwise face unfair foreign competition. Protectionists also exploited the clandestine activities of Confederate agents who operated out of Canada as an excuse to repeal the reciprocity treaty that had permitted free trade with that nation since 1854. By war's end, average duties had risen to 47 percent and the free list had been cut in half, effectively stifling foreign competition.

Even before the southern states seceded, Republicans had officially embraced the Whig policy of federally funded internal improvements (as had northern Democrats as well). Their 1860 platform called upon the federal government "to render immediate and efficient aid" to construct "a Railroad to the Pacific Ocean."[12] Sectional rivalry had prevented government sponsorship of a transcontinental railroad before the war, but in 1862 the Republicans were able to pass the Pacific Railway Act. It chartered two private corporations, the Union Pacific and Central Pacific. They received ten square miles of public land for every mile of track constructed along a central route, supplemented by generous loans from the public treasury. Considerations of military defense helped assure the act's adoption. "You have some seven hundred miles of coast to defend," declared on Oregon Congressman, "and with no iron-clad steamers and no forts there, we are at the mercy of any foreign Power, and especially at the mercy of England."[13] Two years later Congress doubled the lands granted to the Union and Central Pacific and made new grants for a second transcontinental, the Northern Pacific.

The Union's relationship with existing railroads was also intimate. Congress authorized the President to seize any rail and telegraph line at his discretion, and all the railways in occupied portions of the South were under full military management. Inside the North, however, the War Department directly controlled only a few tracks close to the front; the government's influence derived primarily from being the rail companies' largest customer. As a result, some of the North's subsidized and over-expanded rail lines paid dividends to stockholders for the first time.

The Lincoln Administration enlisted other interests with a shower of legislative and administrative favors. Farmers were courted with a new cabinet-level Department of Agriculture in 1862. The Contract Labor Law of 1864 attempted to help employers offset the wartime decline in immigration. It established the post of Commissioner of Immigration and gave government sanction— until its repeal four years later—to twelve-month labor contracts for immigrants, resurrecting a practice that had died with indentured servitude. The Morrill Act of 1862 bestowed huge tracts of the public domain upon the loyal state governments for the purpose of endowing colleges that would offer agricultural, mechanical, and military instruction. This was not simply the first national support for education; it also promoted military training in an arena where such training had been rare.

Because a state's educational grant depended upon its population—30,000 acres for each Senator and Congressman—the eastern states got title to more land in the west than the western states. Furthermore, both the Morrill and Pacific Railway Acts dampened the benefits of the Homestead Act, the only wartime measure that could be said to be consistent with the Democratic Party's traditional ideology. The state governments and the railroad companies engrossed twice the acreage that was given free to homesteaders, and got the choicer plots at that. Almost unnoticed, Congress also took the first small step toward pulling unsettled wilderness off the market entirely to create expansive reaches for government-managed conservation and parks; in 1864 it granted the Yosemite lands to California as a nature preserve.

There were a few government-run enterprises that operated in the North during the war. Of the two federal armories that existed beforehand, only the one at Springfield continued to fashion rifles, the Confederates having put the other at Harper's Ferry out of operation. The Ordnance Department controlled four other manufacturing arsenals that produced accoutrements and ammunition, including the new arsenal at Rock Island, Illinois. The Union set up clothing factories in Cincinnati and Philadelphia; several drug and medicine laboratories; and meat-packing houses in Tennessee and Kentucky. Establishing the Government Printing Office and the Bureau of Engraving and Printing allowed the national government to conduct its own printing and publishing. And in 1863, Congress created the National Academy of Sciences to seek out technological innovations useful for the war effort.

The Union mobilization of the economy, however, relied generally upon profitable war contracts. These forged a new and close partnership between private businesses and governments at every level. Because the tax structure and contract awards tended to favor economically integrated firms, the Civil War encouraged corporate concentration. Industrialists and financiers such as Andrew Carnegie, J. Pierpont Morgan, and John D. Rockefeller all started their fortunes during the war. Charges of graft and profiteering became widespread, especially with respect to the strictly licensed trade in occupied territory. A special congressional committee uncovered one early case where the War Department had paid $117 for horses, when the market price was $60. Worse still, out of one lot of 250 horses, all but 27 were diseased, maimed, or otherwise unfit. Such revelations contributed to the departure in January 1862 of Lincoln's first Secretary of War, Simon Cameron, a venal, machine politician from Pennsylvania. Cameron's replacement, Edwin M. Stanton, was a former Democrat from the same state whose rock-solid public integrity was counterbalanced by obsequious devious-ness and vindictive paranoia. But no matter what the extent of corruption, the war ended up creating an intimacy between the military and industry that brought back the abandoned and discred-ited policies of seventeenth-century mercantilism.

An economic boom in the northern war industries fostered an illusion of general prosperity. "Everybody admits that, in the main, the industry of the North is very flourishing," said the *New York Times* of July 2, 1863. "The farms teem, the workshops and the factories whir, and the bustle of trade fills the streets. Labor was never in greater demand, or more largely paid. The industry of the country has recovered from the terrible shock given it by the first outbreak of the war." The *Times*'s euphoria was unbounded. It claimed that industry "is putting forth its energies with an activity, and with a success, seldom if ever surpassed before."[14]

The war prosperity, in reality, did not extend to all sectors of the northern economy. Adjusting for inflation, workers' wages actually fell by one-third. Laborers sometimes organized unions to keep abreast of living costs, but the Lincoln Administration introduced the policy of employing federal troops against strikers: at the Parrott armaments factory in Cold Springs, New York; at mines in Tioga County, Pennsylvania; and in the border states throughout the conflict. The War Department in July 1864 operated the Philadel-phia and Reading Railroad because striking engineers had inter-rupted the delivery of coal to Philadelphia. This marked the first presidential seizure of private property during a labor dispute.

Modern historians have discovered that the Civil War in fact retarded economic growth. The 1860s saw the American economy's worst performance of any decade between 1840 and 1930, with real income per capita falling by 3 percent. Some of this loss stemmed from wartime destruction in the South. But if the North is considered in isolation, the Civil War still hampered prosperity. Even most of the war industries, outside of woolens, experienced a slump, despite increased participation of women in the work force. Iron production for arms went up, but that was more than offset by declining production for railways. Output in the Massachusetts boot and shoe industry fell by 30 percent, because military contracts did not counteract the loss of southern markets. Overall the war erased at least five years of wealth accumulation.

Economic Mobilization in the South

While the Civil War saw the triumph in the North of Republican neo-mercantilism, it saw the emergence in the South of full-blown State socialism. Nowhere did the Confederacy have greater disadvantages than in industrial output. A single county in Connecticut manufactured firearms in 1860 worth ten times more than that produced in all southern states. Except for the Tredegar Iron Works in Richmond, the South did not even have a cannon foundry. With little native industry to call upon, the Rebel government moved immediately and directly into its own war production.

General Josiah Gorgas, the Pennsylvania-born Chief of Confederate Ordnance, took the lead in establishing government-owned facilities. By 1863 his diary revealed justifiable pride in this forced industrialization: "It is three years ago today since I took charge of the Ordnance Department. . . . I have succeeded beyond my utmost expectations. . . . Large arsenals have been organized at Richmond, Fayetteville, Augusta, Charleston, Columbus, Macon, Atlanta and Selma, and smaller ones at Danville, Lynchburgh, and Montgomery. . . . A superb powder mill has been built at Augusta. . . . Lead smelting works were established by me at Petersburg, and turned over to the Nitre and Mining Bureau, when that Bureau was at my request separated from mine. A cannon foundry established at Macon for heavy guns, and bronze foundries at Macon, Columbus, Ga., and at Augusta; a foundry for shot and shell at Salisbury, N.C.; a large shop for leather work at Clarksville, Va.; besides the

Armories here and at Fayetteville, a manufactory of carbines has been built up here; a rifle factory at Asheville; . . . a new and very large armory at Macon, including a pistol factory; . . . a second pistol factory at Columbus, Ga. . . . Where three years ago we were not making a gun, pistol nor a sabre, no shot nor shell (except at the Tredegar Works)—a pound of powder—we now make all these in quantities to meet the demands of our large armies."[15]

In addition to the powder mill, chemical plant, small-arms factories, and foundries belonging to Gorgas's Ordnance Bureau, the Confederate Navy set up its own cannon foundry and powder mill, as well as numerous shipyards. The Nitre and Mining Bureau extracted and refined coal, iron, copper, nitre, and lead. The Confederate Quartermaster Bureau ran its own clothing, shoe, and wagon factories. The southern state governments also operated arsenals, powder mills, textile mills, flour mills, saltworks, and a variety of other enterprises.

When the authorities did purchase supplies from private firms, they dictated prices and profits. The Rebel government sometimes loaned one-half the start-up capital to businesses, which in turn had to sell two-thirds of their production to the government. Because rigid regulations and soaring inflation made genuine profits impossible, private owners, one after another, turned their factories over to the public officials. Right from the conflict's beginning, the Confederacy had violated its constitution by loaning money for the completion of strategic railway links. Seven-eighths of the freight and two-thirds of the passengers transported on the Virginia Central Railroad during one year, to cite just one example, were for the government's account. Toward the very end, President Davis took possession of all un-captured southern railroads, steamboats, and telegraph lines outright, incorporating their employees and officers into the military.

Managing the ubiquitous system of war socialism was a central government bureaucracy that had grown from nothing to 70,000 civilians in 1863. The Confederate Constitution, moreover, in an effort to limit political patronage, had inadvertently laid the basis for an entrenched civil service by denying the president authority to fire most of these government employees. A quick glance at Augusta, Georgia, one of the new urban centers in the Confederate South, shows the results of this expansion. The Ordnance Bureau's powder works there was the second largest in the world, after the famed Waltham Abbey Works in England. An army clothing factory employed 1,500 female workers. The government ran two cotton presses; a manufacture of clothing, uniforms, and shoes for the Navy; flour mills; meat packing and vegetable canning factories; distilleries; a military bakery with twelve ovens; and an ordnance manufacture. The city's major private firm, the Augusta Textile Factory, did 92 percent of its work for the government.

Confederate war socialism was not merely confined to manufacturing and transportation. The states, in their efforts to stimulate food production and help enforce the cotton embargo, imposed limits upon the acreage of cotton and tobacco that planters could grow, and prohibited the distillation of liquor. The central government meanwhile acquired such large stockpiles of cotton through its produce loans and the tax in kind that it quickly became the market's largest cotton merchant.

Although this staple could not directly feed or equip southern soldiers, it provided collateral for the foreign Erlanger loan. It also brought in vast quantities of war supplies through an illicit but flourishing trade with the enemy. Both sides formally banned the trade. But whereas the Lincoln Administration gave exemptions to private businesses, the Davis government allowed military commanders to monopolize the exchange of cotton across the lines. When the embargo proved a diplomatic failure, the government dominated the reopened export trade in this commodity as well.

The Rebel government moved from its command over cotton into shipping. The Navy Department and North Carolina already were competing against private blockade-runners with one vessel each. The Confederate War Department in 1863 bought its own ships, acquired majority interest in others, and commandeered one-third to one-half the outbound cargo space on the remainder. The following year, the Confederate Congress granted President Davis total regulatory control over foreign exports and banned the importation of any goods it considered "non-essential." The South had now completely nationalized its foreign commerce.

Forced industrialization guaranteed that the agrarian South never lacked for arms and ammunition, even as it verged on starvation. By 1864 the state of Alabama, for instance, was producing four times more iron than had any other state, North or South, prior to the war. Accompanying all these policies were public exhortations for sacrifice to the common cause. *De Bow's Review*, a southern journal that had been in the forefront of the secessionist movement, printed one such call in 1862: "Every man should feel that he has an interest in the State, and that the State in a measure leans upon him; and he should rouse himself to efforts as bold and heroic as if all depended upon his single right arm. . . . It is implied in the spirit which times demand, that all private interests are sacrificed to the public good. The State becomes everything, and the individual nothing."[16]

One of the Civil War's enduring myths is that the South's unbending commitment to states' rights paralyzed its war effort. In actuality, Confederate war socialism was more economically centralized than the Union's neo-mercantilism, which at least relied heavily on private initiative. A North Carolinian serving in the Rebel Congress complained toward the war's close that the land was "alive" with government officials, "thick as locusts in Egypt." Richmond was "full of them," and even in his small hometown, he "could not walk without being elbowed off the street by them." Furthermore, Rebel central planning, while adequately serving the single-minded goal of supplying conventional armies, otherwise misallocated resources and fostered inefficiencies. What paralyzed the Confederacy was not a central government with too little power but one with too much. As the North Carolina Congressman belatedly realized, Southerners had permitted "too much of brass button and bayonet rule in the country."[17]

Chapter 9
Bibliographical Essay

The most succinct statement of the pervasive thesis that the South lost the war because its government was less centralized and more feeble than the North's is David Donald, "Died of Democracy," from Donald, ed., *Why the North Won the Civil War* (cited in ch. 7). "The real weakness of the Confederacy," he writes, "was that the Southern people insisted upon retaining their democratic liberties during wartime." While Donald himself offered this thesis partly to remind us that America's most cherished values were not all embodied in the Civil War's victor, so instinctive is the nationalism of most historians that they condemn those Southerners striving to preserve liberty during wartime, whether or not they accept Donald's conclusion about the actual results. As Joseph Stromberg observes (on p. 45 of "The War for Southern Independence: A Radical Libertarian Perspective," cited prologue), "Unionists pityingly dismiss Richmond's war effort as not measuring up to Lincolnian statism" and "criticize the people" for their "perverse state-rights fetish." These historians feel no discomfort about endorsing centralizing measures that would allegedly have helped the Confederacy win the war at the same time that they condemn southern secession. Their operative precept appears to be: if an omnipotent Union government is impossible then we will settle for an omnipotent Confederate government.

A major new study that analytically compares the growth of State power in the Union and Confederacy, suggesting quite the opposite of Donald, is Richard Franklin Bensel, *Yankee Leviathan: The Origins of Central State Authority in America, 1859–1877* (Cambridge, U.K.: Cambridge University Press, 1990). In two recent works that look only at the northern homefront, the growth of government through finance and economics figures prominently: Phillip Shaw Paludan, " 'A People's Contest': The Union and the Civil War, 1861–1865" (New York: Harper & Row, 1988), part of the New American Nation series; and J. Matthew Gallman, *The North Fights the Civil War: The Home Front* (Chicago: Ivan R. Dee, 1994), a more concise volume. All of these studies are equally relevant for the next chapter as well.

Bert W. Rein, *An Analysis and Critique of the Union Financing of the Civil War* (Amherst, MA: Amherst College Press, 1962), is a brief summary. Longer but weaker is Bray Hammond, *Sovereignty and an Empty Purse: Banks and Politics in the Civil War* (Princeton, NJ: Princeton University Press, 1970), which covers more than its subtitle implies. Robert P. Sharkey, *Money, Class and Party: An Economic Study in Civil War and Reconstruction* (Baltimore: Johns Hopkins Press, 1959), presents the political milieu of Union finance, demonstrating the underlying harmony between protectionist and inflationist interests and charting the Democracy's drift away from its hard-money heritage.

Sidney Ratner, *Taxation and Democracy in America* (New York: John

239

Wiley, 1967), is a historical survey of American taxation that gives good coverage to both the Union and the Confederacy, despite its unfortunate infatuation with government redistribution. (It is actually the second edition, under a different title, of Ratner's *American Taxation, Its History as a Social Force in Democracy* [New York: W. W. Norton, 1942].) An extremely detailed description of the Union's wartime taxes is Harry Edwin Smith, *The United States Federal Internal Tax History from 1861 to 1871* (Boston: Houghton, Mifflin, 1914). The classic history of American tariff duties remains Frank W. Taussig, *The Tariff History of the United States*, 8th edn. (New York: G. P. Putnam's Sons, 1931), whereas the older two volumes of Edward Stanwood, *Tariff Controversies in the Nineteenth Century* (New York: Russell & Russell, 1903), fill in the political background. For the way strained relations with Canada contributed to the end of trade reciprocity, see Robin W. Winks, *Canada and the United States: The Civil War Years* (Baltimore: Johns Hopkins Press, 1969).

The standard condemnation of the free-banking era is most readily accessible in Bray Hammond, *Banks and Politics in America* (cited in ch. 3). Subsequent research has overturned nearly everything Hammond had to say about the politics of banking in antebellum America, which could be tolerated if the author had not been so abysmally innocent of any sound monetary or financial theory. Most of the revisionist research on free banking has been spread through journal articles, and two summaries based on this literature are Kevin Dowd, "US Banking in the 'Free Banking' Period," in Dowd, ed., *The Experience of Free Banking* (London: Routledge, 1992), and Hugh Rockoff, "Lessons From the American Experience With Free Banking," in Forrest Capie and Geoffrey E Woods, eds., *Unregulated Banking: Chaos or Order* (New York: St. Martin's Press, 1991). Most contributions to this revision are either by Hugh Rockoff—"Money, Prices, and Banks in the Jacksonian Era," in Robert W. Fogel and Stanley L. Engerman, eds., *The Reinterpretation of American Economic History* (cited ch. 2); "American Free Banking Before the Civil War: A Reexamination," *Journal of Economic History*, 32 (March 1972), pp. 417–420; and "The Free Banking Era: A Reexamination," *Journal of Money, Credit and Banking*, 6 (May 1974), pp. 141–676—or by Arthur J. Rolnick and Warren E. Weber— "Free Banking, Wildcat Banking, and Shinplasters," Federal Reserve Bank of Minneapolis, *Quarterly Review* (Fall 1982), pp. 10–19; "New Evidence on the Free Banking Era," *American Economic Review*, 73 (December 1983), pp. 1080–091; "The Causes of Free Bank Failures: A Detailed Examination," *Journal of Monetary Economics*, 14 (November 1984), pp. 267–291; "Banking Instability and Regulation in the U.S. Free Banking Era," Federal Reserve Bank of Minneapolis, *Quarterly Review* (Summer 1985), pp. 2–9; and "Explaining the Demand for Free Bank Notes," *Journal of Monetary Economics*, 21 (Winter 1986), pp. 877–890. I should hastily add that these authors may not entirely share the positive assessment of free banking that I and many other economists think their research warrants. The best general profile of the antebellum financial system remains Peter Temin, *The Jacksonian Economy* (New York: W. W. Norton, 1969).

On the crucial role of Jay Cooke in marketing Union bonds and paving the way for the National Currency Acts, see Henrietta Larson, *Jay Cooke, Private Banker* (Cambridge, MA: Harvard University Press, 1936), and the first volume of Ellis Parson Oberholtzer, *Jay Cooke, Financier of the Civil War* (Philadelphia: George W. Jacobs, 1907). Among the few studies exclusively treating the Union's nationalization of the banks are Andrew McFarland Davis, *The Origin of the National Banking System* (Washington: Government Printing Office, 1910), and David M. Gische, "The New York City Banks and the Development of the National Banking System, 1860–1870," *American Journal of Legal History*, 23 (January 1979), pp. 21–67. Although the Civil War acts that created this system are invariably mistitled in historical accounts, their name at the time of passage was National *Currency* Acts. The government did not officially adopt the label of National *Banking* System until 1874. Often overlooked is that Congress started out in 1863 with a 2 percent tax on state bank notes, compared with half that on national bank notes. The fact that jacking up the rate to 10 percent was necessary to drive state notes out of circulation eloquently testifies to their superior efficiency and desirability. A great deal of additional literature pertains to the postwar operation of national banks, on which I will have much to say in chapter 13.

Union paper money gets thorough consideration in Wesley Clair Mitchell, *A History of the Greenbacks: With Special Reference to the Economic Consequences of Their Issue, 1862–65* (Chicago: University of Chicago Press, 1903). The same author covers northern inflation in *Gold, Prices and Wages Under the Greenback Standard* (Berkeley: University of California Press, 1908). Don C. Barrett, *The Greenbacks and Resumption of Specie Payments, 1862–1879* (Cambridge, MA: Harvard University Press, 1931), is also helpful.

Much misunderstood by non-economists is the legal tender provision of the Greenbacks. Some attribute the Confederacy's monetary problems to a failure to make its currency legal tender in private transactions. In fact, as the monetary history of the American colonies makes clear, all that is necessary to get government paper money to circulate is making it payable for taxes, along with some restraint on the amount issued and good prospects that the government will survive. As Charles W. Calomiris, one of the practitioners of the new monetary economics, has pointed out in "The Motives of U.S. Debt-Management Policy, 1790–1880: Efficient Discrimination and Time Consistency," in Roger L. Ransom and Richard Sutch, eds., *Research in Economic History: A Research Annual*, v. 13 (Greenwich, CT: JAI Press, 1991), the Union made Greenbacks legal tender not to support the currency but to assist the banks. This facilitated bank suspension by making Greenbacks legal substitutes for specie. Bank liabilities would now fall in value at the same rate as their primary assets, Treasury bonds and notes.

The only work I know with general coverage of Civil War counterfeiting generally is Lynn Glaser, *Counterfeiting in America: The History of an American Way to Wealth* ([New York]: Clarkson N. Potter, 1968), but Walter

S. Bowen and Harry Edward Heal, *The United States Secret Service* (Philadelphia: Chilton, 1900), contains the officially approved version of that agency's founding. (This agency should not be confused with the military-intelligence operations of General Lafayette C. Baker, which are sometimes over-glorified under the same appellation. See Edwin C. Fishel, "The Mythology of Civil War Intelligence," reprinted in John T. Hubbell, ed., *Battles Lost and Won* [cited ch. 5].) Also neglected are the private mints of the antebellum monetary system, but some facts about their vital role are available in B. W. Barnard, "The Use of Private Tokens for Money in the United States," *Quarterly Journal of Economics*, 31 (August 1917), pp. 600– 634; and chapter 3 of William C. Woolridge, *Uncle Sam, The Monopoly Man* (New Rochelle, NY: Arlington House, 1970).

Although there is no good single study of Union economic mobilization, particularly on the crucial, but overlooked, contribution of northern states, much can be gleaned from Emerson David Fite, *Social and Industrial Conditions in the North During the Civil War* (New York: Macmillan, 1910). John Niven, *Connecticut for the Union* (cited ch. 6), details at least one state. Also examine the relevant portions of James A. Huston, *The Sinews of War: Army Logistics, 1775–1953* (Washington: Office of the Chief of Military History, U.S. Army, 1966). Or the subject can be approached through contrasting biographies of Lincoln's two Secretaries of War: Erwin Stanley Bradley, *Simon Cameron, Lincoln's Secretary of War: A Political Biography* (Philadelphia: University of Pennsylvania Press, 1966), and Benjamin P. Thomas and Harold M. Hyman, *Stanton: The Life and Times of Lincoln's Secretary of War* (New York: Alfred A. Knopf, 1962). Merritt Roe Smith, "Military Arsenals and Industry Before World War I," in Benjamin Franklin Cooling, ed., *War, Business, and American Society: Historical Perspectives on the Military-Industrial Complex* (Port Washington, NY: Kennikat Press, 1977), has information on the government-run enterprises in the North. Although war contracts offer numerous instances of corruption, not all such charges are automatically true. One false accusation that some historians still repeat unawares (I know, because I almost did) is exposed in R. Gordon Wasson, *The Hall Carbine Affair: A Study in Contemporary Folklore*, 2nd edn. (New York: Pandick Press, 1948). On the political triumph of neo-mercantilism, see Leonard P. Curry, *Blueprint for Modern America: Nonmilitary Legislation of the First Civil War Congress* (Nashville: Vanderbilt University Press, 1968).

Union involvement with railroads is exhaustively examined in Thomas Weber, *The Northern Railroads in the Civil War, 1861–1865* (New York: King's Crown Press, 1952), while their military role is treated in George Edgar Turner, *Victory Rode the Rails: The Strategic Place of Railroads in the Civil War* (Indianapolis: Bobbs-Merrill, 1953). There are many books that boost the first transcontinental from a business or engineering angle—for instance James McCague, *Moguls and Iron Men: The Story of the First Transcontinental Railroad* (New York: Harper & Row, 1964)—but one of the few serious economic analyses is Robert William Fogel, *The Union Pacific Railroad: A Case of Premature Enterprise* (Baltimore: Johns Hopkins

Press, 1969). Fogel proves what is almost economically obvious: that government promotion of the transcontinental was an inefficient diversion of resources. A few older legislative histories of the first transcontinental or of national aid to railroads generally are John P. Davis, *The Union Pacific Railway: A Study in Railway Politics, History, and Economics* (Chicago: S. C. Griggs, 1894); John Bell Sandborn, *Congressional Grants of Land in Aid of Railways* (Madison: Democratic Printing, 1910); and Lewis Henry Haney, *A Congressional History of Railways in the United States, 1850–1887* (Madison: University of Wisconsin, 1919).

Paul W. Gates, *Agriculture and the Civil War* (New York: Alfred A. Knopf, 1965), covers government intervention into this sector by both sides during the conflict. Charlotte Erickson, *American Industry and the European Immigrant, 1860–1885* (Cambridge, MA: Harvard University Press, 1957), relates to the contract labor law. Illuminating the Union's use of the military to help employers maintain labor discipline is Grace Palladino, *Another Civil War: Labor, Capital, and the State in the Anthracite Regions of Pennsylvania, 1840–1868* (Urbana: University of Illinois Press, 1990). Benjamin F. Andrews explores the *Land Grant Act of 1862 and Land Grant Colleges* (Washington: Government Printing Office, 1918), and for the neglected militarism of the Morrill Land Grant Act, see Willard Nash, *A Study of Stated Aims and Purposes of the Departments of Military Science and Tactics and Physical Education in the Land-Grant Colleges of the United States* (New York: Columbia University, 1934).

Vernon L. Carstensen, ed., *The Public Lands: Studies in the History of the Public Domain* (Madison: University of Wisconsin Press, 1968), collects articles that debate the relative economic import of Civil War homestead legislation and congressional land grants. Many historians misjudge the Mining Act of 1866, passed after the conflict was over, as another Republican use of the public domain to subsidize a special interest. In fact, this act did not promiscuously hand out huge, empty tracts of government land. Close inspection reveals that it approximated giving title to those actually mining. It therefore applied Lockean principles to a technology that differed from farming. The Mining Act, like the Homestead Act, was a *laissez-faire* solution to problems of unowned resources.

Among popular economic fallacies, perhaps most absurd is that war, with all its destruction and waste, promotes economic prosperity. The Civil War's version of this fallacy is known as the Beard-Hacker thesis, after Charles and Mary Beard, *The Rise of American Civilization* (cited prologue), and Louis M. Hacker, *The Triumph of American Capitalism: The Development of Forces in American History to the End of the Nineteenth Century* (New York: Columbia University Press, 1940). Thomas C. Cochran published the first substantial objection in the September 1961 issue of the *Mississippi Valley Historical Review*. His article, "Did the Civil War Retard Industrialization?", is reprinted in Ralph Andreano, ed., *The Economic Impact of the Civil War*, rev. edn. (Cambridge, MA: Schenkman, 1967), a collection of writings from the ensuing debate. David T. Gilchrist and W. David Lewis, eds., *Economic Change in the Civil War Era: Proceedings of a Conference on*

American Economic Institutional Change, 1850–1873, and the Impact of the Civil War Held March 12–14, 1964 (Greenville, DE: Eleutherian Mills-Hagley Foundation, 1965), is another, related anthology. But the definitive refutation of the Beard-Hacker thesis is Stanley L. Engerman's 1966 article from *Explorations in Entrepreneurial History*, "The Economic Impact of the Civil War," reprinted in the Andreano collection and in Fogel and Engerman's *Reinterpretation of American Economic History*.

Since Wesley Clair Mitchell published his data on inflation, no one has doubted the wartime decline in real wages in the North, but causes are still under discussion. See especially Reuben Kessel and Armen Alchian, "Real Wages in the North During the Civil War: Mitchell's Data Reinterpreted," reprinted in both the Andreano and the Fogel and Engerman anthologies; and Stephen DeCanio and Joel Mokyr, "Inflation and the Wage Lag During the American Civil War," *Explorations in Economic History*, 14 (October 1977), pp. 311–336.

Although the notion that growth accelerated during the war itself is now dead as far as scholars are concerned, there is still some life in the back-up proposition that the war's political and economic transformations indirectly fostered subsequent development, which is closer to what the Beards and Hacker had in mind anyway. The fact that real income on a per capita basis (although not on a total basis) did achieve higher annual increases after the war's end, however, does not confirm this proposition, because the same outcome is what would be expected from demobilization and the reallocation of resources to civilian production. Every attempt to pin down any specific war-induced change that might have accelerated growth has ultimately failed; most of the increases in government intervention, such as the tariff and the railroad subsidies, imposed deadweight loss on the economy. If anything, this welfare burden probably retarded growth. Defenders of the Beard-Hacker thesis have come up with only one possible exception: the war's financial legislation, which as mentioned above, we will deal with later. Denying the long-term economic benefits of the Civil War's increases in State power, however, is not the same as denying their long-term political significance. Unfortunately, much of the historical debate has heedlessly careened between the two propositions. There is no doubt that the wartime triumph of Republican neo-mercantilism represented a major political watershed in American history, as I will argue more extensively later. But this political counter-revolution brought economic losses, not gains.

The "Died of Democracy" thesis is dispatched in the two best surveys of Confederate war socialism—Emory M Thomas, *The Confederacy as a Revolutionary Experience* (Englewood Cliffs, NJ: Prentice-Hall, 1971), and Raimondo Luraghi, *The Rise and Fall of the Plantation South* (New York: Franklin Watts, 1978). Although Luraghi's earlier chapters on the antebellum South are blemished by an implausible Marxism, he was the first to see the striking similarities between forced industrialization in the Confederacy during the Civil War and in Stalinist Russia under the Five-Year Plans. Stalin was more ruthless, extracting savings through the terror-famine that starved millions of Soviet peasants, but even this distinction can be overdrawn. Only because the war ended too soon did the South escape widespread starvation.

Luraghi, moreover, helps us identify the fundamental cause for the Rebel economy's collapse. It was not the blockade, although the blockade made a contribution. Nor was it inept leadership, despite the South's ample share of that. If every Confederate leader had been as talented as Josiah Gorgas, the Confederacy would have done better, but an economic system that will succeed only under managers who are more than human is a poor system. Confederate war socialism, like central planning wherever implemented, made rational economic allocation all but impossible. Yet in the final analysis, we cannot even put the primary blame for the South's wartime impoverishment on faulty bureaucratic incentives, despite piles of unused food rotting at collection points. The key factor was the South's Napoleonic military strategy, which necessitated huge transfers of resources from the civilian economy. This parasitic burden ultimately would have killed its host no matter how delicately the transfers had been extracted. Toombs, when he penned the epitaph, "Died of West Point," was more right than he realized.

Frank Lawrence Owsley, *State Rights in the Confederacy* (Chicago: University of Chicago Press, 1925), is a schizophrenic book; one of the first to argue that the Confederacy "Died of State Rights," it is excellent on Confederate centralization with respect to impressment, conscription, and *habeas corpus*. Also countering the Donald thesis is Frank E. Vandiver, *Jefferson Davis and the Confederate State* (Oxford: Clarendon Press, 1964). Curtis Arthur Amlund, *Federalism in the Southern Confederacy* (Washington: Public Affairs Press, 1966), tracks political centralization. John Christopher Schwab, *The Confederate States of America, 1861–1865: A Financial and Industrial History of the South During the Civil War* (New York: C. Scribner's Sons, 1901), treats the wartime South's domestic policies generally, with special emphasis on finance.

One volume serves Confederate finance well: Richard Cecil Todd, *Confederate Finance* (Athens: University of Georgia Press, 1954). A newer, quite thorough study, Douglas B. Ball, *Financial Failure and Confederate Defeat* (Urbana: University of Illinois Press, 1991), provides more narrative details and ranges widely into cotton diplomacy and blockade running. But Ball's reduction of Southern defeat to a single financial cause turns into a diatribe against Secretary of the Treasury Christopher Memminger. This is a throwback to an older political economy that mindlessly insists on raising taxes high enough to cover all expenditures, without any sensitivity to political constraints or potential drag on the economy.

Judith Fenner Gentry, "A Confederate Success in Europe: The Erlanger Loan," *Journal of Southern History*, 36 (1970), is a look at Confederate borrowing abroad that has been supplemented by Richard I. Lester, *Confederate Finance and Purchasing in Great Britain* (Charlottesville; University Press of Virginia, 1975). A welcome study of southern banking is Larry Schweikart, *Banking in the American South: From the Age of Jackson to*

Reconstruction (Baton Rouge: Louisiana State University Press, 1987).

Eugene M. Lerner wrote three articles that are required reading about the South's wartime hyperinflation: "Monetary and Fiscal Programs of the Confederate Government, 1861–65," *Journal of Political Economy*, 62 (December 1954), pp. 506–522; "Money, Prices, and Wages in the Confederacy," *Journal of Political Economy*, 63 (February 1955), pp. 20–40; and "Inflation in the Confederacy, 1861–65," in Milton Friedman, ed., *Studies in the Quantity Theory of Money* (Chicago: University of Chicago Press, 1956), pp. 161–175. Lerner's estimates of Confederate currency, however, differ from those of Todd and others. The best attempt to sort out this confusion and construct reliable, systematic time series is the published dissertation, John Munro Godrey, *Monetary Expansion in the Confederacy* (New York: Arno Press, 1978). A numismatic study that pays special attention to state currency issues is James F. Morgan, *Graybacks and Gold: Confederate Monetary Policy* (Pensacola, FL: Perdido Bay, 1985).

An overview of Confederate economic mobilization is Charles W. Ramsdell, *Behind the Lines in the Southern Confederacy* (Baton Rouge: Louisiana State University Press, 1944). Viewing the economy from the military's insatiable perspective, Richard D. Goff, *Confederate Supply* (Durham, NC: Duke University Press, 1969), would naturally agree with Donald that there was too little centralization. But May Spencer Ringold, *The Role of the State Legislatures in the Confederacy* (cited ch. 6), details the extensive government intervention at the state level, and Paul Escott, " 'The Cry of the Sufferers': The Problem of Welfare in the Confederacy," *Civil War History*, 23 (September 1977), pp. 228–240, covers specifically government welfare. One recent state study that compares wartime policies with what went before and came after is Peter Wallenstein, *From Slave South to New South: Public Policy in Nineteenth-Century Georgia* (Chapel Hill: University of North Carolina Press, 1987). War socialism's impact on one southern city is vividly told in Florence Fleming Corley, *Confederate City: Augusta, Georgia 1860–1865* (Columbia: University of South Carolina Press, 1960).

Lester J. Cappon, "Government and Private Industry in the Southern Confederacy," in *Humanistic Studies in Honor of John Calvin Metcalf* (Charlottesville: University of Virginia, 1941), surveys government-run industries. The extended reach of the Ordnance Bureau is reviewed in Frank E. Vandiver, *Ploughshares Into Swords: Josiah Gorgas and Confederate Ordnance* (Austin: University of Texas Press, 1952). Ella Lonn, *Salt as a Factor in the Confederacy* (New York: Columbia University Press, 1933), looks at government production of one vital commodity. See Paul P. Van Riper and Harry N. Scheiber, "The Confederate Civil Service," *Journal of Southern History*, 25 (November 1959), pp. 450–470, on the Rebel bureaucracy. Robert C. Black, III, *The Railroads of the Confederacy* (Chapel Hill: University of North Carolina Press, 1952), is splendid despite the author's bemoaning the failure to nationalize southern railroads sooner. Louise B. Hill, *State Socialism in the Confederate States of America* (Charlottesville, VA: Historical, 1936), is devoted mainly to cotton marketing and blockade-running.

Ludwell H. Johnson has uncovered details about the illicit cotton trade with the enemy in four articles: "Contraband Trade During the Last Year of the Civil War," *Mississippi Valley Historical Review*, 49 (March 1963), pp. 635–653; "The Butler Expedition of 1861–1862: The Profitable Side of War," *Civil War History*, 11 (September 1965), pp. 229–236; "Northern Profit and Profiteers: The Cotton Rings of 1864–1865," *Civil War History*, 12 (June 1966), pp. 101–115; and "Trading With the Union: The Evolution of Confederate Policy," *Virginia Magazine of History and Biography*, 78 (July 1970), pp. 308–325. But of all the writers on the Confederate economy, only one, Jack Hirshleifer, in a chapter from his U.S. Air Force study, *Disaster and Recovery: A Historical Survey* (Santa Monica, CA: Rand Corporation, 1963), has taken notice of the self-inflicted damage resulting from the Confederacy's ban on enemy trade. Similar to the self-defeating cotton embargo, this ban was tantamount to helping the Union enforce the blockade. Because of the South's weaker industrial base, an unrestricted exchange of cotton across the lines clearly would have helped its war effort. Indeed, as Hirshleifer points out, "much of the cotton run through the blockade to Cuba or Bermuda was transshipped to the North anyway" (p. 39). Stanley Lebergott, "Through the Blockade: The Profitability and Extent of Cotton Smuggling, 1861–1865," *Journal of Economic History*, 41 (December 1981), pp. 867–888, estimates that overall planters sold twice as much cotton to the Union as abroad.

10

Dissent and Disaffection—North and South

Confederate Conscription

"Civil War troops were the worst soldiers and the best fighters that America has ever produced." So concludes James I. Robertson, Jr., from his close study of these citizen soldiers, North and South.[1] Neither took kindly to military discipline. The obvious analogy with slavery was not lost on Southerners. "I am tired of being bound up worse than a negro," wrote one.[2] Straggling without leave was endemic in all campaigns on both sides, and somewhere between one out of nine and one out of seven deserted. Well over half the deserters were never apprehended, and on August 1, 1863, Jefferson Davis resorted to a general amnesty for any who returned to duty within twenty days.

Under most circumstances, however, punishment could be cruel and capricious. In general, severity increased as the war progressed. The Union and the Confederacy executed a total of five hundred of their own troops, more than in all other American wars combined. Two-thirds of the executions were for desertion. Yet "a soldier might be sentenced to death," observes historian Bell Irvin Wiley, "for an offense for which . . . one of his comrades had to pay only a token fine."[3] Although routine flogging had been abolished in the U.S. Navy in 1850 and in the U.S. Army after the War of 1812,

Union and Confederate courts-martial continued to mete out this punishment. One of Stonewall Jackson's brigade commanders, during campaigning that would lead to the second battle of Bull Run in the summer of 1862, ordered thirty stragglers "bucked" from sunrise to sunset. Bucking and gagging was a particularly brutal procedure, in which the victim sat with his wrists bound together, his arms pulled down over his knees, and a pole or musket barrel slipped above his arms and under his knees, while a piece of wood or bayonet gagged his mouth. Half of those the brigade commander had punished promptly deserted for good, while others vowed that their commander's next battle would be his last. (It was, but as the result of Yankee artillery.) Later during the same campaign Jackson himself ordered three stragglers court-martialed and then executed in front of their entire division.

The Civil War was just one year old when the flow of volunteers willing to put up with this treatment and do the fighting began drying up. The Confederacy, with its smaller population, noticed the drought first. Because most southern states had retained compulsory militia laws, they were able to draft men for short durations to bolster local defenses. As General McClellan's Union forces approached Richmond, four state governments revised these laws to permit drafts for longer periods in order to fill quotas in the Confederate army.

But General Robert E. Lee and other West Pointers wanted a centralized system of conscription. Over half the Confederacy's soldiers had enlisted for only twelve months, and the promise of monetary bounties and sixty-day furloughs was not inducing many to reenlist. With their terms approaching expiration, Davis told the Rebel Congress that conscription was "absolutely indispensable." "We need a large army," declared Louis T. Wigfall, a former United States Senator from Texas who was now serving in the same capacity in the Confederate Senate. "The people will not volunteer to fill up the old regiments." Castigating congressional critics of the administration's request, Wigfall maintained that "no man has any individual rights, which come in conflict with the welfare of the country. The government has as much right to exact military service as it has to collect a tax to pay the expenses of the government."[4]

The Rebel legislature complied with Davis's request in April of 1862. This was not, as so often stated, the first conscription in American history. We have already observed that men had been drafted into the state militias since the country's beginning. Nor was this even the first *national* conscription in American history. Militia laws passed during the Washington Administration had required the states to draft men for national service, which they had done not only during the War of 1812 but even previously during peacetime—for instance, to provide troops for the infamous Watermelon Army, which suppressed resistance to Alexander Hamilton's whiskey excise. But it was the first *centrally administered* conscription in American history, and for that reason represents a momentous step.

The Confederacy's conscription initially applied to all able-bodied men between the ages of eighteen and thirty-five. Yet exemptions were numerous and included clergymen, teachers, state officials, railroad workers, and those employed in war industries. Men could also avoid the draft by paying a substitute to serve for them, a feature carried over from the militia laws. Although much maligned by historians, this practice made conscription more efficient, equitable, and palatable—not less. The primary function of these early Southern acts was to prolong the terms of all draft-age veterans to three years. Later legislation, however, made Confederate conscription steadily tougher. Eventually the eligible ages were extended to cover all males between seventeen and fifty. The Rebel legislature repealed substitution in December 1863. Conscientious objectors still could pay a $500 exemption fee, but only if they were Quakers, Dunkers, or Mennonites as of October 1862. Several who failed to meet these criteria died in the Confederate army from the harsh treatment inflicted upon them after they refused to fight.

Conscription furnished somewhere between one-fifth and one-third of southern military manpower.[5] Nearly every soldier, whether volunteer or conscript, was held in the army until the war ended—or he was wounded or killed. Conscription furthermore was a crucial cog in Confederate war socialism. Draft exemptions were the mechanism for manipulating the labor market. Any southern business that did not conform to military priorities found itself without workers. War Department control over labor became still more overt in February 1864. The Rebel Congress abolished many occupational exemptions and replaced them with the discretionary assignment of soldiers to industrial jobs. Insofar as these detailed soldiers were conscripts, the Confederacy was running its factories on coerced labor. The internal logic of military conscription had led the nation of black agricultural slavery to the ironic but appropriate adoption of white industrial slavery.

No Confederate war measure aroused more popular resentment than conscription. Non-slaveholders were particularly galled by an exemption for one white man on each plantation of twenty or more slaves. This precaution against servile insurrection and declining labor discipline was derisively denounced as the "twenty-nigger law." It led to the widespread quip, "rich man's war—poor man's fight." Southern opponents of the draft could count among their numbers Governors Zebulon B. Vance of North Carolina and Joseph E. Brown of Georgia. "We entered into this revolution in defense of the rights and sovereignty of the States," Governor Brown reminded the Georgia legislature. The conscription act was unconstitutional; "at one fell swoop, [it] strikes down the sovereignty of the States, tramples upon constitutional rights and personal liberty of the citizen, and arms the President with imperial power." Worse still warned the governor, "this action of the Government . . . tends to crush out the spirit of freedom and resistance to tyranny which was bequeathed to us by our ancestors of the Revolution of 1776."[6] Both governors obstructed the draft's implementation in their states. Brown created 15,000 bogus state jobs—mostly in the militia, but including 2,000 unneeded justices of the peace and 1,000 unneeded constables—where men would be exempt. Meanwhile the Chief Justice of the North Carolina Supreme Court routinely freed arrested draft evaders with writs of *habeas corpus*.

Union Conscription

The Union enacted a new, national militia law in July of 1862, shortly after the Confederacy's first conscription act. The President could now call the state militias into federal service for nine instead of three months. Each state received a troop quota. If state officials failed to meet it, either with volunteers or draftees, then national authorities would step in. This awkward measure induced many northern states to reimpose or reactivate compulsory militia duty. State drafts touched off violent resistance among Irish-Americans in the Pennsylvania oil fields and German-Americans in Wisconsin.

Federal officials, however, did no drafting themselves until passage of the Enrollment Act in March of 1863. Men between twenty and forty-five were now made liable for three years of military service, and this eventually would apply to non-citizens residing in the country too. Anyone could hire a substitute or pay the government a flat $300 commutation fee, and although there were no occupational exemptions, those who had already served could not be called again. In contrast to the Confederacy, the Union honored a soldier's original enlistment and did not prevent him from going home when his term expired.

The resulting turnover, however, required the Union to find a greater number of fresh recruits. Moreover, these recruits were often organized into new regiments rather than becoming replacements in older regiments, as in the South. Not only did the North therefore have a smaller proportion of battle-hardened veterans in its armies, but they were concentrated in regiments that dwindled away to skeleton units. Wisconsin was an exception, and General William Tecumseh Sherman attested that, as a result, "we estimated a Wisconsin regiment equal to an ordinary brigade" on the battle-field. "I believe that five hundred new men added to an old and experienced regiment were more valuable than a thousand men in the form of a new regiment, for the former, by association with good experienced captains, lieutenants, and non-commissioned officers, soon became veterans, whereas the latter were generally unavailable for a year."[7]

Congress mainly designed the Enrollment Act, like the militia law a year earlier, to stimulate volunteering. Each congressional district received a troop quota. Along with the stick of conscription, national, state, and local authorities tried to raise the troops with the carrot of monetary bounties. Ranging from $300 all the way up to $1,500, these incentives gave rise to professional bounty brokers as well as the charming vice of bounty jumping, where a man would enlist in one community, get his bounty, desert, and enlist in another area. The bounty jumping record of the North went to John O'Connor, who succeeded in thirty-two desertions before being apprehended and jailed in 1865. Other less fortunate bounty jumpers were shot or hung when caught. Another way to fill quotas, beginning in July of 1864, was to send agents into the occupied areas of the South to recruit blacks. Moreover, approximately 800,000 immigrants arrived in the North during the war, and some of them had enlisted in the military before crossing the ocean. Nearly one-fourth of the those who served in the Union armies would be foreign born.

Only if a district failed to meet its quota with volunteers would federal enrollment officers take over. Rather than obligating citizens to come forward and register, as in the military drafts of more recent times, the Enrollment Act sent these officers on a house-to-house canvass. The intense northern hatred of conscription could make this extremely hazardous. Enrollment officers were killed in Illinois and Indiana. Anti-draft riots engulfed Troy, New York, and Newark, New Jersey. Infantrymen fired into a crowd of resistors in Holmes County, Ohio. When a Boston mob one thousand strong descended upon the National Guard Armory, the local commander ordered artillery to fire canister and grapeshot into the crowd, killing two dozen. At one point in 1863, Secretary of War Edwin M. Stanton faced simultaneous calls from about two hundred cities, towns, and counties throughout the loyal states for troops to suppress draft disturbances.

But nothing matched the fury of the outbreak in New York City during July of 1863. The drawing of the first draftees' names touched off four days of uncontrolled rioting, mostly among the city's teeming population of Irish workingmen and women. The rioters first destroyed the local draft headquarters. Then, mauling any police sent against them, they vented their rage on the city's hapless free blacks, whom the rioters blamed for the war. Any who fell into their hands were lynched from the nearest tree or lamppost. The mob also burned down the Colored Orphan Asylum and sacked the homes of wealthy Republicans. The riot was only suppressed with a contingent of four thousand troops rushed from the battle of Gettysburg.

One Union officer, Lieutenant B. Franklin Ryer, described in his official report the riot-control techniques employed. After marching his command, "numbering about fifty men . . . , to the scene of the disturbance," which was on Forty-second Street between Tenth and Eleventh Avenues, "we were saluted with groans, hisses, etc., and . . . received a storm of bricks and missiles of every description, and shots from the roofs and windows of the buildings." Ryer formed the platoons "so as to sweep the streets and avenue in all directions." Warning the rioters to go home, he gave them one minute. Then "I ordered my troops to fire, and had to fire at least five volleys before I could disperse the mob."[8] With well over one hundred dead and as many wounded, it was the worst urban riot in American history.

After inspiring all this commotion, conscription directly provided only about 6 percent of the men who served in the Union armies.[9] Monetary payments through generous bounties or, secondarily, through substitution remained the main inducements for enlistment. Many military-age men paid fees to insurance clubs that would hire substitutes for those called up. Perhaps as many as 160,000 Northerners illegally evaded the draft altogether. Ezra Heywood, a young abolitionist who was one of the few to remain true to Garrisonian principles throughout the war, declared in the pages of the *Liberator* that "the right to draft men is as purely imaginary as the right to enslave them." The Enrollment Act, like the Fugitive Slave Law, should "be disobeyed and trod under foot." It was "wicked and despotic," not to mention "plainly in conflict with the Divine Law."[10] And draft resistance was hardly the only opposition to the war that President Lincoln had to confront.

Political Opposition in the North

Stephen A. Douglas died less than a year after losing the 1860 presidential election to Abraham Lincoln. He was forty-eight years old. But before passing away, the Illinois Democrat wholeheartedly endorsed Lincoln's efforts to preserve the Union. When fellow members of Douglas's party asked him what course they should follow, he replied firmly that "there are only two sides to the question. Every man must be for the United States or against it. There can be no neutrals in this war, *only patriots—or traitors.*"[11]

Not every northern Democrat shared these sentiments. The

party gradually divided into peace and war factions. Opposition to emancipation and other policies of the Lincoln Administration led increasing numbers of Democrats to question the war altogether. Northern sympathy for the Confederacy was particularly strong among Catholic immigrants in the cities and rural residents of the lower Midwest. Prior to Fort Sumter, New York's Democratic mayor had even proposed that the city secede from the Union. Some Copperheads, as northern peace advocates were derisively labeled, formed secret societies such as the Knights of the Golden Circle and the Order of American Knights.

To intimidate and control these groups, the President employed the same techniques that had held the border states within the Union. He extended the suspension of *habeas corpus*, previously limited to certain areas, throughout the North in September of 1862, just after issuing the preliminary Emancipation Proclamation. This was a response to the first draft disturbances, but even before this blanket suspension, Union authorities were routinely arresting without trial or charges any Northerners they suspected of disloyalty. First the State Department and later the War Department loosely coordinated surveillance through a network of special agents, U.S. marshals, Pinkerton detectives, local police, private informers, and above all, military officials. One widely circulated story claimed that Secretary of State William Seward bragged about his arbitrary power to the British Ambassador: "I can touch a bell on my right hand and order the arrest of a citizen of Ohio. I can touch a bell again, and order the imprisonment of a citizen of New York, and no power on earth, except that of the President of the United States, can release them. Can the Queen of England do as much?"[12]

To be sure, many of those arrested secured release within a month or two, usually after swearing a loyalty oath. The greater number were citizens of either the border states or the Confederacy itself. The Union's provost marshals found summary imprisonment an excellent way to intimidate the local citizens in enemy territory. Only rarely did occupation authorities go as far as General Benjamin Butler in New Orleans, who in June 1862 summarily hanged one headstrong Southerner for tearing down the United States flag from a public building. This act, along with an order that any southern woman who insulted Federal soldiers should be treated as "a woman of the town plying her avocation," earned the general international denunciation and the epithet "Beast Butler."

Nevertheless, the Lincoln Administration imprisoned at least 14,000 civilians throughout the course of the war, and state and local authorities probably seized many more. Seward even took preliminary steps toward the arrest of former President Franklin Pierce. Quite often these jailings were for other than political reasons, as when four leaders of a munitions workers strike at West Point in 1864 were held without trial for seven weeks. Congress finally sanctioned Lincoln's suspension of *habeas corpus* in an act of March, 1863, which added some procedural safeguards for those arrested. But the President neglected to implement the safeguards. Congress had also passed earlier conspiracy and treason acts to facilitate the prosecution of antiwar activities in civilian courts. But Lincoln preferred to employ military courts or, better yet, dispense with courts entirely.

The federal government simultaneously monitored and censored both the mails and telegraphs, and for the first time demanded passports of those entering and leaving the country. No one eligible for the draft could depart. It also suppressed newspapers. Over three hundred, including the *Chicago Times*, the *New York World*, and the *Philadelphia Evening Journal*, had to cease publication for varying periods. If the Postmaster General banned an antiwar paper from the mail, it had received the kiss of death. Early in the war, a special congressional committee, relying primarily upon anonymous informants, conducted sweeping investigations in order to root out disloyalty among government employees.

Lincoln was not reticent about justifying these invasions of liberty. One of his arguments was based upon the danger of desertion. "Long experience has shown that armies can not be maintained unless desertion shall be punished by the severe penalty of death. . . . Must I shoot a simple-minded soldier boy who deserts," the President asked, "while I must not touch a hair of a wiley [*sic*] agitator who induces him to desert?" Sometimes the agitator's antiwar propaganda might insidiously persuade "a father, or brother, or friend . . . to write the soldier boy, that he is fighting in a bad cause, for a wicked administration of a contemptable [*sic*] government. . . . I think that in such a case, to silence the agitator, and save the boy, is not only constitutional, but, withal, a great mercy."[13]

Nor did the President have any constitutional reservations about ignoring the legislative branch if convenient. Starting with his initial militia call, Lincoln repeatedly invoked the war emergency to increase presidential power. He had enlarged the regular army, clamped down the blockade, dispersed government funds, authorized government borrowing, suspended *habeas corpus*, and instituted postal censorship before Congress even convened. After that body met, Lincoln still did not bother with its approval for the emancipation proclamation, for rules governing the army in the field, for setting up courts in the occupied South, and for initiating the reconstruction of southern states.

One civil liberties case, that of Clement L. Vallandigham, a Democratic Congressman from Ohio, became a *cause célèbre*. Vallandigham had denounced "King Lincoln" frequently on the House floor. "Talk to me, indeed, of the leniency of the Executive!" he had exclaimed while debating against conscription. "Too few arrests! too much forbearance by those in power! Sir, it is the people who have been too lenient. They have submitted to your oppressions and wrongs as no free people ought ever to submit." The Ohio Congressman went on to point out the parallels between Lincoln's arrests and religious persecution: "Sir, some two hundred years ago, men were burned at the stake, subjected to the horrors of the Inquisition, to all the tortures that the devilish ingenuity of man could invent—for what? For opinions on questions of religion—of man's duty and relation to his God. And now, today, for the opinions on questions political, under a free government, in a country whose liberties were purchased by our fathers by seven years' outpouring of blood, and expenditure of treasure—we have lived to see men, the born heirs of this precious inheritance, subjected to arrest and cruel imprisonment at the caprice of a President or a secretary or a constable."[14]

Although defeated for reelection to a House seat, Vallandigham decided to run for governor of his state and delivered a speech in May 1863 that accused the President of unnecessarily prolonging the conflict. The Union commander in Ohio rousted Vallandigham from his home at night and jailed him. A military court handed down a sentence of confinement for the war's duration, but public indignation forced Lincoln to commute the sentence to exile behind Confederate lines. After being released in the South, Vallandigham sailed to Canada and then reentered the Union. His travails became the basis for a prowar *Atlantic Monthly* story, "The Man Without a Country," published in December, 1863.

Northern dissatisfaction was so intense by this time that the Republicans had come close to losing control of Congress, despite the total absence of southern Democrats. New York, Ohio, Pennsylvania, Indiana, and Illinois—states that had all voted for Lincoln in 1860—went Democratic in the 1862 elections. Helping Lincoln's party to maintain its congressional majority was military manipulation of the border-state elections. Republican vote totals in these areas, unlike those in the rest of the country, had miraculously risen.

With the Republican governor of Indiana now facing a hostile state legislature, the President helped him illegally run the state government with funds from Washington. Illinois's chief executive, in similar straits, revived the colonial practice of proroguing the legislature—that is, suspending its session by decree. These actions fit within Lincoln's general policy of stripping political and military autonomy away from the war governors. Congress's accelerated and sometimes irregular admission of new states—Kansas in 1861, West Virginia in 1863, and Nevada in 1864—also worked to the advantage of the embattled Republicans. And let us not ignore tampering with the soldiers' vote. This was before the secret ballot, and most of the army's junior officers and paymasters were members of the Republican Party. Any American who has served in the modern military knows how this kind of informal pressure can be quite persuasive.

As the next presidential election approached, the Republicans attempted to broaden their appeal by changing their name to the Union Party. Their convention nominated for Vice-President a War Democrat from Tennessee, Andrew Johnson, who had cosponsored the Crittenden-Johnson resolutions on the Union's war aims and was now serving as the occupation governor of his state. But

Lincoln did not just have to defeat a resurgent Democratic Party to stay in office. He also had to overcome opposition within his own party. Americans had grown accustomed to single-term Presidents. No incumbent had served a second term since 1836, and none had even been renominated by his party since 1840. Moreover, the failure to achieve military victory after three years of murderous conflict had made the President so unpopular throughout the North that few thought he could win. Several Radical Republicans tried to replace him as their party's standard bearer with Secretary of the Treasury Salmon P. Chase. When that effort fizzled, some promoted the third-party candidacy of General John C. Frémont.

Only well after the Democrats had nominated General George B. McClellan did Frémont pull out of the 1864 race. McClellan was the presidential choice of those War Democrats who had not gone over to the Republicans. But in exchange, the Peace Democrats, including Vallandigham, got to write the party's platform. It called for a negotiated armistice to bring the South back. "After four years of failure to restore the Union by the experiment of war," the platform declared, "under the pretense of a military necessity, . . . the Constitution itself has been disregarded in every part, and public liberty and private right alike trodden down." Therefore, "justice, humanity, liberty, and the public welfare demand that immediate efforts be made for a cessation of hostilities."[15] The Democracy's hope was that a peaceful settlement might restore "The Constitution as it is, and the Union as it was." A small Democratic faction, under the leadership of Congressman Alexander Long of Ohio, went so far as to call for immediate and unconditional recognition of Southern independence.

Whether Northerners in fact were weary enough of the war to give Democrats the presidency would ultimately depend upon events at the front. Lincoln himself gloomily concluded that without a major military victory his reelection prospects were dim.

Political Opposition in the South

Jefferson Davis did not have to worry about reelection. The Confederate Constitution had established a single six-year term for the President, and the Confederacy was never blessed with organized political parties. Nonetheless, Davis's haughty leadership aroused bitter opposition. The opinions expressed in correspondence by the fire-eater Robert Toombs of Georgia were typical of a growing southern faction. "The real control of our affairs is narrowing down constantly into the hands of Davis and the old army," he foretold, "and when it gets there entirely the cause will collapse. They have neither the ability nor the honesty to manage the revolution." Not only would the West Point leadership "ruin the cause of independence," in Toombs's opinion, but "it will make the recovery of public liberty hereafter impossible without another bloody revolution."[16]

The Confederate Vice-President, Alexander Stephens, publicly condemned even the slightest increase in executive power. The Vice-President's brother, Linton Stephens, prominent in the Georgia legislature, savagely attacked Davis's character. "How God has afflicted us with a ruler! He is a *little, conceited, hypocritical, snivelling, canting, malicious, ambitious, dogged,* knave and fool."[17] Many southern governors, including Joseph Brown of Georgia and Zebulon Vance of North Carolina, jealously guarded state prerogatives. After the Confederacy's Congressional elections in 1863, open opponents of Davis numbered 41 out of 106 House members and 12 out of 26 Senate members. This disaffection grew in spite of the fact that the Davis Administration could count on firm support from representatives of districts under Union conquest, who faced no political pressures from their constituents.

Because of all these watchdogs, the Rebel government had to be more circumspect in its restrictions upon civil liberties. Unlike Lincoln, Davis rarely acted without congressional authorization. But this just made Confederate suppression more decentralized than the Union's. As early as 1862 the Confederate Congress empowered the President to suspend *habeas corpus* and declare martial law in threatened areas. Richmond was one of the first sectors where Davis exercised this option. General John H. Winder, assuming command of the capital, prohibited the sale of liquor and seized all privately owned firearms. Within the first two weeks of Winder's rule, he had arbitrarily arrested thirty persons, including a former two-term Congressman. A passport system regulated movement in and out of the city. Hotels and railroads were required to provide lists of all guests and passengers. Winder soon threatened to stop the *Richmond Whig* from publishing for undermining confidence in the government. He also tried price-fixing for a few weeks until he discovered that farmers would no longer bring products into the city.

Davis put other areas under martial law at one time or another, while Confederate commanders occasionally instituted martial law at their own discretion. Only military force, mass arrests, and several executions for sabotage held the strongly Unionist eastern part of Tennessee in the Confederacy. In other sections bordering upon the North, the authorities imposed loyalty oaths and arrested those who refused to comply. Indeed, in August 1861, the Confederate Congress had given all individuals born in the North forty days to swear loyalty or go into exile, with their property forfeit. The courts viewed anyone not supporting the Confederacy as an enemy alien, outside any legal protections accorded to citizens. In Virginia, disloyal families were deported beyond Rebel lines and had their homes destroyed, while in Florida, the military burned down one community that harbored deserters and confined its women and children to refugee camps.

The South had always relied upon local and private vigilance committees to monitor community norms, and such groups now imposed, to the point of lynching, their own versions of loyalty. During the early secession crisis, an Arkansas mob had dragged a St. Louis newspaper distributor off a steamboat and hanged him for selling Horace Greeley's *New York Tribune*. By October of 1862, an outbreak of war hysteria in east Texas culminated in rump trials and the execution of well over fifty victims.

The Confederate Congress at intervals renewed and revised the suspension of *habeas corpus*, making it general throughout the Confederacy for certain disloyal acts in February of 1864. Although the government left southern newspapers generally unmolested, Tennessee officials did banish the Unionist editor of the *Knoxville Whig*. The military's provost marshals required passports of travelers in nearly all Confederate-held territory. These Southern travel restrictions, analogous to the pass system already employed to control the slaves, were far more stringent than in the North.

Violations of civil liberties only fueled the mounting opposition to the Confederate government. "Constitutional liberty will go down, never to rise again on this continent, I fear," was the gloomy, private prediction of Vice-President Stephens. The suspension of *habeas corpus* "is the worst that can befall us. Far better that our country should be overrun by the enemy, our cities sacked and burned, and our land laid desolate, than that the people should thus suffer the citadel of their liberties to be entered and taken by professed friends."[18]

Fed up with inflation, impressments, conscription, and arbitrary arrests, secret peace societies flourished. William Holden, a candidate openly demanding that North Carolina make a separate and immediate settlement with the Union, ran against Governor Vance. Soldiers received letters from home encouraging them to desert. "The people is all turning to Union here since the Yankees has got Vicksburg," wrote the wife of a poor North Carolina farmer. "I want you to come home as soon as you can after you git this letter . . . I want you to come home the worst that I ever did."[19]

A similar letter was introduced as evidence in the desertion trial of Private Edward Cooper. *"My dear Edward*—I have been always proud of you, and since your connection with the Confederate army, I have been prouder of you than ever before. I would not have you do anything wrong for the world, but before God, Edward, unless you come home, we must die. Last night, I was aroused by little Eddie's crying. I called and said, 'what is the matter, Eddie?' And he said, 'O Mamma! I am so hungry.' And Lucy, Edward, your darling Lucy; she never complains, but she is growing thinner and thinner every day. And before God, Edward, unless you come home, we must die."[20] This letter saved Private Cooper from a firing squad.

The German areas of Texas, the mountains of Appalachia and the Ozarks, and the swamps of Louisiana and Florida became centers for deserters and other armed opponents of the war. Confederate officials could not safely traverse these locales without military escort. Southern guerrillas sometimes turned upon regular Confederate detachments as readily as they harassed Northern troops. Organized resistors in Jones County, Mississippi, defeated a company of Confederate cavalry, and the authorities were never able to subdue the county. Over 100,000 white males from eastern Tennessee and other parts of the upper Confederacy went and joined the Union armies outright, adding to those serving from the border slave states.

Morale was thus rapidly plummeting in both the South and the North. The Civil War had become an inverted contest where victory would go to the side that gave up last.

Chapter 10
Bibliographical Essay

Most of the general works from the previous chapter on either the Union or Confederacy also cover conscription, civil liberties, and politics. So far we have no book-length study of military discipline during the Civil War, either the lack thereof on the part of the troops or its capricious and cruel enforcement by officers. What makes this omission unfortunate is that these citizen soldiers stand out as such striking counter-examples to the militarist insistence that combat effectiveness requires harsh discipline. But among the works mentioned in chapter 7, James I. Robertson, Jr., *Soldiers Blue and Gray,* has one excellent chapter on the subject, as does each of Bell Irvin Wiley's two books, *The Life of Johnny Reb* and *The Life of Billy Yank,* although Wiley exhibits a bizarre obsession with the "undue leniency" of punishments, to the point of evincing overt disappointment that no Union or Confederate sentries were executed for sleeping while on guard, as military regulations prescribed. Ella Lonn's classic, *Desertion During the Civil War* (New York: The Century Company, 1928), covers both sides. Robert I. Alotta, *Civil War Justice: Union Army Executions Under Lincoln* (Shippensburg, PA: White Mane, 1989), is a preliminary and undiscriminating compendium of Union executions that tentatively concludes that the 275 reported is incomplete. Much better is Alotta's *Stop the Evil: A Civil War History of Desertion and Murder* (San Rafael, CA: Presidio Press, 1978), a heart-rending report on a well meaning but hapless Union soldier executed for desertion to set an example. An eye-opening discussion of the uniquely severe discipline endured by black troops can be found in Joseph T. Glatthaar, *Forged in Battle* (cited ch. 8).

The standard account of Confederate conscription is Albert Burton Moore, *Conscription and Conflict in the Confederacy* (New York: Macmillan, 1924). Moore, however, does not investigate Confederate conscription at the state level. Indeed, its existence might have escaped general notice but for the intriguing contradiction posed by Governor Joseph E. Brown of Georgia, who bitterly denounced and resisted the central government's draft and yet had earlier on his own authority drafted men into the state forces. See for instance William Harris Bragg, *Joe Brown's Army: The Georgia State Line, 1862–1865* (Macon, GA: Mercer University Press, 1987). William L. Shaw, "The Confederate Conscription and Exemption Acts," *American Journal of Legal History,* 6 (October 1962), pp. 368–405, offers a detailed case study of state conscription in Civil War Louisiana, whereas Memory F. Mitchell's important *Legal Aspects of Conscription and Exemption in North Carolina, 1861–1865* (Chapel Hill: University of North Carolina Press, 1965) implies that North Carolina only enlisted volunteers prior to the central government's draft.

The sometimes brutal treatment of southern conscientious objectors is recounted in Fernando G. Cartland, *Southern Heroes: Or the Friends in War*

Time (Cambridge, MA: Riverside, 1895). A more recent work that covers conscientious objection in both the South and the North is Edward Needles Wright, *Conscientious Objectors in the Civil War* (Philadelphia: University of Pennsylvania, 1931). Peter Brock, *Pacifism in the United States* (cited ch. 8) also gives the Civil War's principled opponents of military service significant attention.

The most recent work on the Union draft, James W. Geary, *We Need Men: The Union Draft in the Civil War* (DeKalb: Northern Illinois University, 1991), exonerates substitution and commutation from charges of unfairness. One of the few economists to look at these practices in early American conscription—Jack L. Rafuse—has done so only sketchily in "United States' Experience With Volunteer and Conscript Forces," from v. 2 of *Studies Prepared for the President's Commission on an All-Volunteer Armed Force* (Washington: Government Printing Office, 1970). But the analysis for the most part is straightforward. Because substitution or commutation allow a tax-in-kind to be converted into a monetary tax, they increase the efficiency of the wartime labor market. Those whose skills are more valuable outside the military will be able to afford exemption. Substitution, with or without commutation, is also more equitable and palatable because it permits those being taxed greater options, in particular the option of paying money to avoid a low-wage, life-threatening job. Northern Democrats pilloried the commutation fee until Congress considered repealing it in 1864. Realizing that the draft itself was unfair, and that if they had to submit to a draft, better with this escape than without, congressional Democrats lined up solidly against both repeal of substitution (which failed to pass) and repeal of commutation (which passed anyway).

Present-day egalitarians might argue that conscription is progressive; draftees with higher civilian incomes lose more. Substitution converts this into a regressive head tax for those who can afford replacements. But for those who now have the added option of hiring themselves out, a draft with substitution is *more* progressive, directly transferring money from the rich to the poor. Someone wealthier has been taxed to pay the substitute a better wage than he could earn as a civilian. Without substitution, conscription's progressive feature is ridiculously inefficient, because the monetary losses of those with greater incomes does not end up transferred to government—or to anyone else. It is all deadweight loss. (The relative efficiency of substitution with a flat commutation fee versus substitution without it raises some fascinating economic questions too technical to go into here.)

A survey that traces the Enrollment Act's ideological sources is in the opening chapters of John Whiteclay Chambers, II's, study of the World War I conscription, *To Raise an Army: The Draft Comes to Modern America* (New York: Free Press, 1987), although Whiteclay underrates the extent and importance of antebellum militia drafts. Other accounts of the North's draft include the second part of John Franklin Leach, *Conscription in the United States: Historical Background* (Rutland, VT: Charles E. Tuttle, 1952);

the last part of the first volume and all of the second volume of Fred Albert Shannon, *The Organization and Administration of the Union Army* (cited ch. 6); William L. Shaw, "The Civil War Federal Conscription and Exemption System," *Judge Advocate Journal*, no. 32 (February 1962), pp. 1–32; and Eugene Murdock, *One Million Men: The Civil War Draft in the North* (Madison: State Historical Society of Wisconsin, 1971). Murdock's *Patriotism Limited, 1862–1865: The Civil War Draft and the Bounty System* (Kent, OH: Kent State University Press, 1967) focuses primarily upon New York state. On the reimposition of compulsory militia duty in the loyal states, see Robert S. Chamberlain, "The Northern State Militia," *Civil War History*, 4 (June 1958), pp. 105–118.

The latest work on New York City's conscription-inspired insurrection, Iver Bernstein, *The New York City Draft Riots: Their Significance for American Society and Politics in the Age of the Civil War* (New York: Oxford University Press, 1990), fits the riots within a class-conflict view of New York City politics. Also worth examination is Ernest A. McKay, *The Civil War and New York City* (Syracuse: Syracuse University Press, 1990). Bernstein relies heavily on Adrian Cook, *The Armies of the Street: The New York City Draft Riots of 1863* (Lexington: University Press of Kentucky, 1974), which remains unsurpassed for events during the rioting itself. Prior to Cook's research, estimates of the number killed ranged wildly between 12,000 and 18. Cook's appendices painstakingly lists all possible casualties by name, as well as all known rioters. James McCague, *The Second Rebellion: The Story of the New York City Draft Riots of 1863* (New York: Dial, 1968), is an undocumented journalistic account. On less spectacular forms of draft resistance throughout the Union, consult Peter Levine, "Draft Evasion in the North During the Civil War, 1863–1865," *Journal of American History*, 67 (March 1984), pp. 816–834.

James A. Rawley, *The Politics of Union: Northern Politics During the Civil War* (Hinsdale, IL: Dryden Press, 1974), is a skillful and brief survey that applies to economics and finance as well. Allan G. Bogue, *The Congressman's Civil War* (Cambridge, U.K.: Cambridge University Press, 1989), provides an analytical study of Union Congressmen. On the role of state governors in the northern war effort and their increasing loss of power to Washington, see William B. Hesseltine, *Lincoln and the War Governors* (New York: Alfred A. Knopf, 1948). Harry J. Carman and Reinhard H. Luthin, *Lincoln and the Patronage* (New York: Columbia University Press, 1943), show how Lincoln was able to turn the wartime explosion in federal employment to his political advantage. The notorious corruption and inefficiency of the Union bureaucracy was an inevitable result, but then the wealthier Union could afford more of this than the embattled Confederacy. The mechanics of voting by soldiers is treated in Josiah Henry Benton, *Voting in the Field: A Forgotten Chapter of the Civil War* (Boston: privately printed, 1915).

Joel H. Silbey, *A Respectable Minority: The Democratic Party in the Civil War Era, 1860–1868* (New York: Norton, 1977), is a balanced history of the North's opposition party. An examination of those Democrats who supported the war effort is Christopher Dell, *Lincoln and the War Democrats: The Grand Erosion of a Conservative Tradition* (Rutherford, WI: Farleigh Dickinson University Press, 1975). Two older works on northern dissent, Wood Gray, *The Hidden Civil War: The Story of the Copperheads* (New York: Viking, 1942), and George Fort Milton, *Abraham Lincoln and the Fifth Column* (New York: Vanguard, 1942), manage to get caught up in Republican war hysteria, probably because they came out in the midst of World War II. A good bibliographical criticism of Gray and Milton is Richard O. Curry, "The Union as It Was: A Critique of Recent Interpretations of the 'Copperheads'," *Civil War History*, 18 (March 1967), pp. 25–39. Level-headed about the Copperheads are two works by Frank L. Klement: *The Copperheads in the Middle West* (Chicago: University of Chicago Press, 1960) and *Dark Lanterns: Secret Political Societies, Conspiracies, and Treason Trials in the Civil War* (Baton Rouge: Louisiana State University Press, 1984). Klement also wrote a good biography of the leading peace Democrat, *The Limits of Dissent: Clement L. Vallandigham and the Civil War* (Lexington: University Press of Kentucky, 1970). William Frank Zurnow, *Lincoln and the Party Divided* (Norman: University of Oklahoma Press, 1954), is a superb look at opposition to Lincoln's reelection from within Republican ranks.

The best-researched investigation of the Union's arbitrary arrests is Mark E. Neely, Jr., *The Fate of Liberty: Abraham Lincoln and Civil Liberties* (New York: Oxford University Press, 1991). Neely attempts to absolve the Lincoln Administration from charges of dictatorship by invoking what has became the standard defense: contrasting Union policies favorably with all the conceivable repression that did *not* occur. Most of those arrested, Neely discovers, were border-state or Confederate citizens, and few were incarcerated for outright political motives. I call this the "Not as bad as Hitler-Stalin-Mao" school of historical evaluation. Despite his military incompetence, Lincoln was a consummate politician, well aware that overt tyranny might redound to his political disadvantage. That he was only as ruthless as necessary to stay in power and crush rebellion is hardly an excuse.

John A. Marshall, *American Bastille: A History of the Illegal Arrests and Imprisonment of American Citizens During the Late Civil War* (Philadelphia: Thomas W. Hartley, 1869), is a contemporary compendium of individual cases that went through over thirty printings and made no effort to spare Lincoln's reputation. It is sobering reading because it concretizes the soulless statistics into real-world personal tragedies. A legislative history of this issue is George Clarke Sellery, *Lincoln's Suspension of Habeas Corpus as Viewed by Congress* (Madison: University of Wisconsin, 1907). With respect to the Lincoln Administration's imposition of direct military rule over civilians, George M. Dennison, "Martial Law: The Development of a Theory of Emergency Powers, 1776–1861," *American Journal of Legal History*, 18 (January 1974), pp. 52–79, demonstrates that this represented a significant and sweeping legal innovation dating back only as far as the Dorr Rebellion of 1842 in Rhode Island.

The "Not as bad as Hitler-Stalin-Mao" standard, recently reaffirmed in Herman Belz's short pamphlet, *Lincoln and the Constitution: The Dictator-*

ship Question Reconsidered (Fort Wayne, IN: Louis A. Warren Library and Museum, 1984), reflects ingrained American nationalism and as such predates those three monstrous tyrants, cropping up as early as the turn of the century in the multi-volume general history of James Ford Rhodes (cited prologue). Working against the backdrop of World War I and the Kaiser's Germany, James G. Randall applied it in the first edition (1926) of *Constitutional Problems Under Lincoln*, rev. edn. (Urbana: University of Illinois Press, 1951). Randall's study is a legalistic treatment of many more civil-liberties issues than just arbitrary arrests.

Actually, Harold M. Hyman's *To Try Men's Souls: Loyalty Tests in American History* (Berkeley: University of California Press, 1960), provides an excellent account of domestic liberty in the North, whereas his *Era of the Oath: Northern Loyalty Tests During the Civil War and Reconstruction* (Philadelphia: University of Pennsylvania Press, 1954), is as narrowly focused as its title suggests. Only Hyman has called attention to the House Loyalty Investigating Committee chaired by Congressman John Fox Potter of Wisconsin, which is not the same as the better-known and longer-lived Joint Committee on the Conduct of the War, which also conducted a few loyalty investigations, albeit less sweeping. *To Try Men's Souls* also contained one of the best general treatments of Union occupation practices, until the recent appearance of Stephen V. Ash's definitive *When the Yankees Came: Conflict & Chaos in the Occupied South, 1861–1865* (Chapel Hill: University of North Carolina Press, 1995). A local study of the severity of these practices is Peter Maslowski, *Treason Must Be Made Odious: Military Occupation and Wartime Reconstruction in Nashville, Tennessee* (Millwood, NY: KTO Press, 1978).

Northern newspaper censorship is touched upon in Robert S. Harper's study of the journalistic reaction to the President, *Lincoln and the Press* (New York: McGraw-Hill, 1951), and in J. Cutler Andrews's study of news reporting, *The North Reports the Civil War* (Pittsburgh: University of Pittsburgh Press, 1955). Chapter 3 of Dorothy Ganfield Fowler, *Unmailable: Congress and the Post Office* (Athens: University of Georgia Press, 1977), presents details on Union mail censorship not found elsewhere.

The Confederacy, unlike the Union, lacked a two-party system. Scholars who think this a major weakness are David Potter, "Jefferson Davis and the Political Factors in Confederate Defeat," from David Donald, ed., *Why the North Won the Civil War* (cited ch. 7); and Eric L. McKitrick, "Party Politics and the Union and Confederate War Efforts," in William Nisbet Chambers and Walter Dean Burnham, eds., *The American Party Systems: Stages of Political Development*, 2nd edn. (New York: Oxford University Press, 1975). Richard Franklin Bensel, on the other hand, in *Yankee Leviathan* (cited the previous chapter) finds this contention odd, given that the Confederacy was in reality more centralized than the Union. Why should the opposition's inability to organize have hindered the Rebel war effort?

Regardless of the answer to that question, the absence of formal parties results in the conventional portrayal of Confederate politics as a fever swamp of petty jealousies and personality clashes. Three additional factors have reinforced this portrayal. First, the Rebel Congress usually met in secret, as did the Montgomery convention. Second, most general histories of the Confederacy obscure political conflict with a topical rather than chronological organization (Emory M. Thomas's *The Confederate Nation: 1861–1865,* cited ch. 5, being the major exception). And third, many Southerners had imbibed an older hostility to the corruption of political factions and therefore initially tried to submerge their political differences within an overarching demand for unity.

I believe, in contrast, that we can discern nascent ideological factions reaching back to disputes at the Montgomery convention between radical fire-eaters and their moderate opponents. A new major study that leans toward the same view, treating Davis's opponents as ideologically serious, is George C. Rable, *The Confederate Republic: A Revolution Against Politics* (Chapel Hill: University of North Carolina Press, 1994). Drew Gilpin Faust, *The Creation of Confederate Nationalism: Ideology and Identity in the Civil War South* (Baton Rouge: Louisiana State University Press, 1988), describes the South's wartime ideology, whereas Paul D. Escott, *After Secession: Jefferson Davis and the Failure of Confederate Nationalism* (Baton Rouge: Louisiana State University Press, 1978), chronicles the mounting opposition to the government.

Wilfred Buck Yearns, *The Confederate Congress* (Athens: University of Georgia Press, 1960), is a traditional narrative; Thomas B. Alexander and Richard E. Beringer, *The Anatomy of the Confederate Congress: A Study of the Influence of Member Characteristics on Legislative Voting Behavior, 1861–1865* (Nashville, TN: Vanderbilt University Press, 1972), is more quantitative. An excellent collection of essays on state leaders in the wartime South is W. Buck Yearns, ed., *The Confederate Governors* (Athens: University of Georgia Press, 1985). Among the Confederacy's heroic defenders of liberty, the governor of Georgia is very difficult to admire. His inconsistencies and opportunism come across blatantly in a recent biography, Joseph H. Parks, *Joseph E. Brown of Georgia* (Baton Rouge: Louisiana State University Press, 1977). J. Cutler Andrews, *The South Reports the Civil War* (Princeton, NJ: Princeton University Press, 1979), examines the operations of the southern press.

For internal dissent, and the Confederate government's reaction, see Georgia Lee Tatum, *Disloyalty in the Confederacy* (Chapel Hill: University of North Carolina Press, 1934), and Carleton Beals, *War Within a War: The Confederacy Against Itself* (Philadelphia: Chilton Books, 1965). Particularly outstanding is William M. Robinson, Jr., *Justice in Grey: A History of the Judicial System of the Confederate States of America* (Cambridge, MA: Harvard University Press, 1941), with one of the best discussions of martial law and *habeas corpus* within the Confederacy. Also excellent at exploding the myth of southern respect for civil liberties is, again, Harold Hyman's *To Try Men's Souls.* And Ella Lonn, *Foreigners in the Confederacy* (Chapel Hill: University of North Carolina Press, 1940), contains sections on the treatment of foreigners suspected of disloyalty.

Three books that recount incidents of localized suppression are Phillip

Shaw Paludan, *Victims: A True Story of the Civil War* (Knoxville: University of Tennessee Press, 1981), about a Confederate atrocity in the Appalachian mountains; Wayne K. Durrill, *War of Another Kind: A Southern Community in the Great Rebellion* (Oxford: Oxford University Press, 1990), about Rebel measures to combat disloyalty in close proximity to Union troops along the North Carolina coast; and Richard B. McCaslin, *Tainted Breeze: The Great Hanging at Gainesville, Texas, 1862* (Baton Rouge: Louisiana State University Press, 1994), about the mass executions in east Texas. Richard Nelson Current, *Lincoln's Loyalists: Union Soldiers From the Confederacy* (Boston: Northeastern University Press, 1992), relates the story of those Southerners who actually joined the North's armies.

11

The Ravages of
Total War

Grant Takes Command

During the summer of 1863 the Confederacy suffered four major setbacks. In the eastern theater, General Robert E. Lee had launched a second invasion of Northern territory. Rather than stopping at the border state of Maryland, he had pushed deeper into the free state of Pennsylvania. Irrespective of its military merits, this would have been an enormous political mistake. Lee's Army of Northern Virginia immeasurably hurt the peace movement in the North as it seized provisions, levied tribute, and enslaved free blacks. But these political costs were dwarfed by the campaign's military climax at the small town of Gettysburg. Lee's three-day effort to crush decisively the Union Army of the Potomac resulted in his worst defeat yet.

Far to the west, the day after the battle of Gettysburg, the Confederate stronghold of Vicksburg capitulated to General Ulysses S. Grant. After consistently failing for nearly a year to capture this objective on the Mississippi River, Grant had succeeded only by boldly abandoning his lines of communication and supplying his army off the southern countryside. Several days later, a separate Federal army that had come up the Mississippi from New Orleans finally captured Port Hudson. With the entire river now in Union hands, the Confederacy was effectively divided in two.

This separation was probably not the most debilitating result of the twin defeats at Vicksburg and Port Hudson. The Confederacy's semi-autonomous Trans-Mississippi Department may have been just as well off freer from the central government's meddlesome direction. Far more serious was the loss of over 35,000 Rebel troops besieged within the two cities. While Civil War battles were rarely decisive, sieges ending in surrender most certainly were. Grant had eliminated an entire enemy army from further action yet had sustained fewer than 10,000 casualties himself. Three months later, the South's Army of Tennessee almost turned the tables, pulling off a similar strangulation of 45,000 Federal troops that had managed to get bottled up on quarter-rations within Chattanooga, on the upper Tennessee River in the mountains near the Georgia border. But Grant arrived with fresh forces and opened a supply line, saving the beleaguered Union army.

Along with the military reversals at Gettysburg, Vicksburg, and Port Hudson, the Rebels suffered a diplomatic reversal. The Confederacy had so far contracted with private English shipyards for its most successful warships. But the continuing pressure from American minister Charles Frances Adams finally had compelled the British government to view such construction as violation of its neutrality laws. In early September it seized the two ironclad Laird rams that were nearly completed. The South had been counting upon these powerful ships to pry open the Union blockade.

Because of these four setbacks, historians frequently refer to the summer of 1863 as the Civil War's turning point. The previous military stalemate seemed to be broken. After Grant had consolidated the victories in the west, President Lincoln appointed him general in chief. Grant planned a coordinated offensive of all Union armies for the spring of 1864. He came east to lead the attack against Lee, while his trusted subordinate, General William Tecumseh Sherman, assumed command of the main Federal effort in the west.

Yet the military stalemate was not really broken. Even after the victories of 1863, the Union hardly controlled any more Southern territory than a year previously. Mastery of the oceans and rivers had permitted Federal forces to operate in every Confederate state, but all the hard fighting had resulted in the complete conquest of only one state: Tennessee. The Rebels, moreover, still fielded two large armies, Lee's Army of Northern Virginia in the east and the Army of Tennessee in the west.

The Army of Northern Virginia, although drained of offensive power, had hardly been destroyed. Now forced to remain on the defensive against an opponent twice as numerous, Lee conducted what many military experts consider his finest campaign. Prepared positions repeatedly anticipated every one of Grant's advances. "The great feature of this campaign is the extraordinary use made of earthworks," reported a Union staff officer to his wife. "When we arrive on the ground, it takes of course a considerable time to put troops in position for attack, in a wooded country. . . . Meantime what does the enemy? Hastily forming a line of battle, they then collect rails from fences, stones, logs and all other materials, and pile them along the line; bayonets with a few picks and shovels, in the hands of men who work for their lives, soon suffice to cover this frame with earth and sods; and within one hour, there is a shelter against bullets, high enough to cover a man kneeling, and extending often for a mile or two."

The entrenchment process repeated itself over and over. "It is a rule that, when the Rebels halt, the first day gives them a good rifle-pit; the second, a regular infantry parapet with artillery in position; and the third a parapet with an abattis in front and entrenched batteries behind. Sometimes they put this three days' work into the first twenty-four hours. Our men can, and do, do the same; but remember, our object is offense—to advance." Describing the campaign's effect upon the Virginia landscape, the officer told his wife that "you would be amazed to see how this country is intersected with field-works, extending for miles and miles in different directions and marking the different strategic lines taken up by the two armies, as they warily move about each other."[1]

Federal assaults were rarely able to penetrate and hold Confederate works. But unlike prior commanders of the Army of the Potomac, Grant refused to retreat after one or two repulses. He maneuvered forward and attacked again. The Union general in chief knew he could rely upon the North's more plentiful manpower to maintain the superior strength of his own formations. "We had been accustomed to a programme which began with a Federal advance, culminating in one great battle, and ended in the retirement of the Union army, the substitution of a new Federal commander for the one beaten, and the institution of a more or less offensive campaign on our part," recorded Sergeant-Major George Cary Eggleston of Lee's army. "This was the usual order of events, and this was what we confidently expected when General Grant crossed into the Wilderness. But here was a new Federal general, fresh from the West, and so ill-informed as to the military customs in our part of the country that when the battle of the Wilderness was over, instead of retiring to the north bank of the river and awaiting the development of Lee's plans, he had the temerity to move by his left flank to a new position, there to try conclusions with us again."

Grant's change of strategy soon become clear to Lee's rank and file. "We had begun to understand what our new adversary meant; . . . that the policy of pounding had begun, and would continue until our strength should be utterly worn away. . . . We began to understand that Grant had taken hold of the problem of destroying the Confederate strength in the only way that the strength of such an army, so commanded, could be destroyed, and that he intended to continue the plodding work till the task should be accomplished, wasting very little time or strength in efforts to make a brilliant display of generalship in a contest of strategic wits with Lee."[2]

Grant's constant pounding cost his army dearly. After little more than a month, it had suffered a hideous 60,000 casualties, as many men as the total under Lee's command. Yet the Army of the Potomac was no closer to the Confederate capital than General McClellan had brought it two years earlier. Federal veterans were particularly pessimistic about an assault that Grant ordered at the crossroads of Cold Harbor, within nine miles of Richmond. The night before, many wrote their names and addresses upon slips of paper which they pinned to their uniforms. This precursor to the modern dog tag would allow their dead bodies to be more readily identified. One soldier fatalistically composed his diary entry in advance: "June 3. Cold Harbor. I was killed."[3] The diary was found on his corpse after the battle. Such were the losses that made Lincoln's reelection problematic.

Sherman's March to the Sea

The enhanced range and accuracy of the rifle was turning the Civil War into a war of bloody attrition. While General Grant slowly pounded his way toward Richmond in the east, General Sherman was likewise blocked by successive defensive works as he inched toward Atlanta in the west. This compulsive, forty-four-year-old, red-headed West Pointer had lived many of his adult years in the South. But his brother was one of Ohio's Senators. At one point early in the conflict Sherman had been so incapacitated by depression and anxiety that he was removed from command so his wife could nurse him back to emotional health. Widespread newspaper allegations about his temporary insanity, however, did not prevent reassignment to active duty.

Despite now having three separate Union armies totaling 100,000 soldiers at his disposal, Sherman relied more upon maneuver and less upon assault than did Grant. Western losses were therefore less spectacular. This relative lack of combat led the Confederate government to possibly its greatest miscalculations of the war. Jefferson Davis was still attached to a conventional strategy of offensive defense. Already Bedford Forrest had not been permitted to take the Rebel cavalry on a raid against Sherman's ever lengthening rail line because that would have left Mississippi unguarded. When Joseph E. Johnston, the Southern general defending Atlanta, failed to attack Sherman's much larger force and steadily fell back, Davis replaced him with a general who was more aggressive. After frittering away precious Rebel strength in furious but futile attacks, Johnston's replacement found himself compelled to relinquish Atlanta to the Federals at the beginning of September in 1864. As one embittered Tennessee veteran remembered, "Jeff Davis acted the fool and removed Joseph E. Johnston and put Gen. [John B.] Hood in comand [*sic*], which quickly demoralized the whole Army. . . . All the men . . . Hood failed to see Slaughtered at the Battle of Atlanta on the 22nd of July 1864 he got rid of at" later battles in his "attempt to immortalize himself."[4]

The premature fall of Atlanta had a profound effect upon the morale of both sides. Southern despondency plunged to new lows, whereas northern hopes soared. This was exactly the kind of victory

Lincoln needed to save his administration at the polls. Although the Democrats still received 45 percent of the North's popular vote, the Republicans won a lopsided victory in the electoral college, swept to overwhelming control of Congress, and regained every state legislature they had lost in 1862. The reelected President had a mandate to continue the war.

Losing Atlanta, however, was still not a military catastrophe for the South. Without a city to protect, the Army of Tennessee was free to threaten the fragile Union supply line that extended well over a hundred miles through the mountains of northern Georgia. General Sherman realized that no matter how great his numerical superiority, he did not have enough troops to guard the railroads, garrison enemy territory, and chase down the Rebel forces, all at the same time. The South could never be subdued as long as its people resisted. He therefore proposed to wage war against them directly. "This war differs from European wars in this particular," the general pointed out: "We are not only fighting hostile armies, but a hostile people, and must make old and young, rich and poor, feel the hard hand of war, as well as their organized armies."[5]

Learning from his personal observation of the U.S. Army's counter-insurgency campaign against the Seminole Indians in Florida some twenty years earlier, Sherman determined that the prevailing niceties of civilized warfare must go. Grant himself, with President Lincoln's hearty encouragement, had already discarded any respect for the property of southern civilians when provisioning Union soldiers. "Up to the battle of Shiloh," the general in chief later revealed, "I, as well as thousands of other citizens, believed the rebellion against the Government would collapse suddenly and soon, if a decisive victory be gained over any of its armies. But when Confederate armies assumed the offensive and made such a gallant effort to regain what had been lost, then, indeed, I gave up all idea of saving the Union except by complete conquest. Up to that time it had been the policy of our army, certainly of that portion of it commanded by me, to protect the property of the citizens whose territory was invaded, without regard to their sentiments, whether Union or Secession. After this, however, I regarded it as humane to both sides to protect the persons of those found at their homes, but to consume everything that could be used to support or supply armies."[6]

Sherman went a step further toward a policy of total war. Often during his previous campaigns in Mississippi, Tennessee, and Georgia, his forces had systematically destroyed any supplies that his army could not use. Sherman wanted, in his words, to "make war so terrible" to the people of the South that "generations would pass away before they would again appeal to it."[7] So he now proposed to do this on a grand scale, completely severing his links to the railroads. "By attempting to hold the roads, I will lose one thousand men monthly." Therefore, "until we can repopulate Georgia, it is useless to occupy it, but the utter destruction of its roads, houses, and people will cripple their military resources. . . . I can . . . make Georgia howl."[8] No pleas or protests would be able to move the implacable Federal commander, who originated the adage: "war is hell." "If the people raise a howl against my barbarity and cruelty, I will answer that war is war, and not popularity seeking."[9]

Beginning in mid-November of 1864, Sherman turned his back on the enemy army and marched 60,000 soldiers through the heart of Confederate territory to the sea. Before departing Atlanta, he had ordered the entire civilian population to leave and burned much of the city. Discipline was lax among Sherman's foragers, called "bummers," who cut a swath of plunder and pillage sixty miles wide. Encountering very little organized resistance, they almost never physically harmed white civilians—primarily women, children, and old men. But they invariably took or destroyed all food and valuables and often set fire to dwellings as well. Occasionally Rebel prisoners were summarily executed as reprisals for guerrilla attacks. Eventually Sherman issued direct orders that "should a Union man be murdered then a rebel selected by lot will be shot. . . . In aggravated cases retaliation will be extended as high as five for one."[10]

A young white woman, Eliza Andrews, traveling through an area just after Sherman's troops left, described the desolation: "We struck the 'Burnt Country,' as it is well named by the natives, and then I could better understand the wrath and desperation of these poor people. I almost felt as if I should like to hang a Yankee myself. There was hardly a fence left standing all the way from Sparta to

Gordon. The fields were trampled down and the road was lined with carcasses of horses, hogs, and cattle that the invaders, unable either to consume or to carry away with them, had wantonly shot down, to starve out the people and prevent them from making their crops. The stench in some places was unbearable. . . . . The dwellings that were standing all showed signs of pillage, and on every plantation we saw the charred remains of the ginhouse and packing screw, while here and there, lone chimney stacks, 'Sherman's Sentinels,' told of homes laid in ashes. The infamous wretches! . . . Hay ricks and fodder stacks were demolished, corn cribs were empty, and every bale of cotton that could be found was burnt by the savages. I saw no grain of any sort except little patches they had spilled when feeding their horses, and which there was not even a chicken left in the country to eat."[11]

This is where the Confederacy's Napoleonic strategy revealed its ultimate inadequacy. Such a large-scale Federal campaign through Georgia should have been logistically tenuous. If lavish losses from offensive assaults had not denuded the southern countryside of military-age males, irregular Rebel warfare could have turned Sherman's march into the same kind of military debacle that British General John Burgoyne suffered during the American Revolution, when he invaded the colonies from Canada and was then forced to surrender after the battles of Saratoga. Even without significant military opposition, Federal troops were starting to feel supply strains before they reached the Atlantic coast in December of 1864 and made contact with Union warships.

One indication of this strain was Sherman's efforts to discourage "contrabands." He found it difficult to feed blacks flocking to his columns unless they were males who could provide labor. One Union corps commander took the admonition too literally and ordered his men to pull up a pontoon bridge immediately after crossing it. Five hundred slaves, mostly women and children, were left trapped on the opposite side of a swollen creek that flowed into the Savannah River. Not wishing to trust their fates to the tender mercies of pursuing Confederate cavalry, many plunged into the water and perhaps a dozen drowned. At least 25,000 runaways in all joined Sherman's columns temporarily, but fewer than 7,000 reached the coast. Once safely in Savannah, the Yankee general issued Special Field Order No. 15 in order to rid himself of this nuisance in future operations. Land within 30 miles of the coast was turned over to the freedmen in forty-acre plots for each family.

Rebels Abandon Slavery

Total war was taking its toll. Whereas there were few civilian casualties for the Union, the Confederacy endured over 50,000. The Rebels' scorched-earth policy merely added to enemy devastation. Retreating Confederate forces had torched such villages as Hampton, Virginia, and Brunswick, Georgia, and the authorities had contemplated doing the same to Savannah, Mobile, and Galveston. The unconquered portion of the South overflowed with 200,000 homeless refugees. Food was so scarce that President Davis extolled the virtues of eating rats, which he claimed were "as good as squirrels."[12] The collapse of southern railroads, either through enemy destruction or friendly overuse, made feeding the cities and armies doubly hard.

One gruesome manifestation of the war's growing harshness was the condition of prisoners. The Union resolution against exchanges hardened when some of the captured Rebels who had been paroled after the surrenders at Vicksburg and Port Hudson turned up again within Confederate ranks. Grant furthermore realized that the refusal to exchange prisoners worked to the North's military advantage. "It is hard on our men held in Southern prisons," he admitted, "but it is humanity to those left in the ranks to fight our battles." Every exchanged Rebel only "becomes an active soldier against us at once," thereby prolonging the war.[13]

Since Southerners were already unable to care for their own, they had little left for the enemy captives that accumulated during 1864. Andersonville prison in Georgia became the South's most notorious. An open stockade built to hold 10,000 was eventually packed with a writhing mass of 33,000 unsheltered men. One hundred per day died from starvation, disease, exposure, sadistic guards, or other causes—more than one-fourth of all inmates there. Yet sanitation in many Northern prisons was also poor, certainly not much better than in the opposing armies, and Stanton reduced prisoner rations to what the Confederacy fed its soldiers. The death rate at the worst Union camp, Elmira Barracks, located in upstate New York, with its freezing winters, was not too far below that at Andersonville. Overall, 12 percent of 215,000 Southerners died while imprisoned in the North, which is only marginally better than the conservative estimate of 16 percent deaths among the 195,000 northern prisoners in the South.

The Confederacy was having difficulties even holding its military forces together. The Army of Northern Virginia's desertion rate rose from 8 percent a year until it would peak at 8 percent a month. "An army cannot be . . . supported in Virginia," complained Lee, because of "communications received by the men from their homes, urging their return and the abandonment of the field."[14] The fact that Rebel soldiers still got the same pay as before the hyperinflation of prices, if they got any pay at all, did not help. By 1865, many Confederate units were left with less than half their enrolled strength.

Both sides had sent out peace feelers before the 1864 election in the North, mostly as symbolic gestures to disable the war's opponents. Later aboard a steamer in Hampton Roads, Virginia, the President and William Seward informally met with Alexander Stephens and two other Confederate commissioners. Lincoln offered an armistice that left open possible compensation for former slaveholders in the South, in spite of the certain objections that Radical Republicans would raise. He appeared to have elevated slavery's abolition into one of the North's war goals, but he and Seward simultaneously hinted that the southern states, if they rejoined the Union, could prevent or postpone ratification of an antislavery amendment. The Republican President was inflexible on one condition, however. Reuniting the country was still nonnegotiable.

Jefferson Davis summarily rejected Lincoln's demands, yet he might have given in on southern emancipation in return for Southern independence. His countrymen were already debating the revolutionary expedient of arming slaves to fight for the Confederacy, even though they knew that this meant an end to their peculiar institution. As early as August 1863, an editorial in the *Jackson Mississippian* declared that slavery should not be "a barrier to our independence. If it is found in the way—if it proves an insurmountable object of the achievement of our liberty and separate nationality, away with it! Let it perish!" This was a drastic step, but "we must make up our minds to one solemn duty, the first duty of the patriot, and that is to save ourselves from the rapacious North, whatever the cost."[15]

General Lee added his prestige to the proposal. "We must decide whether slavery shall be extinguished by our enemies and the slaves be used against us, or use them ourselves at the risk of the effects which may be produced upon our social institutions," he warned. "My own opinion is that we should employ them without delay. I believe that with proper regulations they can be made efficient soldiers. . . . [T]he best means of securing the efficiency and fidelity of this auxiliary force would be to accompany the measure with a well-digested plan of gradual and general emancipation."[16] In March of 1865, the Confederate Congress narrowly authorized the recruitment of 300,000 slaves, while the Davis Administration promised full emancipation to the British and French governments in exchange for diplomatic recognition. With the black obstacle removed, the exchange of prisoners of war recommenced at the beginning of 1865. But otherwise these desperate measures came too late.

Collapse of the Confederacy

After completing the March to the Sea and capturing Savannah, Georgia, before Christmas of 1864, Sherman had headed north to spread havoc in the Carolinas. "The whole army is burning with an insatiable desire to wreak vengeance upon South Carolina," he reported; "I almost tremble at her fate." Despite "many friends in Charleston, . . . I would not restrain the army lest its vigor and energy should be impaired."[17] Coastal expeditions meanwhile shut down the last Confederate ports—Mobile the previous August, Wilmington in January, Charleston in February—and ended blockade running. Additional Union raids brought the blight of total war to other sections of the South. Grant, for instance, ordered Virginia's Shenandoah Valley ravaged so thoroughly that "crows flying over it for the balance of this season will have to carry their provender with them."[18]

By the spring of 1865, nine harrowing months of relentless siege around Richmond and Petersburg, a major railroad junction twenty-three miles south, had finally battered and stretched Lee's trenches to the breaking point. The Confederate forces evacuated the capital and tried to flee into the hinterland. But Grant's quick pursuit closed off all possible escape for large units. On April 9, 1865, Lee surrendered what remained of his army to the Union general at Appomattox Courthouse, seventy miles west of Richmond. All other Confederate commands capitulated within seven weeks.

Jefferson Davis had wanted to disperse the troops and continue the struggle. At the last hour, he addressed the people with a plea for guerrilla warfare: "Relieved from the necessity of guarding cities and particular points, important but not vital to our defence with our army free to move from point to point, and strike in detail detachments and garrisons of the enemy; operating in the interior of our own country, where supplies are more accessible, and where the foe will be far removed from his own base and cut off from all succor in case of reverse, nothing is now needed to render our triumph certain, but the exhibition of our own unquenchable resolve. Let us but will it, and we are free."[19]

The Confederate President's plan may have been still feasible *militarily*. Although total war had consumed one-third of southern wealth, not counting the emancipated slaves, and many southern cities were in ashes, including Richmond, Atlanta, and Columbia, capital of South Carolina, no Confederate army had yet lost a battle for lack of arms, equipment, or even food. Sherman's mobile campaigns had left no permanent Federal presence to control Rebel territory. In many respects, southern fortunes had sunk no lower than those of the American revolutionaries in the winter of 1778, when Washington's army shivered and starved at Valley Forge, while at Philadelphia, the new nation's capital, the British sat comfortably. Southerners had suffered proportionally much greater loss of life—about 4.5 percent of the white population. But adjusting for the number of military age men, this figure is comparable to French losses during World War I and less than German losses during World War II.[20]

Many Union leaders feared just what Davis proposed, but Lee

and the other Confederate generals rejected taking to the hills. They clearly recognized that Southerners had lost the will to fight. "While in Richmond I was told that the 'passage of the enemy thro' the country was like the flight of an arrow thro' the air,' that 'overrunning was not subjugation,'" wrote one Confederate Congressman. "Well, this may be true in some sections of the country, but is far different here. Our people are *subjugated*—they are crushed in spirit—they have not heart to do anything but meet together and recount their losses and suffering."[21]

Historians have long pondered the sudden disintegration of Confederate will. Many believe that its causes transcend purely military factors. Southerners, after all, had seceded from the Union either to preserve slavery or to defend states' rights. But the fight for independence cost them both these goals. One Mississippi newspaper concluded that arming the slaves made the entire conflict senseless, "a total abandonment of the chief object of this war, and if the institution is already irretrievably undermined, the rights of the States are buried with it. When we admit this to be true beyond adventure, then our voice will be for peace; for why fight one moment longer, if the object and occasion of the fight is dying, dead, or damned?"[22]

Some historians argue that Southerners had unconsciously imbibed too much of America's revolutionary heritage to feel completely at ease with the brazen prewar justifications for human bondage. This devoutly Protestant people thus interpreted their military defeats as unmistakable evidence of God's wrathful judgment. Deep-seated guilt about the sin of slavery was what ultimately undermined the Confederate cause. Even those Southerners undisturbed by the peculiar institution *per se* could feel morally uneasy about their failure to ameliorate the bondsman's station with Christian charity and Biblical teachings. By the war's second year, a significant movement within southern churches was agitating for such reforms as prohibiting the separation of slave children from their mothers, admitting slave testimony in courts, and permitting slave religious assemblies.

Alexander Stephens, in contrast, remained convinced that the Confederate government's centralization of power had sapped the people's morale. "I knew that our people had gone into the struggle with no other view than to maintain and preserve the principles of the Constitution as established by their fathers. . . . If . . . Government and people should prove true to this cause, I doubted not that, finally, after great sacrifices, much tribulation and suffering, war would be brought to a close upon some settlement securing the rights and sovereignty of the States and perpetuating the principles of self-government." But on the other hand, lamented the Confederate Vice-President, "if this great object should be abandoned by the Government, our cause would be hopeless."[23]

Regardless of the explanation, white Southerners had generally concluded in early 1865 that they could do better back within the Union. With a combination of dread and hope, they waited to see what terms their conquerors would exact.

Chapter 11
Bibliographical Essay

The evolution of the North's military strategy can be traced in Russell F. Weigley's general survey, *The American Way of War* (cited ch. 7), or in Edward Hagerman's more specific *The American Civil War and the Origins of Modern Warfare: Ideas, Organizations, and Field Command* (Bloomington: Indiana University Press, 1988). Most military historians view the move toward total war as some kind of progress rather than as an "advance to barbarism," to use an appropriate phrase from a work by F. J. P. Veale of the same title: *Advance to Barbarism: The Development of Total Warfare From Sarejevo to Hiroshima* (New York: Devin-Adair, 1968). T. Harry Williams, for instance, describes Grant as "the first of the great moderns" in *Lincoln and His Generals* (p. 314, cited ch. 7). The prime criterion for celebrating this so-called progress appears to be military success. These historians' nationalist presuppositions have induced uncritical acceptance of any measures thought necessary for Federal victory, no matter how ruthless. Yet the same authors would presumably refrain from applauding chattel slavery, concentration camps, or simple plunder in cases where these "worked" to their practitioners' advantage.

Whether inevitable or not, the loss of the nineteenth-century's aspirations to an ideal of civilized warfare, limiting the carnage and devastation among non-combatants (however imperfectly realized in practice), is a development to be mourned. One book that does indict the Union for initiating the decline toward Hiroshima and My Lai is James Reston, Jr.'s, meandering travelogue, *Sherman's March and Vietnam* (New York: Macmillan, 1985). At the other extreme, a variation on the "Not as bad as Hitler-Stalin-Mao" standard of historical evaluation has entered the discussion, most notably in Mark E. Neely, Jr., "Was the Civil War a Total War?" *Civil War History*, 37 (March 1991), pp. 5–28, which correctly points out that Union efforts never attained the implacable ferocity of the Allies during World War II. Mark Grimsley also reminds us in *The Hard Hand of War: Union Military Policy Toward Southern Civilians, 1861–1865* (Cambridge, U.K.: Cambridge University Press, 1995) that there remained still worse measures that Federal forces never adopted. But Grimsley does document the increasing harshness, and this marks the Civil War as a major departure.

Not that the Confederacy was blameless. After all, General Jubal B. Early's cavalry reduced to ashes two-thirds of Chambersburg, Pennsylvania, on July 30, 1864, in retaliation for Yankee acts in the Shenandoah Valley. Charles Royster, *The Destructive War: William Tecumseh Sherman, Stonewall Jackson, and the Americans* (New York: Alfred A. Knopf, 1991), finds these tendencies inherent in wartime rhetoric and argues that Stonewall Jackson would have instituted similar practices given the opportunity. For the neglected outrages by Lee's army during the Gettysburg campaign, see the appropriate sections of W. P. Conrad and Ted Alexander, *When War Passed This Way* (Greencastle, PA: Lilian S. Besore Memorial Library, 1982), Edwin B. Coddington, *The Gettysburg Campaign* (cited ch. 7), and Wilbur Sturtevant Nye, *Here Come the Rebels!* (Baton Rouge: Louisiana State University Press, 1965).

A classic study of Lee versus Grant is John F. C. Fuller, *Grant and Lee: A Study in Personality and Generalship*, 2nd edn. (Bloomington: Indiana University Press, 1957), which originally appeared in 1932 and touted Grant as the greater of the two commanders. On the other hand, the only modern, full-scale biography of the Union general in chief, William S. McFeely, *Grant: A Biography* (New York: W. W. Norton, 1981), harks back to a portrait of a cold-hearted "butcher," who expended the North's greater manpower simply to reduce the South through relentless attrition. Neither side in this debate, however, has attached sufficient weight to Lincoln's incompetence, yet again, in the eastern theater. The President virtually imposed a bloody slugfest with Lee's Army of Northern Virginia by rejecting Grant's preferred plan to maneuver farther south through North Carolina.

Detailed military accounts of Grant's campaigns are in Bruce Catton's two volumes, *Grant Moves South* (Boston: Little, Brown, 1960), and *Grant Takes Command* (Boston: Little, Brown, 1969). Also, John Keegan, *The Mask of Command* (New York: Viking, 1987), includes an essay on the Union general in chief that is quite good. An intriguing integration of Grant's military and political sides up until his election as President, one which absolves him of charges of racism and callousness, is Brooks D. Simpson, *Let Us Have Peace: Ulysses S. Grant and the Politics of War and Reconstruction, 1861–1868* (Chapel Hill: University of North Carolina Press, 1991).

The most recent study of the Atlanta campaign is Albert Castel's massive *Decision in the West: The Atlanta Campaign of 1864* (Lawrence: University Press of Kansas, 1992). Joseph T. Glatthaar, *The March to the Sea and Beyond: Sherman's Troops in the Savannah and Carolinas Campaigns* New York: New York University Press, 1985), closely examines the attitudes and behaviors of the Union soldiers who conducted Sherman's campaigns of destruction. Lee Kennett, *Marching Through Georgia: The Story of Soldiers and Civilians During Sherman's Campaign* (New York: Harper-Collins, 1995), is more concerned with the impact on civilians. For a favorable biography of Grant's principal lieutenant from a British military analyst, pick up Basil H. Liddell Hart, *Sherman: Soldier, Realist, American* (New York: Dodd, Mead, 1929). Unfriendly is John Bennett Walters, *Merchant of Terror: General Sherman and Total War* (Indianapolis: Bobbs-Merrill, 1973), which covers only the general's Civil War years. Fuller, newer, psychological portraits are John F. Marszalek, *Sherman: A Soldier's Passion for Order* (New York: Free Press, 1993), and Michael Fellman, *Citizen Sherman: A Life of William Tecumseh Sherman* (New York: Random House, 1995).

An original examination of the area west of the Mississippi that the

Union managed to sever from the Confederacy is Robert L. Kerby, *Kerby Smith's Confederacy: The Trans-Mississippi South, 1863–1865* (New York: Columbia University Press, 1972). Also consult James L. Nichols, *The Confederate Quartermaster in the Trans-Mississippi* (Austin: University of Texas Press, 1964). Gary M. Pecquet, "Money in the Trans-Mississippi Confederacy and the Confederate Currency Reform Act of 1864," *Explorations in Economic History,* 24 (April 1987), pp. 218–243, is a fascinating look at the way monetary policies affected differently that portion of the Confederacy.

Historians still argue about Lincoln's precise terms at the Hampton Roads peace conference. Richard N. Current, *The Lincoln Nobody Knows* (cited ch. 4), and Ludwell H. Johnson, "Lincoln's Solution to the Problem of Peace Terms, 1864–1865," *Journal of Southern History,* 34 (November 1968), pp. 576–586, have made the strongest case that the President appeared willing to abandon the constitutional amendment abolishing slavery. Lincoln's defenders have dismissed this charge as an after-the-fact concoction of Alexander Stephens and other Southerners. David Donald's new biography, *Lincoln* (cited ch. 4), gives the most plausible reconciliation. When Lincoln and Seward hinted at peace without universal emancipation, they were lying, in the hopes of generating further dissension within the Confederacy.

An early treatment of the informal peace negotiations both before and after the 1864 presidential election is Edward C. Kirkland, *The Peacemakers of 1864* (New York: Macmillan, 1927). David Long, *The Jewel of Liberty: Abraham Lincoln's Re-election and the End of Slavery* (Mechanicsburg, PA: Stackpole Books, 1994), covers the election from the Union perspective, but has an unfortunate tendency to descend into Lincoln hagiography, while Larry E. Nelson, *Bullets, Ballots, and Rhetoric: Confederate Policy for the United States Presidential Contest of 1864* (University: University of Alabama Press, 1980), looks at Confederate efforts to influence the outcome.

William B. Hesseltine, *Civil War Prisons: A Study in Psychology* (Columbus: Ohio State University Press, 1930), is sadly dated. A new scholarly look at the most infamous Confederate prison, William Marvel, *Andersonville: The Last Depot* (Chapel Hill: University of North Carolina Press, 1994), revises many of the lurid tales of deliberate Rebel brutality, as popularized in MacKinlay Kantor's depressing, Pulitzer-Prize winning *Andersonville* (New York: World, 1955). Although well researched for a novel, Kantor's book relies too heavily on sensational reminiscences published many years after the war. James I. Robertson, Jr., *Soldiers Blue and Gray,* and Reid Mitchell, *Civil War Soldiers,* (both cited in ch. 7) contain sections presenting the soldiers' impressions of Civil War prisons.

Mary Elizabeth Massey has written a pair of fine works on the deprivations suffered by Confederate civilians: *Ersatz in the Confederacy* (Columbia: University of South Carolina Press, 1952) and *Refugee Life in the Confederacy* (Baton Rouge: Louisiana State University Press, 1964). Bell Irvin Wiley, *The Plain People of the Confederacy* (Baton Rouge: Louisiana

State University Press, 1943), charts the resulting disaffection among non-slaveholders, as does Stephen E. Ambrose, "Yeoman Discontent in the Confederacy," *Civil War History*, 8 (September 1962), pp. 259–268. George C. Rable, *Civil Wars: Women and the Crisis of Southern Nationalism* (Urbana: University of Illinois Press, 1989), focuses on the significant contribution of southern women to demoralization. An investigation into the bureaucratic ineptitude surrounding the payment of Rebel troops is Harry N. Scheiber, "The Pay of Confederate Troops and Problems of Demoralization: A Case of Administrative Failure," in John T. Hubbell, ed., *Battles Lost and Won* (cited ch. 5).

Robert F. Durden, *The Gray and the Black: The Confederate Debate on Emancipation* (Baton Rouge: Louisiana State University Press, 1972), is the standard on its topic, although a recent state study which contributes to our understanding is Ervin L. Jordan, Jr., *Black Confederates and Afro-Yankees in Civil War Virginia* (Charlottesville: University Press of Virginia, 1995). Two older speculations about reasons for Confederate defeat are Charles H. Wesley, *The Collapse of the Confederacy* (Washington: Associated Publishers, 1937), and Wiley, *The Road to Appomattox* (Memphis: Memphis State College Press, 1956).

Scholars who believe that southern guilt about slavery was key include Kenneth Stampp, "The Southern Road to Appomattox," in *The Imperiled Union* (cited prologue), and Richard E. Beringer, Herman Hattaway, Archer Jones, and William N. Still, Jr., in *Why the South Lost the Civil War* (cited ch. 7). Others remain skeptical: for instance, George M. Fredrickson, "Blue Over Gray: Sources of Success and Failure in the Civil War," in Fredrickson, ed., *A Nation Divided: Problems and Issues of the Civil War and Reconstruction* (Minneapolis: Burgess, 1975). William W. Freehling offers a synthesis that admits that few slaveholders felt "guilt about slavery per se," but that many believed that "the treatment of slaves was sometimes un-Christian" and inconsistent with their growing sense of paternalism. See his "The Divided South, the Causes of Confederate Defeat, and the Reintegration of Narrative History," in *The Reintegration of American History* (cited prologue).

Unfortunately, too many of these speculations needlessly follow David M. Potter, "The Historian's Use of Nationalism and Vice Versa" (cited prologue), in underrating Confederate nationalism at the war's outset. One surmises that denying the genuineness of the southern desire for self-determination makes it easier to deny its legitimacy. An important corrective, which appallingly remains unpublished, is John M. Murrin, "War, Revolution, and Nation-Making: The American Revolution Versus the Civil War" (Princeton University, Department of History, October 1989). Murrin insightfully points out that "by virtually all measurable standards, the Confederate sense of national identity appears to have been deeper, more profound, more passionate (no doubt more of a national*ism*) than the ties that bound the Thirteen Colonies together from 1775 to 1783 and beyond." Every problem that plagued the Confederate government was more formidable to the Continental Congress. Nor did opposition to the war within the South approach the scale of loyalist opposition to the Revolution.

Thus, the well-established collapse of Rebel morale at the war's end could not have been the result of Richmond's inability to impose sufficient unity, as so often suggested. "Collect more taxes, install more bureaucrats, draft more hillbillies, print more money, seize more crops, shoot more deserters, suspend more *habeas corpus*, declare martial law, override the Governors, and stretch the Constitution," to quote Joseph Stromberg (from p. 45 of "The War for Southern Independence: A Radical Libertarian Perspective," cited prologue)—"this is supposed to have been the road to victory." Indeed, quite the reverse. The government too vigorously coerced loyalty. Although historians sometimes seem unable to decide whether the Confederate government was too strong or too weak, Vice-President Alexander Stephens had it exactly right. The despotic centralization of Jefferson Davis and his West Point cabal alienated the southern people from the cause of independence.

12

The Politics of Reconstruction

The Prospect of Leniency

Whatever opinion Southerners held about the sinfulness of slavery, President Lincoln certainly felt that the bloody Civil War was the nation's atonement. His second inaugural address in early 1865 was filled with Biblical imagery. "Fondly do we hope, fervently do we pray, that this mighty scourge of war may speedily pass away," said the President. "Yet, if God wills that it continue until all the wealth piled by the bondsman's two hundred and fifty years of unrequited toil shall be sunk, and until every drop of blood drawn with the lash shall be paid by another drawn with the sword, as it was said three thousand years ago, so still it must be said, 'the judgments of the Lord are true and righteous altogether.'"

But Lincoln's inaugural also held out the promise of lenient terms for the defeated South. "With malice toward none, with charity for all, with firmness in the right as God gives us to see the right, let us strive on to finish the work we are in, to bind up the nation's wounds, to care for him who shall have borne the battle and for his widow and his orphan, to do all which may achieve and cherish a just and lasting peace among ourselves and with all nations."[1]

The President had already instituted a policy for the reconstruction of loyal state governments that reflected this promise. As soon as Federal forces managed to occupy a sizable portion of a Confederate state, Lincoln had employed his war powers to appoint a military governor. Then in December of 1863 he had announced liberal presidential pardons for former Rebels. When one-tenth of the voters of an occupied state had taken an oath of future loyalty to the Union, they could establish a new government. Lincoln had insisted upon just one major condition. The reconstructed government must abolish slavery.

The two years since the Emancipation Proclamation had stiffened northern determination that the elimination of slavery must be complete, permanent, and uncompensated. The Fugitive Slave Law was at last repealed, and the border states of Maryland and Missouri freed their slaves. But only one step could put emancipation where no state government, no future Democratic administration, nor Supreme Court ruling could reverse it. A little more than two months prior to Lee's surrender at Appomattox, two-thirds of Congress passed a proposed thirteenth amendment to the Constitution. It provided that "neither slavery nor involuntary servitude, except as punishment for crime whereof the party shall have been duly convicted, shall exist within the United States, or any place subject to their jurisdiction." Only five years after proposing a thirteenth amendment that would have guaranteed slavery forever, the Republican-controlled Congress had now endorsed one that would forever abolish it.

Reconstruction, however, raised other thorny political and constitutional questions. Radical Republicans were not entirely pleased with Lincoln's leniency toward the South. The President believed that his terms would entice former southern Whigs into a Republican alliance, but the Radicals were unconvinced that this course would either ensure the future dominance of their party or adequately protect the freed slaves. They furthermore believed that Congress rather than the President should control Reconstruction.

These disagreements were major reasons for opposition in 1864 to Lincoln's renomination. Republican Congressmen had embodied more stringent terms for Reconstruction in the Wade-Davis bill. It differed from the President's policy in two primary respects. First, it required a majority rather than one-tenth of the voters to swear loyalty. Second, it denied to all former Confederate officials, state and federal, the privilege of voting and participating in the new government through what was known as the "iron-clad" test oath. Lincoln was willing to settle, in most cases, for a promise of future loyalty, whereas the Radicals wanted to insist upon past loyalty.

Congress passed the Wade-Davis bill in July of 1864, before the presidential election, but Lincoln refused to sign it. The bill's authors thereupon publicly castigated what they considered to be the President's usurpation; "a more studied outrage on the legislative authority of the people has never been perpetrated." Although refusing to approve the bill, the President "by proclamation puts as much of it in force as he sees fit, and proposes to execute those parts by officers unknown to the laws of the United States! . . . The bill directed the appointment of Provisional Governors by and with the advice and consent of the Senate. The President . . . proposes to appoint without law, and without the advice and consent of the Senate, *Military* Governors for the Rebel States!"

This congressional manifesto foreshadowed growing Radical opposition to Lincoln's continued exercise of extraordinary war powers. "The President has greatly presumed on the forbearance which the supporters of his Administration have so long practiced, in view of the arduous conflict in which we are engaged, and the reckless ferocity of our political opponents," cautioned the bill's authors. "He must understand that our support is of a cause and not of a man; and that the authority of Congress is paramount and must be respected; . . . and if he wishes our support, he must confine himself to his executive duties—to obey and execute, not make the laws—to suppress by arms armed Rebellion, and leave political reorganization to Congress."[2]

By the time Congress submitted the constitutional amendment abolishing slavery to the states, Lincoln had gone ahead and recognized four former Confederate states as reconstructed according to his own policy: Tennessee, Louisiana, Arkansas, and Virginia. Congress, however, refused to seat representatives from these states or to allow their electoral votes to be tabulated in the recent presidential election. Perhaps Lincoln would have come around to the Radical position, as he had on emancipation and so many other issues. Perhaps he could have resolved the impasse with an astute compromise. But he did not get the chance. Five days after Lee's surrender, while Lincoln and his wife were enjoying a play, an assassin's bullet crashed through his skull. A Southern sympathizer named John Wilkes Booth jumped from Lincoln's box to the stage and escaped. The fifty-six-year-old President died the next morning.

Subjugation Without Restitution

Lincoln's murder did not leave the North in a pleasant mood. One of Booth's companions had made a simultaneous attempt upon the life of Secretary of State Seward, and fantastic speculations about vast conspiracies were rife. A tracking party soon caught up with and killed Booth, while a military court convicted eight alleged accomplices. Four were hanged, including a woman, Mary Surratt, who was almost certainly innocent. Most of the top Rebel leaders fell into Union hands by the end of the month. Although only one Confederate officer, Major Henry Wirz, commander at Andersonville prison, was executed for war crimes, many others were jailed. Jefferson Davis was clapped in chains and held for the next two years. The prospects for leniency looked dim.

The national government had already decided that the prostrate South must help cover the Union's war costs. The direct tax of 1861 was levied against the rebellious states, with a 50 percent penalty for their failure to collect it themselves. Special federal tax commissioners assessed the real property of Southerners, selling the land of those unable to pay and keeping all the proceeds—not just the amount due. Under the terms of the Captured and Abandoned Property Act of 1863, the Confederate government's prior acquisition of most of the cotton crop provided a rationale for corrupt Treasury agents to confiscate nearly all cotton in the seceding states at the end of the war, irrespective of whether it really had belonged to the Confederacy or was still the property of private owners. Hugh McCulloch, who had become Lincoln's new Secretary of the Treasury in 1865, observed: "I am sure I sent *some* honest agents South; but it sometimes seems very doubtful whether any of them remained honest very long."[3] From the estimated $100 million worth of captured property sold, the government received only $30 million. A particularly onerous increase in the federal excise on cotton extracted another $68 million from the South before being repealed in 1868. Furthermore, once the South had recovered sufficiently to begin exporting again, it bore a disproportionate burden from the nation's new high tariffs.

At the end of hostilities, the Union was the mightiest military power on the planet. It quickly demobilized its million-strong army, cut back by more than two-thirds its 700-vessel, 5,000-gun navy, and terminated abruptly all outstanding war contracts. The North's resilient market economy made the transition without hardship. After a gigantic, two-day parade down Pennsylvania Avenue in Washington, many of the northern soldiers finally went home. One Illinois veteran affirmed that their readjustment to civilian life was usually rapid. "When I returned home I found that the farm work my father was then engaged in was cutting and shocking corn. So, the morning after my arrival, September 29th, I doffed my uniform of first lieutenant, put on some of my father's old clothes, armed myself with a corn knife, and proceeded to wage war on the standing corn. The feeling I had while engaged in this work was sort of queer. It almost seemed, sometimes, as if I had been away only a day or two, and had just taken up the farm work where I had left off."[4]

But ongoing military occupation of the South required a post-war standing army that hovered near 60,000 men—four times its immediate prewar size. A large proportion of the remaining recruits were black. One of them encapsulated the profound changes that the war had wrought in southern society when he recognized his former master among a group of Confederate prisoners and shouted an effusive greeting: "Hello, massa; bottom rail top dis time."[5] Protection of the former slaves was charged to a special War Department agency, the Bureau of Refugees, Freedmen, and Abandoned Lands. Congress had established the Freedmen's Bureau, as it was commonly known, just before the fighting ended. The first major federal relief agency in American history, it soon was dispensing free food and clothing from surplus army stocks and free medical care to southern refugees, white and black. It also found employment and supervised labor contracts for the freed slaves and provided them with schools. Volunteers and funds from private northern charities supplemented the Bureau's efforts. Yet all this public and private relief combined did not come close to equaling the amount of money extracted through the central government's punitive taxes.

A few Radical Republicans advocated the wholesale redistribution of southern land. The most outspoken of these was the Pennsylvania Congressman, Thaddeus Stevens. The ironworks owned by this legislator had been destroyed when Lee invaded his state, and rumor maintained that his mulatto housekeeper was his mistress. "Forty acres and a mule" for each adult freedman became Stevens's rallying cry. "Four million persons have just been freed from a condition of dependence," he pointed out. If Congress left the freedmen "prey to the legislation and treatment of their former masters, . . . the evidence already furnished shows that they will soon become extinct, or be driven to defend themselves by civil war." The solution was to "make them independent of their old masters, so that they may not be compelled to work for them upon unfair terms." And this "can only be done by giving them a small tract of land to cultivate for themselves." Congress would thereby "elevate the character of the freedman. Nothing is so likely to make a man a good citizen as to make him a freeholder."

The Pennsylvania Congressman was not motivated by modern-day egalitarianism. Rather, he shared the same natural-rights sense of justice that made Lysander Spooner contend before the war that slaves had rightful title to their master's plantations. Blacks were the legitimate owners of the land, just like any victim who has his private property stolen by a thief. "Have they not a right to it?" Stevens demanded to know. "I do not speak of their fidelity and services in this bloody war. I put it on the mere score of lawful earnings. They and their ancestors have toiled, not for years, but for ages, without one farthing of recompense. They have earned for their masters this very land and much more. Will not he who denies them compensation now be accursed, for he is an unjust man?"[6]

Many Northerners denounced the break-up of slaveholder plantations as violating private property. "An attempt to justify the confiscation of Southern land under the pretense of doing justice to the freedmen," declared the *New York Times*, "strikes at the root of all property rights in both sections."[7] But it was Stevens and the radical abolitionists who more consistently applied the natural-law principles governing just property titles and restitution. Even the freedmen who desired land were not, as Eric Foner reveals, challenging "the notion of private property per se; rather, they viewed the accumulated property of the planters as having been illegitimately acquired." One Virginia black proclaimed: "We has a right to the land where we are located. . . . didn't we clear the land, and raise de crops ob corn, ob cotton, ob tobacco, ob rice, ob sugar, ob everything?"[8]

Thaddeus Stevens further believed that land reform was essential to transform the feudal South into a community of yeoman farmers and free laborers. "The whole fabric of southern society *must* be changed, and never can it be done if this opportunity is lost," warned Stevens. "How can republican institutions, free schools, free churches, free social intercourse exist in a mingled community of nabobs and serfs? . . . If the South is ever to be made a safe Republic let her lands be cultivated by the toil of the owners, or the free labor of intelligent citizens. This must be done even though it drive her nobility into exile."[9]

Outside of Senator Charles Sumner of Massachusetts and Congressman George Washington Julian of Indiana, however, very few Radical Republicans endorsed Stevens's proposal. Congress in 1868 passed a bill sponsored by Julian to apply the homestead principle to 44 million acres of federal lands in the South, with former slaves and pro-Union whites getting preferential access, but most of this land was of poor quality and at distant locations. The House of Representatives passed a second Julian bill nullifying railroad grants in four southern states in order to open additional land for homesteading, but it never got through the Senate.

The earlier wartime confiscation acts for the punishment of rebels, the collection of the direct tax on real estate, and the seizure of abandoned plantations did put a lot of southern land into Federal hands. Army officials helped settle many former slaves onto this land. But far more often, the Freedmen's Bureau implemented a paternalistic policy of compelling the former slaves to work, for wages and under supervised conditions to be sure, but still on plantations owned by white Southerners or leased to white Northerners. One official consequently summed up the Bureau's accomplishments as follows: "It has succeeded in making the Freedman work and in rendering labor secure & stable—but it has failed to secure the Freedman his just dues or compensation for his labor."[10]

Struggle Over the Fourteenth Amendment

President Andrew Johnson was himself a Southerner. He came from Tennessee, one of the four reconstructed states that Lincoln had recognized but Congress had not. A self-made man who as a tailor had worked his way up from poverty, the new President was also a former Jacksonian Democrat. During the 1860 presidential contest, Johnson had supported Breckinridge, the candidate of the southern wing of his party. Yet this onetime slaveholder abhorred secession so much that he had become, in the words of one North Carolina woman, a "vulgar renegade."[11] The Republican ticket had added him solely to cultivate wartime unity.

Because Congress was out of session at the time of Lincoln's death, Johnson was able to carry on his predecessor's Reconstruction policy. Johnson's animosity toward the South's planter elite made his slight modifications actually closer to the harsher congressional plan in the Wade-Davis bill. By the time Congress reconvened in December of 1865, it confronted functioning governments in ten of the eleven former Confederate states. All ten of these reconstructed states had abolished slavery within their own borders, and all but two had ratified the anti-slavery amendment. None of them had of course been represented in the Congress that proposed the amendment. But because most Northerners agreed that the seceding states had not legally left the Union, these states counted toward the total for ratifying the amendment. Only their ratifications, coupled with those from the North, provided the necessary three-fourths.

The future status of the Thirteenth Amendment was assured, but paradoxically the future status of the reconstructed states that had ratified it was not. The new governments were riddled with high Confederate officials. A former Rebel brigadier-general was governor of Mississippi, while none other than Alexander Stephens was

United States Senator from Georgia. South Carolina, rather than disavow its secession ordinance, had merely repealed it. Nearly every one of these state governments dragged its feet over repudiating its war debts.

Republicans faced a certain prospect that the leaders from the reconstructed governments would join forces with the northern Democratic Party. Ironically, the abolition of slavery had increased the South's representation in the House of Representatives. Previously only three-fifths of the South's slaves had counted in apportioning Congressmen. Now, all blacks counted fully, even if none of them could vote. With the South's additional fifteen representatives, the Democrats might undo many of the Republicans' hard-won, wartime, political victories.

Even worse, the new governments threatened the very freedom of the former slaves. Presidential pardons had enabled plantation owners to recover nearly all their confiscated and abandoned land and to oust any freedmen who had been settled on it. It goes without saying that nowhere could the freed slaves vote. Indeed, new Black Codes established a racial subjugation at least as rigid as the apartheid system developed in South Africa decades later. Varying from state to state, the codes generally denied blacks the right to marry whites, bear arms, or assemble after sunset. Blacks who were idle or unemployed were subject to imprisonment or forced labor for up to one year. The Mississippi code prohibited blacks from renting either land or homes outside cities. That of South Carolina forbade them from practicing any profession other than servant or agricultural laborer. In Louisiana, unemployed black agricultural workers were given ten days to make new labor contracts, after which they were legally forbidden to leave their place of employment. An editorial in the *Chicago Tribune* voiced the indignation of many Northerners. "We tell the white men of Mississippi that the men of the North will convert the State of Mississippi into a frog-pond before they will allow any such laws to disgrace one foot of soil in which the bones of our soldiers sleep and over which the flag of freedom waves."[12]

Congress remained adamant in its refusal to seat representatives from any of the reconstructed governments. Senator Sumner advanced a "state suicide" theory of secession, under which the rebellious states could be governed as territories, whereas Stevens was for ruling them outright as "conquered provinces." Most Republicans, however, grounded their treatment of the defeated South on the clause in the Constitution guaranteeing "every State in this Union a Republican form of Government." The reconstructed governments were therefore in the anomalous position of being recognized by the President but not by Congress, of being legitimate for the purpose of ratifying the Thirteenth Amendment but not for the purpose of having representation within the national government.

The Reconstruction deadlock soon solidified into three distinct blocs. At one extreme, supporting President Johnson, were the northern Democratic Party, the leaders of the reconstructed southern governments, and a few conservative Republicans, including Secretary of State William Seward, who had long ago abandoned his Radicalism. They stood for strict constitutional limitations upon national power and for white supremacy in the South. "Known facts [and] all reasoning upon evidence" proved that Negroes have "less capacity for government than any other race of people," declared the President in his third annual message to Congress. "Wherever they have been left to their own devices they have shown a constant tendency to relapse into barbarism." Furthermore, "the great difference between the two races in physical, mental, and moral characteristics will prevent an amalgamation or fusion of them together in one homogeneous mass." As a result, argued Johnson, one or the other race must dominate, and "if the inferior obtains the ascendancy," it will "create such a tyranny as this continent has never yet witnessed. . . . Of all the dangers which our nation has yet encountered, none are equal to those which must result from the success of the effort now making to Africanize the half of our country."[13]

At the other extreme were the Radical Republicans. War-engendered vindictiveness and full political equality for blacks were their twin motives, negative and positive. Thaddeus Stevens vigorously attacked the notion of white supremacy: "This is not a 'white man's government.' . . . To say so is political blasphemy, for it violates the fundamental principles of our gospel of liberty. This is man's Government; the Government of all men alike."[14] On another occasion he insisted that "every man, no matter what his race or color . . . has an equal right to justice, honesty, and fair play with every other man; and the law should secure him those rights. The same law which condemns or acquits an African should condemn or acquit a white man. The same law which gives a verdict in a white man's favor should give a verdict in a black man's favor on the same state of facts. Such is the law of God and such ought to be the law of man." Yet Stevens hastily added that he did not insist upon legally enforced social equality. "This doctrine does not mean that a negro shall sit on the same seat or eat at the same table with a white man. That is a matter of taste which every man must decide for himself. The law has nothing to do with it."[15]

The largest political faction in Congress, however, was neither the Radicals nor the conservatives but moderate Republicans. The moderates shared the Radicals' outrage at the Black Codes and a desire to extend the Republican Party into the South. But they shied away from fully equal rights for blacks. Racial prejudice was still quite prevalent throughout the North. Although the legal status of northern blacks had been steadily improving and Massachusetts in 1865 enacted the country's first ban on racial discrimination in public accommodations, five other loyal states rejected proposals for black suffrage soon after the fighting ceased.

The Radical and moderate Republicans in Congress hence agreed upon opposition to the Johnson-recognized governments, despite disagreeing about the alternative. Together they were strong enough to override Johnson's vetoes of two measures designed to provide the freed slaves with some legal protection from the Black Codes. The Civil Rights Act of 1866 defined blacks as United States citizens and guaranteed their rights to own or rent property, to make and enforce contracts, to have access to the courts as parties and witnesses, and generally to enjoy the "full and equal benefit of all laws and proceedings for the security of person and property, as is enjoyed by white citizens."[16] Depriving someone of these civil rights was made a federal crime, enforceable by the national courts and military. A new Freedmen's Bureau Act passed in conjunction extended the life of that agency and gave it the added power of setting up army tribunals to try civil rights cases.

Johnson had objected to these measures because their expansion of the military's jurisdiction violated the right to trial by jury and the traditional prerogatives of the states. So the Republican lawmakers simultaneously framed a constitutional amendment to govern the terms of Reconstruction. Although they believed that the Civil Rights Act was already fully justified by an enforcement clause within the Thirteenth Amendment, they were worried that the federal courts might strike down the act anyway. The first section of the proposed fourteenth amendment was designed to constitutionally enshrine the rights of the freedmen. It provided that "all persons born or naturalized in the United States, and subject to the jurisdiction thereof, are citizens of the United States and of the State wherein they reside." This directly undid the prior Dred Scott ruling that blacks could never be citizens.

The proposed amendment's first section also prohibited any state action "which shall abridge the privileges or immunities of citizens of the United States" or "deprive any person of life, liberty, or property without due process of law" or "deny to any person within its jurisdiction the equal protection of the laws." No other constitutional innovation has proved more momentous. It extended from the national to the state governments nearly all the restrictions on government power contained in the Bill of Rights. Thus at a single stroke it subjected much state legislation to federal review.

One Radical Republican goal that this amendment failed to implement, however, was black suffrage. Instead, the second section merely reduced the representation of the southern states to the extent that blacks could not vote. A similar compromise found its way into the fourteenth amendment's third section. The Radicals wanted to keep all Southerners who had voluntarily supported the Confederacy from voting, whereas the moderates favored a speedy restoration of political rights. The amendment consequently excluded high-ranking Confederates from office, but not from voting, and Congress could lift the disability. Other clauses precluded any repudiation of the Union's Civil War debt, any assumption of the Confederate debt, or any compensation to former slaveholders.

Yet simply because the proposed amendment could win two-thirds of a Republican Congress that barred southern representatives did not assure the amendment's ratification by three-fourths of the states. President Johnson urged the reconstructed governments in the South to reject it, and all of them did so except his home state of Tennessee. This effectively blocked the amendment's ratification. It also drove the moderate Republicans into the arms of the Radicals. The irascible and truculent President in his vetoes had persistently denied the legitimacy of a peacetime Congress that excluded the reconstructed states. But such a constitutional objection called into question every bit of postwar legislation that Republicans had enacted.

Although Johnson tried to rally support in the North, his clumsy coalition with the Democratic Party only served to heighten sensitivity about a Rebel and Copperhead resurgence. Republicans could still tap war-spawned hatreds, a strategy dubbed "waving the bloody shirt." Governor Oliver Morton of Indiana, for instance, denounced the Democratic Party as "a common sewer and loathsome receptacle, into which is emptied every element of treason North and South." "Every bounty jumper, every deserter, every sneak who ran away from the draft calls himself a Democrat," declared the governor. "Every man who labored for the rebellion in the field, who murdered Union prisoners by cruelty and starvation . . . calls himself a Democrat. . . . [E]very New York rioter in 1863 who burned up little children in colored asylums, who robbed, ravished, and murdered indiscriminately in the midst of a blazing city for three days and nights, called himself a Democrat."[17] Major race riots in Memphis and New Orleans, where white mobs aided by local police slaughtered scores of blacks, confirmed such fears.

The bellwether Congressional elections in November of 1866 were a defeat for the conservative coalition. Beginning in early 1867, nearly two years after hostilities had ceased, Congress instituted a new, still harsher Reconstruction policy. A series of four acts dissolved all the Johnson governments except that of Tennessee, which was rewarded for ratifying the proposed fourteenth amendment. The remainder of the old Confederacy was divided into five military districts. The vote was taken away from ex-Confederates and given to blacks, and new governments were established under military supervision. Only after the new governments ratified the amendment did Congress promise to restore them to their former status within the Union.

Impeachment of President Johnson

Congress could pass legislation over the President's veto. But the President still had to enforce it. And Johnson was by no means ready to abandon his resistance to the Radicals. As commander in chief of the army, he technically controlled the very instrument to which they had entrusted Reconstruction. The army's officers, however, from General Ulysses S. Grant on down tended to side with Congress. Johnson's charitable policies had encouraged white Southerners to file law suits making heavy claims for the damages suffered under military rule during and after the war. Congress was the only body willing to give the army some immunity from such civil action.

It looked for a while as if these suits might not only succeed in southern state courts, but in the federal judiciary as well. The composition of the Supreme Court had changed greatly since Chief Justice Roger Taney had issued the infamous Dred Scott decision; Lincoln had appointed a total of five new justices. Among these were the Radical Republican Salmon P. Chase, who replaced Taney as Chief Justice upon the latter's death in 1864. Nonetheless, in the Milligan case of December 1866 the Court unanimously overturned the death sentence of a Confederate sympathizer from Indiana who had been tried for treason before a wartime military court. The majority then went on, with Chase now dissenting, to cut the constitutional ground out from under military rule in the South. "Martial law cannot arise from a threatened invasion," the Court ruled. "The necessity must be actual and present; the invasion real, such as effectually closes the courts and deposes the civil administration." Military rule "can never exist where the courts are open, and in the proper and unobstructed exercise of their jurisdiction" and it must be "confined to the locality of actual war."[18]

Milligan, the vindicated Confederate sympathizer, thereupon won civil damages—of nominal amount—from the general who had first arrested him. Similar cases were making their way through the lower courts. In the same term, a bare majority of the Supreme Court struck down Reconstruction loyalty oaths, one imposed by Missouri on the clergy and other professions and one imposed by Congress on attorneys in federal courts. Some Radicals went so far as to suggest abolishing the high tribunal altogether. Congress responded however by simply using its discretionary authority under Article III of the Constitution to strip the Court of its jurisdiction over *habeas corpus* cases. Afterwards the justices studiously avoided most constitutional issues raised by Reconstruction.

Congress also enacted administrative restrictions upon presidential power. The Tenure of Office Act forbade Johnson's removal of federal officeholders friendly to the Radicals, while the Command of the Army Act curtailed his authority over the military. Because these restrictions tended to shift control of the army from the executive to the legislature, they cemented the political alliance between the Radicals and the officer corps. The President outwardly complied with congressional policy. But he construed the Reconstruction acts as narrowly as possible, and he could still appoint conservative generals to command southern military districts.

Johnson finally decided to test the constitutionality of the Tenure of Office Act by trying to replace Edwin Stanton as Secretary of War. Although a former Democrat, Stanton was a Lincoln appointee who had been steadfast with the Radicals. There soon ensued a political farce where the Secretary of War barricaded himself in his office, refusing to step down. Congress did not hesitate to accept the President's challenge. As one moderate put it, "he has thrown down the gauntlet to the Congress, and says to us as plainly as words can speak it: 'Try this issue now betwixt me and you; either you go to the wall or I do.' And there is nothing left to Congress but to take it up. Can there be any difference of opinion as to this? Most assuredly I can see none."[19] The Republican majority in the House voted unanimously on February 24, 1868, to impeach Johnson for "high crimes and misdemeanors." Violating the Tenure of Office Act was the major charge. Congressman Stevens, himself near death, openly gloated: "Unfortunate man! thus surrounded, hampered, tangled in the meshes of his own wickedness—unfortunate, unhappy man, behold your doom."[20]

For the first and only time, a President of the United States went to trial before the United States Senate. Chief Justice Chase presided, and although a Radical, found himself increasingly in sympathy with the President's defense. Johnson's lawyers denied the constitutionality of the Tenure of Office Act, claimed the act did not apply at the cabinet level, and argued Stanton was unprotected anyway because Johnson had not appointed him. A few other Republicans felt the same way as Chase, for when it came time for the Senators to make their decision, the final tally fell short of the necessary two-thirds to convict by a single vote. Johnson therefore served out the brief remainder of the term. But his opposition to congressional Reconstruction became subdued.

Spurned by the party that had put him in office, the former Vice-President could not even secure nomination for another term from the Democratic Party. Instead, its convention, after twenty-two deadlocked ballots, settled on Horatio Seymour, a War Democrat who had been governor of New York. Yet rejecting the discredited incumbent did not win for the Democracy the 1868 presidential election. The Radical and moderate Republicans agreed upon General Grant as their candidate, and the popular war hero just barely gained victory at the polls.

By the time of Grant's election as President, seven southern states had complied with the terms of congressional Reconstruction and been readmitted to the Union. Their ratifications had formally made the Fourteenth Amendment part of the Constitution. But in Virginia, Mississippi, and Texas, even the combination of military occupation and black enfranchisement could not induce voters to approve state constitutions that followed congressional guidelines. And if these three southern states had not been excluded, or the others had not been under military domination, then Grant would undoubtedly have lost the very close election.

The Radicals meanwhile had enough momentum to go for one constitutional goal that had proved too extreme for the Fourteenth Amendment. Congress sent a proposed fifteenth amendment to the states. Its wording made voting rights for blacks permanent and nationwide, thereby shielding this loyal Republican constituency not just in the former Confederacy, but also in the former slave states of the border and in the free states. The Republican majority then proffered a deal to the three holdout southern states. It would allow ex-Confederate officials from these jurisdictions to cast ballots and hold office if the states would ratify the proposed amendment. Virginia, Mississippi, and Texas accepted the terms. As the Fifteenth

Amendment became official in March 1870, these last states regained their representation in Congress.

The alliance of expediency between moderate and Radical Republicans had outlived its usefulness. Five years later Congress would pass a second Civil Rights Act, framed by Senator Sumner before he died, that outlawed segregation in nearly all public accommodations, whether public or private, except schools. But the Supreme Court eventually overturned this government intrusion into voluntary interactions. The adoption of black suffrage remained the pinnacle of Radical Reconstruction. None of the other nations that had abolished slavery in the nineteenth century had granted their former slaves citizenship rights equal to those of whites. The American Anti-Slavery Society, founded thirty-seven years earlier, when abolition seemed impossible, now disbanded in triumph. Its final resolution honored the Fifteenth Amendment, securing blacks the right to vote in *both* northern and southern states, as "the cap-stone and completion of our movement;—the fulfillment of our pledge to the Negro race."[21] Whether in fact this sanguine estimate was justified, however, depended upon events within the South itself. For only at the state level could the principles of Radical Reconstruction receive concrete implementation.

Chapter 12
Bibliographical Essay

Just as the Civil War has had successive overarching interpretations, so has Reconstruction. Only in the case of Reconstruction, the historical disagreements have been more impassioned, perhaps because they are more blatantly linked to the politics and ideologies of their advocates. The traditional interpretation is summed up in the title of Claude G. Bowers's popular history, *The Tragic Era: The Revolution After Lincoln* (Cambridge, MA: Riverside Press, 1929). It portrays Reconstruction as a national disgrace, in which vindictive Radicals overturned Lincoln's and Johnson's farsighted and charitable reconciliation with the defeated South for sordid, self-serving ends. This was the rendition incorporated in the turn-of-the-century study of James Ford Rhodes, *History of the United States From the Compromise of 1850 to the Restoration of Home Rule in the South in 1877* (cited prologue), becoming the gospel of the nationalist school of Civil War historians. But it received its fullest scholarly adumbration in the works of William Archibald Dunning and his students. See particularly Dunning's *Reconstruction: Political and Economic, 1865–1877* (New York: Harper & Brothers, 1907), his *Essays on the Civil War and Reconstruction*, 2nd edn., (New York: Macmillan, 1904), and Walter Lynwood Fleming's *The Sequel of Appomattox* (New Haven: Yale University Press, 1921).

Less partisan but not inconsistent with the "Dunning School," as it has come to be known, is the interpretation found in Charles and Mary Beard's *The Rise of American Civilization* (cited prologue), where they ascribe economic motives to the Radical Republicans. Howard K. Beale, *The Critical Year: A Study of Andrew Johnson and Reconstruction* (New York: Harcourt, Brace, 1930), fleshes out this reading of Radical Republicans as agents of Yankee industrialism and finance. Civil War historians of the revisionist and the neo-Confederate camps, as might be expected, also found little to quibble about in the traditional story of Reconstruction. Thus, one still hears echoes of this older view in the classic textbook of revisionist James G. Randall, as tempered by David Donald, *The Civil War and Reconstruction* (cited prologue), while perhaps its strongest modern statement is made by neo-Confederate Ludwell H. Johnson, in *Division and Reunion* (likewise cited in the prologue).

The racial sensibilities of the post-World War II era, however, brought forth a rejection of the traditional interpretation. The Radicals now became idealistic proponents of black civil rights battling a racist President and his white supremacist allies. Unfortunately, at this point the terminology can be a bit confusing to the uninitiated. Although this new interpretation of Reconstruction is called "revisionist," it is not the same revisionism that relates to the war's outbreak, discussed in my prologue's bibliographical essay. Rather, it was historians of the neo-abolitionist school, predictably, who brought forth the newer view of Reconstruction. To maintain consistency, I will therefore always refer to this particular revision as the "neo-abolitionist" interpretation.

An outstanding introduction to this interpretation is Kenneth M. Stampp, *The Era of Reconstruction, 1865–1877* (New York: Alfred A. Knopf, 1965). Other fine overviews include John Hope Franklin, *Reconstruction: After the Civil War* (Chicago: University of Chicago Press, 1961); Rembert W. Patrick, *The Reconstruction of the Nation* (New York: Oxford University Press, 1967); Avery O. Craven, *Reconstruction: The Ending of the Civil War* (New York: Holt, Rinehart and Winston, 1969); and Forrest G. Wood, *The Era of Reconstruction, 1863–1877* (New York: Thomas Y. Crowell, 1975). A broader survey that incorporates the latest findings of social historians is in the later chapters of William L. Barney, *Battleground for Union: The Era of the Civil War and Reconstruction, 1848–1877* (Englewood Cliffs, NJ: Prentice-Hall, 1990). Kenneth M. Stampp and Leon F. Litwack, eds., *Reconstruction: An Anthology of Revisionist Writings* (Baton Rouge: Louisiana State University Press, 1969), is a classic compilation of neo-abolitionist journal articles.

The neo-abolitionist interpretation was not without its precursors. John W. Burgess, *Reconstruction and the Constitution, 1866–1876* (New York: Charles Scribner's Sons, 1902), is an old but fairly even-handed pro-Republican account. The Marxist, W. E. Burghardt DuBois, produced a work noted more for its historical data than for its interpretive dependability: *Black Reconstruction: An Essay Toward a History of the Part Which Black Folk Played in the Attempt to Reconstruct Democracy in America, 1860–1880* (New York: Harcourt, Brace, 1935). James S. Allen renders a more concise Marxist variation in *Reconstruction: The Battle for Democracy, 1865–1876* (New York: International, 1937).

Nor do neo-abolitionists exhibit unanimity with respect to so-called "Radical" Reconstruction. They disagree about how radical it *really was* and how radical it *was intended to be*. Both these questions are further muddied by the interjection of strong moralistic convictions about how radical Reconstruction *should have been*. As modern advocates of government assistance and affirmative action, many neo-abolitionist historians are uneasy with the confidence that Radical Republicans and abolitionists displayed in free labor and market competition. A useful guide to these disagreements is Eric Foner's review essay, "Reconstruction Revisited," *Reviews in American History*, 10 (December 1982), pp. 82–100. Eric Anderson and Alfred A. Moss, Jr., eds., *The Facts of Reconstruction: Essays in Honor of John Hope Franklin* (Baton Rouge: Louisiana State University Press, 199), provides more recent historiographical articles.

The works from chapter 8 on Lincoln versus the Radicals or on the treatment of freed slaves are, of course, all relevant to wartime Reconstruction. In addition, Herman Belz has written three books that examine this process under Lincoln from slightly varied angles: *A New Birth of Freedom: The Republican Party and Freedmen's Rights, 1861 to 1866* (Westport, CT: Greenwood Press, 1976); *Reconstructing the Union: Theory and*

Policy During the Civil War (Ithaca, NY: Cornell University Press, 1969); and *Emancipation and Equal Rights: Politics and Constitutionalism in the Civil War Era* (New York: W. W. Norton, 1967). Peyton McCrary, *Abraham Lincoln and Reconstruction: The Louisiana Experiment* (Princeton, NJ: Princeton University Press, 1978), looks at the most important of the states that was reconstructed under Lincoln's plan, whereas Charles Lewis Wagandt, *The Mighty Revolution: Negro Emancipation in Maryland, 1862–1864* (Baltimore: Johns Hopkins Press, 1964), scrutinizes slavery's political abolition in one of the most important border states.

Jim Bishop, *The Day Lincoln Was Shot* (New York: Harper & Brothers, 1955), probably remains the best straight-out narrative of Lincoln's assassination. There are many ridiculous conspiracy theories, but one of the more popular, which implicates Secretary of War Edwin Stanton, is Otto Eisenschiml's *Why Was Lincoln Murdered?* (New York: Little, Brown, 1937). A thorough debunking of these theories is William Hanchett, *The Lincoln Murder Conspiracies . . .* (Urbana: University of Illinois Press, 1983); while Thomas Reed Turner, *Beware the People Weeping: Public Opinion and the Assassination of Abraham Lincoln* (Baton Rouge: Louisiana State University Press, 1982), puts the assassination trials within the context of the North's war hysteria. One new serious work, William A. Tidwell, James O. Hall, and David Winfred Gaddy, *Come Retribution: The Confederate Secret Service and the Assassination of Lincoln* (Jackson: University Press of Mississippi, 1988), does find evidence of Confederate complicity. See also Tidwell's supplemental volume, *April '65: Confederate Covert Action and the American Civil War* (Kent, OH: Kent State University Press, 1995).

Harold M. Hyman's *Era of the Oath* (cited ch. 10) examines the details of Reconstruction loyalty oaths, and Jonathan Truman Dorres covers *Pardon and Amnesty Under Lincoln and Johnson: The Restoration of the Confederates to Their Rights and Privileges, 1861–1898* (Chapel Hill: University of North Carolina Press, 1953). There is no thorough treatment of the national government's postwar finance as it relates to the South, but some details about the punitive taxes are available in both Herbert Ronald Ferleger, *David A. Wells and the American Revenue System, 1865–1870* (New York: Edwards Brothers, 1942), which focuses more heavily on the tariff, and George Ruble Woolfolk, *The Cotton Regency: The Northern Merchants and Reconstruction, 1865–1880* (New York: Bookman Associates, 1958), a Beardian exploration of the economic interests behind Republican policy.

Don T. Carter, *When the War Was Over: The Failure of Self-Reconstruction in the South, 1865–1867* (Baton Rouge: Louisiana State University Press, 1985), is a treatment of the Whig-dominated Reconstruction governments created under Johnson that is not entirely unsympathetic, whereas Michael Perman, *Reunion Without Compromise: The South and Reconstruction, 1865–1868* (Cambridge, U.K.: Cambridge University Press, 1973), examines their efforts to manipulate their alliance with the President. Theodore Brantner Wilson, *The Black Codes of the South* (University: University of Alabama Press, 1965), details how these regimes treated the freed slaves. A look at northern public reaction to these regimes is Patrick W. Riddleberger, *1866: The Critical Year Revisited* (Carbondale: Southern Illinois University Press, 1979).

Neo-abolitionist accounts of Johnson versus Congress include Eric L. McKitrick, *Andrew Johnson and Reconstruction* (Chicago: University of Chicago Press, 1961); LaWanda Cox and John H. Cox, *Politics, Principle, and Prejudice, 1865–1866: Dilemma of Reconstruction in America* (New York: Free Press of Glencoe, 1963); and William R. Brock, *An American Crisis: Congress and Reconstruction, 1865–1867* (London: Macmillan, 1963). Michael Les Benedict, *A Compromise of Principle: Congressional Republicans and Reconstruction, 1863–1869* (New York: W. W. Norton, 1974), is a lengthy account of Congress's role in Reconstruction, while David Donald, *The Politics of Reconstruction, 1863–1867* Baton Rouge: Louisiana State University Press, 1965), is a brief examination of congressional politics. For a quantitative analysis that dismisses the economic theses of Beard and Beale, see Glenn M. Linden, *Politics or Principle: Congressional Voting on Civil War Amendments and Pro-Negro Measures, 1838–69* (Seattle: University of Washington Press, 1976). A panoramic view of Republican efforts to extend their party into the South is in Richard H. Abbott, *The Republican Party and the South, 1855–1877: First Southern Strategy* (Chapel Hill: University of North Carolina Press, 1986), which concludes that this goal was rather haphazardly and ineptly pursued.

Eric Foner presents the best analysis of Stevens's proposal to provide the freedmen with land in his article, "Thaddeus Stevens, Confiscation, and Reconstruction," reprinted in *Politics and Ideology in the Age of the Civil War* (cited prologue). For the biography of a Radical Congressman who was even more single-mindedly devoted to this goal, who was far more ideologically consistent in his support for liberty, especially on economic issues, and who shared none of Stevens's unsavory personality traits, see Patrick W. Riddleberger, *George Washington Julian, Radical Republican: A Study in Nineteenth Century Politics and Reform* (n.p.: Indiana Historical Bureau, 1966). James M. McPherson, *The Struggle for Equality* (cited ch. 8), traces this proposal's abolitionist origins, whereas Willie Lee Rose, *Rehearsal for Reconstruction* (cited ch. 8), recounts its most extensive implementation, as a result of General Sherman's policies in the South Carolina sea islands. Some free-market advocates mistakenly defend the property claims of slaveholding plantation owners, perceiving land restitution for the freedmen to be some kind of socialistic redistribution. An exception is the economist Murray N. Rothbard, who recognizes the demand for "40-acres and a mule" as a just application of *laissez faire* principles, similar to homesteading. See his articles on that subject mentioned in the fourth chapter.

Claude F. Oubre, *Forty Acres and a Mule: The Freedmen's Bureau and Black Land Ownership* (Baton Rouge: Louisiana State University Press, 1978), recounts the halting and half-hearted efforts toward this goal under the auspices of the Freedmen's Bureau. Two histories of this first federal relief agency that make slightly different appraisals are George R. Bentley,

A History of the Freedmen's Bureau (Philadelphia: University of Pennsylvania Press, 1955), and William S. McFeely, *Yankee Stepfather: General O. O. Howard and the Freedmen* (New Haven: Yale University Press, 1968). Carl R. Osthaus recounts the sad saga of an ostensibly private financial institution that the Bureau sponsored in *Freedmen, Philanthropy, and Fraud: A History of the Freedman's Savings Bank* (Urbana: University of Illinois Press, 1976). Donald G. Nieman, *To Set the Law in Motion: The Freedman's Bureau and the Legal Rights of Blacks, 1865–1868* (Milwood, NY: KTO Press, 1979), specifically treats the Bureau's legal activities.

James E. Sefton, *The United States Army and Reconstruction, 1865–1877* (Baton Rouge: Louisiana State University Press, 1967), investigates the military's crucial part in Reconstruction, whereas General Grant's particular role is traced in Martin E. Mantell, *Johnson, Grant, and the Politics of Reconstruction* (New York: Columbia University Press, 1973), and Brooks D. Simpson, *Let Us Have Peace* (cited the previous chapter). Frank W. Klingberg, *The Southern Claims Commission* (Berkeley: University of California Press, 1955), covers the claims of loyalist Southerners for supplying the Union army during the war.

Most of the older biographies of Andrew Johnson adhere to the Dunning School. An example is George Fort Milton, *The Age of Hate: Andrew Johnson and the Radicals* (New York: Coward-McCann, 1930). Hans L. Trefousse, *Andrew Johnson: A Biography* (New York: W. W. Norton, 1989), gives the neo-abolitionist case. Albert Castel offers a balanced history of *The Presidency of Andrew Johnson* (Lawrence: Regents Press of Kansas, 1979). The topic of Johnson's impeachment and trial is a perennial favorite, but two modern, scholarly treatments are Hans L. Trefousse, *Impeachment of a President: Andrew Johnson, the Blacks, and Reconstruction* (Knoxville: University of Tennessee Press, 1975), and Michael Les Benedict, *The Impeachment and Trial of Andrew Johnson* (New York: W. W. Norton, 1973).

Charles H. Coleman provides still the most exhaustive account of *The Election of 1868: The Democratic Effort to Regain Control* (New York: Columbia University Press, 1933). Edward L. Gambill, *Conservative Ordeal: Northern Democrats and Reconstruction, 1865–1868* (Ames: Iowa State University Press, 1981), and Lawrence Grossman, *The Democratic Party and the Negro: Northern and National Politics, 1868–1892* (Urbana: University of Illinois Press, 1976), are all we really have on the opposition party during this era. On the Supreme Court, Stanley I. Kutler, *Judicial Power and Reconstruction Politics* (Chicago: University of Chicago Press, 1968), challenges the prevailing impression of judicial passivity by emphasizing the number of national laws declared unconstitutional. Charles Fairman's massive, two-volume *Reconstruction and Reunion, 1864–88* (New York: Macmillan, 1971–87), from the *History of the Supreme Court of the United States* series, fills in more details.

Jacobus ten Broek, *Equal Under Law* (New York: Collier Books, 1965)— a revised version of *The Antislavery Origins of the Fourteenth Amendment* (Berkeley: University of California Press, 1951)—does a good job at showing how Reconstruction's constitutional amendments embodied many of the abolitionists' prewar ideals. Joseph B. James covers both *The Framing of the Fourteenth Amendment* (Urbana: University of Illinois Press, 1956) and *The Ratification of the Fourteenth Amendment* ([Macon, GA]: Mercer University Press, 1984). Because its far-reaching clauses were compromises between Radical and moderate Republicans, the Fourteenth Amendment has spawned an interminable debate among legal scholars about original intent. Three installments that are worthwhile for historical content are Michael Kent Curtis, *No State Shall Abridge: The Fourteenth Amendment and the Bill of Rights* (Durham, NC: Duke University Press, 1986); William E. Nelson, *The Fourteenth Amendment: From Political Principle to Judicial Doctrine* (Cambridge, MA: Harvard University Press, 1988); and Earl M. Maltz, *Civil Rights, the Constitution, and Congress, 1863–1869* (Lawrence: University Press of Kansas, 1990). Paul Finkelman, "Rehearsal for Reconstruction: Antebellum Origins of the Fourteenth Amendment," from Anderson and Moss, eds., *The Facts of Reconstruction,* is especially important on what the amendment owed to the improving legal status of northern blacks.

The last Reconstruction amendment is the subject of William Gillette, *The Right to Vote: Politics and the Passage of the Fifteenth Amendment* (Baltimore: Johns Hopkins Press, 1965). Still controversial is Gillette's contention that a major motivation behind this amendment was a desire to enfranchise *Northern* blacks. Robert J. Kaczorowksi, *The Politics of Judicial Interpretation: The Federal Courts, Department of Justice, and Civil Rights, 1866–1876* (New York: Oceana, 1985), recounts the courts' early interpretations of Reconstruction amendments and legislation.

13

American Society Transformed

Reconstruction in the South

Southern tradition excoriates the state governments that came to power during congressional Reconstruction. While the Union military supervised elections and imposed loyalty oaths, disfranchising 10 to 15 percent of white voters, the local Republican Party supposedly united illiterate blacks, southern "scalawags," and northern "Carpetbaggers" into an unscrupulous political triumvirate that indulged in an orgy of extravagance, corruption, and debauchery. Carrying all their worldly possessions in carpetbags, Northerners descended upon the prostrate South looking for easy pickings—or so the tradition goes. These Carpetbaggers proceeded to mobilize Negro voters through nocturnal meetings of the clandestine Union League, with local scalawags, a Scottish term applied to scrawny and unfit cattle, as opportunistic white allies. Recent historians have concluded, however, that this account has more color than accuracy.

There were some spectacular cases of graft within the Radical regimes. The South Carolina legislature at one point appropriated $1,000 to cover the gambling losses of the speaker of the house on a horse race. But the South certainly had no monopoly on these vices.

The long war had contributed to a breakdown everywhere both in prevailing ethical norms and in the distinction between public and private spheres. "The demoralising effect of this civil war," wrote Edward Bates, Lincoln's first Attorney General, "is plainly visible in every department of life. The abuse of official powers and the thirst for dishonest gain are now so common that they cease to shock."[1] The same Congress that passed the Fourteenth Amendment also, without a second thought, voted itself a hefty pay raise, and the flagrancy of a subsequent salary grab in 1873 shamed Congress into repealing it. The Grant era became so notorious for its political bribery that it has gone down in history as the Great Barbecue. In the words of a Carpetbag governor of Louisiana: *"I don't pretend to be honest. I only pretend to be as honest as anybody in politics. . . .* Why, damn it, everybody is demoralizing down here. Corruption is the fashion."[2]

Blacks did fill many elected posts throughout the former Confederacy. In addition to two U.S. Senators, the first of their race, they could boast control of one house in the South Carolina legislature. But nowhere did they hold offices in proportion to their numbers, despite constituting the majority of the electorate in three states. Similarly, the so-called scalawags and Carpetbaggers were often distinguished and well-meaning idealists who wanted to modernize the South or help the freedmen, and the Reconstruction regimes could claim credit for a good number of constructive achievements. Their new state constitutions eliminated archaic and undemocratic features. In South Carolina, the Republicans abolished property qualifications for voting, transferred the choice of presidential electors from the legislature to the voters, and provided for the state's first divorce law. Several states revised their penal codes to make them less barbaric or reapportioned the legislatures to give the backcountry fair representation.

Indeed, Radical rule deserves greater censure for some of its vaunted accomplishments. The heaviest state expenditures went not for graft but for internal improvements, public education, and other social services. Postwar state governments, in the South as elsewhere in the Union, promoted private railroads with reckless abandon. These pro-business subsidies always diverted resources away from more urgent needs, but the costs fell particularly heavily upon Southerners. Poor farmers, already destitute from wartime losses and the Union's heavy exactions, found themselves levied upon further by their own states to provide economic tribute to privileged interests. Railroad appropriations, furthermore, were the occasion for most political fraud below the Mason-Dixon line.

The southern states also imported the Yankee system of tax-supported, compulsory schools. This innovation had not even become standard throughout the northern states until the last decade before the Civil War. American public education had its origins in colonial New England, where Puritans set up town schools for Biblical indoctrination. In the late 1830s, a more secular, universal, and uniform system of tax-funded education appeared in Massachusetts, replacing the recently disestablished state church as the prime instrument for molding social conformity. The famed lexicographer and textbook author, Noah Webster, for instance, praised common schools as a "singular machinery" for "correcting the vices and disorders of society" by teaching children subordination to "the laws of the state, to town and parochial institutions."[3] Northern Whigs had heartily promoted state-supported schools in order to instill proper respect for authority among Catholic immigrants and other ethnic outsiders. But they faced stiff resistance from the Democratic Party, and only through war could the Benevolent Empire's reformers impose compulsory school attendance across the North and extend their cultural hegemony over the remainder of the country.

Literacy among white Southerners had exceeded 80 percent before Fort Sumter, slightly below that of Northerners and better than in Britain or any other European country outside of Sweden and Denmark. Admittedly this omits the slaves, whom it was illegal to educate. Blacks hungered for learning after emancipation, and during Reconstruction many Northerners volunteered their services or donated money to provide education, usually through the auspices of the Freedmen's Bureau. To ensure that government schools were permanently fastened upon the South, Congress created a federal Department of Education in 1867, downgraded the next year to a bureau within the Interior Department. National aid to education eventually became a platform plank of the Republican Party, although the proposal never could make it through the Senate. By 1872 every southern state had established a school system, and generally these were more centrally administered and centrally funded than in the North, where local districts played a larger role. Moreover, the public schools created during congressional Reconstruction were all racially segregated, except briefly in New Orleans. Once captured by the forces of white rule, they could be turned into engines of racial exploitation in which the taxes of poor blacks helped pay for white education. Fifteen years after the war ended, the literacy rate among southern whites had shown no noticeable gain, whereas 70 percent of southern blacks still could not read.

Other new expenditures at the state level included orphanages, insane asylums, and homes for the poor. Alabama charged its new commissioner of industries with the task of encouraging commercial activity. Some states set up bureaus of immigration to foster settlement. South Carolina's first land commissioner financially aided those purchasing real estate. All these functions were costly, with the result that the war-ravaged South suffered under some of the heaviest state and local taxation in proportion to wealth in U.S. history. Tax rates in 1870 were three or four times what they had been in 1860, even though property values had declined significantly. Many who had not lost their land already were now forced into bankruptcy. At one point 15 percent of all taxable land in Mississippi was up for sale because of tax defaults.[4] Coming on the heels of war-engendered confiscations, Radical Reconstruction foisted upon the biracial South the worst of two worlds: significant turbulence in white land titles with hardly any compensating distribution to the freedmen.

White Southerners Violently Resist

None of these excesses upset white Southerners so much as the spectacle of former slaves going to the polls. "The people of our State will never quietly submit to negro rule," declared one protest to Congress from South Carolina. "We do not mean to threaten resistance by arms, but . . . by every peaceful means left us, we will keep up this contest until we have regained the political control handed down to us by an honored ancestry. This is a duty we owe to the land that is ours, to the graves that it contains, and to the race of which you and we are alike members—the proud Caucasian race, whose sovereignty on earth God has ordained."[5]

It was not long before resistance to what was denounced as Black Reconstruction turned violent. A secret society called the Ku Klux Klan spread over the South to become one of the world's first paramilitary organizations. Its Grand Wizard was Nathan Bedford Forrest, the Confederate general who had been most successful at unconventional warfare. White-hooded Klansmen mastered the art of political intimidation, terrorizing and murdering Republican voters and leaders. No one knows the total number of dead and injured attributable to the Klan. Albion W. Tourgée, a Yankee who went to North Carolina after the war and became a Republican judge, counted twelve murders, nine rapes, fourteen cases of arson, and over seven hundred beatings in his judicial district alone. He later fictionalized his experiences in a novel entitled *A Fool's Errand: By One of the Fools:* "Of the slain there were enough to furnish forth a battlefield, and all from those three classes, the negro, the scalawag, and the carpet-bagger,—all killed with deliberation, overwhelmed by numbers, roused from slumber at the murk midnight, in the hall of public assembly, upon the river-brink, on the lonely woods-road, in simulation of the public execution,— shot, stabbed, hanged, drowned, mutilated beyond description, tortured beyond conception."[6]

The Klan was already active in the 1868 presidential election. Congress established a federal Justice Department during the Grant Administration and passed three successive force acts, each giving Union military commanders greater power to suppress violence. In some states these measures were temporarily successful, because Klansmen never confronted the army directly. Officially the organization disbanded in 1869, but others quickly took its place. Having been unwilling to practice guerrilla warfare to maintain their independence, Southerners were now employing it with great effect to bring back home rule and white supremacy. In some respects, this violent campaign for local autonomy represented a postwar continuation of Southern resistance to Confederate centralization. As one North Carolinian explained to William Holden, the state's antiwar leader who had risen to be governor during Reconstruction, "I know a great many men who laid out during the war, who were whipped, kicked, and handcuffed by the rebels during the war, who are now among the Ku-Klux, and voted for the men who abused them so badly."[7]

Although white Southerners had speedily given in to emancipation at the war's termination, racial equality was another matter. Kenneth M. Stampp, a prolific and distinguished historian of American slavery, has suggested why. The defeated Rebels had "every reason to assume" that "free Negroes would be an inferior caste" because this, by and large, was the practice "of most of the northern states. . . . White Southerners were understandably shocked, therefore, when Radical Republicans, during the Reconstruction years, tried to impose a different relationship between the races in the South. . . . Now for the first time white Southerners organized a powerful partisan movement and resisted Republican race policy more fiercely than the civilian population had ever resisted the invading Union armies during the war."[8]

The Colfax courthouse in upstate Louisiana became the scene of the bloodiest incident when a white posse attacked a contingent of armed blacks in mid-April of 1873. Suffering only two deaths themselves, the attackers killed between seventy and one hundred of the defenders and mutilated their bodies. Many had been executed after their surrender. The Justice Department indicted ninety-eight whites under the force acts but were able to convict only three. Then several years later, the Supreme Court, in *U.S.* v. *Cruikshank et al.*, threw out the convictions on the grounds that the Reconstruction amendments permitted Congress to protect individual rights from the actions of state governments but not from the actions of private individuals. "That duty was originally assumed by the States; and it still remains there. The only obligation resting upon the United States is to see that the States do not deny the right."[9]

Southern blacks, on the other hand, did not possess the martial or material resilience to fight back effectively, without some on-going Union presence. Liberated into a regime of military paternalism, they had not been required to build the kind of community structures and solidarity necessary to sustain a protracted armed struggle on their own, even though some Reconstruction governments organized Negro militias. And denied compensation for past enslavement by a national government that actively protected the land titles of their former masters, the freedmen were left without economic independence. "Was it well then to shed our blood," despaired abolitionist Moncure Conway, "in order that the negro might be freely lynched?"[10]

Northerners ultimately grew weary of the expense and frustration of maintaining what some self-styled Liberal Republicans were now openly admitting was "bayonet rule." With increased strength in the midwest, the Republican Party no longer considered the South essential for maintaining political ascendancy. The Amnesty Act of 1872 restored the political rights of all but a few former Confederates, and the Freedmen's Bureau was allowed to pass out of existence. Soon other issues diverted northern attention. Economic panic engulfed the country in 1873, just as the scandals of the Grant Administration reached epic proportions. A leading Republican newspaper observed that the North was ready to wash its hands of Reconstruction and the Negro. "People are becoming tired of . . . abstract questions, in which the overwhelming majority of them have no direct interest. The negro question, with all its complications, and the Reconstruction of the Southern States, with all its interminable embroilments, have lost much of the power they once wielded."[11]

The national government consequently turned its back as white Southerners engaged in a process euphemistically labeled Redemption. The continuing physical intimidation, coupled with social ostracism and economic pressures, kept blacks away from the polls, forced scalawags out of Republican ranks, and drove Carpetbaggers back to the North. Many of the poor whites and former Unionists who initially had been receptive to the Republican coalition had become disenchanted with the extravagance of the Reconstruction governments, which had racked up $130 million worth of additional indebtedness. The Redeemers overturned Radical rule in state after state and instituted a regimen of retrenchment, economy, and partial debt repudiation. By the end of Grant's second term, only

South Carolina, Florida, and Louisiana were left in Republican hands.

The End of Reconstruction

Redemption contributed to a nationwide resurgence of the Democratic Party. Political miscalculation was all that had prevented Grant's ouster from the presidency in 1872. Charles Sumner had become one of the first Republicans to break with the Administration—over its unsavory and unsuccessful effort to annex Santo Domingo for black colonization. Under the leadership of Carl Schurz of Missouri, Charles Frances Adams of Massachusetts, and other former Radicals, the Liberal Republicans soon bolted a party they considered hopelessly debased and organized a separate convention. Although they favored lower tariffs and civil-service reform in addition to reconciliation with the South, the only candidate who could secure their nomination was the erratic Horace Greeley, an ardent protectionist. The Democrats, who had already formally accepted the Fourteenth and Fifteenth Amendments under the urging of their former peace leader, Clement L. Vallandigham, reluctantly endorsed the Liberal Republican candidate, but many potential anti-Grant voters from the ranks of both parties just stayed home.

Despite Grant's sweeping reelection, the Republican split was a portent. Reforging the alliance between the South and urban immigrants in the North, the Democrats two years later elected a majority to the House of Representatives for the first time since the war. Their prospects looked promising as they nominated Samuel J. Tilden, the reform governor of New York, for President in 1876. Tilden had earlier achieved fame by bringing down the infamous Tweed Ring, which had plundered the New York City treasury of upwards of $200 million, more than the total public theft in all Reconstructed states combined. The Republican candidate, Rutherford B. Hayes of Ohio, notwithstanding having been a Civil War general, was burdened with the economic depression and his party's scandals.

The election's outcome, however, became intertwined with the fate of Reconstruction. Tilden unquestionably won a majority of the popular votes. But the electoral votes in the three unredeemed southern states, along with one electoral vote from Oregon, were disputed. The Republicans and the Democrats submitted competing sets of returns to Congress. With each house of Congress controlled by a different party, the nation faced a full-fledged electoral crisis. Democrats darkly hinted at armed resistance to what they feared would become a Republican military coup. They needed only one of the disputed electors to put Tilden in the White House. But intricate back-room maneuvering that lasted until two days before the inauguration confirmed for the Republicans all disputed votes. In return for the presidency, "Rutherfraud" B. Hayes, as disgruntled contemporaries now nicknamed him, agreed to remove federal troops from the South and to support bountiful government subsidies for southern railroads.

Thus, the country's centennial ushered in an end to Reconstruction with a peaceful sectional compromise reminiscent of those that had preceded the Civil War. Yet the Compromise of 1877 was simultaneously a raw political deal symptomatic of the new era's corruption. As the last federal troops withdrew from southern statehouses, the last three Republican governments fell to the Redeemers. Four years of conventional warfare during the Civil War had lost white Southerners their political independence, but an average of six years of low-level unconventional warfare during Reconstruction, off and on depending on the state, had regained them their political autonomy. Northern Republicans gave up any further efforts to protect the freedmen.

"What is the President's Southern policy? . . . It consists," complained a former Republican governor of South Carolina, "in the abandonment of Southern Republicans, and especially the colored race, to the control and rule not only of the Democratic party, but of that class at the South which regarded slavery as a Divine institution, which waged four years of destructive war for its perpetuation, which steadily opposed citizenship and suffrage for the negro—in a word, a class whose traditions, principles, and history are opposed to every step and feature of what Republicans call our national progress since 1860."[12] Just as the Republican Party had put the Union ahead of antislavery before the war, so now predictably the party put national reconciliation ahead of equal liberty.

Southern Impoverishment—
Black and White

Political emasculation was not the only problem for ex-slaves. Their economic fortunes were bound within a region that remained the country's poorest. The South's total commodity output did not return to its 1860 level until nearly two decades later, and since population had also risen, output per person in 1880 was still 20 percent below prewar levels. Although Southerners lost between $1 billion and $1.5 billion from property destroyed during the Civil War, a catastrophic sum, economic historians have long realized that this devastation alone cannot explain the persistence of the income gap between North and South. Both Germany and Japan recovered rapidly from much worse destruction after World War II. Such physical damage is usually repaired within less than five years.

To explain the collapse in southern output we must look elsewhere, to social and institutional changes. The most obvious, of course, was the abolition of slavery. Emancipation itself was a transfer, from the slaveholders to their chattels, and did not leave the region with any fewer resources. But we would expect this change to affect how much and how hard blacks worked, and indeed, once free, they decided to enjoy more leisure. Women and children abandoned the fields, and even black males cut back. "Most of the field labor is now performed by men," complained one publication of southern whites, "the women regarding it as the duty of their husbands to support them in idleness."[13] The total labor supplied by former slaves fell by approximately one-third. Here we encounter a dramatic demonstration of the limitations of economic aggregates for measuring well-being. Income per capita went *down* because people were *better* off. They were working less or producing household amenities, both of which represented improvements in the quality of life.

The gain in black leisure, however, does not fully account for the decline in southern income to 40 percent below the country's average. An additional factor was a slowing in the demand for U.S. cotton. Great Britain and other importers had shifted their purchases to India, Brazil, and Egypt during the wartime embargo and blockade, and the South did not recover its market share until the 1880s, at a time when world consumption was growing at half the prewar rate. American tariffs must share some responsibility for this, because they made southern cotton relatively more expensive in terms of the goods and services Europeans had to sell to get dollars. The Republican Party's economic exploitation of the defeated South therefore harmed blacks as well as whites.

Some historians have also put blame on the new arrangement that came to dominate cotton growing: sharecropping. The sharecropper worked small plots of twenty to fifty acres under one-year contracts that split the harvest with the landowner, usually down the middle or somewhere in that vicinity. The fact that southern manufacturing recovered much more rapidly than agriculture, and the fact that states of the deep South, where cotton predominated, remained the region's poorest, both lend credence to the common suspicion that this new way of farming was inefficient. Immediately after the war, plantation owners would have preferred revamping the prewar gang system. But they only succeeded on the sugar plantations of Louisiana. Elsewhere planters could not pay wages high enough, frequently enough, or dependably enough to overcome fierce black determination to avoid anything that smacked of their previous servitude.

"Many have said to me," reported a Freedmen's Bureau agent about Mississippi blacks, "they cared not for the pay if they were only treated with kindness and not overworked."[14] Forcing the freedmen back into the gangs was a major reason for the Black Codes imposed by the state governments reconstructed under Presidents Lincoln and Johnson. But the experience in the West Indies and South America confirms that large plantations almost never survive emancipation—even with vagrancy, debt peonage, or other coercive labor laws—unless land is unavailable or another source of unfree labor is. Whenever southern whites turned to violence or cartels to limit the freedmen's options, the ensuing labor shortage soon caused one or another land owner to break ranks and reopen competition.

Blacks preferred being sharecroppers because they could avoid direct supervision. Cropping also became common among poor whites who had lost their land. As late as 1910, 70 percent of black and 40 percent of white farmers in the South were tenants of some kind. Yet sharing the crop at first glance seems inferior to renting land outright. The renter gets to keep all extra output, whereas the sharecropper keeps only half (or whatever his predetermined share), thereby reducing his incentive to produce more. Sharecrop ping also dampens the incentive of either the owner or the cropper to invest in machinery, land improvements, and other capital that would increase productivity. A good deal of farm land was, in fact, rented in the South, by both blacks and whites. But renting entails greater risk, especially if there is a bad harvest. A farmer's rent remains unchanged, even if his crops will not sell for enough to pay it. Sharecropping pools the risk between the owner and farmer. Moreover, it often gives the farmer access to the owner's tools and knowledge.

Nonetheless, a well developed financial system might have lifted southern agriculture out of sharecropping. Poor farmers could have borrowed capital instead of depending upon landowners, or gone into debt to buy their own land. Or the landowners could have borrowed cash to pay reliable weekly wages. The postwar South, however, lacked adequate financial markets. Croppers and renters relied almost entirely upon credit from the country store. Local merchants sold food, clothing, and agricultural supplies either for cash or on time, with crops pledged as security. Markups for the store's commodity credit were between 30 and 70 percent annually, whereas in cities only 50 to 100 miles away rates of interest were one-fifth that. The combination of exorbitant interest and crop liens kept some tenant farmers perpetually in debt.

The huge discrepancy between rural and urban lending rates, however, did not make the South's eight thousand or so country storekeepers beneficiaries of monopoly power. Few had a net worth over $10,000, and bankruptcy among them was endemic. Economists have learned that price differentials of this magnitude, if not explained by real factors, usually result from government-imposed barriers. In this case, the prime culprit was the new National Banking System. Its adoption stifled recovery of the South's credit markets from their wartime dislocation.

The Union's financial expedients had been riddled with features that ended up interdicting the flow of savings to agriculture. Nationally chartered banks could not legally make real-estate loans at all until 1913. The general prohibition on branch banking made it more difficult to shift credit out of areas where interest rates were low to where the demand was greatest. High capital requirements for bank charters, the Comptroller of the Currency's restriction of entry, and initial ceilings on bank notes also all discriminated against the rural South. After the ceilings were removed, the requirement that national bank notes be matched by investments in an ever shrinking supply of Treasury securities first diverted savings and then made it less profitable to issue these notes where interest rates were highest. State usury laws posed a similar obstacle, and the primary way of evading these laws, compensating deposit balances, were unlikely to be offered to impoverished agricultural borrowers.

State-chartered banks, which might have filled the gap, could no longer issue notes. They could offer deposits and, for that reason, experienced a resurgence by the turn of the century, but modern readers often fail to appreciate how the widespread use of checking accounts—liabilities of private institutions that form the bulk of today's money supply—depends upon advanced technologies of credit verification. Many will remember a time when few merchants would accept checks in payment. During the nineteenth century, the privilege of writing an open-ended draft against a bank was confined to individuals of recognized wealth or unquestioned probity. The poor or undistinguished had to borrow currency, commodities, or nothing at all.

The National Banking System contributed to starving the agricultural South not only for credit but also for cash in small denominations. So long as the price level can freely adjust up and down, there can never be a shortage of money *per se;* but a denominational shortage can seem like one. The United States had long suffered this problem, because the official prewar mint ratio between gold and silver had driven silver, suitable for small transactions, out of circulation, while states often outlawed small bank notes. Although the Coinage Act of 1853 had tried to address the deficiency by authorizing subsidiary silver coins, even these tokens were melted down for their metallic content during the wartime inflation. By 1869, their circulation had dwindled to nearly one-fourth their prewar level of $21 million.

Despite the new bans on private mints, which had manufactured copper coins, and on the paper currency of state banks, many businesses and municipalities began issuing their own notes, tickets, and due bills that circulated as small change, whereas the government facilitated such use for postage stamps. The Comptroller of the Currency complained in 1872 that "savings-banks, railroad, municipal, and other corporations in the States of Florida, Georgia and other southern States have followed the example of the State of Alabama, and have issued" large amounts of currency, "some in the form of receipts and certificates, and others in the form of railroad tickets, but all . . . intended to circulate as money."[15] Yet the privately and locally issued "shinplasters," as they were called, could not completely ease the shortage so long as they remained technically illegal, and the notes of nationally chartered banks were artificially scarce in rural regions, as already observed. Although the government's paper money was printed in fractional denominations even lower than the $1 limit sct for national bank notes, the Treasury initially contracted its total circulation during Reconstruction.

This government-induced derangement inhibited the South's monetary system just at the moment when its needs had leapt upward. The slave plantation was a mini-planned economy, within which food, clothing, and other resources, were allocated through the planter's central direction. Upon emancipation, most blacks entered the market for the first time. Now they had to purchase their own necessities. One Alabama merchant was jubilant over this "impetus to trade that we never had before."[16] But the denominational shortage often reduced freed slaves to an inefficient reliance upon barter. Sharecropping, after all, was a barter transaction— cotton exchanged for the use of land—and many of the farmers who rented land at fixed rates paid not "cash rent" in the form of money but "standing rent" in the form of crops. Even agricultural laborers often received non-monetary "share wages." Indeed, the inability of planters to pay regular wages in cash had been one reason for the freedmen's refusal to work in agricultural gangs. In short, the National Banking System throttled both financial intermediation and monetary exchange in the agricultural sector. Slavery's abolition, nevertheless, entailed immense benefits for the freedmen. By 1879 the average agricultural income of blacks had risen by at least 45 percent, or still more if one attaches a dollar value to their added leisure.[17] Despite the Republican failure to redistribute large plantations, blacks had purchased 10 percent of the South's agricultural land, at a time when many white farmers were losing title. Not only were blacks accumulating real estate and other forms of wealth faster than white Southerners, but even in the face of widespread discrimination, their incomes rose faster too— at a rate of 2.7 percent per year.[18] Landowners and merchants tried to hinder black mobility with laws that prohibited the "enticement" of laborers, that licensed labor brokers, and that made breaching labor contracts a criminal offense. Nonetheless, liberty was working out exactly as the free-labor ideology of the radical abolitionists had predicted. William Jay of New York had conceded back in the 1830s, that immediately after the slave's emancipation, "he is, in fact, . . . absolutely dependent on his late owner." However, "in the course of time, the value of negro labor, like all other vendible commodities, will be regulated by supply and demand: and justice be done both to the planter and his laborers."[19] Without doubt, the market did much better by blacks than government at any level after the Civil War.

The relative gains of the freedmen appeared so threatening that whites eventually resorted to more severe racial oppression. Although the Redeemers had manipulated voters with intimidation, poll taxes, and later the Australian, or secret, ballot, blacks continued to go to the polls in large numbers. Within the majority of southern states, the only form of discrimination legally imposed on private institutions applied to passenger trains. Social segregation was pervasive but mostly informal and often favored by blacks themselves. Not until the 1900s did mandated segregation for railway stations, street cars, workplaces, and other public facilities make widespread appearance. The first southern state to effectively disfranchise the majority of its Negroes was Mississippi, in 1890, with a literacy test—fourteen years after the last federal troops left the South. Louisiana did not do so until 1898, and then North Carolina, Alabama, Virginia, and Georgia stepped into line. At the same time spending on blacks compared with white pupils in public schools further declined to as low as 17 percent in Louisiana. The country's latest State-worshipping reform movement, progressivism, avidly participated in this wave of Jim Crow laws, drawing inspiration from the heightened racism of yet another American war occurring at the time, the Spanish-American. And this was just one particularly ominous example of the new willingness on the part of Americans generally to employ government power to achieve social goals.

One Nation Under Bigger Government

The turmoil of Reconstruction was only the Civil War's most visible legacy. The war had dramatically altered American society and institutions. The South of course would never be the same, but the transformation of the North was also profound and permanent. The national government that emerged victorious from the conflict dwarfed in power and size the minimal Jacksonian State that had commenced the war. The number of civilians in federal employ swelled almost fivefold. A distant administration that had little contact with its citizens had been transformed into an overbearing bureaucracy that intruded into daily life with taxes, drafts, surveillance, subsidies, and regulations. Central government spending had soared from less than 2 percent of the economy's total output to well over 20 percent in 1865, approximately what the central government spends today.[20] It is hard to decide from which angle that statistic is more astounding: that government spending rose from such infinitesimal lows to today's heights in four years, or that today federal authorities regularly spend during peacetime as much as they did during the country's most devastating war.

A contemporaneous surge in nationalism complemented the surge in actual government power. Northerners now viewed the United States as a single nation, rather than a confederation or union of states. William Ellery Channing, a Unitarian minister representing the New England intelligentsia, had complained in 1835 that "most men value the Union as a Means; to me it is an End."[21] But by 1865 the poet James Russell Lowell observed a "national consciousness," in which "every man feels himself a part, sensitive and sympathetic, of a vast organism."[22] A seemingly minor shift in word usage highlights this change. "Before the Civil War," emphasizes Professor David H. Donald, "many politicians and writers referred to the United States in the plural, but after 1865 only a pedant or the most unreconstructed Southerner would dream of saying the 'the United States *are*.'"[23] Abandoning the word "Union," Lincoln instead called the U.S. a "nation" a total of five times during his short Gettysburg address, in contrast to his predecessors, who tended to avoid the term. This unitary nationalism received the endorsement of such diverse political theorists as the mystical-Hegelian Elisha Mulford, the apostate-Jacksonian Orestes Brownson, and the transplanted-Prussian Francis Lieber. American intellectuals generally came to ally themselves with the central authority, and the ideals of state sovereignty and secession were dead.

Although the end of Reconstruction allowed further military cutbacks, total armed forces would never fall below a level half-again higher than before Fort Sumter. Nor did this end political employment of the U.S. Army, which had been fashioned into a reliable enforcer of domestic laws to an extent previously undreamed of. In addition to finishing off the Indians and herding them onto reservations, the post-Reconstruction army restored order during the Colfax County and Lincoln County range wars in New Mexico between 1877 and 1880, assisted in the final stamping out of open polygamy in Utah in 1885, and suppressed anti-Chinese demonstrations on the west coast from 1885 through 1886. The national government used troops most often, however, to break strikes. It militarily intervened in scores of labor disputes, most notably the General Railroad Strike of 1877 and the Pullman Strike of 1894. The state militias went on strike duty even more frequently, as they were transformed, beginning with New York, from their mass-citizen tradition into tax-financed elite professionals. The term "National Guard" was borrowed from the French in an effort to identify these state military formations more closely with national authority.

The war taxes lingered well after the fighting had ended. Congress did not let the inheritance tax lapse until 1870; the income tax until 1872. The latter was reinstituted, declared uncon-stitutional, and finally made permanent with ratification of the Sixteenth Amendment in 1913. The other internal levies were gradually pared down but never completely abolished, especially the sin taxes on alcohol and tobacco. Evasion of these excises by the "Whiskey Ring" tainted even the White House during Grant's last years in office. None of the post-Appomattox campaigns for tariff reform achieved much either. Republican protectionism continued to dominate trade policy mercilessly for the next three quarters of a century.

The Greenbacks bequeathed a continuing source of political discord. Chief Justice Salmon P. Chase, in one of the most astonish-ing cases of intellectual honesty on the part of a public official, implicitly branded his prior actions as Secretary of the Treasury unconstitutional when the Court struck down the Greenbacks' retroactive legal-tender provision in the *Hepburn* decision of 1869. President Grant, however, soon packed the Court so that it effec-tively reversed itself in 1871. Only in 1879, more than a decade after Appomattox, did this paper money finally circulate at par with specie, and did the banks finally resume payments in gold.

The National Banking System's restrictions on privately issued currency and domestic capital flows impinged on northern as well as southern farmers. More national bank notes circulated in post-war Connecticut than in Michigan, Wisconsin, Iowa, Minnesota, Kansas, Missouri, Kentucky, and Tennessee combined. One indica-tion of this financial inefficiency was the appearance of major differentials among regional interest rates, something that had not existed under free banking. The discount rate on commercial paper in the 1890s ranged from less than 4 percent in Boston to 10 percent in Denver. This fueled misguided political crusades for inflationary policies, either through printing Greenbacks or coining silver, and ultimately undid the Democracy's traditional support for hard money and financial deregulation. The wartime banking legislation had also tied note issue to the national debt, so that any debt retirement automatically contracted part of the money stock. By creating an inelastic currency, the banks faced a new source of runs that left the financial system more vulnerable than ever to panics.

The postwar national debt had climbed to $2.8 billion. The interest alone on this debt commanded about 40 percent of the central government's outlays into the mid-1870s. An unbroken string of twenty-eight annual budget surpluses from the war's end to the depression of 1893 could have eliminated this liability. But national expenditures as a percentage of the total economy were often over twice their prewar level and never dipped below 3 percent of output. Since the Confederate debt had been repudiated, the recipients of this interest, paid in gold under the Public Credit Act of 1869, were initially Northerners and tended to remain so. This was one of several ways in which the Republican fiscal regime extracted tax revenue from the southern economy and transferred wealth north.

Although the debt did fall below $1 billion in 1892, the Republicans were more interested in spending the surpluses on internal improvements and other pork-barrel legislation. Already by 1873 Congress had allotted 155 million acres of land and $64 million in credit to four chartered transcontinental railroads. These subsidies and the Crédit Mobilier scandal that surrounded them epitomized the national government's neo-mercantilist coalition with business. The most extravagant appropriations, however, were for soldiers' benefits. The Grand Army of the Republic, a pressure group comprised of Union veterans, became a powerful bulwark of the Republican Party. Every Republican elected President from Grant through William McKinley had served as a Civil War officer. Veterans' pensions grew from 2 percent of all federal expenditures in 1866 to 29 percent in 1884, replacing interest payments on the war debt as the largest single item. They constituted in essence the national government's first system of old-age and disability insurance. And since none of this money was paid to Confederate veterans, it was yet another way the North exploited the South as a colonial dependency.

The war also brought a proliferation in government activism at the state and local levels. War expenditures had added more than $100 million to the indebtedness of northern states, and some means had to be found to finance this. In addition, people had become accustomed to government attempts at solving social problems. Reformers consequently turned more than ever before to local and state authorities, who undertook a myriad of new tasks. These included everything from public-health measures to business regulations, from professional licensing restrictions to anti-liquor and anti-vice controls. "The war . . . has tended, more than any other event in the history of the country," declaimed Republican Governor Richard Yates of Illinois in 1865, "to militate against the Jeffersonian idea, that 'the best government is that which governs least.' The war has not only, of necessity, given more power to, but has led to a more intimate prevision of the government over every material interest of society."[24]

New York City, for instance, instituted a professional fire department in 1865 to replace volunteer companies that Republican lawmakers found too closely tied to the city's Democratic machine. The New York legislature within the next two years enacted the country's first housing regulations, set up a Board of Charities, and established a string of eight teacher-training colleges. Massachusetts created a statewide constabulary in 1865. This formative state police enforced ordinances against prostitution, gambling, and liquor. In 1869 the state erected a Board of Health and a Bureau of Labor Statistics. Chicago city government was so decentralized prior to Fort Sumter that it was run virtually on user-fees and adopted general taxes only to fund wartime expenditures, particularly bounties to fill troop quotas. Overall, Massachusetts, New Hampshire, and New York had each nearly doubled tax collections per person between 1860 and 1870, even after making allowances for price changes. In New Jersey per capita real taxes went up two-and-a-half times, and in Connecticut three-and-a-half times. During the six years prior to the Panic of 1873, city debt in Boston, New York, and Chicago expanded threefold.[25]

Not all government interventions showed their primary effects fiscally. Republican-controlled Illinois brought its postwar controls over freight rates and grain warehouses to an apex in 1871 with the creation of a railroad commission. Starting in 1865, state after state chartered bar associations, which became exclusive licensing agencies for lawyers. Ohio became the first state to restrict effective competition in the practice of medicine in 1868, and from there stronger medical licensing spread north and south. The Supreme Court sanctioned this surge in state "police powers" and simultaneously eviscerated the Fourteenth Amendment—first in the *Slaughterhouse* decision of 1873, where it let stand a state-chartered monopoly that drove out of business most of Louisiana's butchers, and again in the *Granger* decision of 1877, where it allowed states to regulate railroads and other common carriers.

The legacy of the Civil War was even felt in the seemingly unrelated area of obscenity. The first act regulating mail content was passed in March of 1865, just prior to the fighting's end. Responding to complaints that troops were ordering obscene material, Congress made mailing such material a crime. The Republicans demonstrated their ongoing commitment to being the "Party of Piety" by adding a mail ban on lotteries and other schemes deemed fraudulent in 1868. A series of new enactments beginning in 1872 steadily strengthened both bans, which were further reinforced by various state laws combating obscenity and vice. These laws empowered Anthony Comstock, as special postal agent, to conduct a veritable witchhunt, and his most illustrious victim ironically became Ezra Heywood, the veteran abolitionist and individualist anarchist who had opposed the Civil War draft. Heywood served two years at hard labor while in his sixties for mailing pamphlets that criticized marriage and advocated birth control.

Casting his eyes about the country only four years after the conflict had ended, George Ticknor of Harvard could not help but marvel at the magnitude of all these transformations. "The civil war of '61 has made a great gulf between what happened before it in our century and what has happened since, or what is likely to happen hereafter," he mused. "It does not seem to me as if I were living in the country in which I was born, or in which I received whatever I got of political education and principles."[26]

Chapter 13
Bibliographical Essay

There are two single-volumes that offer comprehensive coverage of Reconstruction within the southern states: E. Merton Coulter's contribution to the *History of the South* series, *The South During Reconstruction, 1865–1877* (Baton Rouge: Louisiana State University Press, 1947), which reflects the traditional view of the Dunning School, and Eric Foner's contribution to the New American Nation series, *Reconstruction: America's Unfinished Revolution, 1863–1877* (New York: Harper & Row, 1988), which reflects the modern view of the neo-abolitionist school. Foner's volume has the greater range of the two, covering national and northern events as well, and displays a staggering command of the subject's vast literature.

Abundant studies of individual states invariably fall into one or the other camp, depending upon when they were published. Rather than a broad sample, we will merely call attention to those exceptional works that integrate the postwar period with the prewar: Paul D. Escott, *Many Excellent People: Power and Privilege in North Carolina, 1850–1900* (Chapel Hill: University of North Carolina Press, 1985), Roger W. Shugg, *Origins of Class Struggle in Louisiana: A Social History of White Farmers and Laborers During Slavery and After, 1840–1875* (Baton Rouge: Louisiana State University Press, 1939), and Steven Hahn, *The Roots of Southern Populism* (cited ch. 5). In a special category is Peter Wallenstein's examination of Georgia's prewar, wartime, and postwar state interventions, *From Slave South to New South* (cited ch. 9).

A worthy anthology of articles on particular states is Otto H. Olsen, ed., *Reconstruction and Redemption in the South* (Baton Rouge: Louisiana State University Press, 1980); while the collection edited by Richard O. Curry, *Radicalism, Racism, and Party Realignment: The Border States During Reconstruction* (Baltimore: Johns Hopkins Press, 1969), explores events in slave states that had not joined the Confederacy. Richard Nelson Current provides a neo-abolitionist study of *Those Terrible Carpetbaggers* (New York: Oxford University Press, 1987). Gordon B. McKinney, *Southern Mountain Republicans, 1865–1900: Politics and the Appalachian Community* (Chapel Hill: University of North Carolina Press, 1978), looks at one group of scalawags.

For the black role in Reconstruction, in addition to works mentioned in ch. 8, consult Robert Cruden, *The Negro in Reconstruction* (Englewood Cliffs, NJ: Prentice-Hall, 1969), plus three noteworthy state studies, Joel Williamson, *After Slavery: The Negro in South Carolina During Reconstruction, 1861–1877* (Chapel Hill: University of North Carolina Press, 1965); Peter Kolchin, *First Freedom: The Responses of Alabama's Blacks to Emancipation and Reconstruction* (Westport, CT: Greenwood Press, 1972); and Thomas Holt, *Black Over White: Negro Political Leadership in South Carolina During Reconstruction* (Urbana: University of Illinois Press, 1977). Because the Dunning School put such emphasis on the Union League, neo-abolitionist historians tended to downplay its political importance for organizing blacks. But Michael W. Fitzgerald provides a modern reassessment in *The Union League Movement in the Deep South: Politics and Agricultural Change During Reconstruction* (Baton Rouge: Louisiana State University Press, 1989).

Carter Goodrich, *Government Promotion of American Canals and Railroads, 1800–1890* (cited ch. 4), contains a thorough chapter on the subsidization of southern railroads by the Radical regimes. A business-oriented history is John F. Stover, *The Railroads of the South, 1865–1900: A Study of Finance and Control* (Chapel Hill: University of North Carolina Press, 1955). More insightful is Mark Wahlgren Summers, *Railroads, Reconstruction, and the Gospel of Prosperity: Aid Under the Radical Republicans, 1865–1877* (Princeton, NJ: Princeton University Press, 1984). Although Summers fails to dispel Stover's superstitious animosity toward importing northern capital (the South's major economic albatross being the government barriers to such investments), his data are generally consistent with the economist's understanding that state railroad subsidies constituted wasteful malinvestments. The overall profligacy of Republican rule in the South is compared with the prewar period in J. Mills Thornton, III,'s important article, "Fiscal Policy and the Failure of Radical Reconstruction in the Lower South," from J. Morgan Kousser and James M. McPherson, eds., *Region, Race, and Reconstruction: Essays in Honor of C. Vann Woodward* (New York: Oxford University Press, 1982).

A dogmatic faith in government schools remains steadfast among nearly all historians and many economists. For the South in particular, the desirability of this secular substitute for State religion is never questioned; its efficacy never tested—despite a growing body of skeptical, revisionist literature on common schools in the North. For example: E. G. West, "The Political Economy of American Public School Legislation," *Journal of Law and Economics*, 10 (October 1967), pp. 101–128; Michael B. Katz, *The Irony of Early School Reform: Educational Innovation in Mid-Nineteenth Century Massachusetts* (Cambridge, MA: Harvard University Press, 1968); Katz, *Class, Bureaucracy, and Schools: The Illusion of Educational Change in America*, rev. edn. (New York: Praeger, 1975); Carl Kaestle, *Pillars of the Republic: Common Schools and American Society, 1780–1860* (New York: Hill and Wang, 1983); and Joel Spring, *The American School, 1642–1985* (New York: Longman, 1986). An economist who offers some evidence that the public-school movement had trivial effects on educational attainments in the antebellum United States is Albert Fishlow, "The American Common School Revival: Fact or Fancy?" in Henry Rosovksy, ed., *Industrialization in Two Systems: Essays in Honor of Alexander Gerschenkron by a Group of His Students* (New York: John Wiley & Sons, 1966). See also Fishlow's comparison of prewar and postwar educational expenditures, "Levels of Nineteenth-Century American Investment in Education," *Journal of Economic History*, 26 (December 1977), pp. 418–436. More enthusiastic are

Lee Soltow and Edward Stevens in *The Rise of Literacy and the Common School in the United States: A Socioeconomic Analysis to 1870* (Chicago: University of Chicago Press, 1981).

Donald R. Warren, *To Enforce Education: The History of the Founding of the Office of Education* (Detroit: Wayne State University Press, 1974), is a study of the national educational bureaucracy's establishment that escapes slavish worship of State schooling. James D. Anderson, *The Education of Blacks in the South, 1860–1935* (Chapel Hill: University of North Carolina Press, 1988), provides an overview of its subject, while two works that emphasize the northern desire for social control are Ronald E. Butchart, *Northern Schools, Southern Blacks, and Reconstruction: Freedman's Education, 1862–1875* (Westport, CT: Greenwood Press, 1980), and Robert C. Morris, *Reading, 'Riting, and Reconstruction: The Education of Freedmen in the South* (Chicago: University of Chicago Press, 1981). On state-government provision of education in the Reconstruction South, consult Charles William Dabney, *Universal Education in the South*, v. 1, *From the Beginning to 1900* (Chapel Hill: University of North Carolina Press, 1936). The segregation issue is the focus of William Preston Vaughn, *Schools for All: The Blacks and Public Education in the South, 1865–1877* (Lexington: University Press of Kentucky, 1974). Robert A. Margo, *Race and Schooling in the South, 1880–1950* (Chicago: University of Chicago Press, 1990), is only the most recent examination of the increasing white use of state schools to exploit blacks.

Efforts of Radical governments to create black militias are in Otis A. Singletary, *Negro Militia and Reconstruction* (Austin: University of Texas Press, 1957). Various aspects of the partisan war conducted by southern whites against Republican rule are treated in Allen W. Trelease, *White Terror: The Ku Klux Klan Conspiracy and Southern Reconstruction* (New York: Harper & Row, 1971), and George C. Rable, *But There Was No Peace: The Role of Violence in the Politics of Reconstruction* (Athens: University of Georgia Press, 1984). Michael Perman examines the final overthrow of Reconstruction in *The Road to Redemption: Southern Politics, 1869–1879* (Chapel Hill: University of North Carolina Press, 1984).

The postwar impact of southern representatives on national politics is investigated in Terry L. Seip, *The South Returns to Congress: Men, Economic Measures, and Intersectional Relationships, 1868–1879* (Baton Rouge: Louisiana State University Press, 1983). Earle Dudley Ross, *The Liberal Republican Movement* (New York: Cornell University, 1919), and John G. Sproat, *"The Best Men": Liberal Reformers in the Gilded Age* (New York: Oxford University Press, 1968), look at the split within Republican ranks, while Louis S. Gerteis, *Morality & Utility in American Antislavery Reform* (Chapel Hill: University of North Carolina Press, 1987), explores the abolitionist roots of the Liberal Republicans. Charles Callan Tansill, *The United States and Santo Domingo, 1798–1873: A Chapter in Caribbean Diplomacy* (Baltimore: Johns Hopkins Press, 1938), contains the best account of the Grant Administration's efforts to annex that island.

On the reform issue that ended up diverting and ultimately derailing the

Liberal Republican drive for *laissez faire,* Ari A. Hoogenboom, *Outlawing the Spoils: A History of the Civil Service Reform Movement, 1865–1883* (Urbana: University of Illinois Press, 1961), is definitive. This result may have been ideologically foreordained. Just when socialists were asserting that State intervention could benefit common people instead of elites, Liberal Republicans became the first American advocates of *laissez faire* openly hostile to the masses. Their anti-democratic conservatism, probably more than Horace Greeley's inept presidential bid, doomed the attempted Liberal Republican alliance with the Democratic Party.

Robert L. Kelley, *The Transatlantic Persuasion: The Liberal-Democratic Mind in the Age of Gladstone* (New York: Alfred A. Knopf, 1969), provides unmatched insights into the classical-liberal political philosophy of the Democracy's 1876 presidential candidate, Samuel J. Tilden. Paul Kleppner's *The Cross of Culture: A Social Analysis of Midwestern Politics, 1850–1900* (New York: Free Press, 1970), was an early application of the new political history to this period. A general survey of national politics during Redemption is William Gillette, *Retreat From Reconstruction, 1869–1879* (Baton Rouge: Louisiana State University Press, 1979). Conflicting perspectives on the disputed election and the resulting compromise are C. Vann Woodward, *Reunion and Reaction: The Compromise of 1877 and the End of Reconstruction,* 2nd edn. (Garden City, NY: Doubleday, 1956), and Keith Ian Polakoff, *The Politics of Inertia: The Election of 1876 and the End of Reconstruction* (Baton Rouge: Louisiana State University Press, 1973). Actual implementation of the settlement is recounted in two works of the same title: Kenneth E. Davidson, *The Presidency of Rutherford B. Hayes* (Lawrence: University of Kentucky Press, 1972), and Ari Hoogenboom, *The Presidency of Rutherford B. Hayes* (Lawrence: University Press of Kansas, 1988).

Paul H. Buck, *The Road to Reunion, 1865–1900* (New York: Alfred A. Knopf, 1937), a social history of cooling wartime hatreds, is heavily influenced by the Dunning School. Vincent P. De Santis, *Republicans Face the Southern Question—The New Departure Years, 1877–1897* (Baltimore: Johns Hopkins Press, 1959), and Stanley P. Hirshon, *Farewell to the Bloody Shirt: Northern Republicans & the Southern Negro, 1877–1893* (Bloomington: Indiana University Press, 1962), look into the evolving attitude of northern Republicans. Two works describe the South's development of a Cult of the Lost Cause, in which slavery was comfortably forgotten as a motive for secession: Rollin G. Osterweis, *The Myth of the Lost Cause, 1865–1900* (Hamden, CT: Archon Books, 1973), and Gaines M. Foster, *Ghosts of the Confederacy: Defeat, the Lost Cause, and the Emergence of the New South, 1865 to 1913* (New York: Oxford University Press, 1987).

Roger L. Ransom and Richard Sutch, *One Kind of Freedom: The Economic Consequences of Emancipation* (Cambridge, U.K.: Cambridge University Press, 1977), is a cliometric analysis funded by the National Science Foundation that almost has become for postbellum sharecropping what Robert Fogel and Stanley L. Engerman's *Time on the Cross* (cited ch. 2) is for antebellum slavery. It has inspired at least one collection—*Market*

Institutions and Economic Progress in the New South 1865–1900: Essays Stimulated by One Kind of Freedom: The Economic Consequences of Emancipation (New York: Academic Press, 1981)—articles reprinted from *Explorations in Economic History* and edited by Gary M. Walton and James F. Shepherd. Engerman previously had compiled the basic numbers on the South's postwar economic performance in "Some Economic Factors in Southern Backwardness in the Nineteenth Century," from John F. Kain and John R. Meyer, eds., *Essays in Regional Economics* (Cambridge, MA: Harvard University Press, 1971), while Claudia Dale Goldin and Frank D. Lewis had calculated wartime destruction in the South in "The Economic Cost of the American Civil War: Estimates and Implications," *Journal of Economic History*, 35 (June 1975), pp. 299–322. Patrick K. O'Brien, *The Economic Effects of the American Civil War* (Basingstoke, U.K.: Macmillan Education, 1988), is a brief historiographical review with particular emphasis on the economic ramifications of emancipation.

Ransom and Sutch's most robust finding is that wartime losses cannot fully explain southern backwardness. They also document the postemancipation increase in black leisure. Gavin Wright, on the other hand, in "Cotton Competition and the Post Bellum Recovery of the American South," *Journal of Economic History*, 34 (September 1974), pp. 610–635, blames the postwar weakening of worldwide cotton demand for the South's lagging output. Peter Temin unifies the two factors in "The Post-Bellum Recovery of the South and the Cost of the Civil War," *Journal of Economic History*, 36 (December 1976), pp. 898–907. But in my opinion, no economic historian has paid sufficient heed to the Republican tariffs. One attempt to assess their *fiscal* impact is Jeffrey Williamson, "Watersheds and Turning Points: Conjectures on the Long-Term Impact of Civil War Financing," *Journal of Economic History*, 34 (September 1974), pp. 631–661. Williamson suggests that by taxing consumption to pay back the war debt, tariffs increased American saving and thereby accelerated capital accumulation. Even if correct (and I remain dubious), his analysis should display a bit more sensitivity to exactly whose consumption was curtailed, since it most likely was impoverished freedmen, among others.

In keeping with their opinions about slavery's efficiency, Fogel in *Without Consent or Contract* (cited ch. 2) and Engerman in "Economic Adjustments for Emancipation in the United States and the British West Indies," *Journal of Interdisciplinary History*, 13 (Autumn 1982), pp. 191–200, reject both the fall in labor hours and stagnant cotton demand as primary factors in the South's economic decline. They instead pinpoint emancipation's destruction of plantation agriculture, with its scale economies. Ralph Shlomowitz performs an economic analysis of "The Origins of Southern Sharecropping" in *Agricultural History*, 53 (July 1979), pp. 557–575. Edward Royce has recently given us a more traditional synthesis in *The Origins of Southern Sharecropping* (Philadelphia: Temple University Press, 1993). The two works confirm that sharecropping was a concession both for planters, who would have preferred gang labor, and for the freedmen, who would have preferred renting or owning land.

This brings us to another of Ransom and Sutch's contentions: the purported inefficiency of sharecropping. Neo-classical defenses of this agricultural system include Joseph D. Reid, Jr., "Sharecropping as an Understandable Market Response: The Postbellum South," *Journal of Economic History*, 33 (March 1973), pp. 106–130; Stephen J. DeCanio, *Agriculture in the Postbellum South: The Economics of Production and Supply* (Cambridge, MA: MIT Press, 1974); and Lee J. Alston and Robert Higgs, "Contractual Mix in Southern Agriculture Since the Civil War: Facts, Hypothesis and Tests," *Journal of Economic History*, 42 (June 1982), pp. 327–353. These will lead you to economists' purely theoretical writings on the subject. The literature is well developed and highly technical, so I will mention only Steven N. S. Cheung's minor classic, *The Theory of Share Tenancy: With Special Application to Asian Agriculture and the First Phase of Taiwan Land Reform* (Chicago: University of Chicago Press, 1969).

If sharecropping was noticeably inefficient, the inevitable question arises: why could more productive agricultural arrangements not compete effectively? The innovative answer offered in *One Kind of Freedom* is that malfunctioning credit institutions bestowed local monopolies on country merchants. Claudia Goldin and Joseph Reid, in their contributions to Walton and Shepherd's *Market Institutions and Economic Progress in the New South 1865–1900*, have made two of the most telling demonstrations that the high differential between rural and urban interest rates reflected default risk and transaction costs rather than territorial monopolies. Ransom and Sutch themselves allude to the role of the National Currency Acts in creating such transaction costs and thereby stifling investment in the rural South, and several neglected articles point in the same direction: William J. Laird and James R. Rinehart, "Deflation, Agriculture, and Southern Development," *Agriculture History*, 42 (April 1968), pp. 115–245; and John A. James, "Financial Underdevelopment in the Postbellum South," *Journal of Interdisciplinary History*, 11 (Winter 1981), pp. 443–454. But no cliometrician has given the National Banking System's role the systematic exploration it warrants. Even more neglected is the possible role of state banking laws, which are briefly reviewed in Davis R. Dewey, "Banking in the South," from v. 6 of *The South in the Building of the Nation* . . . (Richmond: Southern Historical Publication Society, 1909).

Economist Gerold David Jaynes, in *Branches Without Roots: Genesis of the Black Workingclass in the American South, 1862–1882* (New York: Oxford University Press, 1986), has buttressed the argument that sharecropping prevailed because of inadequate credit and money. Although unduly contentious (probably to over-differentiate his product) and often obscure (from futilely striving to square neoclassical theory with Marxist conclusions), Jaynes's book is rich in both useful data and fresh perspectives. Contra Fogel and Engerman, Jaynes finds no scale economies in cotton farming, but if the South's agricultural sector could have paid regular, monetary wages, productivity might have risen 35 percent. He also attributes the rise in transaction costs for the South's credit market to emancipation, because laborers who cannot be enslaved also could not use their future income as collateral for loans. Only a well-specified cliometric study can determine whether this factor was really as significant as banking restrictions.

Class-based indictments of sharecropping attempted by non-economists are Jay R. Mandle, *The Roots of Black Poverty: The Southern Plantation Economy After the Civil War* (Durham, NC: Duke University Press, 1978), and Jonathan M. Wiener, *Social Origins of the New South: Alabama, 1865–1885* (Baton Rouge: Louisiana State University Press, 1978). Wiener's effort, the more historically worthwhile of the two, reveals political and social conflict between landowners and storekeepers. Thomas D. Clark, *Pills, Petticoats and Plows: The Southern Country Store* (Indianapolis: Bobbs-Merrill, 1944), is a traditional and well-balanced history of this business. A broader survey of cotton marketing, going back to antebellum years, is Harold D. Woodman, *King Cotton and His Retainers: Financing and Marketing the Cotton Crop of the South, 1800–1925* (Lexington: University of Kentucky Press, 1968). Woodman's claim that southern agriculture was always starved for capital, however, should be contrasted with the findings of Larry Schweikart, *Banking in the American South* (cited ch. 9), about the South's high degree of financial sophistication before the Civil War's dislocations.

No doubt the lamest of all the charges resuscitated in *One Kind of Freedom* is that country merchants made sharecroppers grow an irrational mix of crops: too much cotton and too little corn or other food. What appears to have been Ransom and Sutch's original formulation, that this cotton overproduction somehow lowered the monetary income of individual farms, was thoroughly refuted—not only in the contributions to *Market Institutions and Economic Progress in the New South 1865–1900* of Claudia Goldin, Peter Temin, and Joseph Reid, but also in *Journal of Economic History* articles by Stephen J. DeCanio, "Cotton 'Overproduction' in Late Nineteenth-Century Southern Agriculture," 33 (September 1973), pp. 608–633, and William W. Brown and Morgan O. Reynolds, "Debt Peonage Reexamined," 33 (December 1973), pp. 862–871.

Ransom and Sutch were compelled to fall back, with some hemming and hawing, on a more defensible formulation of the cotton-overproduction charge, best articulated by Gavin Wright and Howard Kunreuther, "Cotton, Corn and Risk in the Nineteenth Century," *Journal of Economic History*, 35 (September 1975), pp. 526–551. The Wright-Kunreuther version has two independent contentions: (1) Sharecroppers and other small farmers would have preferred to forgo some expected monetary income in order to attain self-sufficiency in food, but their creditors forced them to produce the most profitable mix for the market. (2) Because the worldwide demand for southern cotton was, in economists' jargon, nearly unit elastic, a reduction in total output would have jacked up prices enough to compensate farmers. Cotton restrictions would have worked similar to the oil restrictions of the OPEC cartel. Therefore, by sheer coincidence, if those farmers who had wanted to grow more corn and less cotton had gotten their way, their *collective* incomes might have risen, although each *individual* farmer could still expect to profit monetarily by shifting from corn to cotton.

Yet Robert McGuire and Robert Higgs, "Cotton, Corn, and Risk in the Nineteenth Century: Another View," *Explorations in Economic History*, 14 (April 1977), pp. 167–182, have raised serious theoretical challenges to this version. And Price V. Fishback, "Debt Peonage in Postbellum Georgia," *Explorations in Economic History*, 26 (April 1989), pp. 219–236, presents some empirical evidence that contradicts the common perception of perpetually indebted sharecroppers. We should note that the Wright-Kunreuther thesis, if perchance correct, drives one extra nail in the intellectual coffin of railroad subsidies. If the South was producing too much cotton, poor farmers certainly did not need to be taxed to build railroads to bring that cotton to market.

The same year that *One Kind of Freedom* appeared, Robert Higgs brought forth *Competition and Coercion: Blacks in the American Economy* (Cambridge, U.K.: Cambridge University Press, 1977), the most solid investigation of black economic gains within the South after emancipation. No writer more carefully distinguishes between market relations and racist coercion. Higgs shows that blacks invariably benefited from the market unless private or public violence hindered its operation. Ransom and Sutch, of course, dispute Higgs's optimistic data, and a review essay that remains useful despite its simplistic Marxist animus against economic theory is Harold D. Woodman, "Sequel to Slavery: The New History Views the Postbellum South," *Journal of Southern History*, 43 (November 1977), pp. 523–554. Everyone agrees that emancipation itself was a major economic boon; disagreement is over how rapidly blacks improved afterwards, particularly relative to white Southerners. Two recent statistical analyses of Georgia data appearing in the *American Economic Review*—Higgs, "Accumulation of Property by Southern Blacks Before World War I," 72 (September 1982), pp. 725–735; and Robert A. Margo, "Accumulation of Property by Southern Blacks Before World War One: Comment and Further Evidence," 74 (September 1984), pp. 777–781—are consistent with the relative gains found by Higgs.

Investigations of the coercive disabilities that blacks faced after emancipation include William Cohen, "Negro Involuntary Servitude in the South, 1865–1940: A Preliminary Analysis," *Journal of Southern History*, 42 (February 1976), pp. 31–60, and Daniel A. Novak, *The Wheel of Servitude: Black Forced Labor After Slavery* (Lexington: University Press of Kentucky, 1978). Jaynes tries to show in *Branches Without Roots* that these disabilities were far more effective and harmful than Higgs makes allowance for. To the extent that anti-enticement laws, labor-broker licenses, vagrancy statutes, and the convict-lease system successfully mimicked antebellum slavery, they clearly did so at much higher cost, contributing to the South's postwar poverty.

Irrespective of what happened during the nineteenth century, Richard Vedder, Lowell Gallaway, and David C. Klingaman intriguingly hint that, with the twentieth century's arrival, southern blacks ceased to experience any improvement relative to whites, even though the average income of both races continued to rise. See the authors' "Black Exploitation and White Benefits: The Civil War Income Revolution," from Richard F. America, ed., *The Wealth of Races: The Present Value of Benefits From Past Injustices* (Westport, CT: Greenwood Press, 1990), which suggests that this relative stagnation motivated black migration to the North. What makes this suggestion so historically appealing is that it dates mounting economic obstacles with the mounting politically imposed discrimination we know that blacks faced.

Gavin Wright takes the logic of labor flows even further in *Old South, New South: Revolutions in the Southern Economy Since the Civil War* (New York: Basic Books, 1986), a Malthusian explanation for southern poverty. Agreeing with Higgs that competition within the South usually surmounted racial obstacles, Wright identifies the real problem as lack of competition between the South and the rest of the country. Without interregional labor mobility, population growth ate up all increases in southern output. The South remained an isolated, low-wage labor market for both blacks and whites. Not until the two sections became economically integrated after World War II did the South's income begin to match the North's. The movement of workers, however, is not the only way to equalize wage rates. Another way is through capital mobility, which increases per capita investment and therefore output, bringing us back again to the South's financial system.

An earlier Higgs study, *The Transformation of the American Economy, 1865-1914: An Essay in Interpretation* (New York: John Wiley & Sons, 1971), contends that "scholars have too often exaggerated the problems of Southern development" (p. 108). The South's rate of growth between 1880 and 1900 matched the rest of the country's, and given emancipation's "revolutionary restructuring of property rights" and its "blow to the Southern asset structure," the equilibrating adjustment of regional incomes was going to take time; "it is perhaps most remarkable that the Southern economy managed to rebound as quickly as it did" (p. 114). Worth observing is that this equilibration was only completed after the demise of protectionist trade duties.

The work that called attention to the late origins of Jim Crow legislation was C. Vann Woodward, *The Strange Career of Jim Crow*, 3rd edn. (New York: Oxford University Press, 1974), characterized by two of the author's students as "unquestionably the single most influential book ever written on the history of American race relations" (J. Morgan Kousser and James M. McPherson, "C. Vann Woodward: An Assessment of His Work and Influence," in Kousser and McPherson, eds., *Region, Race, and Reconstruction*, p. xv). Since its first publication in 1955, Woodward's milestone has come in for its share of criticism, but nearly all of this revolves around the causes of segregation and the extent to which *de facto* segregation predated Jim Crow laws. Woodward's basic thesis remains sound, although he stresses political factors whereas more recent writing has added other dimensions. For a review of the controversy, see Woodward, "The Strange Career of a Historical Controversy," in *American Counterpoint: Slavery and Racism in the North-South Dialogue* (Boston: Little Brown, 1971).

An excellent monograph on suffrage restrictions is J. Morgan Kousser, *The Shaping of Southern Politics: Suffrage Restrictions and the Establishment of a One-Party South, 1880–1910* (New Haven: Yale University Press, 1974). Harold N. Rabinowitz looks at *Race Relations in the Urban South, 1865–1890* (New York: Oxford University Press, 1978). A general treatment of the period after Reconstruction is in Woodward, *Origins of the New South, 1877–1913* (Baton Rouge: Louisiana State University Press, 1951), part of the *History of the South* series. Unfortunately Woodward's handling of such economic issues as sharecropping is simple-minded and out-dated. Edward L. Ayers, *The Promise of the New South: Life After Reconstruction* (New York: Oxford University Press, 1992), is a more current study that covers the same ground.

Comparisons of the American South after slavery's abolition with other countries that abolished the institution include Engerman's *Journal of Interdisciplinary History* article mentioned above, "Economic Adjustments for Emancipation in the United States and the British West Indies"; the contributions of George M. Fredrickson and C. Vann Woodward to David G. Sansing, ed., *What Was Freedom's Price?* (Jackson: University Press of Mississippi, 1978); Eric Foner, *Nothing But Freedom: Emancipation and Its Legacy* (Baton Rouge: Louisiana State University Press, 1985); and Roger L. Ransom and Kerry Ann Odell, "Land and Credit: Some Historical Parallels Between Mexico and the American South," *Agricultural History*, 60 (Winter 1986), pp. 4–31. Whatever else might be said, "Reconstruction stands as a unique and dramatic experiment," concludes Foner ("Reconstruction Revisited," p. 91 [cited ch. 12]), "the only instance when blacks, within a few years of emancipation, achieved universal manhood suffrage and exercised a real measure of political power."

Allan Nevins, *The Emergence of Modern America, 1865–1878* (New York: Macmillan, 1927), is a general examination of post-Civil War America. Margaret S. Thompson exposes *The "Spider Web": Congress and Lobbying in the Age of Grant* (Ithaca, NY: Cornell University Press, 1985), while Mark W. Summers, *The Era of Good Stealings* (New York: Oxford University Press, 1993), studies corruption as a political issue. The politics of government finance is dealt with in Clifton K. Yearly, *The Money Machines: The Breakdown and Reform in Governmental and Party Finance in the North, 1860–1920* (Albany: State University of New York Press, 1970), a revisionist evaluation of patronage and corruption. Figures on the Union's civilian bureaucracy are taken from Paul P. Van Riper and Keith A. Sutherland, "The Northern Civil Service, 1861–1865," *Civil War History*, 11 (December 1965), pp. 351–369.

On the domestic employment of the military, see Frederick T. Wilson, *Federal Aid in Domestic Disturbances, 1787–1903* (Senate Document No. 209, 57th Cong., 2nd sess., 1903); Bennett Milton Rich, *The Presidents and Civil Disorder* (Washington: Brookings Institution, 1941); Jerry M. Cooper,

The Army and Civil Disorder: Federal Military Intervention in Labor Disputes, 1877-1900 (Westport, CT: Greenwood Press, 1980); and Robin Higham, ed., *Bayonets in the Streets: The Use of Troops in Civil Disturbances,* 2nd edn. (Manhattan, KS: Sunflower University Press, 1989). Jim Dan Hill, *The Minute Man in Peace and War,* challenges the standard view, found in William H. Riker, *Soldiers of the States,* and John K. Mahon, *History of the Militia and the National Guard* (all three cited in ch. 6), that the desire to suppress labor disputes was decisive in the transformation from militia to National Guard. The coolness of Republicans toward labor unions is explored in David Montgomery, *Beyond Equality: Labor and the Radical Republicans, 1862-1872* (New York: Alfred A. Knopf, 1967).

The premier treatise on money after the Civil War comes from the National Bureau of Economic Research: Milton Friedman and Anna Jacobson Schwartz, *A Monetary History of the United States, 1867-1960* (Princeton, NJ: Princeton University Press, 1963). This model integration of sound economics and scholarly history remains breathtaking in scope and authority. The works mentioned in chapter 9 on Union monetary policy are also relevant for the Reconstruction period. Additional studies of Greenback politics are Irwin Unger, *The Greenback Era: A Social and Political History of American Finance, 1865-1879* (Princeton, NJ: Princeton University Press, 1964); and Walter T. K. Nugent, *The Money Question During Reconstruction* (New York: W. W. Norton, 1967). Together they overhaul Charles Beard's older portrait of the Republican Party as an anti-inflationist, hard-money phalanx and substitute a complex tapestry of jockeying special interests, much more in keeping with modern public-choice analysis. Allen Weinstein looks into the *Prelude to Populism: Origins of the Silver Issue, 1867-1878* (New Haven: Yale University Press, 1970).

Unfortunately, despite the great attention nineteenth-century Americans paid to the lack of cash in small denominations, monetary economists have mostly dismissed the problem. Richard H. Timberlake, Jr., is one of the few to take it seriously—in a 1974 *Journal of Economic History* article that was incorporated as chapter 9 in his *The Origins of Central Banking in the United States* (Cambridge, MA: Harvard University Press, 1978), further revised under the title, *Monetary Policy in the United States: An Intellectual and Institutional History* (Chicago: University of Chicago Press, 1993). The most advanced theoretical consideration of denominational problems that I have been able to locate is in Sui-ki Leung's unpublished paper, "Money Scarcity and the Cause of the American Free Banking Movement" (University of South Carolina, Department of Economics, December 1991). Both Timberlake and Leung offer an explanation for the secular behavior of money's velocity that is more satisfactory than the standard one of Friedman and Schwartz. As denominational shortages became less severe the velocity of the measured money stock declined, because this increased money's utility and therefore its demand relative to output. According to Gary M. Pecquet, "The Change Shortage and Private and Public Provision of Small Currency Denominations in the Trans-Mississippi States, 1861–1865," *Southern Studies,* 25 (Spring 1986), pp. 102–110, this problem also plagued the Confederacy until severe inflation reduced the currency's real value. Historical details about small denomination issues, public and private, are in Neil Carothers, *Fractional Money: A History of the Small Coins and Fractional Paper Currency of the United States* (New York: John Wiley & Sons, 1930).

The impact of postwar deflation upon the denomination and intermediation crises that afflicted the South and other rural regions is ambiguous. By increasing the purchasing power of each unit of money, the steady decline in prices would have made shortages of small change worse. On the other hand, deflation brought back subsidiary silver, although the postwar increase in silver output and consequent decline in silver prices would have done that anyway. With respect to intermediation, to the extent that deflation was unanticipated, creditors gained at the expense of debtors. If deflation was anticipated, adjustments in interest rates would have offset this redistribution. Since this was one of the periods at which famed-economist Irving Fisher was looking when he discovered the long-term correlation between nominal interest and the price level (dubbed by economists the "Fisher effect"), we may tentatively conclude that the postwar deflation was somewhat anticipated. Richard Roll, "Interest Rates and Price Expectations During the Civil War," *Journal of Economic History,* 32 (June 1972), pp. 470–495, finds that nominal interest rates adjusted for price changes at least during the war years. One financial advantage of falling prices is that it assists small, unsophisticated savers by reducing the interest they would otherwise lose by hoarding cash.

An outstanding analysis of the National Banking System is John A. James, *Money and Capital Markets in Postbellum America* (Princeton, NJ: Princeton University Press, 1978). James contends that its pernicious effects receded as most of the legal restrictions were successfully evaded. Phillip Cagan, "The First Fifty Years of the National Banking System—An Historical Appraisal," in Deane Carson, ed., *Banking and Monetary Studies* (Homewood, IL: Richard D. Irwin, 1963), is a succinct statement of the conventional case in favor of the National Banking System, whereas Richard E. Sylla, "The United States 1863–1913," in Rondo Cameron, ed., *Banking and Economic Development: Some Lessons of History* (New York: Oxford University Press, 1972), was an influential reevaluation. A recent exploration of how regulations perversely inhibited the circulation of bank notes is Bruce W. Hetherington, "Bank Entry and the Low Issue of National Bank Notes: A Re-examination," *Journal of Economic History,* 50 (September 1990), pp. 669–675.

Lance E. Davis wrote the original study of regional differences among interest rates during this era: "The Investment Market, 1870–1914: The Evolution of a National Market," *Journal of Economic History,* 25 (September 1965), pp. 355–393. Richard Sylla, "Federal Policy, Banking Market Structure and Capital Mobilization in the United States, 1863–1913," *Journal of Economic History,* 29 (December 1969), pp. 657–686, placed responsibility squarely on the National Banking System. More recently, Howard Bodenhorn and Hugh Rockoff, "Regional Interest Rates in Antebellum America," from Claudia Goldin and Hugh Rockoff, eds., *Strategic Factors in Nineteenth Century American Economic History: A Volume to Honor Robert W. Fogel* (Chicago: University of Chicago Press, 1992), have fortified the case against Republican finance by verifying the absence of such differentials before the war.

Alternative explanations for these interest rate differentials, not all mutually exclusive, are found in Gene Smiley, "Interest Rate Movement in the United States, 1888–1913," *Journal of Economic History*, 35 (September 1975), pp. 591–620; Jeffrey G. Williamson, *Late Nineteenth Century American Development: A General Equilibrium History* (London: Cambridge University Press, 1974); Hugh Rockoff, "Regional Interest Rates and Bank Failures, 1870–1914," *Explorations in Economic History*, 14 (January 1977), pp. 90–95; Marie Elizabeth Sushka and Brian W. Barrett, "Banking Structure and the National Capital Market, 1869–1914," *Journal of Economic History*, 44 (June 1984), pp. 463–477; and John J. Binder and David T. Brown, "Bank Rates of Return and Entry Restrictions, 1869–1914," *Journal of Economic History*, 51 (March 1991), pp. 47–66.

At least since the work of Friedman and Schwartz, economic historians have been aware that the National Banking System's "absence of interconvertibility of deposits and currency" (p. 295) was a serious macroeconomic problem. The best theoretical explanation of why this inelastic currency contributed to bank panics is contained in George A. Selgin, *The Theory of Free Banking: Money Supply Under Competitive Note Issue* (Totowa, NJ: Rowman & Littlefield, 1988). The inelasticity resulted from requirements that national banks collateralize their notes with holdings of Treasury securities, and the standard work on Treasury borrowing remains Robert T. Patterson, *Federal Debt-Management Policies, 1865–1879* (Durham: Duke University Press, 1954). John A. James, "Public Debt Management Policy and Nineteenth-Century American Growth," *Explorations in Economic History*, 21 (April 1984), pp. 192–217, finds that steady retirement of the war debt probably contributed to private capital accumulation.

William Henry Glasson, *Federal Military Pensions in the United States* (New York: Oxford University Press, 1918), is a general history of veterans' benefits up to World War I. Books that delve into the Grand Army of the Republic and its political clout include Mary R. Dearing, *Veterans in Politics: The Story of the G.A.R.* (Baton Rouge: Louisiana University Press, 1952); Wallace Evan Davies, *Patriotism on Parade: The Story of Veterans' and Hereditary Organizations in America, 1783–1900* (Cambridge, MA: Harvard University Press, 1955); and Stuart McConnell, *Glorious Contentment: The Grand Army of the Republic, 1865–1900* (Chapel Hill: University of North Carolina Press, 1992). William W. White treats the impact at the state level in the South of *The Confederate Veteran* (Tuxcaloosa, AL: Confederate, 1962). Theda Skocpol, *Protecting Soldiers and Mothers: The Political Origins of Social Policy in the United States* (Cambridge, MA: Harvard University Press, 1992), has emphasized that Civil War pensions constitute the foundation for the modern welfare state.

A comprehensive history of social welfare from 1850 through Reconstruction is Robert H. Bremner, *The Public Good: Philanthropy and Welfare in the Civil War Era* (New York: Alfred A. Knopf, 1980). Although Bremner appreciates the extent and efficacy of voluntarism during this period, his narrative makes clear that this was when Americans began to turn away from that principle. George H. Miller, *Railroads and the Granger Laws* (Madison: University of Wisconsin, 1971), is a solid exposition of the development of railroad regulation at the state level, and William R. Brock, *Investigation and Responsibility: Public Responsibility in the United States, 1865–1900* (Cambridge, U.K.: Cambridge University Press, 1984), traces the general development of state regulatory and data collecting agencies. An indispensable anthology on the postbellum northern states is James C. Mohr, ed., *Radical Republicans in the North: State Politics During Reconstruction* (Baltimore: Johns Hopkins University Press, 1976). It should come as no surprise that the Republican Party, then known as the Party of Piety, was in the vanguard of expanding government functions, whereas the Democratic Party, the Party of Personal Liberty, usually remained committed to *laissez faire*. Robin L. Einhorn, "The Civil War and Municipal Government in Chicago," from Maris A. Vinovskis, ed., *Toward a Social History of the American Civil War* (cited ch. 7) is a pioneering, suggestive study of the war's impact on urban government.

The development of medical licensing can be traced through William G. Rothstein, *American Physicians in the Nineteenth Century: From Sect to Science* Baltimore: Johns Hopkins Press, 1972), and Ronald Hamowy, "The Early Development of Medical Licensing Laws in the United States, 1875–1900," *Journal of Libertarian Studies*, 3 ([Spring] 1979), pp. 73–119. Hamowy includes a valuable historical table on the various medical laws enacted in all states. Joseph F. Kelt, *The Formation of the American Medical Profession: The Role of Institutions, 1780–1860* (New Haven: Yale University Press, 1968), confirms the lack of medical regulation before Fort Sumter. Although the American Medical Association had been founded in 1847, and twenty states plus the District of Columbia had experimented with some form of medical licensing prior to 1860, none of these effectively restricted entry.

On postal censorship laws, in addition to Dorothy Ganfield Fowler, *Unmailable* (cited ch. 10), see James C. N. Paul and Murray L. Schwartz, *Federal Censorship: Obscenity in the Mail* (New York: Free Press of Glencoe, 1961). David J. Pivar, *Purity Crusade: Sexual Morality and Social Control, 1868–1900* (Westport, CT: Greenwood Press, 1973), exposes the general drive for vice controls. A sardonic biography of perhaps America's most zealous and malicious bluenose is Heywood Broun and Margaret Leech, *Anthony Comstock: Roundsman of the Lord* (New York: Literary Guild of America, 1927). The best account of Comstock's persecution of Ezra Heywood is in Hal D. Sears, *The Sex Radicals: Free Love in High Victorian America* (Lawrence: Regents Press of Kansas, 1977). Sears notes that the radicals such as Heywood who took principled stands against government involvement with sexual matters were usually quite chaste in their personal morality.

Works that pursue the general operations of postwar American government are Leonard D. White, *The Republican Era, 1869–1901: A Study in Administrative History* (New York: Macmillan, 1958); Morton Keller, *Affairs of State: Public Life in Late Nineteenth Century America* (Cambridge, MA: Harvard University Press, 1977); and Richard Franklin Bensel, *Yankee Leviathan* (cited ch. 9). A good preliminary summary of government's expansion at all levels is Daniel J. Elazar's comment in the collection edited by David T. Gilchrist and W. David Lewis, *Economic Change in the Civil War Era* (cited ch. 9). Elazar appears to retreat from this original position in his new book, *Building Toward Civil War: Generational Rhythms in American Politics* (Latham, NY: Madison Books, 1992), which pushes back government expansion to the Mexican War, but his failure to adjust magnitudes for economic growth and sometimes even for population growth make his revised contention shaky.

Two examinations of the profound changes that the Civil War and Reconstruction wrought upon the U.S. Constitution are Bernard Schwartz, *From Confederation to Nation: The American Constitution, 1835–1877* (Baltimore: Johns Hopkins University Press, 1973), and Harold M. Hyman and William M. Wiecek, *Equal Justice Under Law: Constitutional Development, 1835–1875* (New York: Harper & Row, 1982), the latter part of the New American Nation series. The subtitle of another Hyman book, *A More Perfect Union: The Impact of the Civil War and Reconstruction on the Constitution* (cited ch. 5) is strangely misleading. Far more than a constitutional history, this conceptual treatise ranges through the war's impact at the state and local level as well as the national. Philip S. Paludan, *A Covenant With Death: The Constitution, Law, and Equality in the Civil War* (Urbana: University of Illinois Press, 1975), presents the views of Francis Lieber and other political thinkers of the period, while George M. Fredrickson, *The Inner Civil War* (cited ch. 8), surveys northern intellectuals generally. Although many of these historians, including White, Hyman, and Paludan, formally disagree with Fredrickson and belittle the nationalizing impact of the Civil War, this represents one of those classic cases where a glass can be described as half empty or half full. There was retrenchment after Appomattox and again during the Panic of 1873. From the perspective of the Franklin Roosevelt's New Deal or Lyndon Johnson's Great Society, post-Civil War government may seem feeble, especially if one focuses on the Supreme Court's rear-guard and half-hearted restraints on federal authority. To truly appreciate the immensity of the postwar gains in power, one must measure them against the virtually non-existent central, state, and local governments that preceded the conflict.

Epilogue

America's Turning Point

*The historian should be a hanging judge, for the muse of history is
not Clio but Rhadamanthus, the avenger of innocent blood.*

LORD ACTON[1]

The Civil War represents the simultaneous culmination and repudiation of the American Revolution. Four successive ideological
surges had previously defined American politics: the radical republican movement that had spearheaded the revolution itself; the
subsequent Jeffersonian movement that had arisen in reaction to
the Federalist State; the Jacksonian movement that followed the War
of 1812; and at length the abolitionist movement. Although each
was unique, each in its own way was hostile to government power.
Each had contributed to the secular erosion of all forms of coercive
authority.

Just one manifestation of this erosion, but a crucial one, related
to taxes. The United States Constitution was a counter-revolutionary
retreat from the far more libertarian Articles of Confederation.
Indeed, the American nationalists who gathered at Philadelphia in
1787 had hoped to grant the central government plenary powers.
Their dream was partially thwarted, just as America's Constitutional myth has it, through compromises worked out within the
convention itself. More effectual was Anti-Federalist reaction
when the new document was placed before the public. Majorities in
six state ratifying conventions, and minorities in two others, in-

sisted upon further amendments to circumscribe the new government's sphere. These proposals found their way into the Bill of Rights.

The Bill of Rights, however, artfully omitted one change universally desired by the states requesting amendments. Most Anti-Federalists, although willing to let the central government collect import duties, wanted internal taxes confined to the states. Without this limitation enshrined in the new Constitution, George Washington's Secretary of the Treasury, Alexander Hamilton, was able to impose a variety of internal levies as part of his ambitious financial program. Yet in the long run, popular opposition to the whiskey tax and other excises was the Federalists' undoing. All the internal taxes were repealed once Thomas Jefferson was elected President in 1800. Except for a brief span during the War of 1812, the central government's sole sources of revenue remained—until the Civil War—import duties and land sales. The opponents of national authority had not secured a written amendment confining the two levels of government to independent sources of revenue, but this came to be the exact way the system operated in practice: external taxes for the central government and internal taxes for the states. This structural independence, probably as much as any other factor, made state secession a realistic option.

"Nowhere was the American rejection of authority more complete than in the political sphere," writes historian David Donald. "The decline in the powers of the Federal government from the constructive centralism of George Washington's administration to the feeble vacillation of James Buchanan's is so familiar as to require no repetition here. . . . The national government, moreover, was not being weakened in order to bolster state governments, for they too were decreasing in power. . . . By the 1850's the authority of all government in America was at a low point."[2] The United States, already one of the most prosperous and influential countries on the face of the earth, had practically the smallest, weakest State apparatus. The great irony of the Civil War is that all that changed at the very moment that abolition triumphed. As the last, great coercive blight on the American landscape, black chattel slavery, was finally extirpated—a triumph that cannot be overrated—the American polity did an about face.

Insofar as the war was fought to preserve the Union, it was an explicit rejection of the American Revolution. Both the radical abolitionists and the South's fire-eaters boldly championed different applications of the revolution's purest principles. Whereas the abolitionists were carrying on the assault against human bondage, the fire-eating secessionist embodied the tradition of self-determination and decentralized government. As a legal recourse, the legitimacy of secession was admittedly debatable. Consistent with the Anti-Federalist interpretation of the Constitution that had come to dominate antebellum politics, it undoubtedly contravened the framers' original intent. But as a revolutionary right, the legitimacy of secession is universal and unconditional. That at least is how the Declaration of Independence reads. "Put simply," agrees William Appleman Williams, "the cause of the Civil War was the refusal of Lincoln and other northerners to honor the revolutionary right of self-determination—the touchstone of the American Revolution."[3]

American nationalists, then and now, automatically assume that the Union's break up would have been catastrophic. The historian in particular "is a camp follower of the successful army," to quote David Donald again, and often treats the nation's current boundaries as etched in stone.[4] But doing so reveals lack of historical imagination. Consider Canada. The United States twice mounted military expeditions to conquer its neighbor, first during the American Revolution and again during the War of 1812. At other times, including after the Civil War, annexation was under consideration, sometimes to the point of private support for insurgencies similar to those that had helped swallow up Florida and Texas. If any of these ventures had succeeded, historians' accounts would read as if the unification of Canada and the United States was fated, and any other outcome inconceivable. In our world, of course, Canada and the United States have endured as separate sovereignties with hardly any untoward consequences. "Suppose Lincoln did save the American Union, did his success in keeping one strong nation where there might have been two weaker ones really entitle him to a claim to greatness?" asks David M. Potter. "Did it really contribute any constructive values for the modern world?"[5]

The common refrain, voiced by Abraham Lincoln himself, that

peaceful secession would have constituted a failure for the great American experiment in liberty was just plain nonsense. "If Northerners . . . had peaceably allowed the seceders to depart," the conservative London *Times* correctly replied, "the result might fairly have been quoted as illustrating the advantages of Democracy; but when Republicans put empire above liberty, and resorted to political oppression and war rather than suffer any abatement of national power, it was clear that nature at Washington was precisely the same as nature at St. Petersburg. . . . Democracy broke down, not when the Union ceased to be agreeable to all its constituent States, but when it was upheld, like any other Empire, by force of arms."[6]

As an excuse for civil war, maintaining the State's territorial integrity is bankrupt and reprehensible. Slavery's elimination is the only morally worthy justification. The fact that abolition was an unintended consequence in no way gainsays the accomplishment. "The nineteenth century was preeminently the century of emancipations," explains C. Vann Woodward. Small-scale emancipations began in the northern states during the previous century, and chattel slavery was not ended in coastal Kenya until 1907. But starting with the British colonies in 1833 and finishing with Brazil in 1888, over six million slaves achieved some kind of freedom in the Western Hemisphere. Four million were blacks in the United States. "The emancipation experience of the South," Woodward concludes, "dwarfs all others in scale and magnitude."[7]

Yet this justification holds only if war was indeed necessary. No abolition was completely peaceful, but the United States and Haiti are just two among twenty-odd slave societies where violence predominated. The fact that emancipation overwhelmed such entrenched plantation economies as Cuba and Brazil suggests that slavery was politically moribund anyway. An ideological movement that had its meager roots in the eighteenth century eventually eliminated everywhere a labor system that had been ubiquitous throughout world civilizations for millennia. Historical speculations about an independent Confederacy halting or reversing this overwhelming momentum are hard to credit.

When Lincoln took the presidential oath in 1861, letting the lower South secede in peace was a viable antislavery option. At the moment of Lincoln's inauguration the Union still retained more slave states than had left. Radical abolitionists, such as William Lloyd Garrison, had traditionally advocated northern secession from the South. They felt that this best hastened the destruction of slavery by allowing the free states to get out from under the Constitution's fugitive slave provision. Passionately opposing slavery and simultaneously favoring secession are therefore quite consistent. Yet hardly any modern account of the Union's fiery conflagration even acknowledges this untried alternative.

Revisionist Civil War historians at one time argued that slavery was *economically* doomed. Economists have subjected that claim to searching scrutiny, discovering in fact that American slavery was profitable and expanding. But as Eric Foner has perceptively noted, "plantation slavery had always been both a political and economic institution. It could not have existed without a host of legal and coercive measures designed to define the status of the black laborer and prevent the emergence of competing modes of social organization."[8] In the United States these measures included restrictions on manumission, disabilities against free blacks, compulsory slave patrols, and above all fugitive slave laws.

Slavery was doomed *politically* even if Lincoln had permitted the small Gulf Coast Confederacy to depart in peace. The Republican-controlled Congress would have been able to work toward emancipation within the border states, where slavery was already declining. In due course the Radicals could have repealed the Fugitive Slave Law of 1850. With chattels fleeing across the border and raising slavery's enforcement costs, the peculiar institution's final destruction within an independent cotton South was inevitable.

Even future Confederate Vice-President Alexander Stephens had judged "slavery much more secure in the Union than out of it."[9] Secession was a gamble of pure desperation for slaveholders, only attempted because the institution clearly had no political future within the Union. The individual runaway both helped provoke secession—northern resistance to fugitive recapture being a major southern grievance—and ensured that secession would be unable to shield slavery in the end. Back in 1842, Joseph Rogers Underwood, representing Kentucky in the House of Representatives, warned his fellow Southerners that "the dissolution of the Union was the dissolution of slavery." Why? "Just as soon as Mason and Dixon's line and the Ohio river become the boundary between independent nations, slavery ceases in all the border states. How could we retain our slaves, when they, in one hour, one day, or a week at furthest, could pass the boundary?" Once across, the slave could "then turn round and curse his master from the other shore." Nor would the peculiar institution's collapse stop at the border states. "Do you not see that sooner or later, this process would extend itself farther and farther south, rendering slave labor so precarious and uncertain that it could not be depended upon; and consequently a slave would become almost worthless; and thus the institution itself would gradually, but certainly, perish?"[10]

Just such a process later accelerated the demise of slavery in Brazil. This slave economy was in 1825 the New World's second largest, holding in bondage only slightly fewer than the American South. Yet even before Brazil's abolition, manumission caused free blacks to exceed slaves in total numbers, with an estimated half those manumissions through self-purchase. By 1850 free blacks were 43 percent of the population, making a large constituency opposed to slavery. Although the government instituted gradual emancipation in 1871, the law freed only slaves born after its enactment, and only when they reached the age of twenty-one. Brazil also established a tax fund to purchase the freedom of those to whom the law did not apply, but during its operation three times as many purchased their own freedom or were granted manumission.

Brazilian abolitionists meanwhile succeeded in outlawing slavery in the northeastern state of Ceará in 1884. An underground railroad immediately came into existence. Planters retaliated with a fugitive slave law, but the law was widely evaded. The state of Amazonas and many cities joined Ceará. Slavery rapidly disintegrated in the coffee growing region of São Paulo. The value of slaves fell by 80 percent despite the fact that none was slated to be liberated through gradual emancipation. Finally in 1888 the government accepted a *fait accompli* and decreed immediate and uncompensated emancipation. The total number of slaves had already declined from two and half million, or 30 percent of the population in 1850, to half a million, or less than 3 percent.

"Slavery could not last if the slaves had freedom within arm's length," recalled American abolitionist Moncure Conway. Slavery in the Cape Colony of southern Africa, for instance, depended upon the transportation of blacks from Mozambique and Madagascar and of east Indians. The so-called Hottentots, indigenous to the area, were nearly impossible to keep enslaved because they could escape too easily. Civil War runaways so weakened the peculiar institution that the Confederacy itself turned toward emancipating and arming blacks. Slavery thus neither explains nor justifies Northern suppression of secession. The Union war effort reduces, in the words of Conway, to "mere manslaughter."[11]

Brazilian abolitionists had also encouraged resistance by distributing arms to the slaves. An independent Confederacy still faced the specter of John Brown, who merely wished to bring the revolutionary right of secession down to the plantation. The massive uprising that Brown, Lysander Spooner, and David Walker each hoped for would obviously have resulted in much loss of life, but worth speculation is whether it could ever have approached the Civil War's unmatched toll: one dead soldier for every six freed slaves. The war took nearly as many lives as the total number of slaves liberated without bloodshed in the British West Indies. Those who complacently accept this as a necessary sacrifice for eliminating an evil institution inexplicably blanch at the potential carnage of slave revolts.

Violence ultimately ended slavery, but violence of a very different nature. Rather than revolutionary violence wielded by bondsmen themselves from the bottom up, a violence that at least had the potential to be pinpointed against the South's minority of guilty slaveowners, the Civil War involved indiscriminate State violence directed from the top down. Nor would an insurgency's economic devastation likely have reached the war's $6.6 billion cost (in 1860 prices), about evenly divided between the two sides.[12] The North's portion alone was enough to buy all slaves and set up each family with forty acres and a mule. John Brown's plan had the added advantage of actively mobilizing blacks in their own liberation. The social institutions that the revolutionaries would have ineluctably created could have altered the subsequent history of the southern race relations. On what consistent grounds can anyone find war between two governments morally superior to slave rebellion?

"War is the health of the State," proclaimed Randolph Bourne, the young progressive, disillusioned by the Wilson Administration's grotesque excesses during the First World War.[13] Bourne's maxim is true in two respects. During war itself, the government swells in size and power, as it taxes, conscripts, regulates, generates inflation, and suppresses civil liberties. Second, after the war ends there is what economists and historians have identified as a ratchet effect. Postwar retrenchment never returns government to its prewar levels. The State has assumed new functions, taken on new responsibilities, and exercised new prerogatives that continue long after the fighting is over. Both of these phenomena are starkly evident during the Civil War.

Yet the Civil War did something more. Despite wars and their ratchets, governments must *sometimes* recede in reach, else all would have been groaning under totalitarian regimes long ago. Both conservatives and liberals date the major political turning point in American history at the Great Depression of 1929. Previously Americans are supposed to have self-reliantly resisted the temptations of government largess and confined federal power within strict constitutional limits. Although Franklin D. Roosevelt's New Deal is responsible for Social Security, which now ranks as the national government's primary expense, this legend ignores several inconvenient facts. The New Deal to begin with simply emulated the Wilson Administration's previous war collectivism. Roosevelt's keystone agency, the National Recovery Administration, was a re-creation of the War Industries Board of the First World War; F.D.R.'s Agricultural Adjustment Administration was a reactivated wartime Food Administration; the New Deal's National Labor Relations Board trod the path blazed by the Wilson's National War Labor Board and War Labor Policies Board; and the Tennessee Valley Authority grew out of the government-owned nitrate and electric-power plants at Muscle Shoals built under the authority of the 1916 National Defense Act. Moreover, the growth of government under the New Deal was trivial in comparison to its growth during the United States' next major conflict: World War II. Between 1928 and 1938, annual national expenditures slightly more than doubled, from \$3.1 to \$6.8 billion. During the Second World War, federal spending peaked at \$98.3 billion in 1945. Overall, the national government spent about twice as much while fighting the war as during the preceding 150 years combined.

More astute analysts push the watershed in U.S. history back to the progressive era. Progressivism emerged at the beginning of the twentieth century as a diverse inclination, varying in different parts of the country and including members of all political parties. But it became the country's first dominant mindset to advocate government intervention over the free market and personal liberty at every level and in every sphere. My contention, however, is that America's decisive transition must be dated even earlier.

Let us put into evidence one more example, subtle but profound, of how the Civil War altered attitudes about government. Many of the American women who had thrown themselves into the abolitionist crusade had noticed obvious parallels between the slaves' legal status and their own. The 1830s were a time when women, in addition to being unable to vote, hold public office, or serve on juries, were considered wards of their nearest male relative or chattels of their husbands, who legally controlled all their property, earnings, and children. Female abolitionists had good cause to be grateful to the slave, remarked Abby Kelley. "In striving to strike his irons off, we found most surely that *we* were manacled-*ourselves.*"[14] As women embarked on public activity against slavery, they faced social discrimination not only from the public but also from male abolitionists. The issue helped split the American Anti-Slavery Society into warring factions in 1840. Because of these experiences, a group of female abolitionists organized the first women's rights convention in Seneca Falls, New York, in 1848, and the convention issued a declaration patterned upon the Declaration of Independence.

Although the new women's movement called attention to these inequities, it achieved on the whole paltry gains before the Civil War. But with emancipation, the movement's leaders expected this to change abruptly. The National Women's Loyal League collected over 400,000 signatures on petitions favoring the Thirteenth Amendment. They were therefore sorely disappointed when the

Fourteenth Amendment's second section, dealing with representation, confined its penalties to states that denied "male inhabitants" the vote. For the first time the word "male" had been put into the Constitution. Similarly feminists had suggested that the Fifteenth Amendment mention "sex" along with "race, creed, and previous condition of servitude" as illegitimate grounds for denying suffrage. Yet in its final form the amendment did no such thing.

Disillusioned, Elizabeth Cady Stanton and Susan B. Anthony organized the National Woman Suffrage Association in 1869. Concentrating nearly to the point of obsession on the right to vote, this organization signaled a dramatic conservative shift in the women's movement. Previously feminists had relied upon principled arguments demanding equality before the law as their natural right. Now they preferred pragmatic arguments that emphasized the moral superiority of women and the salutary effect their votes would have on public life. Leading suffragists were not above even appealing to white supremacists with assurances that white women were more likely to cast ballots than black. This change in emphasis partly resulted from women's postwar gains in areas other than suffrage, particularly with respect to property rights. But it also represented the incorporation of mainstream feminism into the broader drive for enlarged government guardianship. Woman's suffrage became intimately intertwined with progressivism and prohibition in a statist alliance for social purity. The defense of reproductive rights, sexual liberty, and free speech from government paternalism was left to a scattered remnant of individualists, such as Lillian Harman, Angela Heywood, and Ezra Heywood, who to this day remain forgotten in the mainstream histories of feminism.

The Yankee Leviathan co-opted and transformed feminism the same way it had co-opted and transformed abolitionism. It had shattered the prewar congruence between antislavery, anti-government, and anti-war radicalism. It had permanently reversed the implicit constitutional settlement that had made the central and state governments revenue-independent. It had acquired for central authority such new functions as subsidizing privileged businesses, managing the currency, providing welfare to veterans, and protecting the nation's morals—at the very moment that local and state governments were also expanding. And it had set dangerous precedents with respect to taxes, fiat money, conscription, and the suppression of dissent.

These and the countless other changes that fill the previous pages mark the Civil War as America's real turning point. In the years ahead, coercive authority would wax and wane with year-to-year circumstances, but the long-term trend would be unmistakable. Henceforth there would be no more major victories of Liberty over Power. In contrast to the whittling away of government that had preceded Fort Sumter, the United States had commenced its halting but inexorable march toward the welfare-warfare State of today.

Epilogue
Bibliographical Essay

Donald Livingston—in his essay "The Secession Tradition in America," from David Gordon, ed., *The Political Economy of Secession* (Auburn, AL: Ludwig von Mises Institute, forthcoming)—has called secession "the most under-theorized concept in political philosophy." That is what makes Allen Buchanan's *Secession: The Morality of Political Divorce From Fort Sumter to Lithuania and Quebec* (Boulder, CO: Westview Press, 1991) so notable, even though Buchanan qualifies his moral endorsement of secession with the hairsplitting typical of philosophers. Harry Beran does a similar, if much shorter, analysis in "A Liberal Theory of Secession," *Political Studies,* 32 (March 1984), pp. 21–31, whereas Anthony H. Birch, "Another Liberal Theory of Secession," *Political Studies,* 32 (December 1984), pp. 596–602, criticizes even Beran's limited defense of this principle as too permissive. A prior discussion concerned mostly with secession under international law is Lee C. Bucheit, *Secession: The Legitimacy of Self Determination* (New Haven: Yale University Press, 1978).

The reader may have figured out that my support for this revolutionary right is unconditional. Unfortunately, a history book does not provide the appropriate forum to defend such a theoretical position at length. Robert W. McGee, however, begins to outline the case in "Secession Reconsidered," *Journal of Libertarian Studies,* 11 (Fall 1994), pp. 11–33. Allen Buchanan at least agrees that preserving the Union cannot morally justify preventing secession. Only the abolition of slavery suffices.

The nationalism of most historians, on the other hand, is usually an "unstated major premise," to borrow a phrase from Oliver Wendell Holmes, Jr., although David M. Potter has explored "The Historian's Use of Nationalism and Vice Versa" (cited prologue). Three other writings from the prologue share my unqualified support for southern self-determination: William Appleman Williams's *America Confronts a Revolutionary World;* John S. Rosenberg's *American Scholar* article "Toward a New Civil War Revisionism"; and Joseph R. Stromberg's *Journal of Libertarian Studies* article, "The War for Southern Independence: A Radical Libertarian Perspective." An older critique of nationalism disfigured by paternalistic racism is Richard H. Shryock, "The Nationalistic Tradition of the Civil War," *South Atlantic Quarterly,* 32 (July 1933), pp. 294–305. With respect to the Civil War's ending slavery, the patriarch of New Left historians, Williams put it best (p. 113): "it is the right and responsibility of Blacks—and any other people, including ourselves—to self-determine themselves."

Phillip S. Paludan attempts to answer Rosenberg's article in "The American Civil War: Triumph Through Tragedy," *Civil War History,* 20 (September 1974), pp. 239–250. The strongest of Paludan's arguments relate to slavery. He thinks slave revolts in an independent Confederacy highly unlikely. Paludan ignores the impact of fugitive slaves, but his speculations are far better grounded than the fantastic scenario of Robert Fogel in the Afterword of *Without Consent or Contract* (cited ch. 2). Fogel foresees the Confederacy, if permitted to survive, leading a worldwide reaction against liberalism that, among other transgressions, would have blocked passage within Great Britain of the Reform Bill of 1867.

Discussing what would have happened if secession had been triumphant unfortunately raises the bugaboo of "counterfactual history." Such speculations are supposed to be *verboten* among serious historians. Yet every causal statement, historical or otherwise, contains an implicit counterfactual. As economic historian William N. Parker reasons (in "The South in the National Economy, 1865–1970," *Southern Economic Journal*, 46 [April 1980], p. 1039), "an historian has no [other] choice if he wants to think about history, unless he wishes to accept a fatalistic position of sheer determinism." The more precise and complete the causation in any historian's account, the more definite the implied counterfactuals. Without the stipulated causes, something would have turned out differently. Mindless description is the only alternative.

As for Fogel's international repercussions, one could more plausibly contend that, whatever might have happened, in actuality Northern victory dealt classical liberalism a mortal blow. To follow a cue from Potter's contribution on the "Civil War," in C. Vann Woodward, ed., *The Comparative Approach to American History* (cited ch. 2), the war brought about an early conjunction of liberalism and nationalism, which was soon emulated elsewhere and (although Potter would not go this far) was fatal to liberalism. We do know that Republican protectionism was the first major step away from the fragile ascendancy of international free trade, only recently achieved via repeal of Britain's Corn Laws and the Cobden-Chevalier Treaty. High tariffs were picked up by the Prussian corporate-State, which then became an inspiring model for American progressives.

For my account of Brazilian emancipation, I have drawn heavily on Herbert S. Klein, *African Slavery in Latin America and the Caribbean* (cited ch. 2), which provides an excellent introduction to slave societies throughout the New World. More particulars are in Robert Conrad, *The Destruction of Brazilian Slavery, 1850–1888* (Berkeley: University of California Press, 1972), and Robert Bren Toplin, *The Abolition of Slavery in Brazil* (New York: Atheneum, 1972).

The historical literature on the republicanism of the American Revolution and its Jeffersonian and Jacksonian successors is too overwhelming to do justice to here. Some important works have been mentioned in previous chapters, especially those relating to slavery or the Jacksonian period. Just a few highlights: Bernard Bailyn, *The Ideological Origins of the American Revolution* (cited ch. 1), on the radicalism of the revolution; Gordon S. Wood, *The Creation of the American Republic, 1776–1787* (Chapel Hill: University of North Carolina Press, 1969), on the Constitution as ideological counter-revolution; E. James Ferguson, *The Power of the Purse: A History of American Public Finance, 1776–1790* (Chapel Hill: University of North

Carolina Press, 1961), on Federalist fiscal ambitions; and Thomas P. Slaughter, *The Whiskey Rebellion: Frontier Epilogue to the American Revolution* (New York: Oxford University Press, 1986), on the importance of tax resistance to the Jeffersonian movement. Special mention goes to Herbert J. Storing, *What the Anti-Federalists Were FOR* (Chicago: University of Chicago Press, 1981), not only as the best survey of the ideas of the Constitution's opponents but also for calling attention to the Anti-Federalist desire for revenue independence.

In addition to her seminal work on Garrison and abolitionism, Aileen S. Kraditor is responsible for the first study to emphasize the Civil War transformation of feminism: *The Ideas of the Women's Suffrage Movement, 1890–1920* (New York: Columbia University Press, 1965). Since then Ellen Carol Dubois has supplied greater detail on the transition period in *Feminism and Suffrage: The Emergence of an Independent Women's Movement in America, 1848–1869* (Ithaca, NY: Cornell University Press, 1978). Blanche Glassman Hersh, *The Slavery of Sex* (cited ch. 1), covers women abolitionists, and Catherine Clinton, *The Other Civil War: American Women in the Nineteenth Century* (New York: Hill and Wang, 1984), gives a general background on the changing status of women. An important new biography, Dorothy Sterling, *Ahead of Her Time: Abby Kelley and the Politics of Antislavery* (New York: W. W. Norton, 1991), is about one of the founders of the women's movement, who was practically written out of its history by Susan B. Anthony and Elizabeth Cady Stanton because of her consistent hostility to voting. For the postwar period's all-but-forgotten individualist feminists, see Hal D. Sears, *The Sex Radicals* (cited last chapter), and Wendy McElroy, "The Roots of Individualist Feminism in 19th-Century America," in McElroy, ed., *Freedom, Feminism, and the State: An Overview of Individualist Feminism*, 2nd edn. (New York: Holmes & Meier, 1991).

On war as the health of the State there is no better place to start than Randolph Bourne's writings. "The War and the Intellectuals" first appeared in *The Seven Arts*, 2 (June 1917), pp. 133–146. "The State" was first published, posthumously and in incorrect sequence, under the title "Unfinished Fragment on the State," in *Untimely Papers* (New York: B. W. Huebsch, 1919), a collection of Bourne's essays edited by James Oppenheim. A later collection, *War and the Intellectuals: Essays by Randolph Bourne, 1915–1919* (New York: Harper & Row, 1964), includes both and corrects the earlier version of "The State." The essays also appear in the most useful Bourne anthology, Olaf Hansen, ed., *The Radical Will: Selected Writings, 1911–1918* (New York: Urizen Books, 1977). Louis Filler's older biography, *Randolph Bourne* (Washington: American Council on Public Affairs, 1943), perpetuates exaggerated legends, whereas John Adam Moreau, *Randolph Bourne: Legend and Reality* (Washington: Public Affairs Press, 1966), is more objective.

One of the most profound discussions of war and government is Murray Rothbard's compact "War, Peace and the State," reprinted in his *Egalitarianism as a Revolt Against Nature: And Other Essays* (cited ch. 3). Bruce D.

Porter, *War and the Rise of the State: The Military Foundations of Modern Politics* (New York: Free Press, 1994), is a new work that explores this connection throughout history. Excellent on the war-related origins of European States are the articles in the collection edited by Charles Tilly, *The Formation of National States in Western Europe* (Princeton, NJ: Princeton University Press, 1975), and his own, "War Making and State Making as Organized Crime," from Peter B. Evans, Dietrich Rueschemeyer, and Theda Skocpol, eds., *Bringing the State Back In* (Cambridge, U.K.: Cambridge University Press, 1985).

There is so far no single survey on the relationship between war and the power of the United States government. The closest is Robert Higgs, *Crisis and Leviathan: Critical Episodes in the Growth of American Government* (New York: Oxford University Press, 1987). Higgs, however, only covers from the 1890s, and includes both wars and depressions among his crises. This obscures the fact that, prior to the Great Depression, economic slumps generally brought government retrenchment rather than expansion. Yet no work deserves more credit than *Crisis and Leviathan* for popularizing knowledge of war's ratchet phenomenon, although its naming dates back at least to Bruce D. Porter, "Parkinson's Law Revisited: War and the Growth of Government," *The Public Interest*, no. 60 (Summer 1980), pp. 50–68, an examination of the federal bureaucracy in the twentieth century. A technical exploration of potential causes is Higgs, "Crisis, Bigger Government, and Ideological Change: Two Hypothesis on the Ratchet Phenomenon," *Explorations in Economic History*, 22 (January 1985), pp. 1–28.

Good on divulging the fiscal effect of U.S. wars is M. Slade Kendrick, *A Century and a Half of Federal Expenditures* (New York: National Bureau of Economic Research, 1955). Arthur A. Ekirch, Jr., *The Civilian and the Military: A History of the American Antimilitarist Tradition* (New York: Oxford University Press, 1965), is primarily concerned with war's impact on antimilitarist movements but also provides a somewhat sketchy account of its impact on government activity. Deservedly obscure is James L. Abrahamson, *The American Home Front: Revolutionary War, Civil War, World War I, World War II* (Washington: National Defense University Press, [1988]), an economically illiterate effort to show war's social benefits. For a comparison of the wartime growth of State power in the U.S., Britain, France, and Germany, see Clinton Rossiter, *Constitutional Dictatorship: Crisis Government in Modern Democracies* (Princeton, NJ: Princeton University Press, 1948). Rossiter credits the United States with the least bad record of any Western democracy.

In contrast, some of the standard overviews—Howard White, *Executive Influence in Determining Military Policy in the United States*, 2v. (Urbana: University of Illinois, 1925); Louis Smith, *American Democracy and Military Power: A Study of Civil Control of the Military Power in the United States* (Chicago: University of Chicago Press, 1951); Samuel P. Huntington, *The Soldier and the State: The Theory and Politics of Civil-Military Relations* (Cambridge, MA: Harvard University Press, 1957); Abraham D. Sofaer and

Henry Bartholomew Cox, *War, Foreign Affairs, and Constitutional Power*, 2v. (Cambridge, MA: Ballinger, 1976–1984); and Francis D. Wormuth and Edwin B. Firmage, *To Chain the Dog of War: The War Power of Congress in History and Law*, 2nd edn. (Urbana: University of Illinois Press, 1989)—are overwhelmingly preoccupied with the purely administrative and secondary questions of civilian control over the military or of which civilians— President, Congress, or the states—dictate policy.

Higgs's *Crisis and Leviathan* is noteworthy for another reason. It brings ideology back into economic analysis. The discipline has slighted ideology, although public-choice theory is still responsible for one outstanding service to the study of political history. It has developed a rigorous explanation for what we repeatedly observe in the real world: the inordinate influence of special interests on governments, including democratic governments. By consistently applying the free-rider problem to political action, public choice demonstrates that the State has strong incentives to respond to concentrated groups but weak incentives to respond to the general public. It therefore leaves us unsurprised that the Slave Power dominated the antebellum U.S. government.

Public choice, however, raises an across-the-board objection to almost all genuine improvements in policy. According to its predictions, rent seeking should leave every country sunk in the gravity well of a client-centered, power-broker State. Mancur Olson, for instance, in *The Rise and Decline of Nations: Economic Growth, Stagflation, and Social Rigidities* (New Haven: Yale University Press, 1982), has to rely upon unexplained historical accidents—wars, revolutions, and particularly conquests—to sweep away existing distributional coalitions, so that politics can start afresh with a clean slate. Douglass C. North, *Structure and Change in Economic History* (New York: W. W. Norton, 1981), concedes that "the economic historian who has constructed his model in neoclassical terms has built into it a fundamental contradiction since there is no way for the neoclassical model to account for a good deal of the change we observe in history" (pp. 10–11).

"Casual observation . . . confirms the immense number of cases where large group action does occur and is a fundamental force for change," he adds. To explain those cases where public-spirited mass movements overcome the free-rider problem and achieve significant gains against State power, North must join Higgs to rediscover ideology. Ideology, which historians have known is vital all along, motivates people to do more for social change than the material rewards to each individual would justify. Abolitionism was just such an ideological movement. Like the American revolutionaries, the Jeffersonians, and the Jacksonians, the abolitionists overcame free-rider disincentives in order to roll back coercive authority. Their ideological altruism generated a cascade of what economists call "positive externalities" that eventually destroyed chattel slavery.

The tragedy of American abolitionism is that victory came through a nationalistic war, rather than a peaceful separation as originally envisaged. Before Fort Sumter, to couch my epilogue's argument in public-choice phraseology, ideology had always in the long run trumped political rent seeking. The Civil War not only exhibited what had been witnessed in all previous American wars: an explosion in State power that was not completely undone by postwar cutbacks. It also enfeebled the country's ideological sinews, ravaged its ideological immune system, and left it politically susceptible to special interests. Liberty lost the revolutionary momentum of prewar years and was thereafter on the defensive.

Conventional wisdom often contrasts wild-eyed, intransigent, and fanatical abolitionists with a moderate, temporizing, and humane Abraham Lincoln. Yet before Lincoln was elected President, the radical abolitionists never proposed extinguishing slavery in a war of self-immolation. Although most of them eventually were seduced by the conflict's nationalism, ultimate responsibility for the enormous bloodshed rests squarely on the President's shoulders. Conventional wisdom should be turned on its head. The Civil War directly resulted from Lincoln's policy of political compromise, as harnessed in the interests of the nation-State, and not from the ideological radicalism of principled abolitionists.

Notes

Prologue: America's Crisis

1 Address before the Young Men's Lyceum of Springfield, Illinois, 27 January 1838, in Roy P. Basler, ed., *The Collected Works of Abraham Lincoln* (New Brunswick, NJ: Rutgers University Press, 1953), v. 1, p. 114. The young Lincoln was warning about the potential danger of a future Napoleon subverting the United States Constitution. The full quotation reads: "Towering genius disdains a beaten path. It seeks regions hitherto unexplored. It sees *no distinction* in adding story to story, upon the monuments of fame, erected to the memory of others. It *denies* that it is glory enough to serve under any chief. It *scorns* to tread in the footsteps of *any* predecessor, however illustrious. It thirsts and burns for distinction; and, if possible, it will have it, whether at the expense of emancipating slaves, or enslaving freemen. Is it unreasonable then to expect, that some man possessed of the loftiest genius, coupled with ambition sufficient to push it to its utmost stretch, will at some time, spring up among us? And when such a one does, it will require the people to be united with each other, attached to the government and laws, and generally intelligent, to successfully frustrate his designs."

2 *Philadelphia Morning Pennsylvanian* (4 March 1861), as quoted by Kenneth M. Stampp, *And the War Came: The North and the Secession Crisis, 1860–61* (Baton Rouge: Louisiana State University Press, 1950), p. 197.

3 James D. Richardson, ed., *A Compilation of the Messages and Papers of the Presidents* (Washington: Bureau of National Literature, 1922), v. 7, pp. 3214–15.

4 Grady McWhiney, "Preface," from McWhiney, ed., *Grant, Lee, Lincoln and the Radicals* ([Evanston, IL]: Northwestern University Press, 1964), p. v.

5 Eric Foner, *Free Soil, Free Labor, Free Men: The Ideology of the Republican Party Before the Civil War* (New York: Oxford University Press, 1970), p. 316. Kenneth M. Stampp, in the introduction to the collection he edited, *The Causes of the Civil War*, rev. edn. (Englewood Cliffs, NJ: Prentice-Hall, 1974), p. 3, poses the same two questions but adds a third preliminary one: "What caused the North and South to engage in ceaseless controversy for more than a generation?"

Chapter 1: Slavery and States' Rights in the Early Republic

1 Jay to the English Anti-Slavery Society, [1788], Henry P. Johnston, ed., *The Correspondence and Public Papers of John Jay* (New York: G. P. Putnam's Sons, 1890–93), v. 3, p. 342.

2 Jefferson, "Autobiography," in Merrill D. Peterson, ed., *Thomas Jefferson: Writings* (New York: Library of America, 1984), p. 44.

3 Jefferson to John Holmes, 22 April 1820, *ibid.*, pp. 1433–35.

4 Charles R. King, ed., *The Life and Correspondence of Rufus King: Comprising His Letters, Private and Official, His Public Documents, and His Speeches* (New York: G. P. Putnam's Sons, 1894–1900), v. 6, pp. 699–700.

5 *Annals of Congress*, 18th Cong., 1st sess. (30 January 1824), p. 1308.

6 Resolution of 19 December 1828, reprinted in Henry Steele Commager and Milton Cantor, eds., *Documents of American History*, 10th edn. (Englewood Cliffs, NJ: Prentice-Hall, 1988), v. 1, p. 251.

7 Fort Hill address, 26 July 1831, Robert L. Meriwether, *et. al.*, eds., *The Papers of John C. Calhoun* (Columbia: University of South Carolina Press, 1959–), v. 11, p. 415.

8 *Ibid.*

9 *Congressional Register*, 21st Cong., 1st sess. (27 January 1830), v. 1, p. 74.

10 *Ibid.*, p. 80.

11 Calhoun to Virgil Maxcy, 11 September 1830, Meriwether, *The Papers of John C. Calhoun*, v. 11, p. 229.

12 *The Liberator*, 1 (1 January 1831), p. 1.

13 *The Liberator*, 1 (13 August 1831), p. 129.

14 Speech delivered at Rochester, New York, 5 July 1852, John W. Blassingame, ed., *The Frederick Douglass Papers; Series One: Speeches, Debates and Interviews* (New Haven: Yale University Press, 1979–1992), v. 2, p. 383.

15 D. W. Siler to Governor Z. B. Vance, 3 November 1862, U.S. War Department, *The War of the Rebellion: A Compilation of the Official Records of the Union and Confederate Armies* (Washington: Government Printing Office, 1880–1901), ser. 1, v. 18, pp. 772–73.

16 *Congressional Globe*, 25th Cong., 2nd sess. (10 January 1838) appendix, pp. 61–62.

17 *Ibid.*, 35th Cong., 1st sess. (4 March 1858), p. 962.

18 George Fitzhugh, *Sociology for the South: Or the Failure of Free Society* (Richmond: A. Morris, 1854), p. 245. Incidentally, this was one of the first books in English to employ the term "sociology."

19 *Ibid.*, pp. 30, 170, 179. Jefferson's original statement, "the mass of mankind has not been born with saddles on their backs, nor a favored few booted and spurred, ready to ride them legitimately," appears in his letter to Roger C. Weightman, 24 June 1826, Peterson, *Thomas Jefferson*, p. 1517.

20 As quoted in "Late Southern Convention at Montgomery," *De Bow's Review*, new ser., 24 (June 1858), p. 585.

21 As quoted in William Goodell, *The American Slave Code in Theory and Practice: Its Distinctive Features Shown by its Statutes, Judicial Decisions, and Illustrative Facts* (New York: American & Foreign Anti-Slavery Society, 1853), p. 384.

22 Alexis de Tocqueville, *Democracy in America*, trans. by George Lawrence (New York: Harper & Row, 1969), v. 1, p. 342.

23 Congressman John S. Chipman of Michigan, *Congressional Globe*, 29th Cong., 2nd sess. (8 February 1847), appendix, p. 322.

24 Introduction to Owen and Joseph C. Lovejoy, *Memoir of the Reverend Elijah P. Lovejoy* (New York: John S. Taylor, 1838), p. 12.

25 Liberty Party Platform of 1844, in Donald Bruce Johnson, ed., *National Party Platforms*, rev. edn. (Urbana: University of Illinois Press, 1978), v. 1, p. 5.

26 *Ibid.*, p. 4.

Chapter 2: The Political Economy of Slavery and Secession

1 C. F. McCay, "Cultivation of Cotton," in *Eighty Years' Progress of the United States: A Family Record of American Industry, Energy and Enterprise* (Hartford: L. Stebbins, 1867), p. 116.

2 Robert William Fogel and Stanley L. Engerman, *Time on the Cross*, v. 2, *Evidence and Methods—A Supplement* (Boston: Little, Brown, 1974), p. 117, estimate $34.13 per year at 1860 prices for the average slave, and $48.12 per year for adult males. Roger L. Ransom and Richard Sutch, *One Kind of Freedom: The Economic Consequences of Emancipation* (Cambridge, U.K.: Cambridge University Press, 1977), p. 3, estimate an average of $28.95. Richard K. Vedder, "The Slave Exploitation (Expropriation) Rate," *Explorations in Economic History*, 12 (October 1975), 453–57, uses $30 per year. We should note that all dollar figures in this chapter are at 1860 prices unless otherwise indicated.

3 Jonathan Hughes, *American Economic History*, 3rd edn. (New York: HarperCollins, 1990), p. 234.

4 Frederick Douglass, *My Bondage and My Freedom* (1855; reprint edn., Chicago: Johnson, 1970), p. 115.

5 Address before the South Carolina Institute, 1850, *De Bow's Review*, old ser., 8 (June 1850), p. 518.

6 Thomas Sowell, *Markets and Minorities* (New York: Basic Books, 1981), p. 94.

7 David Brion Davis, "Slavery," in C. Vann Woodward, ed., *The Comparative Approach to American History* (New York: Basic Books, 1968), p. 128.

8 Bureau of the Census, Department of Commerce, *Negro Population: 1790–1815* (Washington: Government Printing Office, 1918), p. 55.

9 John E. Moes, "The Economics of Slavery in the Ante Bellum South: Another Comment," *Journal of Political Economy*, 68 (April 1960), p. 184.

10 Edmund Ruffin, *The Political Economy of Slavery; or, The Institution Considered in Regard to Its Influence on Public Wealth and General Welfare* ([Washington]: Lemuel Towers, 1853), p. 4.

11 Fogel and Engerman, *Time on the Cross*, v. 2, pp. 160–61. Fogel and Engerman estimate that an annual wage of $128 would have been necessary to get free workers to provide gang labor on large plantations. The imputed annual wage that free farmers earned on their family farms was $53, while the annual increase in labor's marginal value product resulting from economies of scale on large plantations was $23. Thus $128 − ($53 + $23) = $52. Unfortunately, this hinges on Fogel and Engerman's debatable contention that in the South agricultural slaves were 28 percent more productive per hour of labor than free workers.

12 Robert William Fogel and Stanley L. Engerman, *Time on the Cross*, v. 1, *The Economics of American Negro Slavery* (Boston: Little, Brown, 1974), p. 245. The extra output was worth $30 million, the total non-pecuniary loss to the slaves was $90 million, for a deadweight loss of $60 million *worldwide*. But according to Fogel and Engerman's calculations, $14 million of the $30 million gain went to cotton consumers outside the South, driving up the net loss for the South alone to $74 million.

13 *Ibid.*, p. 246.

14 George Fitzhugh, *Sociology for the South: Or the Failure of Free Society* (Richmond: A. Morris, 1854), pp. 144–45.

15 Frances Henderson, as quoted in Benjamin Drew, *The Refugee: Or the Narratives of Fugitive Slaves in Canada* (Boston: John P. Jewett, 1856), p. 156–57.

16 These estimates come from Robert William Fogel and Stanley L. Engerman, "The Economics of Slavery," in Fogel and Engerman, eds., *The Reinterpretation of American Economic History* (New York: Harper & Row, 1971), pp. 333–38, which in turn are based upon the work of Richard A. Easterlin, "Regional Income Trends, 1840–1950," in Seymour Harris, ed., *American Economic History* (New York: McGraw-Hill, 1961), pp. 185–243, and also reprinted in the Fogel and Engerman collection, pp. 38–49.

17 John A. James, "The Optimal Tariff in the Antebellum United States," *American Economic Review*, 71 (September 1981), pp. 726–734, especially Figure 2.

18 Claudia Goldin, "The Economics of Emancipation," *Journal of Economic History*, 33 (March 1973), pp. 66–85, provides the more often cited lower figure. The higher comes from Louis Rose, "Capital Losses of Southern Slaveholders Due to Emancipation," *Western Economic Journal*, 3 (Fall 1964), pp. 39–51. Roger L. Ransom and Richard Sutch, "Capitalists Without Capital: The Burden of Slavery and the Impact of Emancipation," *Agricultural History*, 62 (Summer 1988), pp. 133–160, put the number at $3.1 billion, midway between the two.

19 "Letter to an English Abolitionist [Thomas Clarkson]," 28 January

1845, Drew Gilpin Faust, ed., *The Ideology of Slavery: Proslavery Though in the Antebellum South, 1830–1860* (Baton Rouge: Louisiana State University Press, 1981), p. 198.

20 "Prigg *v.* The Commonwealth of Pennsylvania," 16 *Peters* 539 (1842).

21 Faulkner to John C. Calhoun, 15 July 1847, Chauncey C. Boucher and Robert P. Brooks, eds., *Correspondence Addressed to John C. Calhoun, 1837–1849* (Washington: American Historical Association, 1929), pp. 385–87.

22 *Ibid.*

23 Charles M. Wiltse, ed., *David Walker's Appeal, in Four Articles; Together with a Preamble, to the Coloured Citizens of the World, But in Particular, and Very Expressly, to Those of the United States of America* (New York: Hill and Wang, 1965), pp. 25, 69–70.

24 " 'Abolition Insolence'," reprinted in Lawrence H. White, ed., *Democratick Editorials: Essays in Jacksonian Political Economy by William Leggett* (Indianapolis: LibertyPress, 1984), pp. 228–230.

25 As quoted in Bertram Wyatt-Brown, "William Lloyd Garrison and Antislavery Unity: A Reappraisal," *Civil War History*, 13 (Mar 1967), p. 17. Spooner's actual circular, "A Plan for the Abolition of Slavery," is reprinted in Charles Shively, ed., *The Collected Works of Lysander Spooner* (Weston, MA: M & S Press, 1971), v. 4.

Chapter 3: The Slave Power Seeks Foreign Conquest

1 *Annals of Congress*, 18th Cong., 1st sess. (31 March 1824), p. 1978.

2 10 July 1832, James D. Richardson, ed., *A Compilation of the Messages and Papers of the Presidents* (Washington: Bureau of National Literature, 1922), v. 3, p. 1153.

3 [Benjamin Lundy], *The War in Texas: A Review of Facts and Circumstances, Showing That This Contest Is the Result of a Long Premeditated Crusade . . .*, 2nd edn. (Philadelphia: Merrihew and Gunn, 1837), p. 64.

4 Jackson to Major William B. Lewis, 8 April 1844, John Spencer Bassett, ed., *Correspondence of Andrew Jackson* (Washington: Carnegie Institution of Washington, 1926–1933), v. 6, p. 278.

5 Calhoun to William R. King, 12 August 1844, Robert L. Meriwether, *et. al.*, eds., *The Papers of John C. Calhoun* (Columbia: University of South Carolina Press, 1959–), v. 19, p. 571.

6 *Ibid*, pp. 574–76.

7 Address to the people of the free states of the Union, 3 March 1843, as reprinted in Frederick W. Merk, *Slavery and the Annexation of Texas* (New York: Alfred A. Knopf, 1972), p. 205.

8 *Ibid*, p. 210.

9 Ralph H. Orth and Alfred R. Ferguson, eds., *The Journals and*

Miscellaneous Notebooks of Ralph Waldo Emerson (Cambridge: Harvard University Press, 1971), v. 9, pp. 430–31.

10 *Congressional Globe,* 29th Cong., 1st sess. (8 August 1946), p. 1217.

11 *Ibid.,* p. 1214.

12 *Ibid.,* 29th Cong., 2nd sess. (19 February 1847), p. 454.

13 James G. Blaine, *Twenty Years of Congress: From Lincoln to Garfield, With a Review of Events Which Led to the Political Revolution of 1860* (Norwich, CT: Henry Bill, 1884), v. 1, p. 272

14 Letter from Samuel J. May, 4 August 1848, *National Anti-Slavery Standard,* 9 (17 August 1848), p. 47.

15 Speech at Albany, New York, Nov 1847, as quoted in Richard H. Sewell, *Ballots for Freedom: Antislavery Politics in the United States, 1837–1860* (New York: W. W. Norton, 1976), p. 173.

16 *Congressional Globe.,* 31st Cong., 1st sess. (13 December 1849), p. 28.

17 *Ibid.,* (4 March 1850), pp. 453–55.

18 *Ibid.,* (7 March 1850), p. 476.

19 Murat Halstead in William B. Hesseltine, ed., *Three Against Lincoln: Murat Halstead Reports the Caucuses of 1860* (Baton Rouge: Louisiana State University Press, 1960), p. 119.

20 Annual message to Congress, 2 December 1850, Richardson, *A Compilation of the Messages and Papers of the Presidents,* v. 6, p. 2629.

21 "The Author's Introduction," added to later editions of *Uncle Tom's Cabin: Or, Life Among the Lowly,* as reprinted in *The Writings of Harriet Beecher Stowe* (Boston: Houghton, Mifflin, 1896), v. 1, pp. lxii–iv.

22 Herbert Mitgang, ed., *Abraham Lincoln; A Press Portrait: His Life and Times From the Original Newspaper Documents of the Union, the Confederacy, and Europe* (Chicago: Quadrangle Books, 1971), p. 373.

23 Speech at Pittsburgh, Pennsylvania, 11 August 1852, John W. Blassingame, ed., *The Frederick Douglass Papers; Series One: Speeches, Debates and Interviews* (New Haven: Yale University Press, 1979–92), v. 2, p. 390.

24 *Congressional Globe,* 30th Cong., 1st sess (5 May 1848), appendix, p. 599.

25 Speech at Hazlehurst, Massachusetts, 11 September 1858, M. W. Cluskey, ed., *Speeches, Messages and Other Writings of the Hon. Albert G. Brown: A Senator in Congress From the State of Mississippi* (Philadelphia: Jas. B. Smith, 1859), p. 595.

26 Richardson, *Compilation of the Messages and Papers of the Presidents,* v. 6, pp. 2731–32.

27 Aix la Chapelle, 18 October 1854, 33rd Cong., 2nd sess., *House Executive Document No. 93,* p. 128.

Chapter 4: Emergence of the Republican Party

1 Douglas to J. H. Crane, D. M. Johnson, and L. J. Eastin, 17 December 1853, Robert W. Johannsen, ed., *The Letters of Stephen A. Douglas*

(Urbana: University of Illinois Press, 1961), p. 270.

2 19 January 1854, J. W. Schuckers, *Life and Public Services of Salmon Portland Chase: United States Senator and Governor of Ohio; Secretary of the Treasury, and Chief Justice of the United States* (New York: D. Appleton, 1874), pp. 141–17.

3 Buchanan to Nahum Capen, 27 August 1856, John Bassett Moore, ed., *The Works of James Buchanan: Comprising His Speeches, State Papers, and Private Correspondence* (Philadelphia: J. B. Lippincott, 1908–11), v. 10, p. 88.

4 *Congressional Globe*, 33rd Cong., 1st sess. (25 May 1854), appendix, p. 769.

5 *Missouri Republican* (31 August 1853), as quoted by William E. Parrish, *David Rice Atchison of Missouri, Border Politician* (Columbia: University of Missouri Press, 1961), p. 128; Atchison to Robert M. T. Hunter, 4 [April] 1855, Charles Henry Ambler, ed., *Correspondence of Robert M. T. Hunter, 1826–1876* (Washington: American Historical Association, 1918), p. 161.

6 Message to Congress, 2 February 1858, James D. Richardson, ed., *A Compilation of the Messages and Papers of the Presidents* (Washington: Bureau of National Literature, 1922), v. 7, p. 3010.

7 *Congressional Globe*, 35th Cong., 1st sess. (9 December 1857), p. 18.

8 "Dred Scott *v.* Sandford," 19 *Howard* 393 (1856).

9 *New York Daily Tribune*, 16 (7 March 1857), p. 4.

10 Springfield, Illinois, 16 June 1858, Roy P. Basler, ed., *The Collected Works of Abraham Lincoln* (New Brunswick, NJ: Rutgers University Press, 1953), v. 2, pp. 465–66.

11 Murat Halstead in William B. Hesseltine, ed., *Three Against Lincoln: Murat Halstead Reports the Caucuses of 1860* (Baton Rouge: Louisiana State University Press, 1960), p. 119.

12 Springfield, Illinois, 16 June 1858, Basler, *The Collected Works of Abraham Lincoln*, v. 2, pp. 461–62.

13 Alton, Illinois, 15 October 1858, Harold Holzer, ed., *The Lincoln-Douglas Debates: The First Complete, Unexpurgated Text* (New York: Harper-Collins, 1993), pp. 356–57. This phrasing differs slightly from previous renditions of the debate, because nearly all have been based on published transcripts that were edited and cleaned up for public circulation.

14 Ottawa, Illinois, 21 August 1858, *ibid.*, p. 55.

15 Charleston, Illinois, 18 September 1858, *ibid.*, p. 189.

16 *Ibid.*

17 Ottawa, Illinois, 21 August 1858, *ibid.*, p. 63.

18 Freeport, Illinois, 27 August 1858, *ibid.*, p. 106.

19 William Boyce, *Congressional Globe*, 36th Cong., 1st sess. (3 January 1860), p. 308.

20 Speech delivered at Cincinnati, Ohio, 27 April 1852, George W. Julian, *Speeches on Political Questions* (New York: Hurd and Houghton, 1872), pp. 74–75.

21 *Columbus* (Mississippi) *Democrat*, 22 July 1854, as quoted in Avery

Craven, *An Historian and the Civil War* (Chicago: University of Chicago Press, 1964), p. 38. I should mention that the order of Craven's footnotes 32 and 33 appears to have been inverted.

22 Hammond to Francis Lieber, 19 April 1860, in Thomas Sergeant Perry, ed., *The Life and Letters of Francis Lieber* (Boston: James R. Osgood, 1882), p. 310.

23 *Congressional Globe*, 33rd Cong., 1st sess. (16 March 1854), p. 648. Southerners suggested that Giddings actual remarks had been even more incendiary; see *ibid.*, 34th Cong., 3rd sess. (10 December 1856), p. 79. Nor was this the first time that Giddings had tormented southern colleagues with predictions about slave uprisings. Earlier occasions are *ibid.*, 29th Cong., 1st sess. (5 January 1846), p. 140, appendix, pp. 73–74, and 30th Cong., 1st sess. (25 April 1848), appendix, p. 523.

24 2 November 1859, John D. Lawson, ed., *American State Trials* (St. Louis: F. H. Thomas Law Books, 1914–1936), v. 6, p. 801.

25 Henry David Thoreau, "A Plea for Captain John Brown," *The Writings of Henry David Thoreau: With Bibliographical Introductions and Full Indexes* (Cambridge: Riverside Press, 1894), v. 10, p. 234.

26 Rochester, New York, 25 October 1858, George E. Baker, ed., *The Works of William Seward* (Boston: Houghton, Mifflin, 1884), v. 4, pp. 800–02.

Chapter 5: The Confederate States of America

1 "Declaration of Causes Which Induced the Secession of South Carolina," 24 December 1860, reprinted in Frank Moore, ed., *Rebellion Record: A Diary of American Events* (New York: G. P. Putnam and D. Van Nostrand, 1861–71), v. 1, documents, p. 4.

2 Speech at Free Soil Convention, Cleveland, Ohio, July 1849, *New York Times*, 1 (2 October 1851), [p. 4].

3 10 July 1860, as reprinted in Dwight Lowell Dumond, ed., *Southern Editorials on Secession* (New York: Century, 1931), p. 141.

4 As quoted in William Barney, *The Road to Secession: A New Perspective on the Old South* (New York: Praeger, 1972), p. 200.

5 Benjamin to Samuel L. M. Barlow, 9 December 1860, as quoted in James M. McPherson, *Battle Cry of Freedom: The Civil War Era* (New York: Oxford University Press, 1988), p. 237.

6 Savannah, Georgia, 11 March 1861, in Henry Cleveland, *Alexander H. Stephens in Public and Private: With Letters and Speeches Before, During, and Since the War* (Philadelphia: National, 1866), p. 721.

7 Letter written from California as quoted in Eli N. Evans, *Judah P. Benjamin: The Jewish Confederate* (New York: Free Press, 1988), p. 108.

8 As quoted in Roger W. Shugg, *Origins of Class Struggle in Louisiana: A Social History of White Farmers and Laborers During Slavery and After, 1840–1875* (Baton Rouge: Louisiana State University Press, 1939), p. 167.

9 Augusta, Georgia, 10 October 1864, Roland Dunbar, ed., *Jefferson Davis, Constitutionalist: His Letters, Papers and Speeches* (Jackson: Mississippi Department of Archives and History, 1923), v. 6, p. 357.

10 *New York Daily Tribune*, 20 (9 November 1860), p. 4.

11 First inaugural address, 4 March 1861, James D. Richardson, ed., *A Compilation of the Messages and Papers of the Presidents* (Washington: Bureau of National Literature, 1922), v. 7, pp. 3208–09.

12 *Ibid*, p. 3210.

13 *Ibid.*, pp. 3212–13.

14 Entry for 12 April 1861, C. Vann Woodward, ed., *Mary Chesnut's Civil War* (New Haven: Yale University Press, 1981), p. 46.

15 W. Dennison to Abraham Lincoln, 15 April 1861, U.S. War Department, *The War of the Rebellion: A Compilation of the Official Records of the Union and Confederate Armies* (Washington: Government Printing Office, 1880–1901), ser. 3, v. 1, p. 73.

16 Letcher to Simon Cameron, Secretary of War, 16 April 1861, *ibid.*, p. 76.

17 Resolution of 10 May 1861, reprinted in J. Thomas Scharf, *History of Maryland From the Earliest Period to the Present Day* (Baltimore: John B. Piet, 1879), v. 3, pp. 428–29.

18 "Ex parte Merryman," 17 *Federal Cases* 144–53 (1861).

19 Reprinted in Henry Steele Commager, ed., *The Blue and the Gray: The Story of the Civil War as Told by Participants* (Indianapolis: Bobbs-Merrill, 1950), v. 1, pp. 567–67.

20 Uriel Wright, as quoted in William E. Parrish, *Turbulent Partnership: Missouri and the Union, 1861–1865* (Columbia: University of Missouri Press, 1963), p. 24.

21 30 August 1861, *The War of the Rebellion*, ser. 1, v. 3, pp. 466–67.

22 Albert Castel, *A Frontier State at War: Kansas, 1861–1865* (Ithaca, NY: Cornell University Press, 1958), p. 63.

23 Colonel Bazel F. Lazear to his wife, 17 September 1863, in Vivian Kirkpatrick McLarty, ed., "The Civil War Letters of Colonel Bazel F. Lazear," *Missouri Historical Review*, 44 (July 1950), p. 391.

24 Lincoln to Orville H. Browning, 22 September 1861, Roy P. Basler, ed., *The Collected Works of Abraham Lincoln* (New Brunswick, NJ: Rutgers University Press, 1953), v. 4, p. 532.

25 26 May 1861, *War of the Rebellion*, ser. 1, v. 2, pp. 48–49.

Chapter 6: Mobilizing for Conflict

1 Speech at Springfield, Illinois, 14 & 26 August 1852, Roy P. Basler, ed., *The Collected Works of Abraham Lincoln* (New Brunswick, NJ: Rutgers University Press, 1953), v. 2, pp. 149–150.

2 Russell F. Weigley, *History of the United States Army*, enl. edn., (Bloomington: Indiana University Press, 1984), p. 157.

3 Ticknor to Sir Edmund Head, 21 April 1861, Anna Ticknor and George S. Hilliard, eds., *Life, Letters, and Journals of George Ticknor* (Boston: James R. Osgood, 1876), v. 2, p. 433.

4 Frank P. Peak, as quoted in Bell Irvin Wiley, *The Life of Johnny Reb: The Common Soldier of the Confederacy* (Indianapolis: Bobbs-Merrill, 1943), p. 15.

5 Anthony Trollope, *North America* (1862; reprint edn., New York: Alfred Knopf, 1951), p. 181.

6 *New York Times*, 10 (20 April 1861), p. 4.

7 *New York Daily Tribune*, 21 (26 Jun 1861), p. 4.

8 Henry N. Blake, *Three Years in the Army of the Potomac* (Boston: Lee and Shepard, 1865), pp. 22–23.

9 *Charleston Mercury*, 25 July 1861, as quoted in Douglas Southall Freeman, *Lee's Lieutenants: A Study in Command* (New York: Charles Scribner's Sons, 1946), v. 1, pp. 81–82. The actual events on the battlefield at the time are obscure, and Freeman has a review of various versions in Appendix V.

10 Message of 14 January 1863, *Journal of the Congress of the Confederate States of America* (Washington: Government Printing Office, 1905), v. 6, p. 3 [58th Cong., 2nd sess., Document No. 234].

11 George Hamilton Perkins, letter of 27 April 1862, in Susan G. Perkins, ed., *Letters of Captain Geo. Hamilton Perkins, U.S.N., Edited and Arranged: Also a Sketch of His Life*, 2nd edn. (Concord, NH: Rumford Press, 1901), pp. 73–75.

12 Major Joseph M. Bell, as quoted by Benjamin F. Butler, *Butler's Book: Autobiography and Personal Reminiscences of Major-General Benjamin F. Butler* (Boston: A. M. Thayer, 1892), p. 366.

13 Colonel John Taylor Wood, "The First Fight of Iron-Clads," in Robert Underwood Johnson and Clarence Clough Buel, eds., *Battles and Leaders of the Civil War* (New York: Century, 1884–89), v. 1, pp. 701–02.

14 *Congressional Globe*, 35th Cong., 1st sess. (4 March 1858), p. 961. Hammond, however, was not the first Southerner to declare "cotton is king."

15 London *Times* (7 November 1861), p. 6.

16 As quoted in Allan Nevins, *The War for the Union: The Improvised War* (New York: Charles Scribner's Sons, 1959), v. 1, p. 388.

17 Benjamin Moran, entry for 3 December 1861, in Sarah Agnes Wallace and Frances Elma Gillespie, eds., *The Journal of Benjamin Moran, 1857–1865* (Chicago: University of Chicago Press, 1949), v. 2, pp. 916–17.

Chapter 7: The Military Struggle

1 P. G. T. Beauregard, "The First Battle of Bull Run," in Robert Underwood Johnson and Clarence Clough Buel, eds., *Battles and Leaders of the Civil War* (New York: Century, 1884–88), v. 1, p. 222.

2 G. W. Randolph to Molly Randolph, 10 October 1861, as quoted in Richard E. Beringer, Herman Hattaway, Archer Jones, and William N. Still, Jr., *Why the South Lost the Civil War* (Athens: University of Georgia Press, 1986), p. 52.

3 London *Times* (18 July 1861), p. 8.

4 Toombs to Alexander H. Stephens, [30?] September 1861, Ulrich Bonnell Phillips, ed., *The Correspondence of Robert Toombs, Alexander H. Stephens, and Howell Cobb* (Washington: American Historical Association, 1913), p. 577.

5 Stephens as quoted in Richard Malcolm Johnston and William Hard Browne, *Life of Alexander H. Stephens*, rev. edn. (Philadelphia: J. B. Lippincott, 1883), p. 414; Mytra Lockett Avary, ed., *Recollections of Alexander H. Stephens: His Diary Kept When a Prisoner at Fort Warren, Boston Harbour, 1865* . . . (New York: Doubleday, Page, 1910), p. 350; Stephens to his brother, Linton Stephens, 18 February 1862, as quoted in Rudolph Von Abele, *Alexander H. Stephens: A Biography* (New York: Alfred A. Knopf, 1957), p. 207.

6 Stephens to Professor Richard M. Johnson, 14 November 1861, in Henry Cleveland, *Alexander H. Stephens, in Public and Private: With Letters and Speeches Before, During, and Since the War* (Philadelphia: National, 1866), pp. 175–76.

7 Avary, *Recollections of Alexander H. Stephens*, pp. 349–350.

8 Lee to General Gustavus W. Smith, 4 January 1863, Clifford Dowdey, ed., *The Wartime Papers of R. E. Lee* (Boston: Little Brown, 1961), p. 384.

9 John H. Brinton, *The Personal Memoirs of John H. Brinton, Major and Surgeon, U.S.V., 1861–1865* (New York: Neale, 1914), p. 239.

10 Ulysses S. Grant, *Personal Memoirs of U.S. Grant* (New York: Charles L. Webster, 1886), v. 1, p. 311.

11 William L. Barney, *Flawed Victory: A New Perspective on the Civil War* (New York: Praeger, 1975), p. 10.

12 Sherman to Rear Admiral David D. Porter, 25 October 1863, U.S. Naval War Records Office, *Official Records of the Union and Confederate Navies in the War of the Rebellion* (Washington: Government Printing Office, 1875–83), ser. 1, v. 25, p. 474.

13 Grant, *Personal Memoirs*, v. 2, pp. 44–45.

14 Sherman to his brother, John Sherman, 1 October 1862, Rachel Sherman Thorndike, ed., *The Sherman Letters: Correspondence Between General and Senator Sherman From 1837 to 1891* (New York: Charles Scribner's Sons, 1894), p. 166; Sherman to Colonel John A. Rawlins (8 July 1862), U.S. War Department, *The War of the Rebellion: A Compilation of the Official Records of the Union and Confederate Armies* (Washington: Government Printing Office, 1880–1901), ser. 1, v. 17, pt. 2, p. 84.

15 Sherman to John Sherman, *ibid*.

16 Grant, *Personal Memoirs*, v. 1, p. 95.

17 As quoted in Bell Irvin Wiley, *The Life of Billy Yank: The Common Soldier of the Union* (Indianapolis: Bobbs-Merrill, 1952), p. 63.

18 [United States Surgeon Generals Office], *The Medical and Surgical History of the War of the Rebellion (1861–65)* (Washington: Government Printing Office, 1870–88), pt. 3, v. 2, pp. 685–6. The precise numbers are 922 saber and bayonet wounds out of 246,712 total, or 0.37 percent. See also John Buechler, "'Give 'em the Bayonet'—A Note on Civil War Mythology," in John T. Hubbell, ed., *Battles Lost and Won: Essays From Civil War History* (Westport, CT: Greenwood Press 1975), pp. 135–39.

19 S. Weir Mitchell, "The Medical Department in the Civil War," *Journal of the American Medical Association*, 62 (9 May 1914), p. 1447.

20 Walter Millis, *Arms and Men: A Study in American Military History* (New York: G. P. Putnam's Sons, 1956), p. 125.

21 Lieutenant William Lochren of Company E, as quoted in [Return I. Holcombe], *History of the First Regiment, Minnesota Volunteer Infantry* (Stillwater, MN: Easton & Materson, 1916), p. 345. Lochren actually reported not 178 but 215 casualties, for a rate of 82 percent, a figure that has been accepted and repeated *ad infinitum*. For a careful attempt to determine the actual numbers, see Robert W. Meinhard, "The First Minnesota at Gettysburg," *Gettysburg Magazine*, no. 5 (July 1991), pp. 78–88. As Meinhard emphasizes, the revised numbers do "not diminish the luster of what the First Minnesota did on July 2, 1863." See also the *two* modern unit histories devoted to the regiment: John Quinn Imholte, *The First Volunteers: History of the First Minnesota Volunteer Regiment, 1861–1865* (Minneapolis: Ross and Haines, 1963), and Richard Moe, *The Last Full Measure: The Life and Death of the First Minnesota Volunteers* (New York: Henry Holt, 1993).

22 Archie K. Davis, *Boy Colonel of the Confederacy: The Life and Times of Henry King Burgwyn, Jr.* (Chapel Hill: University of North Carolina Press, 1985), pp. 351–52.

23 Captain Henry O. Dwight, with the 20th Ohio Infantry, "How We Fight at Atlanta," *Harper's New Monthly Magazine*, 29 (1864), p. 665.

24 Daniel H. Hill, "McClellan's Change of Base and Malvern Hill," Johnson and Buel, eds., *Battles and Leaders of the Civil War*, v. 2, p. 394.

25 Hill, "Lee's Attack North of the Chickahominy," *ibid.*, p. 352.

26 Charles Francis Adams, Jr., to his father, 5 September 1863, in Worthington Chauncey Ford, ed., *A Cycle of Adams Letters, 1861–1865* (Boston: Houghton Mifflin, 1920), v. 2, p. 79.

27 Gerald F. Linderman, *Embattled Courage: The Experience of Combat in the American Civil War* (New York: Free Press, 1987), p. 128.

28 Frederic Bancroft and William A. Dunning, eds., *The Reminiscences of Carl Schurz, With a Sketch of His Life and Public Service From 1869 to 1906* (New York: McClure, 1907–08), v. 3, p. 39.

29 As quoted in William Quentin Maxwell, *Lincoln's Fifth Wheel: The Political History of the United States Sanitary Commission* (New York: Longmans, Green, 1956), p. 245.

Chapter 8: The War to Abolish Slavery?

1 The Crittenden Resolutions, House of Representatives, 22 July 1861, reprinted in Henry Steele Commager and Milton Cantor, eds., *Documents of American History*, 10th edn. (Englewood Cliffs, NJ: Prentice-Hall, 1988), v. 1, pp. 395–96. The Johnson Resolutions, which passed the Senate on 25 July 1861, have almost identical wording.

2 Speech given at Ottawa, Illinois, 11 August 1861, as quoted in George M. Fredrickson, *The Inner Civil War: Northern Intellectuals and the Crisis of the Union* (New York: Harper & Row, 1965), p. 62.

3 Child to Gerrit Smith, 7 January 1862, in Patricia G. Holland and Milton Meltzer, eds., *The Collected Correspondence of Lydia Maria Child, 1817–1880* (Millwood, NY: KTO Microform, 1979), p. 1364/1.

4 Lysander Spooner, *No Treason, No. 1* (Boston, 1867), p. iii, reprinted in Charles Shively, *The Collected Works of Lysander Spooner* (Weston, MA: M & S Press, 1971), v. 1.

5 Moncure Conway, *Autobiography: Memories and Experiences of Moncure Daniel Conway* (Boston: Houghton, Mifflin, 1904), v. 1, p. 413.

6 Arthur Reed Hogue, ed., *Charles Sumner: An Essay by Carl Schurz* (Urbana: University of Illinois Press, 1951), p. 104; Frederic Bancroft and William A. Dunning, eds., *The Reminiscences of Carl Schurz, With a Sketch of His Life and Public Service From 1869 to 1906* (New York: McClure, 1907-08), v. 2, p. 312.

7 *Congressional Globe*, 37th Cong., 1st sess. (2 August 1861), p. 415.

8 *New York Daily Tribune*, 22 (11 September 1862), p. 4.

9 Lincoln to Horace Greeley, 22 August 1862, in Roy P. Basler, ed., *The Collected Works of Abraham Lincoln* (New Brunswick, NJ: Rutgers University Press, 1953), v. 5, pp. 388–89.

10 Alexander Hunter, "Battle of Antietam," *Southern Historical Society Papers*, 31 (1903), p. 40.

11 As quoted in Jay Luvaas, *The Military Legacy of the Civil War: The European Inheritance* (Chicago: University of Chicago Press, 1959), pp. 18–19.

12 Preliminary Emancipation Proclamation, 22 September 1862, James D. Richardson, ed., *A Compilation of the Messages and Papers of the Presidents* (Washington: Bureau of National Literature, 1922), v. 7, p. 3298.

13 Donn Piatt, *Memories of the Men Who Saved the Union* (New York: Belford, Clarke, 1887), p. 150.

14 11 October 1862, as quoted in Frederic Bancroft, *The Life of William H. Seward* (New York: Harper and Brothers, 1900), v. 2, p. 339.

15 Mrs. W. H. Neblett to her husband in the spring of 1864, as quoted in Bell I. Wiley, *Southern Negroes, 1861–1865* (New Haven: Yale University Press, 1938), p. 52.

16 As quoted in J. William Harris, *Plain Folk and Gentry in a Slave*

Society: White Labor and Black Slavery in Augusta's Hinterlands (Middletown, CT: Wesleyan University Press, 1985), p. 167.

17 General Orders No. 23, 3 February 1864, U.S. War Department, *The War of the Rebellion: A Compilation of the Official Records of the Union and Confederate Armies* (Washington: Government Printing Office, 1880–1901), ser. 1, v. 34, pt. 2, p. 228.

18 Unfinished draft of letter to Isaac M. Schermerhorn, 12 September 1864, Basler, *Collected Works of Abraham Lincoln*, v. 8, p. 2.

19 Charles G. Halpine, as quoted in William Hanchett, *Irish: Charles G. Halpine in Civil War America* (Syracuse: Syracuse University Press, 1970), p. 355.

20 *Punch, or the London Charivari*, 45 (24 October 1863), p. 168.

Chapter 9: Republican Neo-Mercantilism Versus Confederate War Socialism

1 U.S. Department of Commerce, *Historical Statistics of the United States: Colonial Times to 1970* (Washington: U.S. Government Printing Office, 1975), pt. 2, Series Y335–8, Y457–65, Y493–504, Y671–81. I have used the Composite Consumer Price Index calculated by John J. McCusker in *How Much Is That in Real Money? A Historical Price Index for Use as a Deflator of Money Values in the Economy of the United States* (Worcester, MA: American Antiquarian Society, 1992), supplemented by more recent figures from the Consumer Price Index, to deflate amounts to 1995 prices. Thomas Senior Berry, *Production and Population Since 1789: Revised GNP Series in Constant Dollars* (Richmond: Bostwick Press, 1988), estimates nominal output at $3.7 billion in 1858 and $3.9 billion in 1859, while Thomas Weiss, "Estimates of Gross Domestic Output for the United States," (Working paper, University of Kansas, 1992), revises the latter figure to $4.2 billion. Roger L. Ransom and Richard Sutch have their own similar conjecture, appearing in Ransom, *Conflict and Compromise: The Political Economy of Slavery, Emancipation, and the American Civil War* (Cambridge: Cambridge University Press, 1989), p. 256, of $4.1 billion for 1859. For a comparison of these various estimates, see Charles J. Myers, "A Compilation of Estimates of U.S. GNP, 1790–1840" (unpublished paper, Golden Gate University, 1992), which is an early spin off from his "Retirement of the First Federal Debt: A Test of Vincent Ostrom's Theory of Democratic Administration (Ph.D. dissertation, Golden Gate University, 1994). My results conform with the earlier work of M. Slade Kendrick, *A Century and a Half of Federal Expenditures* (New York: National Bureau of Economic Research, 1955), who put national expenditures at 1.5 percent of GNP in 1859.

Lance E. Davis and John Legler, "The Government in the American

Economy, 1815–1902: A Quantitative Study," *Journal of Economic History*, 26 (December 1966), pp. 514–552, presumably have some numbers on state and local expenditures prior to 1902 in order to arrive at their regional, per capita comparisons of government's impact. But the data they present have been so thoroughly refined that it is almost impossible to work out the original figures. More detailed data on state government expenditures only are presented in Charles Frank Holt's published dissertation, *The Role of State Government in the Nineteenth-Century American Economy, 1820–1902: A Quantitative Study* (New York: Arno Press, 1977). See also U.S. Department of the Interior, Census Office, *Eighth (1860) Census* (Washington: Government Printing Office, 1872), v. 4, p. 511, and *The American Almanac and Repository of Useful Knowledge for the Year 1861* (Boston: Crosby, Nichols, Lee, 1861), pp. 240–41, 248–376.

2 James G. Blaine, *Twenty Years of Congress: From Lincoln to Garfield, With a Review of the Events Which Led to the Political Revolution of 1860* (Norwich, CT: Henry Bill, 1884), v. 1, p. 433.

3 Hugh Rockoff, "The Free Banking Era: A Reexamination," *Journal of Money, Credit and Banking*, 6 (May 1974), pp. 149–151. Rockoff puts the losses to note holders at $1,851,900. Actually, a few of the northeastern states that did not formally enact so-called "free banking" legislation had less regulated banking systems. Although he does not say, I presume that the inflationary losses Rockoff has in mind result from the fall in the money's purchasing power, which is really a transfer, usually to the government whose monetary creation is causing the inflation. The true deadweight loss that results from the inefficient decline in people's desired holdings of real-money balances would be smaller.

4 *Congressional Globe*, 37th Cong., 2nd sess. (13 February 1862), pp. 799–800.

5 The standard estimates, in Eugene M. Lerner, "Monetary and Fiscal Programs of the Confederate Government, 1861–65," *Journal of Political Economy*, 62 (December 1954), pp. 506–522, is 5 percent from taxation, 5 percent from seizures and donations, 30 percent from borrowing, and 60 percent from the seigniorage of fiat money. However, Jack Hirshleifer, *Disaster and Recovery: A Historical Survey* (Santa Monica, CA: Rand Corporation, 1963), pp. 41–43, points out that these percentages ignore the resources gained through uncompensated impressments. Adding them into seizures changes the percentages to 7 percent from taxes, 17 percent from seizures and donations, 24 percent from loans, and 52 percent from seigniorage.

6 As quoted in John Christopher Schwab, *The Confederate States of America, 1861–1865: A Financial and Industrial History of the South During the Civil War* (New York: C. Scribner's Sons, 1901), p. 296.

7 George Cary Eggleston, *A Rebel's Recollections*, 4th edn. (New York: G. P. Putnam's Sons, 1905), p. 100.

8 Robert Garlick Hill Kean, entry for 4 October 1863, in Edward Younger, ed., *Inside the Confederate Government: The Diary of Robert Garlick*

Hill Kean, Head of the Bureau of War (New York: Oxford University Press, 1957), p. 108.

9 Bessie Martin, *Desertion of Alabama Troops From the Confederate Army: A Study in Sectionalism* (New York: Columbia University Press, 1932), p. 128.

10 John W. Hagan to his wife, 23 July 1863, Bell Irvin Wiley, ed., "The Confederate Letters of John W. Hagan," *Georgia Historical Quarterly*, 38 (June 1954), p. 196.

11 Thomas H. Watts to James A. Seddon, Confederate Secretary of War, 19 January 1864, U.S. War Department, *The War of the Rebellion: A Compilation of the Official Records of the Union and Confederate Armies* (Washington: Government Printing Office, 1880–1901), ser. 4, v. 3, p. 37.

12 Republican Party Platform of 1860, in Donald Bruce Johnson, ed., *National Party Platforms*, rev. edn. (Urbana: University of Illinois Press, 1978), v. 1, p. 33.

13 George K. Shiel, *Congressional Globe*, 37th Cong., 2nd sess. (5 May 1862), p. 1944.

14 *New York Times*, 12 (2 July 1863), p. 4.

15 Entry for 8 April 1864, Frank E. Vandiver, ed., *The Civil War Diary of Josiah Gorgas* (University: Alabama University Press, 1947), pp. 90–91.

16 James D. B. De Bow, "Our Danger and Our Duty," *De Bow's Review*, old ser., 33 (May-August 1862), p. 46.

17 James T. Leach, 27 January 1865, "Proceedings of the Second Confederate Congress, Second Session in Part," *Southern Historical Society Papers*, 52 (1959), p. 242.

Chapter 10: Dissent and Disaffection—North and South

1 James I. Robertson, Jr., *Soldiers Blue and Gray* (Columbia: University of South Carolina Press, 1988), p. 122.

2 J. C. Owens to Susannah Owens, 26 April 1863, as quoted in Reid Mitchell, *Civil War Soldiers: Their Expectations and Their Experiences* (New York: Simon & Schuster, 1988), p. 58.

3 Bell Irvin Wiley, *The Life of Billy Yank: The Common Soldier of the Union* (Indianapolis: Bobbs-Merrill, 1952), p. 212.

4 29 March 1862, "Proceedings of the First Confederate Congress, First Session Completed, Second Session in Part," *Southern Historical Society Papers*, 45 (May 1925), pp. 27–28.

5 Although General Jonathan S. Preston, Superintendent of the Confederate Conscription Bureau, in U.S. War Department, *The War of the Rebellion: A Compilation of the Official Records of the Union and Confederate Armies* (Washington: Government Printing Office, 1880–1901), ser. 4, v. 3, p. 1101, reported that 81,993 of less than one million total Southern

soldiers entered as draftees, and another 76,206 were induced by conscription to volunteer, this low-end estimate of under 20 percent is incomplete, covers only east of the Mississippi, and does not take into account those who had their terms of service coercively extended. Albert Burton Moore, *Conscription and Conflict in the Confederacy* (New York: Macmillan, 1924), pp. 356–57, credits the Confederate draft with assigning 300,000 men east of the Mississippi—one-third the total who served.

6 Message to the state legislature, 6 November 1862, in Allen Chandler, ed., *The Confederate Records of the State of Georgia* (Atlanta: Chas. P. Byrd, 1910), v. 2, p. 301.

7 William Tecumseh Sherman, *Memoirs of General William T. Sherman*, 2nd edn. (1886; reprint edn., New York: Library of America, 1990), v. 2, p. 879.

8 Report of 20 July 1863, reprinted in J[oel]. T. Headley, *Great Riots of New York, 1712–1873: Including a Full and Complete Account of the Four Days' Draft Riot of 1863* (New York: E. B. Treat, 1873), pp. 348–49.

9 James W. Geary, *We Need Men: The Union Draft in the Civil War* (DeKalb: Northern Illinois University Press, 1991), pp. 78–84. If hired substitutes are included, then the conscription acts furnished 13 percent of Union soldiers during the last two years of the war. State militia drafts garnered another 87,500 nine-month men, 7 percent of the total during the war's first two years.

10 *The Liberator*, 34 (6 May 1864), p. 76.

11 As quoted in Robert W. Johannsen, *Stephen A. Douglas* (New York: Oxford University Press, 1973), p. 868.

12 As reported in Alvan F. Sanborn, ed., *Reminiscences of Richard Lathers: Sixty Years of a Busy Life in South Carolina, Massachusetts and New York* (New York: Grafton Press, 1907), p. 229.

13 Letter to Erastus Corning and others, 12 June 1863, Roy P. Basler, ed., *The Collected Works of Abraham Lincoln* (New Brunswick, NJ: Rutgers University Press, 1953), v. 6, pp. 266–67. This letter was published in the *New York Tribune* of 15 June 1863.

14 *Congressional Globe*, 37th Cong., 3rd sess. (23 February 1863), appendix, pp. 172–73.

15 Democratic Party Platform of 1864, in Donald Bruce Johnson, ed., *National Party Platforms*, rev. edn. (Urbana: University of Illinois Press, 1978), v. 1, p. 34.

16 Toombs to W. W. Burwell, 29 August 1863, in Ulrich Bonnell Phillips, ed., *The Correspondence of Robert Toombs, Alexander H. Stephens, and Howell Cobb* (Washington: American Historical Association, 1913), pp. 628–29.

17 Linton Stephens to Alexander H. Stephens, 14 October 1863, as quoted in James Z. Rabun, "Alexander H. Stephens and Jefferson Davis," *American Historical Review*, 58 (June 1953), p. 307.

18 Stephens to Richard Malcolm Johnston, 1 January 1864, as quoted in Richard Malcolm Johnston and William Hard Browne, *Life of Alexander H. Stephens*, rev. edn. (Philadelphia: J. B. Lippincott, 1883), p. 453.

19 Martha Revis to H.W. Revis, 20[?] July 1863, *War of the Rebellion*, ser. 1, v. 23, pt. 2, p. 951.

20 Mary Cooper to Edward Cooper, as quoted in John W. Moore, *History of North Carolina: From the Earliest Discoveries to the Present Time* (Raleigh: Alfred Williams, 1880), v. 2, p. 237.

Chapter 11: The Ravages of Total War

1 Theodore Lyman to his wife, 18 May 1864, in George R. Agassiz, ed., *Meade's Headquarters, 1863–1865: Letters of Colonel Theodore Lyman From the Wilderness to Appomattox* (Boston: Atlantic Monthly Press, 1922), pp. 99–100.

2 George Cary Eggleston, "Notes on Cold Harbor," in Robert Underwood Johnson and Clarence Clough Buel, eds., *Battles and Leaders of the Civil War* (New York: Century, 1884–88), v. 4, pp. 230–31.

3 As quoted in Shelby Foote, *The Civil War: A Narrative*, v. 3, *Red River to Appomattox* (New York: Random House, 1974), p. 290.

4 Henry C. Dunavant, as quoted in Fred Arthur Bailey, *Class and Tennessee's Confederate Generation* (Chapel Hill: University of North Carolina Press, 1987), p. 93.

5 Sherman to Major General Henry W. Halleck, 24 December 1864, in U.S. War Department, *The War of the Rebellion: A Compilation of the Official Records of the Union and Confederate Armies* (Washington: Government Printing Office, 1880–1901), ser. 1, v. 44, p 799.

6 Ulysses S. Grant, *Personal Memoirs of U.S. Grant* (New York: Charles L. Webster, 1886), v. 1, pp. 368–69.

7 Sherman to Major General Ulysses S. Grant, 4 October 1862, *The War of the Rebellion*, ser. 1, v. 17, pt. 2, p. 261; Sherman to Major General Henry W. Halleck, 17 October 1863, *ibid.*, v. 30, pt. 3, p. 699.

8 Sherman to Lieutenant General Ulysses S. Grant, 9 October 1964, *ibid.*, v. 39, pt. 3, p. 162.

9 Sherman to Major General Henry W. Halleck, 4 September 1864, *ibid.*, v. 38, pt. 5, p. 794.

10 Special Field Orders No. 12, 14 January 1865, *ibid.*, v. 47, pt. 2, p. 50.

11 Eliza Frances Andrews, *The War-Time Journal of a Georgia Girl* (New York: D. Appleton, 1908), pp. 32–33.

12 As quoted in J[ohn] B[eauchamp] Jones, *A Rebel War Clerk's Diary at the Confederate States Capital* (Philadelphia: J. B. Lippincott, 1866), v. 2, p. 175.

13 Grant to General Benjamin F. Butler, 18 August 1864, *War of the Rebellion*, ser. 2, v. 7, p. 607.

14 Lee to Jefferson Davis, 20 April 1865, Clifford Dowdey and Louis H. Manarin, eds., *The Wartime Papers of R. E. Lee* (Boston: Little, Brown, 1961), pp. 938–39

15 As reprinted in John K. Bettersworth, ed., *Mississippi in the Confeder-*

acy, v. 1, *As They Saw It* (Jackson: Mississippi Department of Archives and History, 1961), pp. 245–46.

16 Lee to Andrew Hunter, Richmond, 11 January 1865, *The War of the Rebellion*, ser. 4, v. 3, p. 1013.

17 Sherman to Major General Henry W. Halleck, 24 December 1864, *ibid.*, ser. 1, v. 44, p. 799; William Tecumseh Sherman, *Memoirs of General William T. Sherman*, 2nd edn. (1886; reprint edn., New York: Library of America, 1990), v. 2, p. 735.

18 Grant to Major General Henry W. Halleck, 14 July 1865, *War of the Rebellion*, ser. 1, v. 40, pt. 3, p. 223.

19 Davis in his last Proclamation to the People, Danville, Virginia, 4 April 1865, reprinted in Dunbar Rowland, ed., *Jefferson Davis, Constitutionalist: His Letters, Papers and Speeches* (Jackson: Mississippi Department of Archives and History, 1923), v. 6, p. 530.

20 Richard E. Beringer, Herman Hattaway, Archer Jones, and William N. Still, Jr., *Why the South Lost the Civil War* (Athens: University of Georgia Press, 1986), p. 477. Deaths from combat only in the Confederacy were 2.2 percent of the population, but including disease raises that to 4.7 percent. France lost 3.3 percent during World War I, and Germany 5.0 percent during World War II.

21 Thomas C. Fuller of North Carolina to William A. Graham, 24 March 1865, in J. G. de Roulhac Hamilton and Max R. Williams, *The Papers of William Alexander Graham* (Raleigh: North Carolina Department of Cultural Resources, 1957–1976), v. 6, p. 287.

22 *Jackson News* (10 March 1865), as reprinted in Bettersworth, *Mississippi in the Confederacy*, v. 1, p. 246.

23 Myrta Lockett Avary, ed., *Recollections of Alexander H. Stephens: His Diary Kept When a Prisoner at Fort Warren, Boston Harbour, 1865* . . . (New York: Doubleday, Page, 1910), p. 349.

Chapter 12: The Politics of Reconstruction

1 4 March 1865, in James D. Richardson, ed., *A Compilation of the Messages and Papers of the Presidents* (Washington: Bureau of National Literature, 1922), v. 8, p. 3478.

2 Senator Benjamin F. Wade of Ohio and Representative Henry Winter Davis of Maryland, *New York Daily Tribune*, 24 (5 August 1864), p. 5.

3 As quoted in Whitelaw Reid, *After the War: A Southern Tour, May 1, 1865 to May 1, 1866* (Cincinnati: Moore, Wilstach & Baldwin, 1866), pp. 204–05.

4 Leander Stillwell of the 61st Illinois, in *The Story of a Common Soldier, of Army Life in the Civil War, 1861–1865*, 2nd edn. ([Erie, KS]: Franklin Hudson, 1920), p. 278.

5 As quoted in Leon F. Litwack, *Been in the Storm So Long: The Aftermath of Slavery* (New York: Alfred A. Knopf, 1979), p. 102.

6 *Congressional Globe*, 40th Cong., 1st sess. (19 March 1867), p. 205.

7 *New York Times*, 16 (9 July 1867), p. 4.

8 Eric Foner, *Nothing but Freedom: Emancipation and Its Legacy* (Baton Rouge: Louisiana State University Press, 1983), p. 56. The quoted freedman is Bayley Wyat, speaking in 1867.

9 Speech at Lancaster, Pennsylvania, 6 September 1865, as quoted in Kenneth M. Stampp, *The Era of Reconstruction, 1865–1877* (New York: Alfred A. Knopf, 1965), p. 127.

10 M. L. Stearns to E. C. Woodruff, 1 March 1867, as quoted in George R. Bentley, *A History of the Freedmen's Bureau* (Philadelphia: University of Pennsylvania Press, 1955), p. 151.

11 Catherine Ann Edmonston, diary, 23 April 1865, as quoted in Francis Butler Simkins and James Welch Patton, *The Women of the Confederacy* (Richmond: Garrett & Massie, 1936), p. 249.

12 *Chicago Tribune*, 19 (1 December 1865), p. 2.

13 3 December 1867, Richardson, *A Compilation of the Messages and Papers of the Presidents*, v. 8, pp. 3763–64.

14 *Congressional Globe*, 39th Cong., 1st sess. (18 December 1865), p. 74.

15 *Ibid.*, 39th Cong., 2nd sess. (3 January 1867), pt. 1, p. 252.

16 *U.S. Statutes at Large*, 14 (9 April 1866), p. 27.

17 Speech at Indianapolis, Indiana, 20 June 1866, as quoted in William Dudley Foulke, *Life of Oliver P. Morton: Including His Important Speeches* (Indianapolis: Bowen-Merrill, 1899), v. 1, pp. 474–75.

18 "Ex parte Milligan," 4 *Wallace* 127 (1866).

19 Austin Blair of Michigan, *Congressional Globe*, 40th Cong., 2nd sess. (22 February 1868), p. 1368.

20 *Ibid.* (2 March 1868), p. 1613.

21 *National Anti-Slavery Standard*, 20 (15 May 1869), p. [2].

Chapter 13: American Society Transformed

1 Entry for 9 March 1864, Howard K. Beale, ed., *The Diary of Edward Bates, 1859–1866* (Washington: Government Printing Office, 1933), p. 344.

2 Henry Clary Warmoth, "Report of the Select Committee on Conditions in the South," 43rd Cong., 2nd sess. (1875), *House Reports*, v. 5, no. 261, p. 973.

3 As quoted in Harry Warfel, *Noah Webster: Schoolmaster to America* (New York: Macmillan, 1936), pp. 21, 335.

4 J. Mills Thornton, III, "Fiscal Policy and the Failure of Radical Reconstruction in the Lower South," in J. Morgan Kousser and James M. McPherson, eds., *Region, Race, and Reconstruction: Essays in Honor of C. Vann Woodward* (New York: Oxford University Press, 1982), p. 371. The year was 1871 and the amount 3,330,000 acres.

5 State Central Executive Committee, Democratic Party of South

Carolina, 1868, as quoted in John S. Reynolds, *Reconstruction in South Carolina, 1865–1877* (Columbia, SC: State, 1905), p. 93.

6 Albion W. Tourgée, *A Fool's Errand: By One of the Fools* (New York: Fords, Howard, & Hulbert, 1879), p. 252.

7 Joel Ashworth to Governor William W. Holden, 28 October 1970, "Report of the Select Committee to Investigate Alleged Outrages in the Southern States," 42nd Cong., 1st sess. (1871), *Senate Reports*, v. 1, no. 1, p. lxiv.

8 Kenneth M. Stampp, *The Imperiled Union: Essays on the Background of the Civil War* (New York: Oxford University Press, 1980), p. 268.

9 "United States *v*. Cruikshank et al.," 92 *U.S. Reports* 555 (1875).

10 Moncure Conway, *Autobiography: Memories and Experiences of Moncure Daniel Conway* (Boston: Houghton, Mifflin, 1904), v. 1, p. 222.

11 *Washington National Republican* (24 January 1874), as quoted in James M. McPherson, *Ordeal by Fire: The Civil War and Reconstruction* (New York: Alfred A. Knopf, 1982), p. 593.

12 Daniel H. Chamberlain, speech at Woodstock, Connecticut, 4 July 1877, *New York Times*, 26 (5 July 1877), p. 2.

13 *De Bow's Review*, new ser., 1 (January 1866), p. 659.

14 Lieutenant James M. Babcock to Major G. D. Reynolds, 30 November 1865, as quoted in Eric Foner, *Politics and Ideology in the Age of the Civil War* (New York: Oxford University Press, 1980), p. 107.

15 "Report of the Comptroller of the Currency, 1872," 42nd Cong., 3rd sess. (1872–73), *House Executive Documents*, v. 5, n. 3, p. xxxiii.

16 As quoted in Gerald David Jaynes, *Branches Without Roots: Genesis of the Black Working Class in the American South, 1862–1882* (New York: Oxford University Press, 1986), p. 43.

17 Kenneth Ng and Nancy Virts, "The Value of Freedom," *Journal of Economic History*, 49 (December 1989), pp. 958–965. Their estimate is a revision of figures found in Roger L. Ransom and Richard Sutch, *One Kind of Freedom: The Economic Consequences of Emancipation* (Cambridge: Cambridge University Press, 1977), pp. 3–7, and applies to blacks who worked large plantations. For the average black slave, on both large and small plantations, the gain is over 60 percent. Including leisure raises the gain for slaves on large plantations to somewhere between 99 and 178 percent. If we accept the higher estimates for prewar slave income in Robert William Fogel and Stanley L. Engerman, *Time on the Cross*, v. 2, *Evidence and Methods—A Supplement* (Boston: Little, Brown, 1974), p. 159, these gains are dampened somewhat but not erased. A different approach that reaches congenial conclusions is in Richard Vedder, Lowell Gallaway, and David C. Klingaman, "Black Exploitation and White Benefits: The Civil War Income Revolution," in Richard F. America, ed., *The Wealth of Races: The Present Value of Benefits From Past Injustices* (Westport, CT: Greenwood Press, 1990), pp. 125–37.

18 Robert Higgs, *Competition and Coercion: Blacks in the American Economy, 1865–1914* (Cambridge: Cambridge University Press, 1977).

19 William Jay, *An Inquiry Into the Character and Tendency of the American Colonization and American Anti-Slavery Societies,* 4th edn., (New York: R. G. Williams, 1837), p. 198.

20 U.S. Department of Commerce, *Historical Statistics of the United States: Colonial Times to 1970* (Washington: U.S. Government Printing Office, 1975), pt. 2, Series Y335–8, Y457–65, puts total national government expenditures in 1865 at $1.3 billion. As mentioned in chapter 9, n. 1, assorted GNP estimates for this period are in Thomas Senior Berry, *Production and Population Since 1789: Revised GNP Series in Constant Dollars* (Richmond: Bostwick Press, 1988); Thomas Weiss, "Estimates of Gross Domestic Output for the United States" (Working paper, University of Kansas, 1992); Roger L. Ransom and Richard Sutch, *Conflict and Compromise: The Political Economy of Slavery, Emancipation, and the American Civil War* (Cambridge: Cambridge University Press, 1989), p. 256; and Charles J. Myers, "A Compilation of Estimates of U.S. GNP, 1790–1840" (Unpublished paper, Golden Gate University, 1992).

21 "Slavery," *The Works of William E. Channing,* 11th edn. (Boston: George G. Channing, 1849), v. 2, p. 144.

22 "Scotch the Snake, or Kill It?" *The Complete Writings of James Russell Lowell: With Portraits, Illustrations, and Facsimiles* (Boston: Houghton, Mifflin, 1904), v. 6, pp. 299–300.

23 David Herbert Donald, *Liberty and Union* (Boston: Little, Brown, 1978), p. 215.

24 Final Message to the Illinois General Assembly, 2 January 1865, *Chicago Tribune,* 18 (5 January 1865), p. [2].

25 The figures on taxation are from U.S. Department of the Interior, Census Bureau, *Ninth (1870) Census* (Washington: Government Printing Office, 1872), v. 3, pp. 10–11; while the figures on city debt are from the *Tenth (1880) Census* (Washington: Government Printing Office, 1884), v. 7, pp. 722–731. Population for each state is in U.S. Department of Commerce, *Historical Statistics of the United States: Colonial Times to 1970* (Washington: U.S. Government Printing Office, 1975), pt. 1, Series A195–209; and the Composite Consumer Price Index is in John J. McCusker, *How Much Is That in Real Money? A Historical Price Index for Use as a Deflator of Money Values in the Economy of the United States* (Worcester, MA: American Antiquarian Society, 1992). All northern states had real, per capita tax increases over the decade.

26 Ticknor to George T. Curtis, 30 July 1869, Anna Ticknor and George S. Hilliard, eds., *Life, Letters, and Journals of George Ticknor* (Boston: Osgood, 1876), v. 2, p. 485.

Epilogue: America's Turning Point

1 I have been unable to find the source for this quotation attributed to John Emerich Edward Dalberg Acton, 1st Baron, so it may be apocryphal.

But if Acton did not actually say it, he should have. It is consistent with his thought and his other writings.

2 David Donald, "An Excess of Democracy," in *Lincoln Reconsidered: Essays on the Civil War Era*, 2nd edn. (New York: Random House, 1956), p. 227.

3 William Appleman Williams, *America Confronts a Revolutionary World: 1776–1976* (New York: William Morrow, 1976), p. 113.

4 David Donald, "Died of Democracy," in Donald, ed., *Why the North Won the Civil War* (Baton Rouge: Louisiana State University Press, 1960), p. 79.

5 David M. Potter, "Civil War," in C. Vann Woodward, ed., *The Comparative Approach to American History* (New York: Basic Books, 1968), p. 141.

6 London *Times* (13 September 1862), p. 8.

7 C. Vann Woodward, "The Price of Freedom," in David G. Sansing, ed., *What Was Freedom's Price?* (Jackson: University Press of Mississippi, 1978), p 93.

8 Eric Foner, *Nothing But Freedom: Emancipation and Its Legacy* (Baton Rouge: Louisiana State University Press, 1983), p. 10.

9 Stephens to J. Henly Smith, 10 July 1860, Ulrich Bonnell Phillips, ed., *The Correspondence of Robert Toombs, Alexander H. Stephens, and Howell Cobb* (Washington: American Historical Association, 1913), p. 487.

10 *Congressional Globe*, 27th Cong. 2nd sess. (27 January 1842), pp. 178, 181; appendix, p. 238. The *Globe*'s body and appendix contain slightly different versions of Underwood's remarks, and I have freely quoted from both.

11 Moncure Conway, *Autobiography: Memories and Experiences of Moncure Daniel Conway* (Boston: Houghton, Mifflin, 1904), v. 1, pp. 222, 241. Conway goes on to disparage his earlier endorsement of disunion as one of the "illusions of those time," but his reasons are ambiguous. It is unclear whether he had by then concluded that disunion would not have brought down slavery or simply that politically it would never have been given the chance.

12 Claudia Goldin and Frank D. Lewis, "The Economic Cost of the American Civil War: Estimates and Implications," *Journal of Economic History*, 35 (June 1975), pp. 299–322. Peter Temin, "The Post-Bellum Recovery of the South and the Cost of the Civil War," *Journal of Economic History*, 36 (December 1976), pp. 898–906, contends that Goldin and Lewis have overstated the South's portion of the war's cost. See also their exchange in *Journal of Economic History*, 38 (June 1978), pp. 487–493.

13 Randolph Bourne, "The State," in Olaf Hansen, ed., *The Radical Will: Selected Writings, 1911–1918* (New York: Urizen Books, 1977), p. 360.

14 Speech in 1838, as quoted in Blanche Glassman Hersh, *The Slavery of Sex: Feminist Abolitionists in America* (Urbana: University of Illinois Press, 1978), p. 34.

INDEX

Numbers in italic refer to pages within bibliographical essays. The titles of books and articles by historians are not listed; only the authors or editors are. The endnotes are not indexed at all, except for persons who are quoted in the text anonymously. The number of the endnote that provides their name is given after the number of the page on which they are quoted.